GERMAN
DICTIONARY

GERMAN – ENGLISH
ENGLISH – GERMAN

REVISED AND UPDATED

The Living Language™ Series
Basic Courses on Cassette

Spanish*
French*
German*
Italian*
Japanese*
Portuguese (Continental)
Portuguese (Brazilian)
Advanced Spanish
Advanced French
Children's Spanish
Children's French
Russian
Hebrew
English for Spanish Speakers
English for French Speakers
English for Italian Speakers
English for German Speakers
English for Chinese Speakers

*Also available on Compact Disc

Living Language Plus®

Spanish
French
German
Italian

Living Language Traveltalk™

Spanish	*Russian*
French	*Japanese*
German	*Portuguese*
Italian	

Living Language Fast & Easy

Spanish	*Inglés/English for Spanish Speakers*
French	*Portuguese*
Italian	*Korean*
Japanese	*Mandarin Chinese*
German	*Hungarian*
Hebrew	*Arabic*
Russian	*Czech*
Polish	

Living Language™

GERMAN
DICTIONARY

GERMAN – ENGLISH
ENGLISH – GERMAN

REVISED AND UPDATED

Revised by Walter Kleinmann
Coordinator of Language Programs
Sewanhaka Central High School District

Based on the original
by Genevieve A. Martin
and Theodor Bertram

CROWN PUBLISHERS, INC., NEW YORK

This work was previously published under the title *Living Language*™ *Common Usage Dictionary—German* by Genevieve A. Martin and Theodor Bertram, based on the dictionary developed by Ralph Weiman.

Published by Crown Publishers, Inc., 201 East 50th Street, New York, New York 10022. Member of the Crown Publishing Group.

Random House, Inc. New York, Toronto, London, Sydney, Auckland

THE LIVING LANGUAGE COURSE is a registered trademark. CROWN, LIVING LANGUAGE and colophon are trademarks of Crown Publishers, Inc.

Manufactured in the United States of America

Library of Congress Catalog Card Number: 56-9318

ISBN 0-517-59044-1

10 9 8 7 6 5 4 3 2 1

Revised Edition

CONTENTS

INTRODUCTION

The *Living Language™ German Dictionary* lists more than 15,000 of the most frequently used German words, gives their most important meanings, and illustrates their use. This revised edition contains updated phrases and expressions as well as many new entries related to business, technology, and the media.

1. More than one thousand of the most essential words are capitalized to make them easy to find.

2. Numerous definitions are illustrated with phrases, sentences, and idiomatic expressions. If there is no close English equivalent for a German word, or if the English equivalent has several meanings, the context of the illustrative sentences helps to clarify the meanings.

3. Because of these useful phrases, the *Living Language™ German Dictionary* also serves as a phrase book and conversation guide. The dictionary is helpful both to beginners who are building their vocabulary and to advanced students who want to perfect their command of colloquial German.

4. The German expressions (particularly the idiomatic and colloquial ones) have been translated to their English equivalents. However, literal translations have

been added to help the beginner. For example, under the entry *Kuh,* cow, you will find: *Er ist bekannt wie eine bunte Kuh.* He is well-known everywhere. ("He's a colorful cow.") This dual feature also makes the dictionary useful for translation work.

EXPLANATORY NOTES

Literal translations are in parentheses. Colloquial is abbreviated to *coll.*

Gender is indicated by *m.* for masculine, *f.* for feminine, and *n.* for neuter.

Case is indicated by *nom.* for nominative, *gen.* for genitive, *dat.* for dative, *acc.* for accusative.

Possessive is abbreviated to *poss.,* pronoun to *pron.,* adjective to *adj.,* preposition to *prep.*

In German, all nouns are capitalized.

German-English

A

AB 1. *adv. off, down, away from, from.*
ab heute   *from today.*
ab und ab   *now and then.*
ab und zu   *to and fro, now and then.*
von hier ab   *from here.*
von nun ab   *henceforth.*
2. *separable prefix (implies a movement down or away, imitation, appropriation, deterioration, destruction).*
Das Flugzeug stürzte ins Meer ab.   *The plane fell down into the sea.*
Einige alte Häuser werden abgebaut.   *Some old houses will be demolished.*
Er hat ihm tausend Mark abgeschmeichelt.   *He got a thousand marks from him by flattery.*
Ich schreibe meine Aufgabe ab.   *I copy my homework.*

Abart *f. variety; variation of species*

abbeissen *to bite off*
sich die Nägel abbeissen   *to bite one's nails.*

abbezahlen *to pay off.*

abbiegen *to turn off*

Abbild *n. copy, image.*

abbinden *to unbind*

Abbitte *f. apology; forgiveness*

abbrechen *to break up, interrupt, deduct, gather*
Blumen abbrechen   *to gather flowers.*
die Arbeit abbrechen   *to cease work.*

abdanken *to dismiss, abdicate.*
Der Fürst hat abgedankt.   *The prince has abdicated.*

abdrehen *to turn off, switch off.*
Drehen Sie das Radio ab!   *Turn off the radio!*

abdrucken *to print*

ABEND *m. evening.*
diesen Abend   *this evening.*
Es wird Abend.   *It is getting dark.*
heute Abend   *tonight*

Abenteuer *n. adventure.*
auf Abenteuer ausgehen   *to look for adventure.*

abenteuerlich *adventurous.*

Abenteurer *m. adventurer*

ABER *but, however, anyway.*
Ich wollte ausgehen aber das Wetter war zu schlecht.   *I wanted to go out but the weather was too bad.*
Das Kind wollte spielen, die Mutter aber wollte nicht.   *The child wanted to play but the mother did not want to.*
Der König aber ...   *The King, however, ...*
Nein aber!   *I say!*
Nun aber!   *But now!*
tausend und aber tausend   *thousands and thousands*

abermals *again, once more.*

abfahren *to set off, depart.*
Der Zug fährt um drei Uhr ab.   *The train leaves at three.*
Sie fuhr übel ab.   *She got the worst of it.*

Abfahrtsort *m. place of departure.*

abfinden *to settle, come to an agreement.*

abführen *to lead away, carry away.*

Abführung *f. removal*

Abgabe *f. tax, tribute, delivery.*
abgabenfrei   *tax free.*
abgabenpflichtig   *taxable; accessible.*

Abgang *m. departure, exit*

ABGEBEN *to give, supply, deliver, pay taxes.*
sich mit etwas abgeben   *to occupy oneself with a matter.*
Wir können die Waren zu diesem Preis nicht abgeben.   *We cannot supply the merchandise on these terms.*

abgehen *to depart, go off.*
Er lässt sich nichts abgehen.   *He denies himself nothing.*
von seinem Vorhaben nicht abgehen   *to persist in one's plans.*

abgemacht *agreed.*

abgewinnen *to win from.*

abgewöhnen *to disaccustom, give up.*
Ich habe mir das Rauchen abgewöhnt.   *I have given up smoking.*

Abgrund *m. abyss, precipice.*

abhalten *to hold off, restrain.*
Lassen Sie sich nicht abhalten!   *Don't let me stop you!*

abhängen *to unhang, hang up (phone). disconnect.*

abhängig *sloping, dependent on.*

abheben *to lift off, uncover, become detached.*
Die helle Gestalt hebt sich auf dem dunkeln Hintergrunde vorteilhaft ab.   *The light figure is brought into relief against the dark background.*

Abhilfe *f. relief*

abholen *to get, collect.*
Das Taxi wird mich abholen.   *The taxi will pick me up.*

Abkunft *f. descent, origin.*

ablenken *to divert, distract.*

ablesen *to pick up, read off.*

abliefern *to deliver.*

ABMACHEN *to remove, loosen, agree, settle.*

Abgemacht! *Agreed!*
abnehmen *to take off, gather, pick up (phone), to lose weight.*
Er nimmt seinen Hut ab. *He takes off his hat.*
er hat zehn Pfund abgenomen. *He lost ten pounds.*
Abneigung *f. dislike, antipathy.*
Abort *m. lavatory; W.C.*
abräumen *to take away, remove*
ABREISE *f. departure*
eine unvorbergesehene Abreise *an unexpected departure*
Absage *f. refusal*
absagen *to refuse, to cancel, call off.*
eine Gesellschaft absagen lassen *to call off a party.*
Falls Sie mir nicht absagen, komme ich. *Unless you call it off, I'll come.*
Abscheu *m. aversion, horror.*
abscheulich *horrible, abominable, nasty.*
Das war abscheulich von ihm. *It was very nasty of him.*
ABSCHIED *m. departure*
Abschied nehmen *to take leave.*
Ich werde Abschied von ihnen nehmen *I am going to leave you.*
den Abschied bekommen *to be dismissed.*
Der Offizier hat seinen Abschied genommen. *The officer has been placed on the retired list.*
abschreiben *to copy, to deduct.*
abseits *prep. (gen) aside, apart, away from.*
ABSICHT *f. intention, purpose, view.*
in der Absicht *with the intention.*
Er tat es in böser Absicht. *He did it with a malicious intention.*
absichtlich *on purpose.*
(sich) abspielen *to occur, to take place*
Abstand *m. distance, interval.*
Er nahm Abstand von seiner Erbschaft. *He gave up his inheritance.*
Er nahm Abstand von dem schnell vorbei fahrenden Zug. *He stood back from the fast passing train.*
Absturz *m. fall, crash*
Er wurde bei einem Flugzeugabsturz getötet. *He was killed in a plane crash.*
ABTEIL *n. compartment, division, section*
Abteil erster Klasse *n. first-class compartment*
Nichtraucherabteil *non-smoking compartment.*
Abteilung *f. department (in a store).*
Schuhabteilung *f. shoe department.*
abtrocknen *to dry off, wipe*
das Geschirr abtrocknen *to dry the dishes.*

abwärts *downward.*
abwechseln *to vary, change, alternate.*
abwesend *absent.*
Abwesenheit *f. absence.*
abzahlen *to pay off.*
abziehen *to retain, take off, subtract*
Der Arbeitgeber zieht die Steuer vom Einkommen ab. *The employer retains taxes from the salary.*
Abzugskanal *m. sewer*
ach! *Ah! Oh!*
ACHT *eight*
heute in acht Tagen *A week from today.*
achtmal *eight times.*
ACHTEL *eighth.*
achten *to esteem, regard, respect.*
ACHTUNG *f. esteem.*
Achtung! *Beware! Attention!*
achtungsvoll *respectful.*
ACHTZEHN *eighteen.*
ACHTZEHNTE *eighteenth.*
ACHTZIG *eighty.*
ACHTZIGSTE *eightieth.*
ACKER *m. field, soil.*
Ackerbau *m. agriculture.*
ackern *to plough.*
Ackersmann *m. ploughman*
addieren *to add up.*
Adel *m. nobility, aristocracy.*
Ader *f. vein.*
Adjektiv *n. adjective.*
adelig *noble.*
ADRESSE *f. address*
Hier ist meine Adresse. *Here is my address.*
adressieren *to address.*
Adverb *n. adverb.*
Affe *m. monkey.*
Affekt *m. excitement.*
affektiert *affected.*
Agent *m. agent.*
ahnen *to have a premonition.*
Es ahnt mir Unglück. *I have a premonition of evil.*
Ich habe keine Ahnung. *I don't have the slightest idea.*
ähnlich *similar, like.*
ähnlich sehen *to look alike.*
Ähnlichkeit *f. similarity, resemblance.*
Akademie *f. academy, university.*
Akten *pl. deeds, documents.*
Aktie *f. share, stock.*
aktiv *active.*
Akzent *m. accent, stress.*
Alarm *m. alarm.*
Alkohol *m. alcohol, liquor.*
ALL (aller, alle, alles) *entire, whole, every, each, any*
all die Leute *everybody.*

all und jeder   *each and every.*

alle Tage   *every day.*

auf alle Fälle   *in any case.*

ohne allen Grund   *for no reason at all.*

ALLEIN *alone, single, solitary, apart, lonesome.*

Ich bin allein.   *I am alone.*

Sie lebt allein.   *She lives alone.*

allerart *diverse.*

allgemein *universal.*

Alphabet *n. alphabet.*

ALS *when, than, as, like.*

Als Bismarck starb, gab es noch keine Flugzuege.   *When Bismarck died, they still didn't have any airplanes.*

Sie ist Grösser als ihr Bruder.   *She is taller than her brother.*

als ob   *as if, as though.*

Er tut, also ob er die Antwort kenne.   *He acts as if he knew the answer.*

so bald als   *as soon as*

ALSO *so, thus, in this way.*

"Also sprach Zarathustra . . ."   *"Thus spoke Zarathustra . . ."*

ALT *old, aged, ancient.*

alte Sprachen   *ancient languages (classics)*

altehrwürdig   *venerable.*

altgläubig   *orthodox.*

altmodisch   *old-fashioned*

eine alte Jungfer   *an old maid.*

ALTER *n. age, old age, antiquity.*

Mittelalter   *n. Middle Ages.*

älter *older, elder, senior.*

Altertum *n. antiquity.*

Altertumshändler   *m. antique dealer.*

älteste *oldest*

am (an dem) *on, at.*

Amerikaner *m.* **-in** *f. American.*

amerikanisch *American.*

AMT *n. office, charge, board. In compound words, the suffix amt designates a government office:*

das Auswärtige Amt   *the Foreign Office.*

Polizeiamt   *n. police station.*

Zollamt   *n. customs.*

in Amt und Würden stehen   *to be a person of position.*

amüsant *amusing.*

AMÜSIEREN *to amuse.*

sich amüsieren   *to enjoy oneself.*

ich habe mich bei der Gesellschaft sehr amüsiert.   *I enjoyed myself at the party.*

AN 1. *prep. (dat. when answering question. Wo?; acc. when answering question. Wohin?, and depending on the idiom).*

an die Arbeit gehen   *to go to work.*

an der Arbeit sein   *to be at work.*

an der Donau   *on the Danube.*

an und für sich   *in itself.*

Er starb an seinen Wunden.   *He died of his wounds.*

Es ist an mir. Ich bin dran.   *It is my turn.*

Ich gehe an die Tür.   *I go to the door.*

Ich weiss, was an der Geschichte dran ist.   *I know what the story is.*

soviel an mir liegt   *as far as I am concerned.*

2. *separable prefix. (implies movement closer to the speaker, proximity, contact, attraction, climbing, beginning).*

Der Hund ist angebunden.   *The dog is tied.*

Der Tag bricht an.   *The day begins.*

Er behielt seine Schuhe an.   *He kept his shoes on.*

Er zieht seine Jacke an.   *He puts his coat on.*

Ich steige langsam den Berg hinan.   *I climb the mountain slowly.*

anbehalten *to keep on.*

Ich will meinen Mantel anbehalten.   *I want to keep my coat on.*

anbieten *to offer, volunteer.*

Anblick *m. sight, view.*

Andenken *n. memory, souvenir.*

zum Andenken an meine Eltern.   *In memory of my parents.*

ANDER *other, another, different, next.*

am anderen Morgen   *the next morning.*

anderer Meinung sein   *to be of a different opinion.*

ein andermal   *another time.*

einen Tag um den andern   *every other day.*

etwas anderes   *another thing, something else, something different.*

nichts anderes als   *nothing but.*

unter anderem   *among other things.*

anderenfalls *otherwise.*

anderseits *on the other side.*

andeuten *to indicate.*

Anerbieten *n. offer, proposal.*

Anfall *m. attack, fit.*

Herzanfall   *m. heart attack.*

Anfang *m. beginning, start.*

anfangen *(to) begin, start.*

von Anfang bis Ende   *from beginning to end.*

Anfrage *f. inquiry.*

anfragen *to inquire.*

anfreunden *(sich) to become friends.*

angemessen *suitable, accurate.*

Angesicht *n. face, countenance.*

von Angesicht zu Angesicht   *face to face.*

angesichts *considering, in view of.*

Angewohnheit *f. habit, custom.*
angrenzen *to border.*
Angriff *m. attack.*
in Angriff nehmen   *to set about.*
Angst *f. anxiety.*
ängstigen *to frighten.*
sich ängstigen vor   *to be afraid of.*
sich ängstigen um   *to feel anxious about.*
anhaben *to wear, have on.*
Er hat einen neuen Anzug an.   *He's wearing a new suit.*
anhalten *to stop, pull up.*
anhören *to listen to.*
Anker *m. anchor.*
anklagen *to accuse.*
ankleiden *to dress.*
anklopfen *to knock at.*
ANKOMMEN *to arrive, approach, reach.*
Es kommt darauf an, ob Sie Zeit haben.   *It depends on whether you have time.*
Der Zug ist um 1500 Uhr ankegommen.   *The train arrived at 3:00 P.M.*
ANKUNFT *f. arrival.*
anmelden *to announce, notify, report.*
Anmut *f. grace, charm.*
anmutig *graceful, charming.*
Annahme *f. acceptance, assumption.*
annehem *to accept, receive, assume, take care of.*
anpassen *to fit, suit, adapt.*
anprobieren *to try on.*
anrechnen *to charge.*
zu viel anrechnen   *to overcharge.*
Ich rechne Ihnen Ihre Hilfe hoch an.   *I appreciate your help very much.*
Anrede *f. address.*
anreden *to address, accost.*
Der Schutzmann redete mich an.   *The policeman spoke to me.*
anregen *to incite, stimulate, excite.*
Ansage *f. announcement, notification.*
ansagen *to announce, notify.*
anschauen *to look at, contemplate.*
anschaulich *evident, clear.*
Anschrift *f. address (letter).*
anschuldigen *to accuse.*
ANSEHEN *to look at, consider, regard.*
dem Ansehen nach   *to all appearances.*
im Ansehen stehen   *to be esteemed.*
vom Ansehen kennen   *to know by sight.*
Ansicht *f. view, sight, opinion.*
nach meiner Ansicht   *according to my opinion.*
Ansichtskarte *f. picture postcard.*
Ansprache *f. speech, address.*
Anspruch *m. claim, pretension.*
Anspruch haben auf   *to be entitled to.*

Anstand *m. manners, decency, etiquette.*
ohne Anstand   *without hesitation.*
anständig *decent, respectable*
ANSTATT (statt) 1. *prep. (gen.) instead of; also conj.*
Anstatt eines Regenschirms nahm er einen Hut.   *Instead of an umbrella, he took a hat.*
anstrengen (sich) *to strain, exert.*
anstrengend *tiring, trying, exacting.*
ANTWORT *f. answer.*
ANTWORTEN *to answer.*
anvertrauen *to entrust, confide.*
Anwalt *m. lawyer, attorney.*
anwesend *present.*
Anwesenheit *f. presence.*
Anzahl *f. quantity, amount.*
anzahlen *to pay on account.*
Anzeige *f. notice, advertisement.*
anzeigen *to notify, report, announce*
Ich halte es für angezeigt.   *I consider it advisable.*
(sich) anziehen *to put on (clothes); to dress oneself.*
ANZUG *m. suit, dress.*
Anzüglichkeit *f. suggestive remark.*
anzünden *to light the fire, set fire to.*
APFEL *m. apple*
in den sauren Apfel beissen   *to swallow a bitter pill.*
APFELSINE *f. orange*
Apotheke *f. pharmacy.*
Apotheker *m. pharmacist.*
Apparat *m. apparatus, appliance, telephone.*
Bleiben Sie am Apparat!   *Hold the wire!*
Appetit *m. appetite.*
applaudieren *to applaud.*
APRIL *m. April*
Äquator *m. equator.*
ARBEIT *f. work, job.*
ARBEITEN *to work, manufacture.*
arbeitsfähig   *able-bodied.*
arbeitsunfähig   *unfit for work.*
Arbeiter *m. (-in, f.) worker, laborer.*
Arbeiterstand   *m. working class.*
Arbeitgeber *m. employer.*
Arbeitnehmer *m. employee.*
arbeitsam *industrious, diligent.*
Architekt *m. architect.*
Architektur *f. architecture.*
arg *bad, mischievous.*
Sie dachte an nichts Arges.   *She meant no harm.*
Ärger *m. annoyance, anger, worry.*
ärgerlich *annoying, angry.*
ärgern *to annoy, irritate, bother.*
sich ärgern   *to be angry.*
Argument *n. argument.*
Aristokrat *m. aristocrat.*

Aristokratie *f. aristocracy.*
aristokratisch *aristocratic.*
ARM *m. arm.*
ARM *poor*
Armband *n. bracelet.*
Armbanduhr *f. wrist watch.*
Ärmel *m. sleeve*
Armlehne *f. arm of chair*
Armut *f. poverty.*
Arrest *m. arrest.*
ART *f. kind, manner, way, type.*
artig *good, well-behaved.*
Artikel *m. article.*
Arznei *f. medicine (drug).*
Arzneikunde *f. pharmacy (profession of).*
Ast *m. branch (tree).*
Atem *m. breath, suspense.*
    Dieser Kriminalroman hält uns in
        Atem. *This detective story keeps us*
        in suspense.
atemlos *breathless.*
atemraubend *breath-taking.*
    Der Film war atemraubend. *The movie*
        was breath-taking.
Athlet *m. athlete.*
atmen *to breathe.*
AUCH *also, too, even.*
    was auch   *whatever.*
    wer auch   *whoever.*
    wo auch   *wherever.*
    Was auch geschieht, Sie sind
        verantwortlich. *Whatever happens,*
        you are responsible.
    Wer auch kommen mag, ich bin nicht zu
        Hause. *Whoever comes, I am not*
        home.
    Wo auch immer er auftauchen mag, man
        wird ihn erkennen. *Wherever he*
        appears, he will be recognized.
AUF 1. *prep. (dat. when answering*
    question, Wo?; acc. when answering
    question, Wohin?, and depending on
    the idion) on, upon, at, in, to, for,
    during.
    Er kommt auf die Strasse hinab. *He*
        comes down to the street.
    Ich kaufe Gemüse auf dem Markt. *I buy*
        vegetables at the market.
    Ich traf sie auf dem Ball. *I met her at the*
        ball.
    Ich fahre auf das Land. *I drive to the*
        country.
    Sie wohnen auf/in diesem Schloss. *They*
        live in that castle.
    Die Jäger gehen auf die Jagd. *The*
        hunters go hunting.
    Der Tag folgt auf die Nacht. *The day*
        follows the night.
    alle bis auf einen   *all except one.*

auf der Rückfahrt von Wien   *during the*
    return from Vienna.
auf deutsch   *in German.*
auf einmal   *suddenly.*
auf keinen Fall   *in no case.*
auf Wiedersehen!   *Good-bye!*
Liebe auf den ersten Blick   *love at first*
    sight.
2. *adv. up, upwards.*
auf und ab   *up and down.*
3. *Separable prefix (implies motion*
    upward or outward, opening,
    completion).
Ich setze meinen Hut auf.   *I put my hat*
    on.
Die Sonne geht auf.   *The sun is rising.*
Bitte, machen Sie das Fenster auf.   *Please*
    open the window.
aufbewahren *to keep, preserve, stock.*
Aufbewahrung *f. preservation, storage.*
aufbrauchen *to use up.*
aufeinander *one on top of the other.*
Aufenthalt *m. stay, residence.*
aufessen *to eat up.*
Auffassung *f. conception, interpretation.*
Aufgabe *f. task, duty, problem.*
aufgeben *to commission, order, lose, give up,*
    resign, check, send.
    die Hoffnung aufgeben   *to lose hope.*
    ein Telegramm aufgeben   *to send a*
    telegram.
aufhängen *to hang up.*
aufheben *to pick up, rise, abolish.*
aufheitern *to cheer up.*
aufklären *to clear, explain.*
Aufklärung *f. explanation.*
aufmachen *to open, unlock, undo.*
aufmerken *to pay attention, attend.*
aufmerksam *attentive.*
Aufmerksamkeit *f. attention.*
Aufnahme *f. taking up, admission,*
    enrollment, snapshot.
aufnahmefähig *receptive.*
Aufnahmeprüfung *f. entrance examination.*
aufnehmen *to lift, take up, admit,*
    photograph, record (a voice).
aufpassen *to adapt, fix, pay attention.*
    Aufgepasst! *Attention!*
Aufpasser *m. watcher, spy.*
aufräumen *to arrange, put in order, clean.*
aufrecht *upright, straight.*
aufregen *to stir up, excite.*
aufregend *exciting, seditious.*
Aufregung *f. excitement, agitation.*
Aufsatz *m. main piece, top, ornament, article*
    (newspaper); composition.
aufschliessen *to unlock.*
Aufschluss *m. opening up, explanation,*
    information.

Aufschluss über eine Sache geben *to give some information about something.*

aufschreiben *to write down.*

Aufsehen *n. sensation, attention.*

Er erregt Aufsehen. *He attracts attention.*

Aufstand *m. tumult, revolt.*

AUFSTEHEN *stand up, rise, get up.*

aufstehen gegen *to rebel against.*

Stehen sie auf! *Get up!*

aufstellen *to set up, erect, draw up, nominate.*

Eine Behauptung aufstellen *to make a statement.*

Auftrag *m. commission, instruction.*

im Auftrage von *by order of.*

einen Auftrag ausführen *to execute an order.*

auftragen *to carry up, serve up, draw, charge.*

Er nat mir viele Grüsse an Sie aufgetragen. *He sends you his regards ("He charged me with many greetings for you.")*

aufwachen *to awaken.*

aufwachsen *to grow up.*

Aufwand *m. expenditure, expense.*

aufwärts *upwards.*

Er schwimmt een Fluss aufwärts. *He swims upstream.*

aufwecken *to wake someone up.*

aufziehen *to bring up, raise, wind a watch, pull up, tease.*

Aufzug *m. procession, parade, attire, outfit, act (play), elevator.*

AUGE *n. eye.*

Er versuchte mir Sand in die Augen zu streuen. *He tried to deceive me ("throw dust into my eyes").*

gute Augen haben *to have good eyesight.*

grosse Augen machen *to look very surprised.*

Ich habe kein Auge zugemacht. *I did not sleep a wink.*

unter vier Augen *privately ("among four eyes").*

Wir haben ihn aus den Augen verloren. *We lost sight of him.*

Augenarzt *m. oculist, eye doctor.*

Augenblick *m. moment.*

im Augenblick *for the moment.*

augenblicklich *immediately.*

Augenbraue *f. eyebrow.*

Augenlid *n. eyelid.*

Augenwimper *f. eyelash.*

AUGUST *m. August.*

Auktion *f. auction, sale.*

AUS 1. *prep. (dat.) out, out of, for, from, in, upon.*

Aus den Augen, aus dem Sinn. *Out of sight, out of mind.*

Er kommt aus dem Theater. *He comes out of the theater.*

Er hat es aus Liebe getan. *He did it for love.*

Meine Uhr ist aus Gold. *My watch is made of gold.*

Sie stammt aus Paris. *She is a native of Paris.*

2. *adv. out, over, up.*

von hier aus *from here.*

von mir aus *for my part.*

3. *separable prefix. Implies the idea of motion out (in this case also combines with him or her), achievement.*

Die Vorstellung ist aus. *The performance is over.*

Ich gehe aus dem Speisezimmer hinaus. *I go out of the dining room.*

ausbilden *to form, develop, cultivate, educate, train.*

ausbleiben *to stay away, fail to appear, escape.*

Ihre Strafe wird nicht ausbleiben. *You will not escape punishment.*

Ausblick *m. outlook, prospect.*

ausbrechen *to break out, vomit.*

in Tränen ausbrechen *to burst into tears.*

Ausbruch *m. outbreak, eruption, escape.*

Ausdauer *f. perseverance, assiduity.*

ausdauern *to hold out, outlast, endure.*

ausdehnen *to expand, prolong.*

ausdenken *to invent, conceive, imagine.*

Ausdruck *m. expression, phrase.*

ausdrücken *to squeeze, express.*

sich kurz and klar ausdrücken *to express oneself briefly and to the point.*

auseinander *apart, separately.*

ausführen *to take out, export, realize.*

ausführlich *adj. detailed, full; in detail, fully.*

Erzählen Sie mir alles ausführlich. *Tell me everything in detail.*

ausfüllen *to fill out, stuff.*

Ausgabe *f. delivery, edition, issue, publication.*

Ausgang *m. way out, exit, end.*

ausgeben *to give out, deliver, issue, deal (cards).*

ausgehen *to go out, come out, run out, proceed, start from, end.*

frei ausgehen *to go free.*

ihm geht die Geduld aus. *He is losing his patience.*

Wie wird diese Sache ausgehen? *How will this matter end?*

AUSGEZEICHNET *excellent, distinguished.*

ausgleichen *to make even, equalize, settle, arrange, compensate.*

aushalten to bear, suffer, support, hold out, last.

Aushang m. notice (posted); poster.

aushängen to hang out, post a notice.

Aushilfe f. aid (temporary); assistant.

auskleiden to undress.

auskommen to manage, get along.
> Es ist schwer mit ihm auszukommen.   It is difficult to get along with him.
> Ich komme nicht mit dem Papier aus.
> I can't manage with the paper.
> (I don't have enough of it.)

Auskunft f. information

Auskunftei f. information bureau.

auslassen to leave out, omit, let out.

Auslese f. choice, selection.

auslesen to select, choose, read through.

ausmachen to put out, constitute, come to, settle, amount.
> Das macht nichts aus.   It does not matter.

Ausmass n. measurement, scale, proportion.
> mit solchem Ausmass   to such an extent.

ausmessen to measure, survey.

Ausnahme f. exception.
> ohne Ausnahme   without exception.

auspacken to unpack.

Ausrede f. excuse, pretense.

ausreden to finish speaking, excuse.
> einem etwas ausreden   to dissuade somebody from something.

ausrichten to execute, deliver, obtain.
> Haben Sie es ihm ausgerichtet?   Did you give him the message?

Ausruf m. cry, exclamation.

ausrufen to cry out, admonish, proclaim.

ausruhen to rest
> sich ausruhen   to rest oneself.

Aussage f. statement, assertion, declaration, evidence.

aussagen to affirm, declare, give evidence.

ausschalten to cry out, switch off.
> Schalten Sie den Motor aus!   Switch off the motor!

ausscheiden to separate, withdraw.

ausschiffen to disembark, land.

ausschliessen to exclude.

ausschliesslich exclusive (of).

ausschmücken to decorate, adorn.

ausschneiden to cut out, snipe.

AUSSEHEN to look out, appear.

Aussehen n. look, air.

aussen on the outside, abroad, without.
> von aussen   from the outside.

aussenden to send out.

AUSSER 1. prep. (dat.) out of, out, besides.
> ausser der Jahreszeit   out of season.
> ausser sich   beside oneself.
> 2. conj. except, unless, but.
> Ausser Sonntags, gehe ich jeden Tag in die Schule.   I go to school every day except Sunday.

ausserdem besides, moreover.

äusserlich external; on the outside.

äussern to express.

äusserst utmost.

aussetzen to set out, put out, offer, bequeath.
> auszusetzen haben   to find fault with.

Aussicht f. view, prospect.

aussöhnen to reconcile.

aussondern to separate, select.

Aussprache f. pronunciation, accent.

aussprechen to pronounce, express.

aussuchen to seek out, search.

Austausch m. exchange.

austauschen to exchange

Auster f. oyster.

austragen to deliver, distribute.

austreten to treat under, trample, retire.

Ausverkauf m. clearance sale.

ausverkaufen to sell out, clear off (a shop).

Auswahl f. choice, assortment, selection.

auswählen to choose, select.

Auswanderer m. emigrant.

auswandern to emigrate.

Auswanderung f. emigration.

auswärtig foreign, abroad.

Ausweg m. way out.

ausweichen to avoid, evade, shun.

Ausweis m. certificate, document, identity card.

ausziehen to undress, pull out, extract, move, remove.

Auszug m. departure, extract, removal.

Auto n. automobile, car.

Autobahn n. parkway.

Autobus m. bus.

Axt f. axe.

B

Bach m. brook.

BACKEN to bake, fry.

Bäcker m. baker.

Backobst n. dried fruit.

Backofen m. oven.

Backpulver n. baking powder.

BAD n. bath, spa.

Badeanstalt f. baths, swimming pool.

Badeanzug m. bathing suit.

Badehose f. swim trunks.

Bademantel m. bathrobe.

Badeort m. spa.

Badetuch n. bath towel.

Badewanne f. bathtub

Badezimmer n. bathroom

BAHN f. track, road, way, railway.

Bahnarbeiter m. railway worker.

Bahnbeamte *m. railroad official.*
Bahngleis *n. track.*
BAHNHOF *m. train station.*
Bahnsteig *m. platform.*
Bahnübergang *m. railroad crossing.*
Balance *f. balance, equilibrium.*
balancieren *to balance.*
BALD *soon, shortly.*
  bald . . . , bald . . . *sometimes . . . ,*
    sometimes . . .
  bald darauf *soon after.*
Balkon *m. balcony.*
Ball *m. ball, dance.*
Ballett *n. ballet.*
Ballon *m. balloon.*
Band *n. ribbon.*
Bande *f. band, gang.*
bändigen *to tame, to break.*
Bandmass *n. tape measure.*
BANK *f.* 1. *bench, seat.*
  auf die lange Bank schieben *to postpone,*
    delay.
  2. *bank.*
  Geld auf der Bank haben *to have money*
    in the bank.
Bankanweisung *f. check.*
Bankbeamte *m. bank clerk.*
BAR *bare, naked, devoid of, pure.*
  barfuss *barefoot.*
  die bare Wahrheit *the bare truth.*
  bar bezahlen *to pay in cash.*
Bär *m. bear.*
Bargeld *n. cash.*
  bar zahlen *to pay cash.*
barmherzig *merciful.*
Barmherzigkeit *f. mercy*
Baron *m.* (-in, *f.*) *Baron* (*ess*).
Bart *m. beard, whiskers.*
BAU *m. building, construction, edifice,*
  frame.
Bauch *m. belly, stomach.*
BAUEN *to build, construct, cultivate.*
  Luftschlösser bauen *to build castles in the*
    air.
Bauer *m. peasant.*
Bauernhof *m. farm.*
Bauernvolk *n. countryfolk.*
baufällig *dilapidated.*
BAUM *m. tree, pole.*
Baumschule *f. nursery* (*trees*).
Baumwolle *f. cotton.*
Baustein *n. brick.*
beabsichtigen *to intend.*
beachten *to observe, notice.*
Beachtung *f. consideration, attention.*
beachtenswert *noteworthy.*
Beamte *m. official, civil servant.*
  Zollbeamte *m. customs officer.*
beängstigen *to alarm.*

beanspruchen *to claim, demand.*
beantworten *to answer, reply.*
beaufsichtigen *to supervise.*
beben *to tremble.*
  vor Angst beben *to tremble with fear.*
Becher *m. cup, goblet, dice box.*
bedacht *thoughtful, considerate.*
bedanken *to thank.*
Bedarf *m. need, requirement.*
bedauerlich *deplorable, regrettable.*
bedecken *to cover.*
  Der Himmel ist bedeckt. *The sky is*
    overcast.
bedenken *to think, think over, reflect, ponder.*
  sich eines andern bedenken *to change*
    one's mind.
bedenklich *doubtful.*
Bedenkzeit *f. time for reflection.*
(sich) bedienen *to help oneself.*
Bedienung *f. service.*
  einschliesslich der Bedienung *service*
    included.
bedürfen *to need, require*
Bedürfnis *n. need, want, necessity.*
(sich) beeilen *to hurry oneself.*
beeindrucken *to impress.*
beerdigen *to bury.*
Beerdigung *f. funeral.*
befassen *to touch.*
  sich befassen mit *to concern oneself with,*
    to deal with.
  Er befässt sich mit Politik. *He is*
    concerned with politics.
Befehl *m. order, command.*
befehlen *to order, command.*
befestigen *to fasten, fortify.*
befolgen *to obey* (*someone*).
befreien *to free, liberate.*
Befreier *m. liberator.*
Befreiung *f. liberation.*
befreunden *to befriend.*
  sich befreunden mit *to become friends*
    with.
befriedigen *to satisfy, content.*
befriedigend *satisfying.*
Befriedigung *f. satisfaction, gratification.*
befürchten *to fear.*
Befürchtung *f. fear, apprehension.*
befürworten *to recommend.*
begabt *gifted.*
begeben (*sich*) *to set about.*
begegnen *to meet, encounter.*
begeistern *to inspire, fill with enthusiasm.*
begeistert *inspired, enthusiastic.*
Begeisterung *f. inspiration, enthusiasm.*
Beginn *m. beginning.*
BEGINNEN *to begin, start.*
beglaubigen *to attest, certify, to authenticate.*
begleiten *to accompany.*

nach Hause begleiten   *to see (someone) home.*

begründen *to found, to prove.*

Behaglichkeit *f. comfort.*

behalten *to keep, retain, remember.*

Behalten Sie das Kleingeld!   *Keep the change!*

behandeln *to handle, deal with.*

behaupten *to maintain, assert, affirm.*

Behelf *m. help, expedient.*

behelfen (*sich*) *to manage, do without.*

BEI 1. *prep.* (*dat.*) *at, by, near, with, because of, in case of.*

bei der Hand   *by hand.*

Bei Feuer müssen wir die Feuerwehr rufen.   *In case of a fire, we must call the fire department.*

Bei ihrem Charakter wird sie unglücklich werden.   *With (because of) her character, she will be unhappy.*

bei Tage   *by day.*

bei weitem   *by far.*

beim Arzt   *at the doctor's.*

Er arbeitet bei Licht.   *He works by light.*

Hast du Geld bei dir (*or* dabei)?   *Do you have any money on you?*

Ich kaufe meine Kleider bei Engels.   *I buy my clothes at Engels.*

Meine Schwester wohnt bei mir.   *My sister lives with me.*

Beichte *f. confession.*

beichten *to confess.*

BEIDE *both.*

wir beide   *both of us.*

einer von beiden   *one of the two.*

keiner von beiden   *neither of them.*

beiderseits   *on both sides, mutually.*

BEIFALL *m. approval, approbation, applause.*

beifolgend *herewith, enclosed.*

beiläufig *accidental, casual; incidentally.*

beilegen *to add, enclose.*

Beileid *n. sympathy.*

Beileid bezeigen   *to console somebody.*

beim (*bei dem*) *at, by.*

BEIN *n. leg, bone.*

sich kein Bein ausreissen   *to take it easy.*

Er ist immer auf den Beinen.   *He's always on his feet.*

beinahe *nearly, almost.*

beisammen *together.*

beiseite *aside, apart.*

BEISPIEL *n. example.*

zum Beispiel   *for example.*

Das ist ein schlechtes Beispiel.   *This is a bad example.*

beispiellos *unheard of, without example.*

beissen *to bite.*

Der Hund beisst nicht.   *The dog does not bite.*

beistehen *to help, stand by.*

beistimmen *to agree with.*

Beitrag *m. contribution, subscription.*

bejahen *to answer in the affirmative, assent, accept.*

bejammern *to lament.*

bejammernswert *deplorable, lamentable.*

bekämpfen *to combat, fight, struggle.*

BEKANNT *well-known, acquainted.*

bekannt machen mit   *to introduce to.*

Bekannte *m./f. acquaintance, friend.*

Bekanntmachung *f. publication, announcement, notice.*

bekennen *to confess, admit, profess.*

sich schuldig bekennen   *to plead guilty.*

beklagen *to complain, lament.*

BEKOMMEN *to get, receive, catch, agree with.*

Das ist nicht mehr zu bekommen.   *You can't get that any more.*

Es bekommt mir nicht.   *It does not agree with me.*

bekräftigen *to confirm, corroborate.*

belächeln *to smile at.*

belachen *to laugh at.*

belästigen *to molest, trouble.*

beleben *to animate, revive.*

Beleg *m. proof, evidence, illustration.*

BELEGEN *to cover, reserve.*

Ich möchte einen Platz belegen.   *I want to reserve a seat.*

belegte Brötchen   *sandwiches.*

eine Vorlesung belegen   *to enroll for a course.*

belehren *to enlighten, instruct.*

eines Besseren belehren   *to correct.*

beleidigen *to offend, insult.*

beliefern *to supply.*

belohnen *to reward.*

Belohnung *f. reward.*

belügen *to lie (falsify).*

belustigen *to amuse, entertain.*

Belustigung *f. amusement.*

bemerkbar *noticeable, perceptible.*

bemerken *to notice, observe, remark.*

bemerkenswert *noticeable, noteworthy.*

Bemerkung *f. remark, observation.*

bemitleiden *to pity, be sorry for.*

bemitleidenswert *deplorable*

benachrichtigen *to inform, advise.*

Benachrichtigung *f. information, advice.*

benachteiligen *to prejudice.*

Benachteiligung *f. prejudice, injury.*

(sich) benehmen *to behave oneself.*

Benimm dich nicht wie ein kleines Kind!   *Don't behave like a child!*

benelden *to envy.*

benötigen *to require.*

benutzen *to use, employ, utilize.*

beobachten *to observe, watch.*
  heimlich beobachten   *to shadow.*
BEQUEM *comfortable, convenient, lazy.*
  Sei nicht so bequem!   *Don't be so lazy!*
  Wir sitzen bequem.   *We are seated comfortably.*
bequemen *to condescend, comply, submit.*
Bequemlichkeit *f. convenience.*
beraten *to advise.*
Berater *m. adviser.*
beratschlagen *to deliberate.*
berechnen *to calculate, estimate.*
bereden *to talk over, persuade.*
Beredsamkeit *f. eloquence.*
Bereich *m. & n. reach, range, area, zone, domain.*
BEREIT *ready, prepared.*
  bereit halten   *to keep ready.*
  bereitwillig   *willing, ready.*
Bereitwilligkeit *f. willingness.*
bereuen *to repent, regret.*
BERG *m. mountain, hill.*
  über alle Berge sein   *to be out of the woods.*
  Mir standen die Haare zu Berge.   *My hair stood on end.*
Bergmann *m. miner.*
berichten *to report.*
berichtigen *to correct, amend, settle (a bill).*
Berichtigung *f. correction, amendment.*
berücksichtigen *to consider.*
Berücksichtigung *f. consideration, regard.*
BERUF *m. profession, occupation.*
beruflich *professional.*
berufstätig *working, employed.*
beruhigen *to quiet, calm*
Beruhigung *f. reassurance, comfort.*
BERÜHMT *famous, celebrated.*
Berühmtheit *f. fame, celebrity.*
besänftigen *to soften, appease, soothe.*
beschädigen *to damage, injure, harm.*
beschäftigen *to occupy, engage, employ.*
  sich beschäftigen   *to occupy oneself.*
Beschäftigung *f. occupation.*
beschäftigungslos *unemployed, out of work.*
Bescheid *m. answer, information.*
  Bescheid geben   *to inform.*
  Ich habe ihm gehörig Bescheid gesagt.   *I told him off.*
bescheiden *modest, moderate.*
Bescheidenheit *f. modesty.*
bescheinen *to shine upon.*
bescheinigen *to certify, attest.*
Bescheinigung *f. certificate, receipt.*
beschleunigen *to hasten, accelerate.*
beschränken *to limit, confine, restrict.*
Beschränkrung *f. limitation, restriction.*
beschreiben *to write upon, describe.*
Beschreibung *f. description.*

beschuldigen *to accuse.*
Beschuldigung *f. accusation.*
Beschwerde *f. complaint, hardship, trouble.*
(sich) beschweren *to complain.*
  Beschwerdebrüro   *n. complaint department.*
Besen *m. broom.*
besetzen *to occupy, trim, set.*
  Es ist alles besetzt!   *All seats are occupied.*
  Besetzt!   *Occupied! Busy!*
Besetzung *f. occupation, cast.*
  Die Besetzung ist aussergewöhnlich gut.   *The cast is outstanding.*
besichtigen *to view, inspect, visit.*
Besichtigung *f. view, inspection.*
besiegen *to conquer, beat, defeat.*
besinnen *to consider, reflect.*
  sich besinnen   *to remember.*
  sich eines Besseren besinnen   *to think better of.*
besinnlich *contemplative, thoughtful.*
Besitz *m. possession, property, estate.*
besorgen *to take care of, fetch, procure, provide.*
Besorgnis *f. fear, alarm.*
Besorgung *f. care, management.*
  Besorgungen machen   *to go shopping.*
besprechen *to discuss, talk over, criticize, review.*
BESSER *better.*
  umso besser   *so much the better.*
bessern *to improve, recover.*
  sich bessern   *to improve oneself.*
Besserung *f. recovery, improvement.*
  Gute Besserung!   *I hope you will get well soon!*
best(er-es) *best.*
beständig *constant, permanent, steady; constantly, all the time.*
Beständigkeit *f. constancy, stability.*
bestätigen *to confirm, ratify.*
bestechen *to bribe, corrupt.*
bestechlich *corruptible.*
Bestechung *f. bribery, corruption.*
Besteck *n. silverware.*
bestellen *to arrange, order, tell, cultivate.*
  Waren bestellen   *to order goods.*
  zu sich bestellen   *to send for.*
BESTIMMEN *to decide, fix, intend, define, induce.*
  bestimmen über   *to dispose of.*
  bestimmt!   *agreed!*
Bestimmtheit *f. certainty, precision.*
bestrafen *to punish.*
Bestrafung *f. punishment.*
BESUCH *m. visit, company, attendance.*
BESUCHEN *to visit, attend.*
Besucher *m. visitor, spectator, audience.*

beteiligen *to give a share, take part, take an interest.*
beteiligt sein   *to participate.*
Beteiligung *f. share, participation.*
betonen *f. to stress, accent, emphasize.*
Betonung *f. stress, emphasis.*
beträchtlich *considerable.*
(sich) betragen *to behave.*
betreffen *to concern.*
was mich betrifft   *so far as I am concerned.*
betreten *to tread on.*
Betreten des Rasens verboten!   *Keep off the grass!*
Betrieb *m. management, plant, factory.*
in Betrieb sein   *to be working.*
ausser Betrieb   *not working, closed.*
in Betrieb setzen   *to set in motion.*
(sich) betrinken *to get drunk.*
betrüben *to grieve, distress.*
Betrug *m. deception, fraud, swindle.*
betrügen *to deceive, defraud, trick.*
BETT *n. bed.*
das Bett hüten   *to be confined in bed.*
früh zu Bett gehen   *to go to bed early.*
Bettdecke *f. blanket, bedspread.*
betteln *to beg.*
Bettlaken *n. sheet.*
Bettler *m. beggar.*
Bettwäsche *f. bed linen.*
beugen *to bend, bow.*
beunruhigen *to disturb, alarm, upset.*
beurlauben *to grant leave, take leave.*
beurlaubt   *absent on leave.*
Beutel *m. bag, purse.*
bevollmächtigen *to empower, authorize.*
BEVOR *before.*
bewachen *to watch over.*
bewältigen *to master.*
bewegen *to move, stir.*
Beweggrund *m. motive.*
Was war der Beweggrund des Verbrechens?   *What was the motive of the crime?*
beweglich *movable, mobile, quick, lively.*
BEWEGUNG *f. movement, agitation, motion.*
Einer politischen Bewegung angehören   *to belong to a political party.*
Beweis *m. proof, evidence.*
beweisen *to prove, demonstrate.*
Beweisführung *f. demonstration.*
bewerben *to apply for, compete.*
sich bewerben um   *to apply oneself for.*
Er bewarb sich um eine neue Stellung.   *He applied for a new job (position).*
Bewerber *m. applicant, candidate.*
Bewerbung *f. application, courtship.*

bewilligen *to consent, concede.*
bewusst *conscious.*
sich einer Sache bewusst sein   *to be conscious or aware of something.*
bewusstlos *unconscious.*
BEZAHLEN *to pay.*
sich bezahlt machen *to pay for itself (be lucrative).*
bezaubernd *charming.*
Bezug *m. covering, cover, case.*
in Bezug auf   *in regard to.*
Bezug nehmen auf   *to refer to.*
unter Bezugnahme auf   *with reference to.*
Bibel *f. Bible.*
Bibliothek *f. library.*
Bibliothekar *m. librarian.*
Biene *f. bee.*
Bier *n. beer.*
BIETEN *to offer.*
sich alles bieten lassen   *to put up with everything.*
BILD *n. image, picture, illustration, portrait, likeness.*
BILDEN *to form, shape, educate.*
Der Präsident hat ein neues Kabinett gebildet.   *The president has formed a new cabinet.*
die bildenden Künste   *fine arts.*
Bildseite *f. face, head (coin).*
Bildung *f. formation, constitution.*
billig *just, reasonable, fair, moderate.*
binden *to bind, tie.*
BIS *until, as far as, about.*
zwei bis drei Pfund.   *About two or three pounds.*
bis an (acc.)   *up to.*
bis in alle Ewigkeit   *till the end of time.*
bis dann/dahin   *until then.*
bis auf (acc.) *except for.*
Mir gefällt der Film bis auf das Ende.   *I like the film except for the ending.*
alle bis weiteres   *until further notice.*
bis zu   (dat.) (down) to.
von dem Kopf bis zu den Füssen   *from head to foot.*
bis jetzt   *so far.*
bisher   *till now.*
bisweilen   *sometimes.*
Bischof *m. bishop.*
bisschen *a bit, a little, a while.*
Das ist ein bisschen stark.   *That's going a bit too far.*
Er kam ein bisschen spät.   *He came a little late.*
Bissen *m. bite, mouthful.*
Bitte *f. request, prayer.*
BITTE *please.*
bitte, bitte schön, bitte sehr.   (In response to a request: Here you are. In

    response to thanks: You are welcome; don't mention it.)
Wie, bitte? *I beg your pardon?*
BITTEN *to ask, beg, implore.*
    Ich bitte um Entschuldigung. *I beg your pardon, I am sorry.*
bitter *bitter.*
blamieren *to expose to ridicule.*
    sich blamieren *to make a fool of oneself.*
BLATT *n. leaf, petal, blade, sheet.*
    sich kein Blatt vor den Mund nehmen *to speak plainly.*
blättern *to leaf through the pages of a book.*
BLAU *blue.*
Blech *n. tin.*
Blei *n. lead.*
BLEIBEN *to stay, remain, keep, last.*
    bleiben lassen *to leave alone.*
    Das bleibt unter uns. *That's between you and me.*
    Es bleibt dabei *Agreed.*
    sich gleich bleiben *to remain the same.*
    stehen bleiben *to stop, stand still.*
bleibend *permanent, lasting.*
bleich *pale, faded, faint.*
bleichen *to bleach.*
Bleistift *m. pencil.*
blenden *to blind, dazzle.*
BLICK *m. glance, look, gaze.*
    auf den ersten Blick *at first sight.*
    Er warf ihm einen bösen Blick zu. *He gave him a dirty look.*
blind *blind, false.*
    ein blinder Alarm *a false alarm.*
Blindheit *f. blindness.*
blinken *to glitter, glimpse, twinkle, signal.*
Blitz *m. lightning, flash.*
blitzen *to lighten, flash, sparkle.*
Block *m. block, log, pad, stocks.*
blond *blond, fair.*
BLOSS *bare, naked, uncovered; merely, only.*
    Ich tue es bloss ihnen zu gefallen. *I am only doing it to please you.*
blühen *to bloom.*
BLUME *f. flower.*
    Lasst Blumen sprechen! *Say it with flowers!*
Blumenkohl *m. cauliflower.*
Bluse *f. blouse.*
BLUT *n. blood, race, parentage.*
blutarm *anemic.*
Blutdruck *m. blood pressure.*
bluten *to bleed.*
Blutprobe *f. blood-test.*
Blutvergiftung *f. blood-poisoning.*
Boden *m. floor, ground, soil, attic.*
Bogen *m. bow, curve, arch.*
BOHNE *f. bean.*

grüne Bohnen *string beans.*
weisse Bohnen *dried beans.*
Bombardement *n. bombardment.*
bombardieren *to bomb.*
Bombe *f. bomb.*
    Atombombe *f. atomic bomb.*
Bonbon *m. & n. candy.*
BOOT *n. boat.*
    Bootsfahrt *f. boatride.*
Börse *f. purse, stock exchange.*
Börsenmakler *m. stockbroker.*
bösartig *ill-natured, wicked, malicious.*
BÖSE *bad, angry, evil.*
boshaft *malicious, mischievous.*
Bote *m. messenger.*
Botschaft *f. news.*
Botschafter *m. ambassador.*
boxen *to box.*
Brand *m. burning, fire, conflagration.*
    in Brand geraten *to catch fire.*
Brandschaden *m. damage by fire.*
BRATEN *m. roast.*
    Brathuhn *n. roast chicken.*
    Bratkartoffeln *pl. fried potatoes.*
    Bratapfel *m. baked apple.*
BRATEN *to roast, grill, fry.*
Brauch *m. usage, use, custom.*
brauchbar *useful, practicable.*
BRAUCHEN *to use, employ, need.*
    Wie lange werden Sie noch brauchen? *How much more time will it take you?*
Brauhaus *n. brewery, tavern.*
BRAUN *brown.*
Brause *f. shower, douche, spray.*
brausen *to storm, rage, roar, rush.*
    sich abbrausen *to take a shower.*
Braut *f. fiancee.*
    Brautführer *m. best man.*
    Brautjungfer *f. bridesmaid.*
    Brautkleid *n. wedding dress.*
    Brautpaar *n. engaged couple.*
Bräutigam *m. bridegroom.*
brav *good, honest, excellent.*
BRECHEN *to break, pick.*
    Er spricht ein gebrochenes Deutsch. *He speaks broken German.*
BREIT *broad, wide, flat.*
    weit und breit *high and low.*
Breite *f. breadth, width, latitude.*
Bremse *f. brake.*
bremsen *to put the brakes on.*
BRENNEN *to burn, brand, bake, roast.*
    darauf brennen *to be anxious.*
    Es brennt in der Stadt. *There is a fire in town.*
Brett *n. board, plank, shelf, stage.*
    am schwarzen Brett *on the board.*
BRIEF *m. letter*

Briefkasten m. letter-box.
Briefmappe f. attaché case.
Briefmarke f. stamp.
Briefpapier n. stationery.
Brieftasche f. wallet, pocket-book.
Briefträger m. mailman.
Briefumschlag m. envelope.
Brille f. glasses.
BRINGEN to bring, fetch, carry, put, take.
  dazu bringen to induce to.
  Er hat sich ums Leben gebracht. He has committed suicide.
  es zu etwas bringen to achieve something.
  Ich werde das in Ordnung bringen. I'll straighten that out.
  Sie hat es auf neunzig Jahre gebracht. She turned ninety years old.
britisch British
BROT n. bread.
  Brötchen roll.
  sein Brot verdienen to earn one's living.
Brötchen n. roll.
Bruch m. break, fracture, fraction.
Bruchteil m. fraction
BRÜCKE f. bridge (also dental).
  Er hat alle Brücken hinter sich abgebrochen. He has burnt his bridges behind him.
BRUDER m. brother.
  Brüderschaft f. fraternity.
Brunnen m. spring, well, fountain.
Brust f. breast, chest, bosom.
Bube m. boy, jack of cards.
BUCH n. book.
Buchdeckel m. cover, binding.
Buchführung f. bookkeeping.
Buchhaltung f. bookkeeping.
Buchhändler m. bookseller.
Buchhandlung f. bookshop.
Büchse f. can.
Büchsenöffner m. can opener.
Buchstabe m. letter, character.
Buchumschlag m. jacket (book).
Bügelbrett n. ironing board.
Bügeleisen n. iron (for pressing).
bügeln to press.
Bühne f. stage, platform.
Bund m. league, confederation.
Bündel n. bundle.
bunt colored, lively, gay.
  Das ist mir zu bunt. I'm fed up with it.
Burg f. castle, citadel.
Bürge f. bail.
bürgen to guarantee, vouch for.
Bürger m. citizen, townsman.
Bürgerkrieg m. civil war.
Bürgermeister m. mayor.
Bürgersteig m. pavement.

BÜRO n. office.
bürokratisch bureaucratic.
Bursch m. youth, lad, fellow.
Burschenschaft f. students' association.
Bürste f. brush.
bürsten to brush.
Busch m. bush.
Busse f. penitence, repentance.
  Busse tun to do penance.
büssen to suffer for, expiate.
Büste f. bust.
Büstenhalter m. brassiere, bra.
BUTTER f. butter.
Butterbrot n. slice of bread and butter.

C

Café n. café.
Cello n. cello.
Cellist m. cellist.
Champagner m. champagne.
Charakter m. character, disposition.
charakteristisch characteristic.
Chauffeur m. chauffeur.
Chef m. head, boss, chief.
Chemie f. chemistry.
chemisch chemical.
Chinese m., **-in**, f. Chinese (person).
chinesisch Chinese.
Chirurg m. surgeon.
Chor m. choir, chorus.
Choral m. chorale.
Chorgesang m. choir singing.
Choristin f. chorus-girl.
Chorknabe m. choir-boy.
Christ m. Christian.
Christenheit f. Christendom.
Christentum n. Christianity.
Chronik f. chronicle.
Commonwealth Unabhängiger Nationen n. Commonwealth of Independent States (former U.S.S.R.)
Cousin m. (Vetter m.) cousin (man).
Cousine f. (Kusine) cousin (woman).
Creme m. cream (cosmetic).

D

DA 1. adv. there, here.
  2. conj. when, because, as, since.
  da sein to be present.
  da stehen to stand near, stand by.
DABEI near, near by, close to, along, moreover.
  Dabei bleibt es there the matter ends.
  Er hat kein Geld dabei. He has no money on him.
dableiben to stay, remain.

Dach *n. roof.*
  unter Dach und Fach *safe.*
Dachkammer *f. attic.*
DADURCH *through it, by it, thereby.*
  dadurch dass *through the fact that.*
  Er ist dadurch berühmt geworden. *That made him famous.*
DAFÜR *for that, for it, instead of it.*
  dafür sein *to be in favor of.*
  Ich kann nichts dafür. *It is not my fault.*
DAGEGEN 1. *adv. against it.*
  nichts dagegen haben *to have no objection.*
  2. *conj. on the other hand.*
DAHEIM *at home.*
DAHER *from there.*
  Ich komme gerade daher. *I am just coming from there.*
DAHIN *to there.*
  bis dahin *by then.*
  Ich gehe sofort dahin. *I am going there right now.*
dahinten *behind.*
damalig *then, of that time.*
Dame *f. lady, queen (cards), checkers.*
  eine Partie Dame spielen *to play a game of checkers.*
DAMIT 1. *adv. with it, by it.*
  Was wollte er damit sagen? *What does he mean by that?*
  2. *conj. so that, in order to.*
  Ich sage es noch einmal, damit Sie es nicht vergessen. *I say it once more so that you won't forget it.*
  damit nicht *for fear that.*
Dämmerlicht *n. dusk.*
Dämmerung *f. twilight, dawn.*
Dampf *m. vapor, steam.*
Dampfbad *n. steam bath.*
dämpfen *to damp, tone down. extinguish, steam (cooking).*
Dampfer *m. steamer.*
DANACH *afterwards, after that, thereafter.*
  Es sieht danach aus. *It looks like it.*
daneben 1. *adv. near it, next to it, close by.*
  2. *conj. besides, moreover, at the same time, also.*
DANK *m. thanks, gratitude, reward.*
  Gott sei Dank! *Thank God!*
  zum Dank *as a reward.*
DANKBAR *grateful, thankful.*
DANKE *thank you*
  Danke schön! *Thank you very much!*
DANKEN *to thank.*
  Nichts zu danken. *Not at all, don't mention it.*
DANN *then, thereupon.*
  dann und wann *now and then.*
DARAN (dran) *at it, of that, in it, in that.*

Ich glaube daran. *I believe in it.*
  nahe daran sein *to be near, on the point of.*
  Wer ist dran? *Whose turn is it?*
DARAUF (drauf) *on, upon it, after that, thereupon.*
  Es kommt darauf an. *It all depends.*
  Ich lege keinen Wert darauf. *I'm not interested in it.*
DARAUS (draus) *of it, of that, from this, from that.*
  Daraus ist nichts geworden. *Nothing came of it.*
darbieten *to offer, present.*
Darbietung *f. entertainment, offering.*
DAREIN (drein) *into it, therein.*
DARIN (drin) *in it, in that.*
  Es ist nichts darin. *There is nothing to it.*
darlegen *to explain.*
Darlegung *f. explanation, exposition.*
Darlehen *n. loan.*
DARÜBER (drüber) 1. *adv. over it, above it, about it.*
  Darüber besteht kein Zweifel. *There is no doubt about that.*
  darüber hinaus *beyond that.*
  2. *conj. meanwhile.*
DARUM (drum) *round it, for it, about it.*
  Ich kann mich nicht darum kümmern. *I can't take care of that.*
DARUNTER (drunter) *under it, underneath, among them, by that.*
  Was verstehen Sie darunter? *What do you mean by that?*
DAS 1. *neuter article (nom. and acc.). the.*
  2. *demons. pron. that*
  3. *rel. pron. which, that.*
  dasjenige das *the one which.*
  dasselbe *the same.*
dasein *to exist, be present.*
Dasein *n. existence, life.*
  Der Kämpf für das Dasein *struggle for life.*
DASS *conj. that.*
  dass doch *if only.*
Datum *n. date.*
Dauer *f. length, duration.*
  auf die Dauer *for long.*
DAUERN *to last, continue.*
  lange dauern *to take a long time.*
Dauerwelle *f. permanent wave.*
Daumen *m. thumb.*
DAVON *for it, from this, from that, of it, of that.*
  Was halten Sie davon? *What do you think of it?*
  Geben Sie mir ein Paar davon. *Give me a pair of them.*
  Das hängt davon ab. *It depends.*

DAVOR in front of it, of it, of that.
   Sie stehen direkt davor. *They stand right in front of it.*
DAZU to it, for it, for that putpose.
   Es ist schon zu spät dazu. *It is already too late for that.*
   dazu gehören *to belong to it.*
dazwischen in between.
Decke f. cover, blanket, ceiling.
Deckel m. cover, lid.
DECKEN to protect, cover, guard, secure.
Deckung f. cover, shelter, protection.
   in Deckung gehen *to take cover.*
Defekt m. defect, deficiency.
Degen m. sword.
DEIN (poss. adj. fam. form.) your.
DEIN (-er, -e, -es) (poss. pron. fam. form.) yours.
DEM dat, sing of der and das to the, to this, to whom, to which.
   demnach *then.*
   demnächst *soon, shortly.*
   demzufolge *accordingly.*
   Wie dem auch sei *be that as it may.*
Demokrat m. democrat.
Demokratie f. democracy.
Demut f. humility.
demütig humble.
demütigen to humiliate.
Demütigung f. humiliation.
DEN acc. sing. of der; dat. pl. of die. the, this, to them, whom, that.
DENEN dat. pl. of die (rel. pron.) to whom, to which.
DENKEN to think, intend, mean.
   Was denken Sie zu tun? *What do you intend to do?*
   denken an *to remember, think of.*
   sich denken *to imagine.*
   Das kann ich mir schon denken. *I can well imagine.*
Denker m. thinker.
DENN for, because, then.
   es sei denn, dass *unless.*
dennoch nevertheless.
deponieren to deposit.
DER 1. masc. article (nom.) the; (fem.) (gen. & dat.) of the, to the; pl. (gen.) of the.
   2. demons. pron. this.
   3. rel. pron. which, who, that.
   derjenige der *the one who, he who.*
   derselbe *the same.*
DEREN gen. fem. and pl. of die, (rel. pron.) whose.
DES yen. sing. of der and das of the.
DESHALB therefore, for that reason.
DESSEN gen. sing. of der and das pron. whose.

Detektiv m. detective.
deuten to point out, explain, interpret.
deutlich distinct, clear; distinctly, clearly.
Deutlichkeit f. distinctness, clearness.
DEUTSCH German.
DEUTSCHE m. & f. German (person)
DEUTSCHLAND n. Germany.
Deutung f. interpretation, explanation.
Devise f. foreign bill, motto.
DEZEMBER m. December.
Dialekt m. dialect.
Diamant m. diamond.
Diät f. diet.
   Diät leben *to diet.*
DICH acc. of du. (fam. form) you.
DICHT thick, dense, tight, close.
dichten to compose, write poetry, invent.
Dichter m. poet.
Dichtung f. poetry, fiction.
DICK thick, stout, fat.
   Er ist dick geworden. *He got fat.*
Dickkopf m. blockhead.
DIE 1. fem. article (nom. and acc.), the. pl. article (noun. and acc.). the.
   2. demons. pron. this.
   3. rel. pron. who, which, that.
diejenige die *she who, the one which.*
   dieselbe *the same.*
DIEB m. thief, burglar.
   Halten Sie den Dieb! *Stop the thief!*
Diebstahl m. theft.
DIENEN to serve.
   Womit kann ich dienen? *Can I help you?*
Diener m. servant.
Dienerin f. maid.
dienlich serviceable.
Dienst m. service, duty, situation, employment.
   ausser Dienst *off duty.*
   zu Diensten stehen *to be at a person's disposal.*
DIENSTAG m. Tuesday.
diensteifrig zealous.
Dienstmädchen n. maid.
Dienststelle f. headquarters.
DIES (-er, -e, -es) this, that.
DIESMAL this time.
DIESSEITS (gen.) on this side.
Diktat n. dictation, treaty.
DING n. thing, object.
   guter Dinge sein *to be in high spirits.*
   vor allen Dingen *first of all.*
Diplom n. diploma, certificate.
Diplomatie f. diplomacy.
diplomatisch diplomatic.
DIR dat. of du (fam. form) you, to you.
direkt direct.
Direktor m. director.
Dirigent m. conductor.

dirigieren *to conduct, direct.*

diskret *discreet, tactful.*

Diskretion *f. discretion.*

diskutieren *to discuss.*

Distanz *f. distance.*

DOCH *however, anyway, nevertheless, but, still, yet; surely, of course, yes* (*in answer to a negative question*)*; indicates a well-known fact.*

Willst du nicht kommen? Doch. *Won't you come? Of course.*

Ich habe doch gewusst, dass er schwer krank war. *I knew* (*very well*) *he was very ill.*

Ich werde doch gehen. *I will go anyhow.*

Ja doch! *Of course.*

Sie werden doch zugeben, dass er recht hatte. *But you will admit he was right.*

Und doch ist es nicht so traurig, wie Sie denken. *And still it is not so sad as you think.*

DOKTOR *m. doctor.*

den Doktor machen *to take the degree of doctor.*

Doktorarbeit *f. thesis for doctorate.*

Dokument *n. document.*

dokumentieren *to prove.*

Dolch *m. dagger.*

dolmetschen *to interpret.*

Dolmetscher *m. interpreter.*

Dom *m. cathedral.*

Donner *m. thunder.*

vom Donner gerührt *thunderstruck.*

donnern *to thunder.*

Donnerschlag *m. thunderbolt.*

DONNERSTAG *m. Thursday.*

Donnerwetter *n. thunderstorm.*

Donnerwetter! *Good heavens!*

doppeldeutig *ambiguous.*

Doppelpunkt *m. colon.*

doppelt *double.*

Doppelbett, *n. double bed.*

Doppelzimmer, *n. room with twin beds.*

DORF *n. village.*

Dorn *m. thorn.*

DORT *there, yonder.*

dorther *from there.*

dorthin *that way, over there.*

Dose *f. box, can, dose, amount.*

DRAHT *m. wire, cable, line.*

Drängen *to push, press, hurry, urge*

Nicht drängen! *Do not push!*

draussen *outside, outdoors, abroad.*

drehen *to turn, rotate, revolve.*

DREI *three.*

Dreieck *n. triangle.*

DREISSIG *thirty.*

DREISSIGSTE *thirtieth.*

DREIZEHN *thirteen.*

DREIZEHNTE *thirteenth.*

dringen *to enter, get in, penetrate.*

dringen auf *to insist on.*

dringend *urgent.*

DRITTE *third.*

Droge *f. drug.*

Drogerie *f. chemist's shop.*

drüben *over there, yonder.*

Druck *m. pressure, compression.*

in Druck gehen *to go to press.*

drucken *to print.*

Druckknopf *m. push button.*

Druckfehler *m. misprint.*

Dschungel *f. jungle.*

DU *pers. pron. fam. form. you.*

Duft *m. scent, smell, fragrance.*

DUFTEN *to smell sweet, be fragrant.*

duftig *sweet-smelling, fragrant.*

dulden *to endure, bear, suffer.*

dumm *stupid, dull, ignorant.*

Sei nicht so dumm! *Don't be so stupid!*

Es wurde mir zu dumm. *I got sick and tired of it.*

Dummheit *f. stupidity, blunder.*

Dummkopf *m. stupid fellow, dunce.*

düngen *to fertilize.*

Dünger *m. fertilizer, manure.*

dunkel *dark, gloomy, vaguely.*

Ich erinnere mich dunkel ... *I vaguely remember ...*

Dunkelheit *f. darkness, obscurity.*

dunkeln *to get dark.*

dünn *thin, weak, rare.*

DURCH 1. *prep.* (*acc.*) *through, across, by, by means of, because of.*

Ich ging durch den Wald. *I walked through the forest.*

Durch den Krieg wurden viele Städte zerstört. *Many cities were destroyed because of the war.*

Er bestand die Prüfung durch viel Arbeit. *He passed the examination by working hard.* (*through much work.*)

Er schickt es durch die Post. *He sends it by mail.*

die ganze Zeit durch *all the time.*

durch und durch *through and through.*

2. *prefix.*

a) *inseparable. through, across, around.*

Die Milchstrasse durchzieht den Himmel. *The milky way goes across the sky.*

b) *separable, implies the idea of accomplishment.*

Ich lese das Buch durch. *I read the book to the end.*

durcharbeiten *to work through, study thoroughly.*

durchaus *thoroughly, absolutely.*

durchaus nicht *not at all, not in the
  least.*
durcheinander *confusedly, in disorder.*
durchfahren *to drive through (without
  stopping).*
Durchfahrt *f. thoroughfare, passage.*
  Keine Durchfahrt! *No thoroughfare!*
durchfechten *to fight out.*
durchfinden *to find one's way through.*
durchführbar *to carry out, accomplish,
  execute.*
Durchführung *f. accomplishment, execution,
  performance.*
Durchgang *m. passageway.*
  Kein Durchgang! *No trespassing!*
durchgehen *to go through, pass through, run
  away.*
durchhalten *to hold out, carry through.*
durchmachen *to go through, suffer.*
  Sie haben viel durchgemacht. *They have
    gone through a lot.*
Durchmesser *m. diameter.*
durchnehmen *to work through, go over.*
Durchreise *f. journey through, passing
    through, transit.*
durchreisen *to travel through, cross.*
Durchreisevisum *n. transit visa.*
durchschauen *to look through.*
Durchschlag *m. colander, strainer, carbon
    copy.*
durchschlagend *powerful.*
Durchschlagpapier *n. carbon paper.*
durchschneiden *to cut through.*
durchsetzen *to achieve, carry out, bring
    about.*
durchsuchen *to search through.*
Durchsuchung *f. search, police raid.*
Durchzug *m. march through, passage
    through.*
DÜRFEN *to be allowed to, be permitted.*
  Darf ich, bitte? *May I, please?*
  Darf ich um den nächsten Tanz bitten?
    May I have the next dance?
  Darf man hier rauchen? *Is smoking
    allowed here?*
dürftig *poor, needy, indigent.*
DÜRR *dry, parched, dried, lean, skinny.*
  dürres Holz *dry wood.*
DÜRRE *f. dryness, drought.*
Durst *m. thirst.*
  Das macht Durst. *That makes (one)
    thirsty.*
dürsten *to be thirsty, long for, crave.*
durstig *thirsty.*
Dusche *f. shower-bath.*
duschen *(sich) to take a shower.*
Düsenflugzeug *n. jet plane.*
Dutzend *n. dozen.*
  dutzendmal *dozens of times.*

E

Ebbe *f. ebb, low tide.*
  die Ebbe und die Flut *the ebb and flow.*
EBEN *even, flat, smooth, just.*
  eben erst *just now.*
  eben deshalb *for that very reason.*
  ebenfalls *likewise, too, also.*
  ebenmässig *symmetrical, proportional.*
  ebenso *just as, just so, quite as.*
  Es geschiet dir eben recht. *It just serves
    you right.*
Ebene *f. plain.*
ebnen *to level, smooth.*
Echo *n. echo.*
ECHT *genuine, true, real, legitimate.*
Echtheit *f. legitimacy.*
Ecke *f. corner, angle.*
eckig *triangular, cornered.*
edel *noble, well-born, generous.*
Efeu *n. ivy.*
Effekt *m. effect, stocks.*
Effekthascherei *f. showing off.*
effektvoll *effective.*
Egoismus *m. egoism.*
Egoist *m. egoist.*
egoistisch *egoistic.*
egozentrisch *egocentric.*
EHE *before, until.*
  ehemals *formerly.*
  eher *sooner, rather.*
Ehe *f. matrimony, marriage.*
Ehefrau *f. wife, spouse.*
Ehegatte *m. husband.*
Ehepaar *n. married couple.*
ehelich *matrimonial, conjugal.*
Ehescheidung *f. divorce.*
Ehescheidungsklage *f. divorce suit.*
Eheschliessung *f. marriage.*
EHRE *f. honor, reputation, respect.*
  Meine Ehre steht auf dem Spiel. *My
    honor is at stake.*
ehren *to honor.*
ehrenamtlich *honorary.*
Ehrenbezeigung *f. mark of respect.*
Ehrenwort *n. word of honor.*
ehrerbietig *respectful.*
Ehrerbietung *f. deference, respect.*
Ehrfurcht *f. respect, awe, reverence.*
Ehrgefühl *n. sense of honor, self-respect.*
Ehrgeiz *m. ambition.*
ehrlich *honorably.*
  ehrlich gesagt *to tell the truth.*
  Ehrlich gesagt, glaube ich ihm nicht. *To
    tell (you) the truth, I don't believe
    him.*
ehrgeizig *ambitious.*
Ehrlichkeit *f. honesty.*

Ehrlosigkeit *f. dishonesty, infamy.*
Ei *n. (pl. Eier) egg.*
  Eigelb *n. egg yolk.*
  Eiweiss *n. egg white.*
  Rühreier *scrambled eggs.*
  Spiegeleier *fried eggs.*
  weiche Eier *soft-boiled eggs.*
Eiche *f. oak.*
Eichhörnchen *n. squirrel.*
Eifer *m. zeal, ardor.*
Eifersucht *f. jealousy.*
eifersüchtig *jealous.*
eifrig *eager, keen, zealous.*
EIGEN *own, proper, particular, special, choosy.*
  Er ist sehr eigen im Essen. *He is very fussy about his food.*
eigenartig *odd, peculiar, strange, queer.*
eigensinnig *stubborn, obstinate.*
eigentlich *real, actual; actually, really, exactly, just, as a matter of fact, indeed.*
  Was heisst das eigentlich? *What does it actually mean?*
Eigentum *n. property.*
eigentümlich *queer, odd, peculiar.*
(sich) eignen *to be suited, qualified.*
EILE *f. hurry, haste, speed.*
  Es hat keine Eile. *There's no hurry about it.*
  Eile mit Weile. *Haste makes waste.*
EILEN *(sich) to hurry.*
  Das eilt sehr. *This is very urgent.*
  Das eilt nicht. *There's no hurry.*
eilig *fast, hasty.*
  es eilig haben *to be in a hurry.*
Eilzug *m. fast train, express.*
EIN, eine, ein 1. *indefinite article. a, an.*
  2. *number. one.*
  3. *pron. one.*
  Eines Tages *some day.*
  ein für allemal *once for all.*
  4. *separable prefix (implies the idea of entrance or reduction in volume).*
  Die Lehrerin trat in das Schulzimmer ein. *The teacher (fem.) entered the classroom.*
  Läuft dieser Stoff ein? *Does this material shrink?*
EINANDER *each other, one another.*
  Wir haben einander jahrelang nicht gesehen. *We have not seen each other for years.*
einarbeiten *to get used to, familiarize with.*
einatmen *to inhale.*
Einbahnstrasse *f. one-way street.*
einbiegen *to turn into.*
  Biegen Sie in diese Strasse ein! *Turn into this street.*

(sich) einbilden *to imagine; fancy, think, believe.*
Einbildung *f. imagination, conceit, presumption.*
einbrechen *to break open, through.*
  Heute Nacht ist ein Dieb bei ihm eingebrochen. *Last night a thief broke into his house.*
Einbrecher *m. burglar.*
Einbruch *m. house-breaking, burglary.*
EINDRUCK *m. impression.*
  Er tut es bloss, um Eindruck zu machen. *He does it only to show off.*
EINFACH *simple, plain, single; simply, plainly, elementary.*
  einfache (Fahrt) *one-way (ticket).*
Einfall *m. idea, collapse, whim.*
  Wie kommen Sie auf den Einfall? *What gave you the idea?*
einfältig *simple.*
Einfluss *m. influence.*
einflussreich *influential.*
Einfuhr *f. importation, import.*
einführen *to introduce, import.*
Einführung *f. importation.*
Einfuhrzoll *m. import duty.*
Eingabe *f. petition, memorial.*
EINGANG *m. entrance.*
  Kein Eingang. *No entrance.*
  Verbotener Eingang! *Keep out!*
Eingemachtes *n. preserves.*
eingebildet *conceited.*
Eingebung *f. inspiration.*
eingestehen *to admit, confess.*
eingewöhnen *to accustom.*
Einhalt *m. stop.*
  Einhalt gebieten *to put a stop to.*
einhalten *to observe, follow, keep to, meet.*
  Wird er den Termin einhalten? *Will he meet the deadline?*
Einheit *f. unity, union, unit.*
einheitlich *uniform.*
einholen *to bring in, collect, gather, make up.*
  einholen gehen *to go shopping.*
einig *in agreement, united, unanimous.*
einigemal *several times.*
einigen *to unite, unify.*
sich einigen *to come to terms, agree.*
einig (-er,-e,-es) *some, any, a few.*
einigermassen *to some extent, somewhat.*
Einigkeit *f. harmony.*
Einigung *f. agreement.*
einjagen *to alarm, frighten.*
EINKAUF *m. purchase, buying.*
EINKAUFEN *to buy, purchase, shop.*
  Einkaufspreis *m. price of purchase.*
Einkommen *n. income.*
Einkommensteuer *f. income tax.*

einladen *to invite.*
EINLADUNG *f. invitation.*
Einlass *m. entrance, admission.*
einlassen *to admit, let in.*
einleben *to settle down, familiarize oneself.*
einleiten *to begin, initiate, introduce, institute.*
Einleitung *f. introduction.*
einmachen *to preserve.*
Einmachglas *n. preserves jar.*
EINMAL *once, formerly.*
  auf einmal *all at once.*
  Es war einmal . . . *Once upon a time there was . . .*
  noch einmal *once more.*
(sich) einmischen *to interfere, to meddle.*
einmütig *unanimous.*
Einnahme *f. occupation, capture, conquest.*
einnehmen *to collect, engage, occupy, receive, captivate.*
einnehmend *captivating.*
einordnen *to arrange, classify, file.*
einpacken *to wrap up.*
einpflanzen *to plant, inculcate.*
einrahmen *to frame.*
einreden *to persuade, talk someone into.*
einreichen *to hand in, deliver, present.*
einreihen *to insert, include, arrange.*
Einreise *f. entry into a country.*
Einreiseerlaubnis *f. permit to enter a country.*
einrichten *to arrange, prepare, manage, furnish.*
  sich einrichten *to plan.*
Einrichtung *f. furniture, layout.*
EINS *one, the same.*
  Es kommt auf eins hinaus. *It comes to the same thing.*
EINSAM *lonely, solitary, lonesome.*
Einsamkeit *f. loneliness, solitude.*
einschläfern *to lull to sleep.*
einschalten *to insert, put in.*
einschenken *to pour in.*
einschlafen *to fall asleep.*
einschlagen *to drive in (nail), break, wrap up.*
  Schlagen Sie mir das, bitte, ein. *Will you please wrap that for me?*
einschliessen *to lock up, enclose.*
einschliesslich *inclusive.*
Einschreibebrief *m. registered letter.*
einschreiben *to enter, note down, register.*
einschüchtern *to intimidate.*
EINSEITIG *one-sided, partial.*
einsetzen *to put in, insert.*
  sich einsetzen für *to speak on behalf of.*
Einspruch *m. protest, objection.*
  Einspruch erheben *to object to, protest against.*

EINST *once, one day.*
  einstmals *once, formerly.*
  einstweilen *meanwhile, for the present.*
  einstweilig *temporary.*
einsteigen *to get in.*
  Nach Düsseldorf einsteigen! (*Passengers*) *to Düsseldorf, all aboard!*
einstellen *to put on, adjust, stop, cease.*
  Arbeit einstellen *to strike.*
  Betrieb einstellen *to close down.*
  sich einstellen auf *to be prepared.*
Einstellung *f. adjustment, enlistment, attitude.*
  Ich verstehe Ihre Einstellung nicht. *I don't understand your attitude.*
einstimmen *to join in.*
einstimmig *unanimous.*
einstudieren *to study, rehearse.*
einteilen *to divide, plan, distribute.*
Einteilung *f. division, distribution, arrangement.*
eintönig *monotonous.*
Eintönigkeit *f. monotony.*
Eintracht *f. harmony, union, concord.*
(sich) eintragen *to register.*
eintreffen *to arrive, happen.*
  Was ich befürchtete, ist eingetroffen. *What I was afraid of has happened.*
EINTRETEN *to go in, enter.*
  Bitte, treten Sie ein! *Won't you come in, please!*
  eintreten für *to intercede.*
  eintreten in *to join.*
EINTRITT *entrance, entry.*
  Eintritt verboten! *No admission!*
  Eintritt frei! *Admission free!*
Eintrittsgeld *n. admission fee.*
Eintrittskarte *f. ticket.*
EINVERSTANDEN *agreed.*
  einverstanden sein *to agree.*
Einverständnis *n. agreement, consent.*
Einwand *m. objection, protest.*
einwandfrei *faultless, perfect.*
Einwanderer *m. immigrant.*
einwandern *to immigrate.*
Einwanderung *f. immigration.*
einwechseln *to change money.*
einwenden *to object.*
einwilligen *to consent.*
Einwilligung *f. consent.*
Einwurf *m. slit, slot.*
Einzahl *f. singular.*
einzahlen *to pay in.*
Einzahlung *f. payment.*
EINZELN *individual, particular, separate, single.*
  Kann man jeden Band einzeln kaufen? *Can I buy each volume separately?*

jeder einzelne   *each and every one.*

einziehen *to pull in, draw, move in.*

Sie sind schon in ihre neue Wohnung eingezogen.   *They have already moved into their new apartment.*

EINZIG *only, sole, unique.*

einzig und allein *solely, entirely.*

Er ist das einzige Kind.   *He is the only child.*

Einzug *m. entry, entrance, moving in.*

EIS *n. ice, ice cream.*

Eisbahn   *f. rink.*

Eisschrank   *m. refrigerator.*

eisig *icy.*

EISEN *n. iron.*

zum alten Eisen werfen   *to junk.*

Eisenbahn *f. railway.*

Eisenbahnwagen *m. railway car.*

Eisenwaren *pl. hardware.*

eisern (er,-e,-es) *of iron, inflexible.*

der eiserne Vorhang   *the iron curtain.*

Er hat einen eisernen Willen.   *He has an iron will.*

eitel *vain, conceited, idle.*

Eitelkeit *f. vanity, conceit.*

Elefant *m. elephant.*

elegant *elegant.*

Eleganz *f. elegance.*

Elektriker *m. electrician.*

elektrisch *electric.*

elektrisieren *to electrify.*

Elektrizität *f. electricity.*

Element *n. element.*

elementar *elementary.*

Elend *n. misery, misfortune, distress.*

elend *miserable, ill; miserably.*

Elfenbein *n. ivory.*

ELFTE *eleventh.*

Ellenbogen *m. elbow.*

elterlich *parental.*

ELTERN *pl. parents.*

elternlos *orphaned.*

Emigrant *m. emigrant.*

Empfang *m. receipt, reception.*

EMPFANGEN *to receive, welcome.*

Empfänger *m. receiver, addressee.*

empfänglich *receptive.*

Empfangsnahme *f. receipt (paper).*

empfehlen *to recommend.*

empfinden *to experience, feel, perceive.*

empfindlich *sensitive; susceptible.*

Empfindlichkeit *f. sensitiveness.*

empören *to rouse, excite, shock.*

sich empören *to be furious; rebel.*

Empörung *f. rebellion.*

ENDE *n. end, result, conclusion, extremity.*

am Ende   *in the end, after all.*

Ende gut, alles gut.   *All is well that ends well.*

letzten Endes   *finally.*

zu Ende führen   *to finish.*

zu Ende gehen   *to come to an end.*

ENDEN *to end, finish, stop, die.*

Endergebnis *n. final result.*

endgültig *final, definite.*

endlos *endless.*

Endstation *f. terminus.*

Energie *f. energy.*

energisch *energetic, vigorous.*

ENG *narrow, tight, close, intimate.*

engherzig   *narrow-minded.*

engagieren *to engage.*

Engel *m. angel.*

Engländer *m. Englishman.*

Engländerin *f. Englishwoman.*

Englisch *n. English.*

auf Englisch   *in English.*

Enkel *m. 1. ankle. 2. grandson.*

Enkelkind *n. grandchild.*

Enkeltochter *f. (Enkelin) granddaughter.*

entbehren *to be without, lack, miss.*

entbehrlich *superfluous, spare.*

Entbehrung *f. privation, want.*

entdecken *to discover, find out, detect.*

Entdecker *m. discoverer.*

Entdeckung *f. discovery.*

Ente *f. duck.*

entehren *to dishonor.*

enteignen *to expropriate, dispossess.*

Enteignung *f. expropriation.*

enterben *to disinherit.*

entfalten *to unfold, develop, display.*

entfernen *to remove, take away, depart.*

sich entfernen   *to leave.*

entfernt *far off, far away, distant.*

Entfernung *f. distance.*

entfliehen *to run away, escape.*

entfremden *to estrange, alienate.*

Entfremdung *f. estrangement, alienation.*

entführen *to carry off, elope, to abduct.*

Entführung *f. abduction, elopement, kidnapping.*

entgegen *toward, opposed to, contrary to.*

entgegen arbeiten *to work against, counteract.*

entgegengehen *to go to meet, face.*

entgegengesetzt *opposite.*

entgegenhalten *to object, contrast.*

entgegenkommen *to come to meet.*

auf halbem Weg entgegenkommen   *to meet halfway.*

entgegenkommend *obliging, kind, helpful.*

entgegennehmen *to accept, receive.*

entgegensetzen (entgegenstellen) *to oppose, contrast.*

entgegentreten *to advance toward, oppose.*

entgegnen *to reply, answer.*

Entgegnung *f. reply.*

entgehen *to escape, elude.*
enthalten *to contain, hold, include.*
  enthalten sein   *to be included.*
  sich enthalten   *to refrain.*
entkommen *to escape.*
entladen *to unload, discharge.*
Entladung *f. discharge.*
entlassen *to dismiss.*
Entlassung *f. dismissal.*
entmutigen *to discourage, dishearten.*
entnehmen *to take from, gather,*
  understand.
enträtseln *to solve, decipher.*
entrüsten *to provoke, irritate, make angry.*
Entrüstung *f. anger, indignation.*
entsagen *to renounce, abandon.*
  dem Thron entsagen   *to abdicate.*
Entscheid *m. answer.*
entscheiden *to decide, make up one's mind.*
  Entscheiden Sie das.   *You decide that.*
entscheidend *decisive, critical.*
Entscheidung *f. decision, judgment, sentence,*
  award.
entscheiden *decided, firm, resolute.*
Entschiedenheit *f. determination, certainty.*
entschliessen *to decide, make up one's mind.*
  Ich habe mich anders entschlossen.   *I've*
  changed my mind.
Entschlossenheit *f. determination.*
Entschluss *m. resolution, decision.*
entschuldbar *excusable.*
ENTSCHULDIGEN *to excuse.*
  Entschuldigen Sie, bitte!   *Please excuse*
  me!
  Ich bitte vielmals um Entschuldigung. *I am*
  awfully sorry.
  sich entschuldigen *to apologize.*
entschwinden *to vanish, disappear.*
entsetzen *to frighten, dismiss from, relieve.*
entsetzlich *terrible, dreadful.*
(sich) entsinnen *to remember, recollect,*
  recall.
entspannen *to relax.*
Entspannung *f. relaxation, rest, recreation.*
entstehen *to arise, originate.*
Entstehung *f. origin, formation.*
entstellen *to distort, misrepresent.*
enttäuschen *to disappoint.*
Enttäuschung *f. disappointment.*
ENTWEDER ... ODER *either ... or.*
entwerfen *to draw up, design.*
entwerten *to depreciate.*
ENTWICKELN *to develop, explain.*
  einen Film entwickeln *to develop a film*
  (*photographic*).
Entwicklung *f. development.*
Entwicklungsjahre *pl. adolescence.*
entwürdigen *to degrade, disgrace.*
Entwurf *m. sketch, draft.*

entziehen *to deprive of, take away from,*
  withdraw.
entzücken *to delight, charm, enchant.*
entzückend *charming, delightful.*
entzwei *in two, torn, broken.*
Episode *f. episode.*
Epoche *f. epoch, era.*
ER *he.*
  er selbst *himself.*
(sich) erarbeiten *to get through hard work.*
erbarmen *to feel pity, have mercy.*
erbärmlich *pitiful, miserable.*
erbarmungslos *merciless, pitiless.*
Erbe *m. heir.*
Erbe *n. heritage.*
erben *to inherit.*
Erbfolge *f. succession.*
(sich) erbieten *to offer, volunteer.*
erblassen *to turn pale.*
erblicken *to catch sight of, perceive.*
erbrechen *to break open.*
  sich erbrechen   *to vomit.*
Erbschaft *f. inheritance, legacy.*
Erbse *f. pea.*
Erbstück *n. heirloom.*
Erbteil *n. portion of inheritance.*
Erdbeben *n. earthquake.*
Erdbeere *f. strawberry.*
Erdboden *m. ground, soil, earth.*
ERDE *f. earth, ground, soil.*
  auf der Erde *on earth.*
Erdgeschoss *n. ground floor.*
  zu ebener Erde *on the ground floor.*
Erdkunde *f. geography.*
erdolchen *to stab.*
Erdteil *m. continent.*
(sich) ereignen *to happen, occur, pass.*
  Wann hat sich das ereignet? *When did that*
  happen?
Ereignis *n. event, occurrence, incident.*
erfahren *to learn, experience.*
  Wo kann ich das erfahren? *Where can I get*
  this information?
Erfahrung *f. experience, information.*
  aus Erfahrung *by experience.*
  erfahrungsgemäss *from experience.*
erfinden *to find out, discover, invent.*
Erfinder *m. inventor.*
Erfindung *f. invention.*
Erfolg *m. success, result, outcome.*
erfolgen *to result, follow.*
erfolglos *unsuccessful, fruitless.*
erfolgreich *successful.*
erforderlich *necessary, requisite.*
erforschen *to explore, investigate.*
Erforschung *f. exploration, investigation.*
ERFREUEN *to give pleasure, gladden, be*
  pleased, rejoice.
sich erfreuen *to enjoy.*

erfreulich *delightful, gratifying, satisfactory.*
ERFREUT *glad, pleased, delighted.*
  Sehr erfreut (*in social introductions*). *How do you do?* (*Delighted.*)
erfrieren *to die of cold, freeze to death.*
erfrischen *to refresh.*
Erfrischung *f. refreshment.*
ergänzen *to complete, restore.*
Ergänzung *f. completion, restoration.*
ergeben *to produce, yield, result in.*
ergeben *devoted.*
  Ihr ergebener *yours faithfully.*
ergreifen *to seize, take hold of.*
ergreifend *moving, touching.*
Ergriffenheit *f. emotion.*
erhalten *to receive, obtain, preserve.*
Erhalter *m. supporter, preserver.*
erhältlich *obtainable.*
Erhaltungszustand *m. condition, state of preservation.*
erheben *to raise, lift up, collect.*
erhebend *elevating, impressive.*
erheblich *considerable.*
Erhebung *f. raising, elevation, revolt.*
erhitzen *to heat, warm.*
(sich) erholen *to recover, get better.*
Erholung *f. recovery, rest, recreation.*
ERINNERN *to remind.*
  Erinneren Sie mich später daran. *Remind me about it later.*
  sich erinnern an *to remember, recall.*
  Ich kann mich nicht mehr daran erinnern. *I can't remember it any more.*
Erinnerung *f. remembrance, recollection, memory.*
  Erinnerung wachrufen *to evoke memories.*
  zur Erinnerung an *in memory of.*
erkälten *to chill.*
  sich erkälten *to catch a cold.*
erkämpfen *to win by fighting.*
erkennbar *recognizable.*
ERKENNEN *to recognize, perceive, realize.*
  zu erkennen geben *to show, indicate.*
erkenntlich *recognizable, grateful.*
Erkenntnis *f. knowledge, perception, understanding.*
ERKLÄREN *to explain, account for, declare.*
ERKLÄRUNG *f. explanation, interpretation, declaration.*
erkranken *to fall ill, be taken ill.*
Erkrankung *f. illness.*
(sich) erkundigen *to inquire, make inquiries.*
Erkundigung *f. inquiry.*
ERLAUBEN *to allow, permit, presume.*
  Erlauben Sie, bitte! *Allow me, please!*
Erlaubnis *f. permission, leave, license.*
erleben *to experience.*
Erlebnis *n. event.*

erledigen *to carry through, wind up, dispatch.*
  erledigt sein *to be dead tired.*
erleichtern *to facilitate, ease, relieve.*
Erleichterung *f. facilitation, relief.*
erlogen *false, untrue, fabricated.*
erlösen *to save, redeem, deliver.*
Erlösung *f. redemption, release, deliverance.*
ermächtigen *to empower, authorize.*
Ermahnung *f. exhortation, admonition.*
ermässigen *to reduce, abate.*
  Ermässigte Preise *reduced prices.*
ermöglichen *to make possible, enable.*
ermorden *to murder, assassinate.*
Ermordung *f. murder, assassination.*
ermüden *to tire out, weary.*
Ermüdung *f. fatigue, weariness.*
ermutigen *to encourage.*
ernähren *to nourish, feed, support.*
Ernährung *f. nourishment, food, support, maintenance.*
ernennen *to nominate, appoint.*
Ernennung *f. nomination, appointment.*
erneuern *to renew, renovate, replace.*
Erneuerung *f. renewal, renovation.*
erniedrigen *to humiliate, depress.*
Erniedrigung *f. humiliation, degradation.*
ERNST *serious, severe, grave, seriously.*
  Sie nimmt die Sache ernst. *She takes the matter seriously.*
  ernst meinen *to be serious about something.*
Ernst *m. seriousness, earnestness, gravity.*
  Ernst machen mit *to put into practice.*
  Ernstfall, *m. emergency.*
Ernte *f. harvest, crop.*
Erntearbeit *f. harvesting.*
ernten *to harvest.*
erobern *to conquer, capture.*
eröffnen *to open, start, disclose.*
erörtern *to discuss.*
Erörterung *f. discussion.*
erpressen *to extort, blackmail.*
Erpressung *f. extortion, blackmail.*
erraten *to guess.*
erregbar *excitable, irritable.*
erregen *to excite, stir up.*
Erregung *f. excitement, agitation.*
erreichbar *attainable, within reach.*
erreichen *to reach, attain, get.*
ERSATZ *m. substitute, equivalent, spare.*
  Ersatzreifen *m. spare tire.*
  Ersatzteil *m. spare part.*
erscheinen *to appear, come out.*
Erscheinung *f. appearance, figure, apparition.*
erschiessen *to shoot; to kill by shooting.*
Erschiessung *f. execution by gunfire.*
erschöpfen *to exhaust.*

erschöpfend *exhaustive.*
Erschöpfung *f. exhaustion.*
erschrecken *to frighten.*
erschrocken *frightened.*
erschüttern *to shake, upset, shock.*
  Die Nachricht hat uns erschüttert. *We were shocked by the news.*
erschweren *to make more difficult, aggravate.*
ersetzen *to replace, compensate, restore.*
ersparen *to save, economize.*
ERST *first, at first, only.*
  der erste beste *the first that comes.*
  eben erst *just now.*
  erst als *not till.*
  erst recht nicht *certainly not.*
  Erst die Arbeit, dann das Spiel. *Business before pleasure.*
Erstaufführung *f. opening night.*
erstaunen *to astonish.*
erstaunlich *astonishing.*
erstenmal (zum) *for the first time.*
erstens *firstly.*
erstgeboren *first-born.*
ersticken *to suffocate.*
erstmalig *first, for the first time.*
Ertrag *m. produce, yield, profit, returns.*
erträglich *bearable, endurable.*
ertränken *to drown.*
ertrinken *to be drowned.*
erübrigen *to save, spare.*
erwachen *to awake.*
erwachsen *to grow up.*
  die Erwachsenen *the grown-ups, adults.*
erwägen *to consider, weigh.*
erwähnen *to mention.*
ERWARTEN *to wait for, await, expect.*
Erwartung *f. expectation, hope.*
  in Erwartung Ihrer Antwort *looking forward to your reply.*
erwartungsvoll *expectant, full of hope.*
erweitern *to widen, expand.*
Erweiterung *f. widening, expansion.*
Erwerb *m. acquisition, gain, profit.*
erwerben *to acquire, gain.*
erwerbslos *unemployed, out of work.*
Erwerbslosenunterstützung *f. unemployment relief.*
ERZÄHLEN *to tell, relate, narrate.*
Erzählung *f. story, tale, narrative.*
erzeugen *to breed, produce, procreate.*
Erzeugnis *n. product.*
  Deutsches Erzeugnis. *Made in Germany.*
Erzeugung *f. procreation, production.*
erziehen *to raise, educate, train.*
erzieherisch *educational.*
Erziehung *f. education, upbringing.*
Erziehungswesen *n. educational system.*
erzwingen *to force, extort.*

ES *it.*
essbar *edible.*
ESSEN *to eat, dine.*
Essen *n. food, dinner, meal.*
Essenszeit *f. mealtime.*
Essig *m. vinegar.*
Esslöffel *m. tablespoon.*
Esswaren *pl. provisions, victuals.*
Esszimmer *n. dining room.*
Etage *f. floor.*
ETWA *nearly, about, by chance.*
ETWAS *some, something, any, anything, a bit, somewhat.*
EUCH *acc. and dat. of ihr (fam. form pl.) you, to you.*
EUER *poss. adj. (fam. pl. form) your.*
EUER(ER,-E,-ES) *poss. pron. (pl. fam. form) yours.*
euerseits *on your part.*
euresgleichen *like you, of your kind.*
euretwegen *for your sake, on account of you.*
Europa *n. Europe.*
evakuieren *to evacuate.*
evangelisch *Protestant.*
Evangelium *n. Gospel.*
EWIG *eternal, forever, all the time.*
Ewigkeit *f. eternity.*
exakt *exact.*
Examen *n. examination.*
examinieren *to examine.*
Excellenz *f. Excellency.*
Exemplar *n. sample.*
exemplarisch *exemplary.*
Existenz *f. existence.*
existieren *to exist, live.*
Experiment *n. experiment.*
experimentieren *to experiment.*
Export *m. export.*
Exporteur *m. exporter.*
exportieren *to export.*
Extrablatt *n. special edition.*
Extrakt *m. extract.*
exzentrisch *eccentric.*

F

Fabel *f. fable, story, plot.*
fabelhaft *fabulous.*
Fabrik *f. factory, mill, plant.*
Fabrikanlage *f. plant.*
Fabrikant *m. manufacturer.*
Fabrikarbeiter *m. factory worker.*
Fabrikat *n. product (manufactured).*
Fabrikation *f. making.*
fabrizieren *to manufacture.*
Fach *n. compartment, shelf, drawer.*
  Was ist Ihr Fach? *What's your line?*
Fachkenntnis *f. technical knowledge.*

Fachmann *m. expert, specialist.*

Fackel *f. torch.*

Faden *m. thread.*
  an einem Faden hängen   *to hang by a thread.*

FÄHIG *able.*
  fähig sein *to be able, capable.*

Fähigkeit *f. capability.*

Fahne *f. flag, banner.*

Fahrbahn *f. road, track.*

fahrbar *passable, navigable.*

Fähre *f. ferry.*

FAHREN *to drive, ride, go, travel.*
  Fahren Sie rechts! *Keep to the right!*
  mit dem Schiff fahren   *to sail.*
  spazieren fahren   *to go for a ride.*

Fahrer *m. driver.*

Fahrgast *m. passenger.*

Fahrgeld *n. fare.*

Fahrkarte *f. ticket (transportation).*

Fahrkartenschalter *m. ticket window.*

fahrlässig *careless, negligent.*

Fahrlässigkeit *f. carelessness, negligence.*

Fahrplan *m. timetable.*

Fahrrad *n. bicycle.*

Fahrschein *m. transportation ticket (bus).*

Fahrstrasee *f. highway.*

Fahrstuhl *m. lift, elevator.*
  Fahrstuhlführer. *m. elevator boy, attendant.*

FAHRT *f. ride, journey, trip.*
  Hin-und Rückfahrt *round trip.*
  in voller Fahrt *at full speed.*
  Was kostet die Fahrt, bitte? *How much is the fare, please?*

Fahrzeug *n. vehicle.*

Fakultät *f. faculty.*

FALL *m. fall, drop, case, accident.*
  auf jeden Fall, auf alle Fälle *in any case.*
  auf keinen Fall! *On no account!*

Falle *f. trap.*

FALLEN *to fall.*
  fallen lassen *to let fall, drop.*
  im Krieg fallen *to be killed in action.*
  in den Rücken fallen *to attack from behind.*
  in Ohnmacht fallen *to faint.*
  Das Fest fällt auf einen Sonntag. *The holiday falls on a Sunday.*
  Das fällt nicht weiter ins Gewicht. *That is of no further consequence.*

falls *in case, in the event.*

Fallschirm *m. parachute.*

FALSCH *wrong, incorrect, false.*
  Sie hat falsche Zähne. *She has false teeth.*
  Das Geld ist falsch. *The money is counterfeit.*
  falsch verstehen *to misunderstand.*

fälschen *to falsify, forge.*

Fälscher *m. forger.*

Falschheit *f. falseness, falsehood.*

Falschspieler *m. cheat (at cards).*

Fälschung *f. forgery.*

Falte *f. pleat, fold, wrinkle.*

falten *to fold.*

familiär *familiar, intimate.*

FAMILIE *f. family.*

Familienname *m. last name.*

Fanatiker *m. fanatic.*

Fang *m. catch, capture, prey.*

fangen *to catch, capture.*

FARBE *f. color, paint.*
  farbenblind *color blind.*

färben *to color, dye.*
  sich die Haare färben *to dye one's hair.*

farbig *colored.*

farblos *colorless, pale.*

Fasching *m. carnival.*

Fass *n. barrel, cask.*
  Das schlägt dem Fass den Boden aus. *That's the last straw.*

Fassade *f. front (of a building).*

FASSEN *to catch, seize, hold, apprehend, grasp, comprehend.*
  Fassen Sie sich kurz! *Make it short!*
  ins Auge fassen *to consider, to keep in mind.*
  einen Entschluss fassen *to make a decision.*

Fassung *f. setting, composure.*
  aus der Fassung bringen *to upset, disconcert.*

fast *almost, nearly.*

faul *lazy, rotten, bad.*
  Das ist eine faule Sache. *This is a shady business.*

faulen *to rot, be lazy.*

Faulheit *laziness.*

Faulpelz *m. idler, lazybones.*

Faust *f. fist.*
  auf eigene Faust *on one own's responsibility.*
  faustdick hinter den Ohren haben *to be sly.*

Fausthandschuh *m. mitten, boxing glove.*

fax *m. fax.*

faxen *to fax (colloq.).*

FEBRUAR *m. February.*

FEDER *f. pen, feather.*
  Federhalter *m. penholder.*
  federleicht *light as a feather.*

fegen *to sweep.*

FEHLEN *to miss, make a mistake, lack, be absent.*
  es an nichts fehlen lassen *to spare no pains.*
  Sie werden mir sehr fehlen. *I'll miss you very much.*

Was fehlt Ihnen? *What's the matter with you?*

FEHLER *m. fault, defect, mistake, blunder.*

Das ist mein Fehler. *That is my fault.*

Fehlschlag *failure.*

Feier *f. festival, celebration, ceremony, party.*

Feierabend *time for the workday to end.*

Wir machen jetzt Feierabend. *Let's call it a day.*

feierlich *solemn, festive, ceremonious.*

Feierlichkeit *f. solemnity, ceremony.*

feiern *to celebrate.*

Sie feiern ihre goldene Hochzeit. *They are celebrating their golden anniversary.*

Feierstunde *f. leisure hour, festive hour.*

Feiertag *m. holiday.*

feige *cowardly.*

Feigheit *f. cowardice.*

feil *for sale, mercenary.*

feil bieten *to offer for sale.*

feil halten *to have for sale.*

FEIN *fine, thin, delicate, refined, distinguished, elegant.*

Feind *m. enemy.*

feindlich *hostile.*

feinfühlig *sensitive.*

Feingefühl *n. sensitivity.*

Feinheit *f. fineness, grace, elegance, refinement, subtlety.*

Feinschmecker *m. gourmet.*

FELD *n. field, plain, ground, square.*

Schlachtfeld, *n. battlefield.*

Feldstecher *m. binoculars.*

Feldzug *m. campaign.*

Fell *n. skin, hide, coat, fur (animals).*

Diese Katze hat ein schönes Fell. *This cat has a beautiful fur.*

Fels *m. rock, cliff.*

felsenfest *firm as a rock.*

felsig *rocky, craggy.*

FENSTER *n. window.*

Fensterbank *f. window-sill.*

Fensterrahmen *m. window-frame.*

Fensterscheibe *f. window pane.*

Ferien *pl. holidays, vacation.*

in die Ferien gehen *to go on vacation.*

FERN *far, distant, remote.*

von fern *from afar, from a distance.*

Ferne *f. distance.*

ferner *further, furthermore, besides.*

Ferngespräch *n. long-distance phone call.*

Fernglas *n. binoculars, field glass.*

fernmündlich *by telephone, over the telephone.*

Das Telegramm wurde mir fernmündlich durchgegeben. *The telegram was given to me over the phone.*

Fernsehen *n. television.*

Fernsprechbuch *n. telephone directory.*

Fernsprecher *m. telephone.*

Fernsprechstelle *f. telephone booth.*

FERTIG *ready, ready-made, finished, done.*

fertigbringen *to bring about, accomplish.*

sich fertig machen *to get ready.*

Werden Sie damit fertig werden? *Will you be able to manage this by yourself?*

FEST *n. festival, feast.*

FEST *firm, hard, rigid, steady, solid, stiff, stable, firmly, stiffly, fully.*

eine feste Stellung *a permanent post.*

fester Schlaf *sound sleep.*

festbinden *to tie, bind, fasten.*

Festessen *n. banquet.*

festfahren *to get stuck.*

Festhalle *f. banqueting hall.*

festhalten *to hold tight.*

sich festhalten an *to hold on to.*

festigen *to make firm.*

Festigkeit *f. solidity, firmness.*

festlegen *to fix, lay down.*

festlich *festive, solemn.*

Festlichkeit *f. festivity.*

festmachen *to fasten, attach, fix, settle.*

Festnahme *f. arrest, seizure.*

festsetzen *to fix, set, settle.*

Der Preis wird auf hundert Mark festgesetzt. *The price has been fixed at one hundred marks.*

festsitzen *to be stuck, fit tightly.*

Festspiel *n. festival performance.*

Feststellung *f. statement, determination, identification.*

Festtag *m. holiday, feast.*

Festung *f. fortress, stronghold.*

FETT *fat, plump, fertile, rich, greasy.*

Fett *n. grease, fat.*

fettig *fatty, greasy.*

FEUCHT *damp, humid, muggy.*

FEUER *n. fire, firing, bombardment.*

Feuer! *Fire!*

Feuer fangen *to catch fire.*

Feuer geben *to give a light.*

feuerfest *fireproof.*

Feuergefahr *f. danger of fire.*

feuergefährlich *inflammable.*

Feuerlöscher *m. fire-extinguisher.*

Feuerung *f. fuel.*

Feuerversicherung *f. fire insurance.*

Feuerwache *f. fire station.*

Feuerwerk *n. firework.*

Feuerzeug *n. lighter.*

Fieber *n. fever, temperature.*

Fieber messen *to take one's temperature.*

fieberhaft *feverish.*

fiebern *to be feverish, have a temperature.*

Fieberthermometer *n. clinical thermometer.*

Fieberwahn *m. delirium.*
Figur *f. figure, form, shape.*
Filiale *f. branch.*
FILM *m. film, picture, movie.*
Filmaufnahme *f. shooting of film.*
filmen *to film.*
Filmstreifen *m. filmstrip.*
Filter *m. filter.*
filtern *to filter, strain.*
Filz *m. felt.*
filzig *stingy.*
Finanz *f. finance.*
Finanzamt *n. revenue office.*
finanziell *financial.*
finanzieren *to finance, support.*
FINDEN *to find, discover, meet with, think, consider.*
Finder *m. finder.*
findig *clever, ingenious.*
Findigkeit *f. cleverness.*
FINGER *m. finger.*
Fingerabdruck *m. fingerprint.*
Fingerfertigkeit *f. dexterity, skill.*
Fingerhut *m. thimble.*
Fingerspitze *f. tip of the finger.*
Fingerspitzengefühl *n. instinct; intuition.*
Fingerzeig *m. hint, tip.*
finster *dark, gloomy, obscure.*
Finte *f. feint, trick.*
Firma *f. firm, business.*
FISCH *m. fish.*
FISCHEN *to fish.*
Fischer *m. fisherman.*
Fischerei *f. fishing, fishery.*
Fischgräte *f. fish-bone.*
Fischhändler *m. fishmonger.*
FLACH *flat, plain, level.*
Fläche *f. surface, plain, area.*
Flachland *n. flat country, plain.*
Flagge *f. flag.*
flaggen *to deck with flags.*
Flamme *f. flame.*
FLASCHE *f. bottle.*
Flaschenbier *n. bottled beer.*
Flaschenöffner *m. bottle opener.*
flatterhaft *fickle, inconsistent.*
flattern *to flutter; wave.*
FLECK *m. place, spot, stain.*
    vom Fleck kommen   *to get on, make headway.*
Flecken *m. spot, stain.*
fleckenlos *spotless.*
fleckig *spotted, stained.*
Flegel *m. boor, impertinent person.*
flegelhaft *rude, insolent.*
Flegeljahre *pl. teenage years.*
flehen *to implore, beseech.*
FLEISCH *n. flesh, meat, pulp.*
Fleischbrühe *f. meat broth.*

Fleischer *m. butcher.*
fleischig *fleshy, plump.*
fleischlos *meatless.*
FLEISS *m. diligence, industry.*
    mit Fleiss   *on purpose.*
fleissig *diligent, industrious.*
flicken *to patch, mend, repair.*
Fliege *f. fly.*
FLIEGEN *to fly, rush.*
    in die Luft fliegen   *to blow up.*
Flieger *m. airman, aviator, pilot.*
fliehen *to run away, flee.*
fliessen *to flow, run.*
    fliessendes Wasser   *running water.*
    fliessend sprechen   *to speak fluently.*
flink *quick, agile, nimble.*
Flinte *f. shotgun, rifle.*
    die Flinte in das Korn werfen   *to give up.*
Flirt *m. flirtation.*
flirten *to flirt.*
Flitterwochen *pl. honeymoon.*
Floh *m. flea.*
Flöte *f. flute.*
flöten *to play the flute.*
flott *afloat, floating.*
Flotte *f. fleet, navy.*
Fluch *m. curse, imprecation.*
fluchen *to curse, swear.*
Flucht *f. flight, escape.*
flüchten *to flee, escape.*
flüchtig *careless, passing, superficial.*
    Er ist nur ein flüchtiger Bekannter.   *He is only a passing acquaintance.*
Flüchtling *m. fugitive.*
FLUG *m. flight (aerial).*
Flugblatt *n. pamphlet.*
Fluggast *m. air passenger.*
Flughafen *m. airport.*
Flugplatz *m. airfield, airport.*
Flugzeug *n. airplane*
Flugzeugträger *m. aircraft carrier.*
Flur *f. field, meadow.*
Flur *m. hall, corridor.*
FLUSS *m. river.*
flüssig *liquid, fluid.*
Flüssigkeit *f. fluidity.*
Flusslauf *m. course of a river.*
flüstern *to whisper.*
Flut *f. tide, flood.*
fluten *to stream, flow.*
FOLGE *f. sequence, succession.*
    Folge leisten   *to comply with.*
Folgeerscheinung *f. consequence, effect.*
FOLGEN *to follow, succeed, obey, mind.*
    daraus folgt   *hence follows.*
folgendermassen *as follows.*
folgern *to infer, conclude, deduce.*
Folgerung *f. inference, conclusion, deduction.*
folglich *consequently.*

folgsam *obedient, docile.*
Folgsamkeit *f. obedience, docility.*
foltern *to torture.*
fordern *to demand, ask, claim, require.*
Forderung *f. demand, claim, challenge.*
Form *f. form, shape.*
Formalität *f. formality.*
Format *n. size, weight, importance.*
Formel *f. formula.*
formell *formal.*
formen *to form, shape.*
förmlich *formal, ceremonious, regular.*
Formlosigkeit *f. formlessness, shapelessness.*
Formular *n. form.*
formulieren *to formulate, define.*
formvollendet *perfect in form.*
forschen *to investigate, search.*
Forschung *f. inquiry, investigation.*
Förster *m. forester, gamekeeper.*
FORT *adv. and separable prefix (implies*
　　movement away from speaker, or
　　continuation). away, off, gone, on
　　(going on).
　　und so fort　*and so forth.*
fortan *henceforth, from this time.*
Fortbildung *f. further study.*
fortfahren *to drive away, remove, continue.*
　　Er ist gestern fortgefahren.　*He left*
　　yesterday.
fortführen *to lead away, go on, continue.*
fortgehen *to go away.*
fortgesetzt *continuous, incessant.*
fortschreiten *to advance, proceed, make*
　　progress.
Fortschritt *m. progress.*
fortschrittlich *progressive.*
fortsetzen *to continue, carry on, pursue.*
Fortsetzung *f. continuation, pursuit.*
　　Fortsetzung folgt *to be continued.*
Fracht *f. freight.*
Frachtdampfer *m. freighter.*
FRAGE *f. question, inquiry, problem.*
　　das ist noch die Frage　*that remains to be*
　　seen.
　　eine Frage stellen　*to ask a question.*
　　ohne Frage　*undoubtedly.*
FRAGEN *to ask, inquire.*
　　fragen nach　*to ask for.*
　　nichts danach fragen　*not to care about*
　　something.
　　sich fragen　*to wonder.*
　　Es fragt sich, ob es der Mühe wert ist.　*It*
　　is a question whether it is worth the
　　trouble.
Fragezeichen *n. question mark.*
fraglich *in question, questionable, doubtful.*
fraglos *unquestionable.*
Franzose, -n *n. Frenchman.*
Französin, -nen *f. Frenchwoman.*

französisch *French.*
FRAU *f. woman, wife, Mrs.*
　　gnädige Frau *Madam.*
　　Ihre Frau (Gemahlin) *your wife.*
Frauenarzt *m. gynecologist.*
FRÄULEIN *n. young lady, girl, Miss.*
fraulich *womanly.*
frech *impudent, insolent.*
Frechheit *f. impudence, insolence.*
FREI *free, vacant, open, liberal,*
　　spontaneous, frank; freely, frankly, at
　　ease.
　　die freie Zeit　*leisure, spare time.*
　　Es ist mein freier Tag.　*This is my day off.*
　　Ist dieser Platz frei?　*Is this seat taken?*
　　unter freiem Himmel, im Freien　*outside,*
　　in the open air.
Freibillett *n. complimentary ticket.*
Freidenker *m. freethinker.*
freigeben *to set free, release, open (to the*
　　public).
freigebig *liberal, generous.*
Freigebigkeit *f. liberality, generosity.*
Freigeist *m. freethinker.*
freihalten *to hold, treat.*
Freiheit *f. freedom.*
freilassen *to release, set free.*
Freilassung *f. release.*
Freimut *m. frankness, candor.*
freimütig *frank, candid.*
freisprechen *to acquit, absolve.*
Freispruch *m. acquittal.*
Freistelle *f. scholarship, free place.*
FREITAG *m. Friday.*
Freizeit *f. leisure time.*
freiwillig *voluntary, spontaneous.*
Freiwillige *m. volunteer.*
FREMD *strange, foreign, unknown, exotic.*
　　fremdes Gut *other people's property.*
fremdartig *strange, odd.*
FREMDE *m. foreigner, tourist, foreign*
　　country.
　　in der Fremde (im Ausland)　*abroad.*
Fremdenführer *m. tourist guide.*
Fremdenverkehr *m. tourist traffic.*
Fremdsprache *f. foreign language.*
Fremdwort *n. foreign word.*
Fressen *n. animal food, feed.*
fressen *to eat (animals), feed.*
FREUDE *f. joy, delight, pleasure, cheer.*
　　Freude haben an *to enjoy, delight in.*
　　freudestrahlend *beaming with joy.*
freudelos *joyless, cheerless.*
freudig *joyful, cheerful.*
freuen *to please, delight.*
　　sich freuen　*to be pleased, rejoice.*
　　Es freut mich sehr, Sie kennenzulernen.
　　I am very glad to meet you.
　　sich freuen auf　*to look forward to.*

FREUND m. -in f. friend.
FREUNDLICH friendly, kind, obliging, pleasant.
Freundlichkeit f. friendliness.
Freundschaft f. friendship.
freundschaftlich friendly, serviceable.
FRIEDE m. peace.
Friedensbruch m. breach of peace.
Friedensvertrag m. peace treaty.
Friedhof m. churchyard, cemetery.
friedlich peaceful.
friedliebend peace-loving.
frieren to freeze, be cold, get cold.
    Die Füsse frieren mir.   My feet are freezing.
    Mich friert (es).   I am cold.
FRISCH fresh, bright, lively, new.
    frisch gestrichen   wet paint.
    frische Eier   fresh eggs.
    frische Wäsche   clean linen.
FRISÖR m. barber, hairdresser.
Friseuse f. hairdresser (female).
frisieren to fix one's hair.
    sich frisieren lassen   to have one's hair done.
Frisur f. hairdressing, hairdo.
froh glad, happy.
frohgemut cheerful.
FRÖHLICH merry, happy.
    Fröhliche Weihnachten!   Merry Christmas!
Fröhlichkeit f. cheerfulness.
Frohsinn m. cheerfulness.
fromm pious, religious, godly.
Front f. front (military).
Frosch m. frog.
Frost m. frost, cold, chill.
frösteln to shiver, feel chilly.
FRUCHT f. fruit, crop, produce.
fruchtbar fruitful, fertile.
Fruchtbarkeit f. fruitfulness, fertility.
fruchtbringend fruit-bearing, productive, fertile.
fruchten to bear fruit, to have effect.
Fruchtsaft m. fruit juice.
FRÜH early in the morning.
    heute früh   this morning.
    morgen früh   tomorrow morning.
Frühe f. morning, dawn.
    in aller Frühe   very early.
früher earlier, sooner, former.
    früher oder später   sooner or later.
frühestens at the earliest.
FRÜHLING m. Spring.
FRÜHSTÜCK n. breakfast.
frühstücken to breakfast.
Fuchs m. fox.
fügen to join, put together, add, submit.
fügsam yielding, submissive.
Fügung f. dispensation, coincidence.

fühlbar tangible, perceptible.
FÜHLEN to feel, sense, be sensitive to.
    sich gut fühlen   to feel well.
FÜHREN to lead, conduct, direct, handle, carry.
    ein Gespräch führen   to have a conversation.
    Wer führt?   Who is ahead?
    Er führt immer das grosse Wort.   He is always bragging.
    Er führt etwas im Schilde.   He is up to something.
Führer m. leader, driver, pilot, guidebook.
Führerschein m. driving license.
Führung f. leadership, command, direction, management, behavior, conduct.
FÜLLEN to fill, stuff.
    sich füllen   to fill up.
    Das Stadion füllt sich langsam.   The stadium is slowly filling up.
Fund m. finding.
Fundament n. foundation.
fundieren to lay a foundation.
FÜNF five.
FÜNFTE fifth.
FÜNFZEHN fifteen.
FÜNFZEHNTE fifteenth.
FÜNFZIG fifty.
FÜNFZIGSTE fiftieth.
Funk m. wireless, radio (communications medium).
Funke m. spark.
funkeln to sparkle.
Funker m. telegraphist.
FÜR prep. (acc.) for, by, to.
    ein für allemal   once for all.
    Er geht Schritt für Schritt vorwärts.   He walks forward step by step.
    Ich arbeite für mich.   I work for myself.
    Ich habe Karten für das Theater.   I have tickets for the theater.
    Stück für Stück   piece by piece.
    Tag für Tag   day by day
    Was für ein?   what kind of?
FURCHT f. fear, fright, dread, anxiety.
furchtbar awful, horrible, terrible: awfully, terribly.
fürchten to fear.
fürchterlich terrible, horrible, frightful.
furchtlos fearless, intrepid.
Furchtlosigkeit f. fearlessness, intrepidity.
furchtsam timid, nervous.
Furchtsamkeit f. timidity.
Fürst m. (-in f.) prince(ss).
Fürwort n. pronoun.
FUSS m. foot, base, bottom.
    auf eigenen Füssen stehen   to be independent.
    auf freien Fuss setzen   to set at liberty.

Er lebt auf grossem Fuss.   *He is living in grand style.*

Ich stehe mit ihm auf gutem Fuss.   *I am on good terms with him.*

zu Fuss   *on foot.*

Fussball *m. soccer.*

Fussbank *f. footstool.*

Fussgänger *m. pedestrian.*

nor für Fussgänger   *for pedestrians only.*

Fusspur *f. footprint.*

Fusstapfe *f. footstep.*

Fusstritt *m. kick.*

Futter *n.* 1. *food, feed* (*animals*). 2. *sheath, lining.*

Futterseide *f. silk for lining.*

G

Gabe *f. present, gift, talent.*

Gabel *f. fork.*

gähnen *to yawn, gape.*

GANG *m. walk, stroll, walk, aisle, course, gear, hall, errand.*

in Gang setzen   *to start, set.*

in vollem Gang   *in full swing.*

die Sache nimmt ihren Gang   *the matter takes/runs its course.*

Gans *f. goose*

Gänseblümchen *n. daisy.*

ganz *all, whole, entire, complete; in full, wholly, entirely, thoroughly, altogether.*

die ganze Stadt   *the whole town.*

ganz anders   *quite different.*

ganz besonders   *more especially.*

ganz gleich   *all the same, no matter.*

ganz und gar   *wholly.*

ganz und gar nicht   *not at all.*

im ganzen   *on the whole.*

im grossen und ganzen   *on the whole.*

von ganzem Herzen   *with all my heart.*

gar *done, cooked through: fully, very, quite, even.*

gar kein . . .   *no . . . whatsoever.*

gar nicht   *not at all.*

gar nichts   *nothing at all.*

Garage *f. garage.*

Garderobe *f. wardrobe, cloakroom.*

Garderobenmarke *f. check* (*cloakroom*).

Garderobennummer *f. check* (*cloakroom*).

Gardine *f. curtain*

Garn *n. yarn, thread.*

garnieren *to trim, garnish.*

Garnitur *f. trimming, outfit.*

garstig *nasty, ugly.*

GARTEN *m. garden.*

Gartenhaus *n. summer house.*

Gartenlaube *f. garden house* (*pavilion*).

Gärtner *m. gardener.*

Gas *n. gas.*

Gashahn *m. gas tap.*

Gasleitung *f. gas pipes, gas supply.*

Gasse *f. narrow street, alley.*

GAST *m. visitor, guest.*

gastfreundich *hospitable.*

Gastfreundschaft *f. hospitality.*

Gastgeber *m. host*

Gasthaus *n. inn, hotel.*

Gasthof *m. inn. hotel.*

gastlich *hospitable.*

Gastspiel *n. guest performance.*

Gastwirt *m. innkeeper.*

Gasuhr *f. gas meter.*

Gatte *m. husband.*

Gattin *f. wife.*

Gaumen *m. palate.*

Geächtete *m. outlaw.*

Gebäck *n. pastry, cookie.*

Gebärde *f. gesture, movement.*

(sich) gebärden *to behave, conduct oneself.*

Gebäude *n. building, structure, edifice.*

GEBEN *to give, present, produce, yield.*

Das gibt mir zu denken.   *That makes me wonder.*

es gibt   *there is, there are*

Was gibt es zum Mittagessen?   *What are they having for lunch?*

gegeben werden   *to play* (*in theater*).

Was wird heute in Theater gegeben?   *What's playing tonight at the theater?*

Gebet *n. prayer.*

Gebiet *n. district, territory, area, field.*

gebieten *to order, command.*

Gebirge *n. mountain chain.*

gebirgig *mountainous.*

Gebiss *n. set of teeth, denture.*

Gebot *n. order, command, law.*

Gebrauch *m. use, customs, rites.*

gebrauchen *to use, make use of.*

gebräuchlich *usual, in use.*

Gebühr *f. duty, tax, fee, rate.*

gebühren *to be due.*

sich gebühren   *to be proper.*

gebührenfrei *tax-free*

gebührenpflichtig *taxable.*

gebührlich *suitable, proper.*

GEBURT *f. birth, origin, extraction.*

Geburtshelferin *f. midwife.*

Geburtsjahr *n. year of birth.*

Geburtsschein *n. birth certificate.*

Geburtstag *m. birthday.*

Gedächtnis *n. memory, remembrance.*

aus dem Gedächtnis   *from memory.*

GEDANKE *m. thought, idea.*

sich Gedanken machen   *to worry.*

Wie kommen Sie auf den

Gedanken? *What gives you that idea?*

gedankenlos *thoughtless.*

Gedankenlosigkeit *f. thoughtlessness.*

Gedeck *n. cover (at table), set of table linens.*

gedeihen *to grow, develop, succeed.*

gedenken *to intend, think of*

Gedenkfeier *f. commemoration.*

Gedicht *n. poem.*

Gedränge *n. crowd, throng.*

gedruckt *printed.*

Geduld *f. patience, endurance.*

(sich) gedulden *to have patience.*

geduldig *patient.*

Gefahr *f. danger, risk.*

gefährden *to endanger, expose to danger.*

gefährlich *dangerous, perilous.*

gefahrlos *safe, secure, without danger.*

gefahrvoll *dangerous, perilous.*

GEFALLEN *to please, suit.*

Das gefällt mir. *I like that.*

sich gefallen lassen *to submit, put up with.*

gefällig *pleasant, agreeable.*

Gefangene *m. prisoner, captive.*

Kriegsgefangene m. prisoner of war.

Gefangenschaft *f. captivity, confinement.*

Gefangensetzung *f. capture, arrest.*

Gefängnis *n. prison, jail.*

Gefäss *n. container, receptacle.*

gefasst *composed, collected, calm.*

sich gefasstmachen auf *to be prepared for.*

Geflügel *n. birds, poultry, fowl.*

Geflüster *n. whispering.*

Gefolge *n. suite, entourage.*

GEFÜHL *n. feeling, sentiment, sense, emotion, sensation.*

gefühllos *numb, heartless.*

Gefühllosigkeit *f. numbness, heartlessness.*

gefühlvoll *tender, sentimental.*

GEGEN *prep. (acc.) against, about, around, toward, for, to, compared with.*

Die Soldaten kämpfen gegen den Feind. *The soldiers fight against the enemy.*

Er schwamm gegen den Strom. *He swam against the current.*

Es ist gegen neun Uhr. *It is about nine o'clock.*

gegen voriges Jahr *compared with last year.*

gegeneinander *against each other.*

Waren gegen Geld tauschen *to exchange goods for money.*

GEGEND *f. country, region, district.*

Gegenseite *f. opposite side.*

gegenseitig *reciprocal, mutual.*

Gegenstand *m. subject.*

gegenstandlos *pointless.*

Gegenteil *n. contrary, opposite.*

im Gegenteil *on the contrary.*

gegenüber *opposite.*

Gegenwart *f. present, presence.*

gegenwärtig *present.*

Gegenwert *m. equivalent.*

Gegner *m. opponent, adversary, enemy.*

Gehalt *m. content.*

Gehalt *n. salary.*

gehaltlos *worthless.*

gehaltvoll *valuable, substantial.*

gehässig *spiteful, malicious.*

Gehässigkeit *f. spite, malice.*

geheim *conceal, hidden, clandestine.*

GEHEIMNIS *n. secret, mystery.*

geheimnisvoll *mysterious.*

Geheimpolizei *f. secret police.*

GEHEN *to go, walk, pass, move, leave; run, work (machinery).*

an die Arbeit gehen *to go to work.*

Das geht nicht. *That won't do.*

Es geht mir gut, danke. *I am fine, thank you.*

Es geht nichts über gutes Bier. *There is nothing like good beer.*

Es geht um Tod und Leben. *It is a matter of life and death.*

gehen auf (nach) *to face on, look out on.*

Das Fenster geht auf den Hof. *The window faces the courtyard.*

gehen lassen *to let go, give up.*

sich gehen lassen *to let oneself go.*

Wie geht es Ihnen? *How are you?*

Gehilfe *m. assistant, clerk, helper.*

Gehirn *n. brain.*

GEHÖR *n. hearing; ear (mus.).*

gehorchen *to obey.*

GEHÖREN *to belong to, be owned by.*

Es gehört ihm. *It belongs to him.*

Das gehört nicht zur Sache. *That's beside the point.*

Dazu gehört Zeit. *That takes time.*

gehorsam *obedient.*

Geige *f. violin.*

geigen *to play the violin.*

GEIST *m. spirit, genius, mind.*

geistesabwesend *absent-minded.*

Geistesgegenwart *f. presence of mind.*

geisteskrank *of unsound mind, insane.*

geistesschwach *feeble-minded.*

geistig *spiritual, intellectual, mental.*

geistlich *religious, spiritual.*

geistlos *spiritless, lifeless, dull.*

geistreich *ingenious, spiritual, witty.*

Geiz *m. stinginess, avarice.*

geizig *avaricious, stingy.*

Gelände *n. country, countryside.*

Geländer *n. railing, banister.*
gelangen *to reach, arrive, attain to.*
gelassen *calm, collected.*
Gelassenheit *f. calmness, composure.*
geläufig *fluent, familiar, current.*
gelaunt *disposed.*
  gut gelaunt *in good humour.*
  schlecht gelaunt *cross, bad-tempered.*
Geläute *n. chime, ringing of bells.*
GELB *yellow.*
gelblich *yellowish.*
Gelbsucht *f. jaundice.*
GELD *n. money.*
  Bargeld *n. cash.*
  Kleingeld *n. change.*
Geldentwertung *f. inflation, devaluation.*
Geldschein *m. paper money, bill.*
Geldschrank *m. safe.*
Geldstück *n. coin.*
Geldtasche *f. purse.*
Gelee *m. jelly.*
gelegen *1. situated. 2. convenient.*
  Er kam gerade zu gelegener Zeit. *He came just at the right time.*
Gelegenheit *f. opportunity, occasion, chance.*
Gelegenheitskauf *m. bargain.*
gelegentlich *occasional, accidental.*
gelehrig *docile, teachable.*
Gelehrsamkeit *f. learning, erudition.*
gelehrt *learned, scholarly, erudite.*
Gelehrte *m. scholar, savant.*
Geleise *n. track.*
Geleit *n. escort, convoy.*
geleiten *to accompany, escort, convoy.*
Geleitwort *n. motto.*
Gelenk *n. joint, articulation.*
Geliebte *m. & f. lover, mistress, beloved.*
gelingen *to succeed, manage.*
gelten *to matter, mean, be worth, have influence, be valid.*
  Das gilt nicht. *That does not count.*
  gelten als *to be considered as.*
Geltungsdauer *f. period of validity.*
gemächlich *comfortable.*
Gemahl *m. husband.*
Gemahlin *f. wife.*
gemäss *suitable.*
GEMEIN *ordinary, general, low, vulgar, common.*
  der Gemeine *the private soldier.*
  Es war gemein von ihm. *It was mean of him.*
  gemeinhaben mit *to have in common with.*
Gemeinde *f. community, congregation, parish, municipality.*
Gemeinheit *f. vulgarity, baseness, bad trick.*
gemeinnützig *beneficial to the community.*
Gemeinschaft *f. community.*

  in Gemeinschaft mit *together with.*
GEMÜSE *n. vegetables.*
Gemüsehändler *m. greengrocer.*
Gemüt *n. soul, mind, heart, feelings.*
Gemütlich *good-natured, cozy.*
Gemütlichkeit *f. comfort, coziness.*
GENAU *close, tight, exact, accurate.*
  Er nimmt es sehr genau. *He is very particular.*
  Nehmen Sie es nicht zu genau! *Don't take it too literally!*
Genauigkeit *f. exactness, accuracy, precision.*
General *m. general.*
genesen *to recover, get better.*
Genesung. *f. recovery, convalescence.*
genial *full of genius.*
Genialität *f. genius, originality.*
Genick *n. nape (of neck).*
Genie *n. genius.*
genieren *to trouble, inconvenience, bother.*
geniessbar *eatable, drinkable.*
geniessen *to eat, enjoy, have the benefit of.*
Genosse *m. companion, colleague.*
GENUG *sufficient, enough.*
Genugtuung *f. satisfaction, compensation.*
Geographie *f. geography.*
GEPÄCK *n. luggage, baggage.*
Gepäckabfertigung *f. luggage dispatch office.*
Gepäckannahme *m. luggage counter.*
Gepäckaufbewahrung *f. left luggage office.*
Gepäckausgabe *f. luggage office.*
Gepäckschein *m. receipt for registered baggage.*
Gepäckstück *n. bag, parcel.*
Gepäckträger *m. porter.*
GERADE *direct, upright, straight, honest; just, exactly, directly.*
  nun gerade *now move than ever.*
  geradeus *straight on.*
Gerät *n. tool, implement, utensil.*
geraten *to succeed, turn out well.*
  sich in die Harre geraten *to come to blows.*
  Ihm gerät nichts. *He never succeeds in anything.*
  in Brand geraten *to catch fire.*
geräumig *roomy, spacious.*
Geräusch *n. noise.*
geräuschvoll *noisy.*
GERECHT *just, fair, equitable.*
Gerechtigkeit *f. justice, righteousness, fairness.*
Gerede *n. talk, rumor, gossip.*
Gereiztheit *f. irritation.*
Gericht *n. dish, course, judgment.*
  Jüngstes Gericht. *Last Judgment.*
  vor Gericht *in court.*

Gerichtshof *m. court of law.*
gering *small, little, unimportant.*
  nicht im geringsten *not in the least.*
  geringfügig *unimportant.*
Gerippe *n. skeleton.*
GERN *gladly, with pleasure, readily, easily.*
  gern essen *to like (to eat something).*
  Gern geschehen! *Don't mention it!*
  gern haben *to like (a person or object).*
  gern tun *(or any verb of action) to like*
    (to do something).
  Ich esse gern Eisbein mit Sauerkraut. *I*
    like pig's knuckles with sauerkraut.
  Sie hat ihn gern. *She likes him.*
  Tanzen Sie gern? *Do you like to dance?*
Geruch *m. smell, scent, odor.*
geruchlos *odorless.*
Gerücht *n. rumor, report.*
Gerüst *n. scaffold, stage.*
GESANG *m. song, singing.*
  Gesanglehrer *m. singing teacher.*
GESCHÄFT *n. business, transaction,*
  commerce, commerical firm, store.
geschäftlich *commercial.*
Geschäftsführer *m. manager.*
Geschäftsmann *m. business man.*
geschäftsmässig *commercial.*
Geschäftsviertel *n. shopping district.*
Geschäftszeit *f. office hours;* **Sprechzeit** *f.*
  doctor's office hours.
GESCHEHEN *to happen, occur, be done.*
  Es geschieht ihm recht. *It serves him*
    right.
  Es ist um mich geschehen. *I am done for.*
  geschehen lassen *to allow, permit, let*
    happen.
gescheit *clever, intelligent, sensible.*
Geschenk *n. present, gift.*
GESCHICHTE *f. story, history.*
Geschichtsbuch *n. history book.*
Geschick *n. fate, destiny.*
geschickt *clever, capable.*
Geschirr *n. crockery, dishes, china,*
  tableware.
GESCHLECHT *n. sex, gender, kind,*
  species, race, family, stock.
geschlechtlich *sexual.*
GESCHMACK *m. taste, flavor.*
  Geschmack finden an *to like.*
geschmacklos *insipid, in bad taste.*
Geschmacklosigkeit *f. bad taste.*
geschmackvoll *tasteful.*
Geschrei *n. shouting, screaming, clamor.*
Geschwätz *n. idle talk.*
geschwätzig *talkative, verbose.*
geschwind *quick, fast, swift, prompt, speedy.*
Geschwindigkeit *f. quickness, rapidity.*
  Geschwindigkeitsgrenze 60 km. *Speed*
    limit 60 kilometers.

Geschwister *pl. brother(s) and sister(s).*
Geselle *m. fellow, companion, journeyman.*
Geselligkeit *f. sociability, social life.*
GESELLSCHAFT *f. society, association,*
  company.
  (jemanden) Gesellschaft leisten *to keep*
    (someone) company.
  in Gesellschaft *socially.*
Gesellschafter *m. partner.*
Gesellschaftsanzug *m. evening clothes.*
Gesellschaftskleidung *f. evening dress.*
  Gesellschaftskleidung erwünscht. *Evening*
    dress requested.
Gesellschaftsspiel *n. party game*
Gesetz *n. law, statute.*
Gesetzbuch *n. code*
gesetzlich *legal, lawful.*
gesetzwidrig *unlawful, illegal.*
GESICHT *n. vision, sight, hallucination,*
  appearance, face.
  Das steht Ihnen gut (zu Gesicht). *It is*
    very becoming to you.
  Gesichter schneiden *to make faces*
  Sie lachte übers ganze Gesicht. *She was*
    all smiles.
Gesichtszug *n. feature.*
Gesinnung *f. mind, way of thinking.*
gesinnungslos *unprincipled.*
gesinnungstreu *loyal*
Gesinnugswechsel *m. change of opinion.*
gesittet *well-mannered.*
gespannt *stretched, strained.*
Gespenst *n. ghost.*
gespenstig *ghostly*
Gespött *n. mockery, derision.*
GESPRÄCH *n talk, conversation, discourse.*
gesprächig *talkative.*
Gesprächsstoff *m. topic of conversation.*
Gestalt *f. form, figure, shape, build, frame,*
  manner, fashion.
gestalten *to form.*
Geständnis *n. confession.*
  ein Geständnis ablegen über *to make a*
    confession.
gestehen *to confess, admit.*
Gesträuch *n. shrubs, bushes, shrubbery.*
Gesuch *n. application, petition, request.*
GESUND *healthy, well, sound, natural.*
  gesunder Menschenverstand *common*
    sense
Gesundheit *f. health*
  Gesundheit! *God bless you!*
gesundheitlich *hygienic, sanitary.*
gesundheitshalber *for the sake of health.*
Getränk *n. drink, beverage.*
Getreide *n. grain.*
Getreidespeicher *m. granary.*
Getümmel *n. bustle, tumult.*
Gewächs *n. plant, growth, produce.*

gewachsen *equal to*
Er ist der Arbeit gewachsen. *He is equal to the task.*
Er ist seinem Gegner gewachsen. *He is a match for his opponent.*
Gewächshaus *n. conservatory (greenhouse).*
gewagt *risky.*
Gewähr *f. security, surety.*
gewähren *to grant.*
jemanden gewähren lassen *to let a person do as he pleases.*
GEWALT *f. power, authority, force. violence.*
in der Gewalt haben *to have command of, master.*
mit aller Gewalt *with all one's might.*
sich in der Gewalt haben *to have self-control.*
Gewaltherrschaft *f. despotism.*
gewaltsam *violent*
gewalttätig *brutal, violent.*
gewandt *agile, skillful, clever.*
gewärtig *expecting, expectant.*
Gewebe *n. weaving, web, tissue, fabric.*
Gewehr *n. rifle, weapon.*
Gewerbe *n. trade, business, profession.*
Gewerbeschein *m. trade license.*
Gewerbeschule *f. trade, technical school.*
gewerbsmässig *professional.*
Gewicht *n. weight.*
ins Gewicht fallen *to weigh with.*
gewichtig *weighty, important.*
Gewinn *m. winning.*
Gewinnanteil *m. dividend.*
gewinnbringend *profitable, lucrative.*
GEWINNEN *to gain, earn, win, produce, extract.*
es sich gewinnen *to bring oneself to.*
Gewinner *m. winner.*
gewinnsüchtig *greedy (for victory).*
Gewirr *n. confusion, mess*
GEWISS *certain, sure, fixed; certainly, indeed, of course, no doubt.*
Gewiss! *Surely!*
In gewissem Sinne hat er recht. *In a sense he is right.*
gewissenlos *unscrupulous.*
gewissermassen *to some extent, so to speak, as it were.*
Gewissheit *f. certainty.*
Gewitter *n. thunderstorm.*
gewittern *to thunder.*
Gewitterregen *m. deluge.*
GEWÖHNEN *to accustom.*
sich an etwas gewöhnen *to get used to something.*
Gewohnheit *f. habit.*
gewöhnlich *usual, ordinary, common.*
gewöhnt *accustomed.*

Gewölbe *n. vault.*
Gewühl *n. turmoil, crowd.*
Gewürz *n. spice, seasoning, condiment.*
gewürzig *spiced.*
geziert *affected.*
giessen *to pour, water, spill.*
Gift *n. poison.*
giftig *poisonous, venomous.*
Gipfel *m. summit, peak, top.*
Gipfelpunkt *m. limit.*
Giraffe *f. giraffe.*
Gitter *n. railing, fence, grating.*
Gianz *m. brightness, glamour.*
glänzen *to shine, glitter, gleam.*
glänzend *shining, lustrous.*
Glanzleistung *f. (top) record, achievement.*
glanzvoll *brilliant, splendid, glorious.*
GLAS *n. glass, jar, pitcher.*
gläsern *of glass, vitreous.*
GLATT *even, smooth, slippery, flat; smoothly, slippery.*
Glatteis *n. slippery ice.*
Glauben *m. faith, confidence, trust, belief.*
GLAUBEN *to believe, trust, think, suppose.*
Sie können ihm aufs Wort glauben. *You can take his word for it.*
glaubhaft *credible, likely, probable.*
gläubig *believing, faithful.*
gläublich *credible, likely.*
glaubwürdig *credible, reliable, authentic.*
Glaubwürdigkeit *f. credibility, authenticity.*
GLEICH *same, similar, alike, even, level, direct, equal, like, equivalent; equally, just, at once, immediately.*
es einem gleich tun *to rival a person.*
Es ist mir gleich. *It is all the same to me.*
gleich darauf *immediately afterwards.*
Gleich und gleich gesellt sich gern. *Birds of a feather flock together.*
gleichberechtigt *entitled to the same rights.*
GLEICHEN *to be equal, resemble.*
gleichfalls *likewise.*
gleichförmig *uniform.*
gleichgesinnt *congenial.*
Gleichgewicht *n. equilibrium, balance, poise.*
gleichgültig *indifferent, unconcerned.*
Gleichgültigkeit *f. indifference.*
Gleichheit *f. equality, identity, similarity.*
gleichmässig *proportional.*
Gleichstrom *m. direct current.*
gleichviel *no matter, just the same.*
gleichwertig *equivalent.*
gleichzeitig *simultaneous.*
Gletscher *m. glacier.*
Glied *n. limb, member.*
gliedern *to articulate, arrange, classify.*
glitzern *to glitter, glisten, twinkle.*
Globus *m. globe.*
Glocke *f. bell, clock.*

Glockenspiel *n. chime.*
Glockenturm *m. steeple.*
GLÜCK *n. fortune, good luck, prosperity.*
  etwas auf gut Glück tun   *to take a chance*
    on something.
  Glück haben   *to be lucky.*
  Glück im Spiel, Unglück in der
    Liebe.   *Lucky at cards, unlucky in*
    love.
  Glück wünschen   *to congratulate.*
  Viel Glück!   *Good luck! Many happy*
    returns!
  zu meinem Glück   *fortunately.*
glücken *to succeed, be lucky.*
GLÜCKLICH *fortunate.*
  Glückliche Reise!   *Have a pleasant trip!*
glücklicherweise *fortunately.*
Glücksfall *m. chance.*
Glücksspeil *n. game of chance.*
Glückwunsch *m. congratulations, good*
  wishes.
Glühbirne *f. electric bulb.*
glühen *to glow.*
glühend *glowing, fervent.*
Glühwurm *m. glowworm.*
Glut *f. glow, heat.*
Gnade *f. favor, mercy.*
  auf Gnade und Ungnade   *at discretion.*
Gnadengesuch *n. petition for clemency.*
GNÄDIG *merciful, gracious.*
  gnädige Frau   *Madam.*
GOLD *n. gold.*
golden *gold, of gold, golden.*
Goldgrube *f. gold mine.*
goldig *shining like gold.*
  jedes Wort auf die Goldwaage legen   *to*
    weigh one's words carefully.
Golf *m. golf.*
gönnen *to wish well, allow, permit; not to*
  begrudge.
Gotik *f. Gothic.*
GOTT *m. God.*
  Gott sei Dank!   *Thank God!*
  Um Gottes willen!   *For Heaven's sake!*
  Gott behüte!   *God forbid!*
  in Gottes Name!   *for heaven's sake!*
Götterdämmerung *f. twilight of the Gods.*
Gottesdienst *m. public worship, service*
  (church).
göttlich *divine, godlike.*
Grab *n. tomb, grave.*
Grabstein *m. tombstone.*
Grad *m. degree.*
Graf *m. count.*
Gräfin *f. countess.*
Gram *m. sorrow, grief.*
grämen *to grieve, worry.*
Gramm *n. gram. (1,000 grams equal 1*
  kilogram.)

Grammatik *f. grammar.*
GRAS *n. grass.*
grässlich *terrible, horrible.*
Gräte *f. fish-bone.*
Gratulant *m. congratulator, well-wisher.*
gratulieren *to congratulate.*
GRAU *gray.*
grauen *to be afraid, shudder, dread.*
  Es graut mir vor.   *I am afraid.*
grauenhaft *horrible, ghastly.*
grauenvoll *awful, dreadful.*
Grauhaar *n. gray hair.*
grausam *cruel.*
Grausamkeit *f. cruelty.*
grausig *gruesome, ghastly.*
Grazie *f. grace, charm.*
graziös *gracious.*
greifbar *tangible, palpable.*
greifen *to seize, grasp, catch, touch, strike.*
  ineinander greifen   *to interlock.*
Greis *m. old man.*
Greisenalter *n. old age.*
Greisin *f. old woman.*
Grenze *f. frontier, boundary, limit.*
grenzenlos *boundless, infinite.*
Grenzverkehr *m. traffic at or across the*
  frontier, frontier trading.
Griff *m. grip, grasp, hold, catch.*
Grimm *m. anger, rage.*
grimmig *furious, grim.*
Grippe *f. grippe.*
grob *thick, rough, coarse, clumsy.*
Grobheit *f. coarseness, rudeness.*
Groll *m. resentment, anger.*
grollen *to be resentful, angry.*
GROSS *big, tall, large, great, huge, grand.*
  die grossen Ferien   *the summer vacation.*
  gross tun   *to boast.*
  gross ziehen   *to bring up.*
  grosse Kinder   *grown-up children.*
  grosser Buchstabe   *capital letter.*
  im grossen und ganzen   *on the whole.*
  das grosse Publikum   *the general public.*
  eine grosse Zahl von   *a great many (of).*
  gross auftreten   *to assume airs.*
grossartig *great, grand.*
GRÖSSE *f. size, dimension, largeness,*
  tallness, celebrity, star.
Grosseltern *pl. grandparents.*
Grosshandel *m. wholesale trade.*
grossjährig *of age.*
Grossmacht *f. great power.*
grossmütig *generous, magnanimous.*
Grossmutter *f. grandmother.*
grosspurig *arrogant.*
Grosstadt *f. metropolis.*
Grosstädter *m. inhabitant of a large town.*
grösstenteils *for the most part, largely.*
Grossvater *m. grandfather.*

grosszügig *generous, on a large scale.*
Grün *n. green, verdure.*
GRÜN *green (adj.).*
   im Grünen   *in country surroundings.*
   vom grünen Tisch aus   *only in theory.*
GRUND *m. ground, bottom, cause, reason.*
   im Grunde   *after all.*
   auf den Grund gehen   *to investigate.*
   Aus welchem Grund?   *For what reason?*
Grundbesitz *m. real estate.*
gründen *to found, establish, promote.*
Grundgedanke *m. fundamental idea.*
Grundlage *f. foundation.*
grundlegend *fundamental.*
gründlich *thorough, solid, profound.*
Gründlichkeit *f. thoroughness, solidity.*
Grundsatz *m. principle.*
grundsätzlich *fundamental.*
Grundstück *n. piece of land, lot.*
Gründung *f. foundation, establishment.*
grünen *to grow green, sprout.*
Gruppe *f. group.*
GRUSS *m. greeting; salute (military).*
GRÜSSEN *to greet, salute.*
   grüssen lassen   *to send one's regards.*
gültig *valid, available, good, current.*
Gültigkeit *f. validity; currency (monetary).*
Gummi *m. rubber, eraser.*
Gummiabsatz *m. rubber heel.*
Gummiband *n. rubber band.*
Gummischuh *m. galosh.*
Gummiwaren *pl. rubber goods.*
Gunst *f. kindness, favor.*
   zu Gunsten von   *in favor of.*
günstig *kind, favorable.*
Gurke *f. cucumber.*
Gürtel *m. belt, girdle.*
Guss *m. torrent, downpour.*
Gut *n. property, good, estate, farm.*
GUT *good, pleasant, kind, full; well,*
     pleasantly, kindly
   es gut haben   *to be well off.*
   Gute Besserung!   *I hope you get well*
     soon!
   Guten Morgen!   *Good morning!*
   kurz und gut   *in short.*
   Schon gut!   *All right!*
Gutachten *n. expert opinion, estimate.*
Gutachter *m. assessor, surveyor, consultant.*
gutartig *good-natured.*
Güte *f. kindness.*
Güterzug *m. freight train.*
gutgelaunt *in a good temper, in good spirits.*
gutgläubig *credulous.*
Guthaben *n. balance, credit.*
gutheissen *to approve, sanction.*
gutherzig *kind-hearted; warmhearted.*
gütig *kind, good.*
gutmachen *to make amends for.*

gutmütig *good-natured.*
Gutmütigkeit *f. good nature.*
Gutsbesitzer *m. landowner, gentleman*
     farmer.
Gutschein *m. token, voucher.*
gutwillig *willing, voluntary.*
Gymnasialbildung *f. classical education.*
Gymnasiast *m. high-school boy.*
Gymnasium *n. high-school.*
Gymnastik *f. gymnastics.*

H

HAAR *n. (Haare pl.) hair.*
   sich die Haare machen   *to do one's hair.*
   sich die Haare schneiden lassen   *to get a*
     haircut.
   Haare auf den Zähnen haben   *to stand up*
     (to opponents).
   um ein Haar   *nearly, narrowly.*
   kein gutes Haar an einem lassen   *to pull a*
     person to pieces.
   sich in die Haare geraten   *to come to*
     blows.
   Lassen Sie sich darüber keine grauen Haare
     wachsen!   *Don't let that give you*
     gray hair!
Haarnadel *f. hairpin.*
Haarspalterei *f. hair-splitting.*
Haarwasser *n. hair tonic.*
Habe *f. property, belongings.*
   Hab und Gut   *good and chattel.*
   habhaft werden   *to obtain possession.*
HABEN *to have, own, possess, get.*
   Den wievielten haben wir heute?   *What is*
     the date today?
   nichts auf sich haben   *to be of no*
     consequence.
   Recht haben   *to be right.*
   unter sich haben   *to be in charge of.*
   Was hast du?   *What is the matter with*
     you?
   zu haben sein   *to be obtainable.*
Habgier *f. greed, avarice.*
habgierig *greedy, avaricious.*
hacken *to chop, mince.*
Hafen *m. port, harbor.*
Hafenstadt *f. seaport.*
Haft *f. custody, arrest, detention.*
haftbar *responsible, liable.*
haften *to stick to, cling to.*
   haften für   *to answer for (bear the*
     responsibility).
Häftling *m. prisoner.*
haftpflichtig *liable, responsible.*
   mit beschränkter Haftung   *with limited*
     liability.
Haftung *f. liability, responsibility.*

Hagel m. hail.
Hagelschlag m. hailstorm.
HAHN m. rooster, cock.
Hai m. shark.
Haken m. hook, mark.
Halb half.
  auf halbem Wege   midway, halfway.
  ein halbes Pfund   half a pound.
  halb durchgebraten   medium done (meat).
  halb so viel   half as much.
  halb zwei   half past one.
  halb geschenkt   practically given away.
halbieren to halve, bisect.
Halbinsel f. peninsula.
Halbmond m. crescent moon, half-moon.
Hälfte f. half.
  Kinder zahlen die Hälfte.   Children pay
    half price.
Halle f. hall, hangar.
HALS m. neck, throat.
  Es hängt mir schon zum Hals heraus.
    I am sick and tired of it already.
  Hals über Kopf   headlong.
  um den Hals fallen   to embrace.
  Es geht um den Hals.   It's a matter of life
    and death.
Halsband n. necklace.
halsbrecherisch dangerous.
Halsschmerzen pl. sore throat.
Halstuch n. scarf.
Halt m. stop, halt, hold, footing.
  Halt!   Stop!
haltbar tenable, lasting, durable.
Haltbarkeit f. durability, defensibility.
HALTEN to hold, support, observe, keep,
    celebrate, last, stop, endure, continue,
    follow.
  an sich halten   to restrain oneself.
  Et hält sich für sehr klug.   He thinks he is
    very clever.
  halt machen   to stop.
  halten für   to consider, to think.
  es halten mit   to side with.
  Halten Sie sich rechts!   Keep to the right!
  halten von   to think of.
  Was halten Sie von ihr?   What do you
    think of her?
  schwer halten   to be difficult.
  sein Wort halten   to keep one's word.
  viel halten auf   to think highly of.
Haltestelle f. stop, station.
haltlos without support, unsteady,
    unprincipled.
Haltung f. behavior, attitude, self-control.
Hammer m. hammer.
HAND f. hand, palm.
  an der Hand führen   to lead someone.
  ihn auf den Händen tragen   to treat him
    with every consideration.

aus zweiter Hand kaufen   to buy
    something secondhand.
die Hände voll zu tun haben   to be very
    busy.
eine Hand wäscht die andere   a good turn
    deserves another.
bei der Hand sein   to be ready.
die Hand im Spiel haben   to have a finger
    in the pie.
einem die Hand geben   to shake hands
    with someone.
Hand und Fuss haben   to be to the
    purpose.
mit Händen und Füssen   with might and
    main (tooth and nail).
unter der Hand   secretly.
von der Hand gehen   to work well.
von der Hand weisen   to decline.
zur Hand   handy.
Handarbeit f. manual work, labor.
HANDEL m. trade, business, affair.
  Handel treiben   to trade.
  handelseinig werden   to come to terms.
handeln to act, do.
  handeln mit   to trade with.
  handeln von   to deal with.
  sich handeln um   to be about, be a matter
    of.
Handelskammer f. chamber of commerce.
Handfertigkeit f. manual skill.
Handgelenk n. wrist.
Handgepäck n. hand luggage.
handgreiflich obvious, manifest.
  handgreiflich werden   to use one's fists.
handhaben to handle, manage.
Handkoffer m. suitcase.
Händler m. trader, dealer.
handlich handy.
Handlung f. act, action, deed, business.
Handlungsweise f. way of acting, method of
    dealing.
Handschrift f. handwriting.
Handschuh m. glove.
Handstreich m. surprise attack.
Handtasche f. handbag.
Handtuch n. towel.
Handwerk n. handicraft, trade.
  einem das Handwerk legen   to stop a
    person's activities.
hängen to hang, suspend, fix, attach.
  hängen bleiben   to be caught.
hänseln to tease.
Harm m. grief, sorrow, insult, injury.
harmlos harmless.
Harmlosigkeit f. harmlessness, innocence.
Harmonie f. harmony.
harmonieren to harmonize, agree.
HART hard, firm, solid.
  hartherzig   hard-hearted.

harthörig *hard of hearing.*
Härte *f. hardness, roughness, cruelty, severity.*
hartnäckig *obstinate, stubborn.*
Hase *m. hare.*
Hasenbraten *m. roast hare.*
Hass *m. hate, hatred.*
hassen *to hate.*
hässlich *ugly, nasty.*
Hässligkeit *f. ugliness.*
Hast *f. hurry, haste.*
hastig *hurried, hasty.*
Haube *f. hood, cap.*
    unter die Haube bringen *to marry off.*
Hauch *m. breath, slight breeze.*
hauchen *to breathe.*
Haufen *m. heap, pile.*
häufen *to heap, pile, accumulate.*
häufig *frequent, abundant.*
HAUPT *n. chief, head; principal.*
Hauptbahnhof *m. main station.*
Hauptmann *m. captain.*
Hauptperson *f. principal person, leading character (theater).*
Hauptpostamt *n. general post office.*
Hauptquartier *n. headquarters.*
Hauptsache *f. main thing.*
hauptsächlich *principal.*
Hauptstadt *f. capital.*
Hauptverkehrszeit *f. rush hour.*
Hauptwort *n. substantive, noun.*
HAUS *n. house, home, building.*
    bei uns zu Hause *where I come from.*
    das Haus hüten *to be confined to the house.*
    nach Hause gehen *to go home.*
    von Haus aus *originally.*
    zu Hause *at home.*
Hausangestellte *m. & f. servant.*
Hausarbeit *f. housework.*
Hausaufgabe *f. homework.*
Häuschen *n. small house.*
Hausflur *m. hall, corridor.*
Hausfrau *f. housewife.*
Haushalt *m. household.*
haushalten *to keep house, to economize.*
Haushälterin *f. housekeeper.*
Hausherr *m. master.*
Hauslehrer *m. private tutor.*
häuslich *domestic.*
Häuslichkeit *f. family life, domesticity.*
Hausmeister *m. janitor.*
Hausschuh *m. slipper.*
Haussuchung *f. police raid.*
Haustier *n. domestic animal.*
Haustür *f. front door.*
Hauswirt *m. landlord.*
HAUT *f. skin, hide, coat.*

    aus der Haut fahren *to lose one's patience.*
    sich seiner Haut wehren *to defend oneself.*
Hautfarbe *f. complexion.*
heben *to lift, raise.*
Heer *n. army.*
Hefe *f. yeast.*
Heft *n. notebook, pamphlet.*
heften *to pin, fasten, stitch, fix.*
heftig *violent, strong.*
Heftigkeit *f. violence, vehemence, intensity.*
heikel *delicate, ticklish, difficult.*
HEIL *unhurt, intact, safe, cured.*
heilbar *curable.*
heilen *to cure.*
heilig *holy, godly, sacred.*
    Heiligabend *Christmas Eve.*
    heilighalten *to hold sacred.*
heilkräftig *curative.*
Heilmittel *n. remedy.*
heilsam *curative.*
Heilsarmee *f. Salvation Army.*
Heilung *f. healing, cure.*
Heilverfahren *n. medical treatment.*
HEIM *n. home.*
heim *homeward.*
Heimat *f. native country, homeland.*
heimatlos *homeless.*
Heimatstadt *f. home town.*
Heimkehr(-kunft) *f. homecoming.*
heimlich *secret, private, comfortable; secretly, privately.*
Heimsuchung *f. trial, misfortune.*
Heimtücke *f. malice.*
heimtückisch *malicious, insidious.*
Heimweg *m. way home, return.*
Heimweh *n. homesickness.*
    Heimweh haben *to be homesick.*
HEIRAT *f. marriage.*
heiraten *to marry, get married.*
Heiratsantrag *m. proposal.*
heiser *hoarse.*
    heiser sein *to be hoarse, have a sore throat.*
Heiserkeit *f. hoarseness, sore throat.*
HEISS *hot.*
HEISSEN *to call, name, be called.*
    das heisst *that is.*
    es heisst *they say.*
    Ich heisse Anna. *My name is Ann.*
    Wie heisst das auf Englisch? *What is that called in English?*
    jemand willkommen heissen *to bid someone welcome.*
heiter *gay, cheerful.*
Heiterkeit *f. brightness, clearness, serenity, cheerfulness.*
heizbar *with heating*

heizen *to heat.*
Heizkissen *n. electric pad.*
Heizung *f heating, firing, radiator.*
Held *m. hero.*
HELFEN *to support, help, assist.*
  Ich kann mir nicht helfen. *I can't help it.*
Helfer *m. helper, assistant.*
Helfershelfer *m. accomplice ("helper's helper")*
HELL *bright, shining, clear, light, fair, pale, sheer.*
Helle *f. clearness, brightness.*
hellhörig *keen of hearing.*
Helm *m. helmet.*
HEMD *n. shirt.*
hemmen *to check, stop, hinder. restrain.*
Hemmung *f. inhibition, check, stoppage restraint*
hemmungslos *free, unrestrained.*
HER 1. *adv. here, from, since, ago.*
  von Alters her *of old, long ago.*
  2. *separable prefix (implies the idea of a movement toward the speaker)*
  Kommen Sie her! *Come here!*
herab *down, downward.*
herablassen *to lower, let down, to stoop.*
Herablassung *f. condescension.*
herabsehen *to look down upon.*
herabsetzen *to lower, degrade, reduce (price).*
Herabsetzung *f. lowering, degradation; reduction (price).*
heran *on, up, near, along.*
heranbilden *to train, educate.*
herankommen *to come near.*
  die Dinge an sich herankommen lassen *to bide one's time.*
heranwachsen *to grow up.*
HERAUF *up, upwards.*
heraufgehen *to go up.*
  Kommen Sie herauf! *Come up!*
HERAUS *out, from within.*
  Sie kommen heraus. *They are coming out.*
herausbekommen *to get back (money); find out.*
herausnehmen *to take out, extract.*
herausstellen *to turn out, appear.*
herbei *here, near, hither.*
herbeischaffen *to bring near, procure, produce.*
HERBST *m. autumn.*
herbstlich *autumnal.*
Herd *m. hearth, fireplace.*
Herdplatte *f. hot plate.*
HEREIN *in.*
  Kommen Sie herein (Herein!) *Come in!*
  Hier herein, bitte! *This way, please!*
hereinfallen *to be taken in, disappointed.*

herkommen *to come near, approach, originate.*
Herkunft *f. origin, descent.*
HERR *m. master, gentleman, lord, sir, Mr.*
  Meine Damen und Herren *Ladies and gentlemen.*
  Ist der Herr Doktor zu sprechen? *Can I see the doctor?*
  eigener Herr sein *to stand on one's own feet.*
  Herr werden *to master, overcome.*
  Herr im Hause sein *to be the master of the house.*
herrichten *to arrange.*
herrisch *imperious, dictatorial.*
Herrschaft *f. power, rule, command, master and mistress (of an estate).*
herrschen *to rule, govern, prevail, exist.*
Herrscher *m. ruler, tyrant, dictator.*
herrschsüchtig *fond of power, tyrannical.*
herüber *across, to this side.*
herüberkommen *to come over,*
HERUM *around, round, near, about.*
  rundherum *all around.*
herumdrehen *to turn round.*
herumführen *to lead.*
herumreichen *to hand around.*
(sich) herumtreiben *to run around.*
HERUNTER *down, off.*
herunterkommen *to come down.*
  Komm gleich herunter! *Come down right away!*
heruntersetzen *to lower.*
hervor *out, forth.*
hervorbringen *to produce, yield.*
hervorheben *to make prominent.*
hervorragen *to stand out, project.*
hervorragend *prominent, excellent.*
(sich) hervortun *to distinguish oneself.*
Herz *n. heart, feeling, mind, courage.*
  ans Herz legen *to recommend to someone's care.*
  ins Herz schliessen *to become fond of.*
  sich ein Herz fassen *to take courage.*
  sich zu Herzen nehmen *to take to heart.*
  von Herzen gern *with the greatest pleasure.*
  Was haben Sie auf dem Herzen? *What's on your mind?*
herzleidend *suffering from heart trouble.*
herzlich *hearty, cordial.*
  mit herzlichen Grüssen *with kindest regards.*
herzlos *heartless.*
Herzschlag *m. heart beat, heart failure.*
Heu *n. hay.*
Heufieber *n. hay fever.*
Heuchelei *f. hypocrisy.*
heucheln *to feign, pretend.*

Heuchler *m. hypocrite.*
HEUTE *today.*
  heute abend *tonight.*
  heute früh; heute morgen *this morning.*
  heute vor acht Tagen *a week ago.*
  heutzutage *nowadays.*
Hexe *f. witch.*
Hier *here.*
  hier und da *here and there.*
hierauf *hereupon.*
hierdurch *through this, this way, thereby.*
hierher *here, hither.*
hierherum *hereabout.*
hiermit *herewith, with this.*
hiernach *after this, thereupon.*
hierüber *over here, about this.*
hiervon *hereof, from this.*
hierzu *to this, moreover.*
HILFE *f. help, assistance, support, relief.*
  Hilfe leisten *to help, assist.*
  erste Hilfe *first aid.*
hilflos *helpless.*
hilfreich *helpful, charitable.*
hilfsbedürftig *indigent, needing help.*
HIMMEL *m. sky, heaven.*
  aus allen Himmeln fallen *to be bitterly disappointed.*
  Himmel und Menschen *a throng; many people.*
Himmelsrichtung *f. quarter, direction, point of compass.*
himmlisch *heavenly, celestial.*
HIN 1. *adv. there, thither.*
  hin und her *to and fro.*
  hin und her überlegen *to turn over in one's mind.*
  hin und wieder *now and then.*
  2. *separable prefix (implies the idea of a movement away from the speaker).*
  Gehen Sie hinaus! *Go out.*
hinab *down, downward.*
HINAUF *up, upward.*
  hinaufarbeiten *to work one's way up.*
  Er geht die Treppe hinauf. *He goes up the stairs.*
HINAUS *out, outside, past.*
  darüber hinaus *beyond that.*
  Ich schicke die Kinder hinaus. *I am sending the children outside.*
hinausgehen *to go out.*
hinauskommen *to come out.*
  auf eins hinauskommen *to come to the same thing.*
hinausschieben *to defer, postpone, put off.*
hinauswerfen *to throw out, expel.*
  hoch hinauswollen *to aim high.*
hinausziehen *to draw out, put off.*
Hinblick *m. look at or toward.*
  im Hinblick auf *with regard to.*

hinbringen *to take, bring, carry.*
hinderlich *in the way, hindering, obstructive.*
hindern *to prevent, hinder, hamper.*
hindurch *through, throughout, across.*
HINEIN *in, into.*
  Ich gehe in das Zimmer hinein. *I go into the room.*
hineingehen *to go into.*
hinfahren *to carry, drive to.*
Hinfahrt *f. trip there.*
hinfallen *to fall down.*
hinfällig *frail, weak.*
  hinfällig werden *to fail, come to nothing.*
hinfort *henceforth, in the future.*
Hingabe *f. surrender, devotion.*
hinhalten *to put off.*
hinlänglich *sufficient, adequate.*
hinnehmen *to take, accept.*
hinsehen *to look at.*
(sich) hinsetzen *to set down, sit down.*
hinsichtlich *with regard to.*
hinstellen *to place, put down.*
hinten *behind, in the rear, at the back.*
HINTER 1. *prep. (dat. when answering question, Wo?; acc. when answering question, Wohin? and depending on the idiom) behind, back, after.*
  Hinter dem Haus ist eine Garage. *There is a garage behind the house.*
  Sie hat schon viel hinter sich. *She has been through a lot.*
  hinter sich bringen *to get over, cover.*
Hinterbliebene *m. & f. survivor.*
hintereinander *one after the other.*
  zwei Tage hintereinander *two days running.*
Hintergedanke *m. underlying thought, unacknowledged motive.*
Hintergrund *m. background.*
Hinterhalt *m. ambush.*
hinterhältig *malicious, devious.*
hinterher *behind, afterwards.*
hinterlassen *to leave, leave behind.*
  Hat er keine Nachricht für mich hinterlassen? *Hasn't he left a message for me?*
hinterlistig *artful, cunning.*
Hinterrad *n. backwheel.*
hinters *hinter das.*
HINÜBER *over, across, over there, to the other side.*
HINUNTER *down, downward, downstairs.*
  Sie geht die Treppe hinunter. *She walks down the stairs.*
Hinweg *m. way there.*
hinweg *away, off.*

hinwegkommen (über) *to get over.*
hinwegsetzen (über) *to disregard.*
Hinweis *m. indication, hint, reference, direction.*
hinweisen *to show, indicate, refer.*
hinwerfen *to throw down.*
hinzu *to, near, there.*
hinzufügen *to add.*
hinzuziehen *to include, consult.*
Hirn *n. brain.*
Hitze *f. heat.*
hitzig *hot, hot-headed.*
HOCH *high, tall, lofty, great, noble.*
    Es geht hoch her.   *Things are getting pretty lively.*
    Hände hoch!   *Hands up!*
    hoch anrechnen   *to value greatly.*
    Hoch leben . . . !   *Long live. . . !*
    hochleben lassen   *to toast.*
hochachten *to esteem, respect.*
Hochachtung *f. esteem, respect.*
    hochachtungsvoll   *yours respectfully.*
Hochbetrieb *m. intense activity.*
Hochdeutsch *n. high German, standard German.*
hochhalten *to cherish, raise.*
Hochhaus *n. skyscraper.*
hochherzig *high-minded, magnanimous.*
Hochmut *m. pride, arrogance.*
hochmütig *arrogant, proud.*
Hochschule *f. university, college.*
Hochsommer *m. midsummer.*
Hochspannung *f. high tension.*
    Vorsicht! Hochspannung!   *Caution! High tension wires!*
HÖCHST *highest, utmost, extreme, maximum; very, extremely.*
Hochstapelei *f. swindling.*
Hochstapler *m. swindler.*
höchstens *at best, at most.*
Höchstgeschwindigkeit *f. top speed, speed limit.*
Höchstgrenze *f. limit.*
Höchstleistung *f. maximum output, record performance.*
höchstwahrscheinlich *most likely.*
hochtrabend *high-sounding.*
Hochverrat *m. high treason.*
Hochzeit *f. wedding, marriage.*
Hochzeitsreise *f. honeymoon trip.*
HOF *m. yard, court, farm.*
    den Hof machen   *to pay court to.*
HOFFEN *to hope.*
    hoffen auf   *to hope for.*
hoffentlich *it is to be hoped.*
Hoffnung *f. hope.*
    sich falsche Hoffnungen machen   *to have illusions.*
hoffnungslos *hopeless.*

hoffnungsvoll *hopeful.*
HÖHE *f. height, altitude, latitude, top, summit, amount.*
    auf der Höhe sein   *to be up to date, to be in top form.*
    auf gleicher Höhe mit   *on the same level with.*
    sich nicht auf der Höhe fühlen   *not to feel up to par.*
    auf der Höhe von   *at the altitude of.*
    aus der Höhe   *from on high.*
    Das ist die Höhe.   *That is the limit.*
    in (der) Höhe von   *in the amount of.*
Höhenstrahlen *pl. cosmic rays.*
höher *higher, superior.*
HOHL *hollow, concave, dull.*
Höhle *f. hole, cave.*
Hohlraum *m. empty space, cavity.*
Hohn *m. scorn, sneer, mockery, insult.*
höhnen *to mock, defy.*
höhnisch *scornful, sneering.*
HOLEN *to get, take, fetch.*
    sich Rat holen   *to consult.*
    sich eine Erkaltung holen   *to catch a cold.*
    Atem holen   *to catch one's breath.*
HÖLLE *f. hell.*
höllisch *hellish, infernal.*
HOLZ *n. wood, timber, lumber.*
hölzern *wooden.*
Honig *m. honey.*
horchen *to listen, lend an ear, listen in, spy.*
    Es horcht jemand.   *Somebody is listening in.*
HÖREN *to hear, listen, attend, obey, understand.*
    schwer hören   *to be hard of hearing.*
Horizont *m. horizon.*
Horn *n. horn, bugle.*
Horoskop *n. horoscope.*
    ein Horoskop stellen   *to cast horoscope.*
Hörspiel *n. radio play.*
Hose *f. trousers, pants.*
    Sie hat die Hosen an.   *She wears the pants.*
Hosenträger *pl. suspenders.*
Hotel *n. hotel, inn.*
hübsch *pretty, charming, nice.*
Huf *m. hoof.*
Hügel *m. hill.*
HUHN *n. hen.*
    gebratenes Hühnchen   *roast chicken.*
    junges Huhn   *young chicken.*
Huld *f. grace, favor, charm.*
huldigen *to pay homage.*
Humor *m. sense of humor.*
humoristisch *humorous.*
HUND *m. dog.*
Hundert *n. hundred.*

zu Hunderten *by hundreds.*

HUNDERT *one hundred (adj.)*

HUNGER *m. hunger.*

Hunger haben *to be hungry.*

hungern *to be hungry, starve.*

Hungersnot *f. famine.*

hungrig *hungry.*

husten *to cough.*

Hustensirup *m. cough syrup.*

HUT *m. hat.*

unter einen Hut bringen *to reconcile.*

hüten *to guard, keep, beware.*

das Zimmer hüten *to be confined to one's room.*

Hütte *f. hut.*

I

ICH *I, self, ego.*

Ideal *n. ideal.*

Idealist *m. idealist.*

Idee *f. idea, notion.*

identifizieren *to identify.*

identisch *identical.*

IHM *dat. of er, es. (pers. pron., masc. and neut.) to him, to it.*

IHN *acc. of er (pers. pron. masc.) him, it.*

IHNEN (ihnen) *dat. of sie (pers. pron. pl). to them.*

IHNEN (ihnen) *dat. of Sie (pers. pron. sing, polite form) to you.*

IHR *dat. of sie (pers. pron. fem.) to her, to it.*

IHR (ihr) *poss. adj. (fem. and pl.) her, its, their.*

IHR (ihr) *poss. adj. (sing. polite form) your.*

IHR(ER,-E,-ES) *poss, pron. (fem. and pl.) hers, its, theirs.*

poss. pron.(sing. polite form) your.

ihretwegen *on her (its, their) account, for her sake.*

Ihretwegen *on your account, for your sake.*

illustrieren *to illustrate.*

imitieren *to imitate.*

IMMER *always, ever.*

auf immer *forever.*

immer mehr *more and more.*

immer wieder *again and again.*

immerfort *continually, constantly.*

wer auch immer *whoever.*

immerhin *for all that, still, nevertheless.*

immerzu *all the time, continually.*

imponieren *to impress.*

Import *m. imports, importation.*

Impuls *m. impulse.*

impulsiv *impulsive.*

IN *prep. (dat. answering question, Wo?; acc. answering question, Wohin?) in, into, to, at.*

Die Besucher gehen in die Oper. *The spectators go to the opera.*

Der Lehrer sitzt in dem Zimmer. *The teacher is sitting in the room.*

Der Lehrer tritt in das Zimmer ein. *The teacher goes into the room.*

Der Sänger singt in der Oper. *The singer sings in the opera.*

Goethe wurde in Frankfurt geboren. *Goethe was born in Frankfurt.*

im Februar *in February.*

im Kreise *in a circle.*

Inbegriff *m. embodiment, essence.*

inbegriffen *including, inclusive, included.*

INDEM *while, by, on, since.*

indirekt *indirect.*

indiskret *indiscreet, tactless.*

Indiskretion *f. indiscretion.*

Industrie *f. industry.*

Industrielle *m. manufacturer, producer.*

Infektionskrankheit *f. infectious disease.*

infolge *in consequence of, as a result of.*

infolgedessen *because of that, consequently, hence.*

Ingenieur(-in) *m. (f.) engineer.*

Inhaber *m. proprietor.*

Inhalt *m. contents, area, extent, volume, capacity.*

inhaltlich *with regard to the contents.*

Inhaltsangabe *f. summary, table of contents.*

inhaltsleer *empty, meaningless.*

inhaltsreich *full of meaning, significant.*

Inhaltsverzeichnis *n. contents, table of contents, index.*

inmitten *in the midst of.*

innen *within, inside, in.*

INNER *interior, internal, inner.*

innerhalb *within, inside.*

innerlich *inward, internal, interior.*

innig *hearty, intimate.*

Innigkeit *f. intimacy, cordiality.*

ins *in das.*

insbesondere *particularly.*

Inschrift *f. inscription, legend.*

Insekt *n. insect.*

INSEL *f. island.*

Inserat *n. advertisement.*

inserieren *to advertise.*

insgesamt *all together, collectively.*

insofern *in so far, as far as that goes.*

insoweit *in so far.*

Instandhaltung *f. upkeep.*

inständig *instant, urgent.*

Instinkt *m. instinct.*

instruieren *to instruct, brief.*

Instrument *n. instrument.*

Intelligent *intelligent.*

Intelligenz f. *intelligence, understanding, intellect.*
interessant *interesting.*
Interesse n. *interest, advantage.*
interessieren *to interest.*
  sich interessieren (für) *to be interested in.*
international *international.*
interviewen *to interview.*
Inventar n. *inventory, stock.*
investieren *to invest.*
inzwischen *in between, in the meantime.*
IRGEND *any, some.*
  wenn irgend möglich *if at all possible.*
irgendetwas *something.*
irgendjemand *somebody, anybody.*
irgendwann *sometime.*
irgendwie *somehow.*
irgendwo *somewhere.*
irgendwoher *from some place or other.*
irgendwohin *to somewhere or other.*
ironisch *ironical.*
irre *astray, wrong, confused, insane.*
  irre werden an *to lose confidence in.*
IRRE f. *wandering, mistaken course.*
  in die Irre gehen *to lose one's way, go astray.*
  Irre machen *to confuse.*
irren *to err, wander, lose one's way, be mistaken, be wrong.*
  sich irren *to be mistaken.*
  irren ist menschlich *To err is human.*
Irrenanstalt f. *lunatic asylum.*
irrereden *to talk incoherently, to rave.*
irritieren *to irritate.*
Irrsinn m. *madness, insanity.*
irrsinnig *mad, insane.*
Irrtum m. *error, mistake*
  Sie sind im Irrtum. *You are mistaken.*
irrtümlich *erroneous, wrong.*
Israeli m. *Israeli (person).*
israelisch *Israeli.*
Italiener m. *Italian (person).*
Italienisch n. *Italian (language).*
italienisch *Italian.*

J

JA *yes, really, indeed, certainly.*
  Da sind Sie ja! *So there you are!*
  Sie wissen ja, dass ich nicht gehen kann. *But you know that I can't go.*
  ja sogar *even.*
Jacke f. *jacket*
Jackenkleid n. *lady's suit.*
JAGD f. *hunt, pursuit, hunting, shooting.*
  auf die Jagd gehen *to go hunting.*
Jagdschein m. *hunting license.*

jagen *to chase, pursue.*
Jäger m. *hunter, huntsman, sportsman.*
jäh *sudden, quick, steep.*
JAHR n. *year.*
  ein halbes Jahr *six months.*
Jahrestag m. *anniversary.*
Jahreswende f. *New Year, turn of the year.*
JAHRESZEIT f. *season.*
Jahrhundert n. *century.*
jährlich *yearly, annual.*
Jahrmarkt m. *fair.*
Jahrtausend n. *thousand years, millennium.*
Jahrzehnt n. *decade.*
Jähzorn m. *sudden anger, violent temper.*
jähzorning *hot-tempered, irascible.*
Jammer m. *misery, wailing.*
  Was für ein Jammer! *What a pity!*
jammern *to lament, wail, moan.*
JANUAR m. *January.*
Japaner m. *Japanese (person).*
japanisch *Japanese (language).*
jauchzen *to exult, shout, rejoice.*
JAWOHL *of course, indeed.*
JE *each, ever, at all times.*
  je zwei *two at a time.*
  Sie erhielten je ein Pfund. *They received a pound each.*
  je nach *according to*
  je nachdem *according as*
  Je eher umso (desto) besser. *The sooner, the better.*
jedenfalls *at all events, in any case.*
JEDER (jede, jedes) *every, each, either, any.*
jedermann *everyone, everybody.*
jederzeit *at any time, always.*
jedesmal *every time.*
  jedesmal wenn *whenever, as often as.*
jedoch *however, nevertheless.*
jeher von jeher *at all times, from times immemorial.*
jemals *at any time.*
jemand *somebody, someone.*
JENER (jene, jenes) *that, that one, the former, the other.*
  jenseitig *opposite, on the opposite side.*
JENSEITS 1. *adv. beyond, on the other side, yonder.*
  2. *prep. (gen). that side, on the other side.*
  Er wohnt jenseits des Flüsses. *He lives on the other side of the river.*
jetzig *present, actual.*
JETZT *now, at present.*
Joch n. *yoke.*
Jod n. *iodine.*
Journalist m. *journalist.*
Jubel m. *rejoicing, jubilation.*
Jude m. *Jew.*
jüdisch *Jewish.*

JUGEND *f. youth, young people.*
Jugendfreund *m. friend of youth.*
jugendlich *youthful*
Jugendliche *m. & f. young boy or girl.*
Jugendliebe *f. first love.*
Jugendzeit *f. youth, young days.*
JULI *m. July.*
JUNG *young, youthful.*
Junge *m. boy, lad.*
jungenhaft *boyish.*
jünger *younger.*
Jungfrau *f. virgin, maid, maiden.*
    alte Jungfer   *old maid.*
Junggeselle *m. bachelor.*
Jüngling *m. young man.*
JUNI *m. June.*
Jura *pl. law.*
    Jura studieren   *to study law.*
Jurist *m. law-student, lawyer.*
Justiz *f. administration of the law.*
Juwel *f. jewel.*
Juwelier *m. jeweler.*

K

Kabarett *n. cabaret.*
Kabine *f. cabin.*
Kachel *f. glazed tile.*
KAFFEE *m. coffee.*
Kaffeekanne *f. coffee-pot.*
Käfig *m. cage.*
kahl *bald, bare, naked.*
kahlköpfig *bald-headed.*
Kai *m. wharf.*
Kaiser *m. emperor.*
Kalb *n. calf.*
Kalbfleisch *n. veal.*
    Kalbsbraten   *m. roast veal.*
Kalender *m. calendar.*
kalkulieren *to calculate.*
KALT *cold, indifferent.*
kaltblütig *cold-blooded.*
Kälte *f. coldness, indifference.*
Kamel, *n. camel.*
Kamera *f. camera*
Kamerad *m. friend, comrade, fellow.*
Kameradschaft *f. fellowship, comradeship.*
Kamin *m. chimney, fireplace.*
Kamm *m. comb.*
kämmen *to comb.*
Kammer *f. small room, chamber*
    (government).
Kammermusik *f. chamber music.*
KAMPF *m. fight, combat, conflict, struggle.*
    Kampf ums Dasein   *struggle for a living.*
KÄMPFEN *to fight.*
Kanadier *m. Canadian (person).*
kanadisch *Canadian.*

Kanal *m. canal, sewer.*
Kanarienvogel *m. canary bird.*
Kandidat *m. candidate.*
kandidieren *to be a candidate.*
Kaninchen *n. rabbit.*
Kanne *f. jug, pot, pitcher.*
Kanone *f. cannon.*
Kante *f. edge, corner.*
kantig *edged, angular.*
Kantine *f. canteen, mess.*
Kanzel *f. pulpit.*
Kapelle *f. chapel, band.*
Kapital *n. capital.*
Kapitalsanlage *f. investment.*
Kapitalismus *m. capitalism.*
Kapitalist *m. capitalist.*
kapitalkräftig *wealthy.*
Kapitän *m. captain.*
Kapitel *n. chapter.*
kapitulieren *to capitulate.*
kaputt *broken, ruined, out of order.*
Karfreitag *m. Good Friday.*
Karikatur *f. caricature.*
Karneval *m. carnival.*
Karotte *f. carrot.*
Karriere *f. career, gallop.*
KARTE *f. card, ticket, map, menu.*
    Karten legen   *to tell one's fortune.*
Kartenspiel *n. card game, pack of cards.*
KARTOFFEL *f. potato*
    Kartoffelpüree   *n. mashed potatoes.*
    Bratkartoffeln   *pl. fried potatoes.*
    Kartoffelsalat   *m. potato salad.*
Karton *m. cardboard, box.*
Karwoche *f. Passion Week.*
KÄSE *m. cheese.*
Kaserne *f. barracks.*
Kasse *f. cash-box.*
    Zahlen Sie, bitte, an der Kasse!   *Please pay the cashier.*
Kassenschein *m. receipt.*
kassieren *to receive money.*
Kassierer *m. cashier.*
Kastanie *f. chestnut.*
Kasten *m. box, chest, mailbox.*
Katalog *m. catalog.*
Katastrophe *f. catastrophe.*
katastrophal *catastrophic.*
Katholik *m. Roman Catholic.*
katholisch *Roman Catholic (adj.).*
Katze *f. cat.*
kauen *to masticate, chew.*
    Kaugummi   *n. chewing-gum.*
KAUF *m. buy, purchase.*
    mit in Kauf nehmen   *to put up with.*
KAUFEN *to buy, purchase.*
    sich etwas kaufen   *to buy oneself something.*
Käufer *m. buyer.*

Kaufhaus n. *department store, store, warehouse.*
Kaufladen m. *store, shop.*
Kaufmann m. *shopkeeper, merchant.*
KAUM *hardly, scarcely, barely.*
Kavalier m. *cavalier, gentleman.*
keck *bold, daring, impudent.*
Keckheit f. *boldness.*
Kegel m. *ninepin.*
   mit Kind und Kegel   *with bag and luggage.*
kegeln *to bowl.*
Kehle f. *throat.*
Kehlkopf m. *larynx.*
KEHREN *turn, to sweep.*
   ihm den Rücken kehren   *to turn one's back to him.*
   kehrtmachen   *to face about, turn back.*
KEIN adj. *no, not one, not any.*
KEIN (ER,-E,-ES) pron. *none, neither.*
   keiner von beiden   *neither of them.*
keinerlei *of no sort.*
KEINESWEGS *no account, not at all.*
Kelch m. *cup, goblet, chalice.*
Keller m. *cellar.*
KELLNER m (-in, f.) *waiter, (waitress).*
KENNEN *to know, be acquainted with.*
   kennenlernen   *to meet, become acquainted with.*
Kenner m. *connoisseur.*
Kennkarte f. *identity-card.*
kenntlich *recognizable, distinguishable.*
KENNTNIS f. *knowledge, information.*
   in Kenntnis setzen   *to inform.*
   zur Kenntnis nehmen   *to take note of.*
Kennzeichen n. *identity, mark.*
Kern m. *kernel, corn, seed, stone (fruit).*
Kerze f. *candle, sparking plug.*
Kessel m. *boiler, kettle.*
Kette f. *chain, necklace.*
Kettenhund m. *watch dog.*
keuchen *to pant, puff.*
Keuchhusten m. *whopping cough.*
Keule f. *club, leg (of lamb, etc.)*
keusch *pure, chaste.*
Keuschheit f. *modesty, purity, chastity.*
Kiefer m. *jaw.*
Kilogramm n. *kilogram (2.204 pounds).*
Kilometer m. *kilometer (.621 miles).*
Kilometerzähler m. *mileage recorder.*
KIND n. *child.*
   kleines Kind   *baby (infant).*
   von Kind auf   *from childhood on.*
Kinderernährung *baby feeding.*
Kindergarten m. *kindergarten, nursery school.*
kinderlos *childless.*
Kindermädchen n. *nursemaid.*
Kinderstube f. *nursery.*

Kinderwagen m. *baby carriage.*
Kindheit f. *childhood.*
kindisch *childish.*
kindlich *childlike.*
Kinn n. *chin.*
Kino n. *cinema, picture show, movies.*
Kirche f. *church, service.*
Kirchhof m. *cemetery.*
Kirchtum m. *church steeple.*
Kirsche f. *cherry.*
Kissen n. *cushion, pillow.*
Kissenbezug m. *cover, pillow-case.*
Kiste f. *box, chest, case.*
kitzeln *to tickle.*
kitzlig *ticklish.*
Klage f. *lament, complaint.*
klagen *to lament, complain, sue.*
Kläger m. *plaintiff.*
kläglich *lamentable, deplorable.*
klamm *numb, stiff, tight.*
klammern *to fasten, clasp, cling to.*
Klang m. *sound, tone, ringing of bell.*
Klangfarbe f. *timbre.*
klanglos *soundless.*
klangvoll *sonorous.*
Klappstuhl m. *folding chair.*
Klapptisch m. *folding table.*
Klaps m. *slap.*
KLAR *clear, limpid, pure, plain, evident.*
   klar und deutlich   *distinctly, plainly.*
   klar zum Gefecht   *ready for action.*
   klar legen (stellen)   *to clear up, explain.*
   sich klar darüber sein   *to realize.*
Klarinette f. *clarinet.*
Klarinettist m. *clarinetist.*
KLASSE f. *class, form, order.*
Klassenlehrer m. *class-teacher.*
Klassenzimmer n. *classroom.*
Klassik f. *classical art, classical period.*
Klatsch m. *smack, crack, slap.*
klatschen *to clap, lash, applaud.*
   Beifall klatschen   *to applaud.*
Klavier n. *piano.*
Klavierspieler m. *pianist.*
kleben *to stick, glue.*
Klee m. *clover, shamrock.*
KLEID n. *dress, frock, gown.*
   die Kleider   pl. *garments.*
kleiden *to dress, clothe, suit, become.*
   Er ist immer gut gekleidet.   *He is always well-dressed.*
Kleiderbügel m. *coathanger.*
Kleiderbürste f. *clothes brush.*
Kleiderschrank m. *wardrobe.*
Kleidung f. *dress, clothes, clothing.*
KLEIN *little, small, tiny, minor.*
   klein schneiden   *to cut in pieces.*
   klein schreiben   *to write with small letters.*
   von klein auf   *from infancy on.*

klein denken *to have narrow views.*
KLEINGELD *n. change (monetary).*
kleingläubig *of little faith.*
Kleinholz *n. sticks, firewood.*
Kleinkram *m. trifle.*
Kleinstadt *f. small provincial town.*
kleinstädtisch *provincial.*
klettern *to climb.*
Klima *n. climate.*
klimatisch *climatic.*
Klingel *f. bell.*
klingeln *to ring.*
Klinke *f. doorknob; handle.*
klipp *snapping sound, snap of the fingers.*
    klipp und klar *quite clear.*
klirren *to clink, jingle.*
klopfen *to beat, knock, tap.*
Kloster *n. monastery, convent.*
Klub. *m. club.*
Klubsessel *m. lounge chair, easy chair.*
KLUG *intelligent, sensible, clever.*
    Ich werde nicht klug daraus. *I can't
    figure it out.*
Klugheit *f. intelligence.*
Klumpen *m. lump.*
KNABE *m. boy, lad.*
Knall *m. bang, detonation, crack.*
knapp *narrow, tight, close, poor.*
    knapp werde *to run short of.*
Knappheit *f. scarcity, shortage.*
Knecht *m. servant, farmhand, slave.*
Knechtheit *f. servitude, slavery.*
kneifen *to pinch, nip.*
Kneipe *f. tavern, public house.*
Knie *n. knee.*
Kniehosen *pl. breeches, shorts.*
knistern *to rustle, crackle.*
KNOCHEN *m. bone.*
knöchern *of bone, bony.*
Knopf *m. button, knob, head.*
knöpfen *to button.*
Knopfloch *n. buttonhole.*
Knospe *f. bud.*
Knoten *m. knot.*
knurren *to growl, rumble.*
knusprig *crisp.*
Koch *m. cook.*
Kochbuch *n. cookbook.*
KOCHEN *to cook, boil.*
Kochgeschirr *n. pots and pans.*
Köchin *f. cook.*
Kochlöffel *m. ladle.*
Kochtopf *m. saucepan, pot, casserole.*
Koffer *m. trunk, bag, suitcase.*
Kognak *m. cognac, brandy.*
Kohl *m. cabbage.*
Kohle *f. coal, carbon.*
    auf Kohlen sitzen *to be on thorns or
    tenterhooks.*

Kohleneimer *m. coal bucket.*
Koje *f. cabin, berth.*
Kollege *m. colleague.*
Kolonialwaren *pl. groceries.*
Kolonialwarenhandlung *f. grocery store.*
Komiker *m. comedian.*
komisch *comical.*
Komma *n. comma.*
kommandieren *to command, order.*
KOMMEN *to come, arrive, get, result,
    happen, occur.*
    Das kommt davon. *That's the result.*
    Das kommt nicht in Frage. *This is out of
    the question.*
    Es kommt darauf an. *It depends.*
    kommen lassen *to send for.*
    kommen sehen *to foresee.*
    nicht dazu kommen *to have no time to.*
    Wann komme ich an die Reihe? *When
    will it be my turn?*
    Wie kommet es, dass *how is it that.*
    zu sich kommen *to recover.*
kommend *next.*
    kommende Woche *next week.*
Kommentar *m. commentary.*
Kommode *f. chest of drawers.*
Komödiant *m. comedian, hypocrite.*
Komödie *f. comedy.*
Kompass *m. compass.*
komplett *complete; completely.*
Kompliment *n. compliment.*
komponieren *to compose.*
Komponist *m. composer.*
Konditor *m. pastry cook.*
Konditorei *f. pastry-shop, cafe.*
Konfekt *n. candy, chocolates, sweets.*
Konfektion *f. ready-made clothes.*
Konferenz *f. conference.*
Konfession *f. confession.*
Konfitüre *f. preserves, jam.*
Konflikt *m. conflict.*
KÖNIG *m. king.*
königlich *royal.*
Konkurrent *m. rival.*
Konkurrenz *f. competition.*
konkurrieren *to be in competition with,
    compete.*
Konkurs *m. bankruptcy.*
    Konkurs anmelden *to declare bankruptcy.*
KÖNNER *to be able to, be possible,
    understand.*
    Das kann sein. *It may be.*
    Das kann nicht sein. *It is impossible.*
    Ich kann nicht mehr. *I am exhausted.*
    Er kann nichts dafür. *It is not his fault.*
konsequent *consistent.*
Konsequenz *f. consistency.*
konservativ *conservative.*
Konservatorium *n. academy of music.*

Konserve f. canned goods.
konstruieren to construct.
Konstrukteur m. constructor.
Konsul m. consul.
Konsulat n. consulat.
Kontinent m. continent.
Konto n. account (financial).
Kontoauszug m. statement (account).
Kontrakt m. contract.
Kontrast m. contrast.
Kontrolle f. control.
Kontrolleur m. controller.
kontrollieren to control.
Kontroverse f. controversy.
Konversationslexikon n. encyclopedia.
Konzert n. concert.
KOPF m. head, brains, intellect, heading.
　auf den Kopf stellen　to turn upside down.
　aus dem Kopf　by heart.
　einem den Kopf waschen　to give a
　　person a dressing-down.
　Es ist mir über den Kopf gewachsen.　It
　　was too much for me.
　im Kopf behalten　to remember.
　Kopf oder Schrift　heads or tails.
　nich auf den Kopf gefallen sein　to be no
　　fool.
　sich den Kopf zerbrechen　to rack one's
　　brains.
　sich etwas aus dem Kopf schlagen　to
　　dismiss something from one's mind.
　sich in den Kopf setzen　to take into one's
　　head.
　vor den Kopf stossen　to hurt, offend.
　den Kopf verlieren　to lose one's head.
　ihm über den Kopf wachsen　to be too
　　much for him.
Kopfarbeit f. brain work.
Kopfkissen n. pillow.
Kopfsalat m. lettuce.
kopfscheu timid.
Kopfschmerzen pl. headache.
　Ich habe Kopfschmerzen.　I have a
　　headache.
Kopfweh n. headache.
Korb m. basket.
Kork m. cork, stopper.
Korkenzieher m. corkscrew.
Korn n. grain.
　aufs Korn nehmen　to aim at.
KÖRPER m. body.
körperlich bodily, physical.
Körperpflege f. physical culture, care of the
　body.
Körperwärme f. body heat.
korrekt correct.
Korrespondenz f. correspondence.
Korridor m. corridor.
korrigieren to correct.

Kosmetik f. cosmetics.
Kost f. food, board.
kostbar precious, costly, valuable.
Kostbarkeit f. preciousness, object of valor.
Kosten f. costs, expenses.
　auf seine Kosten kommen　to recover
　　expenses, be satisfied with the deal.
KOSTEN to cost, require, taste.
Kostenanschlag m. estimate.
kostenlos free.
kostenpflichtig liable for the cost.
Kostenpunkt f. expenses.
köstlich precious, valuable, delicious.
kostspielig expensive.
Kostüm n. costume, tailored suit.
Kostümfest n. fancy dress ball.
Kotelett n. cutlet, chop.
Krabbe f. shrimp, crab.
Krach m. crash, noise, quarrel,
　mit Ach und Krach　with difficulty, just
　　barely.
KRAFT f. strength, energy, power.
　ausser Kraft setzen　to annul, abolish.
　Das geht über meine Kräfte.　That's too
　　much for me.
　in Kraft treten　to come into force, effect.
　nach bestern Kräften　to the best of one's
　　ability.
　zu Kräften kommen　to regain one's
　　strength.
kräftig robust, strong.
kraftlos weak, feeble.
Kragen m. collar.
KRANK ill, sick.
　sich krank lachen　to split one's sides
　　(with laughter).
　krank werden　to be taken ill.
Kranke m. patient.
Krankenauto n. ambulance.
Krankenhaus n. hospital.
Krankenschwester f. nurse.
Krankheit f. illness, disease.
Kranz m. wreath, garland.
kraus crisp, curly.
　die Stirne krausziehen　to knit one's brow.
Kraut n. cabbage.
Krawatte f. necktie.
Krebs m. crawfish, cancer.
Kredit f. credit.
KREIS m. circle, social group.
　einen Kreis ziehen　to describe a circle.
　sich im Kreise drehen　to turn around,
　　rotate.
　in allen Kreisen des Lebens　in every walk
　　of life.
kreisen to circle, revolve, circulate.
Kreislauf m. circulation, course, revolution.
KREUZ n. cross; clubs (cards)
　das Kreuz schlagen　to cross oneself.

das Rote Kreuz *the Red Cross.*
kreuz und quer *in all directions.*
Kreuzung *f. crossing.*
Eisenbahnkreuzung. *Railroad crossing.*
Kreuzverhör *n. cross-examination.*
Kreuzworträtsel *n. crossword puzzle.*
kriechen *to creep, crawl.*
KRIEG *m. war.*
im Krieg *in wartime.*
Krieg führen *to make war.*
Kriegsgefangene *m. prisoner of war.*
Kriegsschauplatz *m. theater of war.*
Kriminalpolizei *f. criminal investigation department.*
Kriminalroman *m. detective-story.*
Kritik *f. criticism.*
Kritiker *m. critic.*
kritiklos *uncritical, undiscriminating.*
kritisch *critical.*
kritisieren *to criticize.*
Krone *f. crown.*
Kronleuchter *m. chandelier.*
Krug *m. pitcher, jar.*
Krümel *n. crumb.*
krümeln *to crumble.*
krumm *crooked, curved, bent.*
krümmen *to bend.*
Krümmung *f. curve.*
Krüppel *m. cripple.*
Kristall *n. crystal.*
KÜCHE *f. kitchen, cooking.*
Kuchen *m. cake, pastry.*
Küchenherd *m. stove.*
Kugel *f. bullet, ball, globe, sphere.*
Kuh *f. cow.*
Er ist bekannt wie eine bunte Kuh. *He is well-known everywhere ("like a colorful cow").*
KÜHL *cool, fresh, chilly.*
Kühlanlage *cold storage plant.*
Kühle *f. coolness, freshness.*
kühlen *to cool.*
Kühler *m. radiator (car).*
Kühlschrank *m. refrigerator.*
Kühlung *f. cooling, freshness.*
kühn *bold, daring, audacious.*
Kühnheit *f. boldness, audacity.*
Kulisse *f. wing*
hinter den Kulissen *backstage; behind the scenes (secretly).*
kultivieren *to cultivate.*
Kultur *f. culture.*
Kummer *m. grief, sorrow.*
kummervoll *sad, sorrowful.*
Kunde *f. customer, client, news.*
Kundgebung *f. announcement.*
kundig *well-informed, experienced.*
kündigen *to give notice (to quit).*
Kundschaft *f. customers.*

künftig *in the future.*
KUNST *f. art.*
Kunstausstellung *f. art exhibition.*
Kunstgalerie *f. art gallery.*
Kunsthandel *m. fine art trade.*
Kunsthändler *m. art dealer.*
Künstler *m. artist.*
künstlich *artificial, false.*
Kunstseide *f. artificial silk.*
Kunststoff *m. plastics, synthetic material.*
Kunststück *n. feat, trick.*
KUR *f. treatment, cure.*
Kurgast *m. visitor, patient.*
Kurhaus *n. casino*
kurios *odd, strange.*
Kurort *m. health resort.*
Kurs *m. course, rate of exchange.*
Kurve *f. curve, bend, turn.*
Gefährliche Kurve! *Dangerous curve!*
KURZ *short, brief, abrupt; in short, briefly.*
den Kürzem ziehen *to be the loser.*
in kurzem *soon, shortly.*
kurz darauf *shortly after.*
kurz oder lang *sooner or later.*
kurz und bündig *concisely, briefly.*
kurz und gut *in short.*
vor kurzem *recently.*
kurz abfertigen *to dismiss abruptly.*
Kürze *f. shortness, brevity.*
kürzen *to shorten, abridge.*
kurzgefasst *concise; in short.*
Kurzgeschichte *f. short story.*
kürzlich *lately, recently.*
Kurzschrift *f. shorthand.*
kurzsichtig *shortsighted.*
Kürzung *f. shortening, abbreviation.*
Kuss *m. kiss.*
Mit Grüssen und Küssen *With love and kisses.*
küssen *to kiss.*
Küste *f. coast, shore.*
Kuvert *n. envelope, cover, wrapping.*

L

Laborant *m. laboratory assistant.*
Laboratorium *n. laboratory.*
lächeln *to smile.*
höhnisch lächeln *to sneer.*
Lachen *n. laugh, laughter.*
LACHEN *to laugh.*
lächerlich *laughable, ridiculous.*
lächerlich machen *to ridicule.*
Laden *m. shop, store, shutter.*
Ladeninhaber *m. shopkeeper.*
Ladenschluss *m. closing time.*
Ladentisch *m. counter.*
Ladeplatz *m. loading point, goods platform.*

Lage *f. situation, position, site, condition, storage.*
Lager *n. bed, couch, layer, support.*
Lageraufnahme *f. inventory.*
Lagergeld *n. storage fee.*
Lagerhaus *n. warehouse.*
lagern *to lie down, camp; to be stored.*
lahm *lame, paralyzed.*
Laie *m. layman.*
Laken *n. sheet.*
LAMPE *f. lamp, light.*
Lampenfieber *n. stagefright.*
Lampenschirm *m. lamp-shade.*
LAND *n. land, mainland, ground.*
  ans Landsteigen *to land, go ashore.*
  aufs Land gehen *to go to the country.*
  ausser Landes gehen *to go abroad.*
landen *to land, put ashore.*
  aus aller Herren Ländern *from all parts of the globe, from all over the world.*
Landesbrauch *m. national custom.*
Landesfarben *pl. national colors.*
Landessprache *f. national language.*
Landestracht *f. national costume.*
Landesverrat *m. high treason.*
Landesverweisung *f. expulsion, banishment, exile.*
Landhaus *n. country house.*
Landkarte *f. map.*
Landschaft *f. landscape, scenery.*
landschaftlich *provincial.*
Landstrasse *f. highway, highroad.*
Landung *f. landing, disembarkation.*
Landwirtschaft *f. farming, agriculture.*
landwirtschaftlich *agricultural.*
LANG *long, tall.*
  auf lange Sicht *long-dated.*
  auf die lange Bank schieben *to put off.*
  den lieben langen Tag *the livelong day.*
  einen Tag lang *for a day.*
  Es dauert lange. *It takes long.*
  es ist schon lange her, dass … *It's been a long time since/that …*
  über kurz oder lang *sooner or later.*
langatmig *long-winded, lengthy.*
Länge *f. length, duration.*
  der Länge nach *lengthwise.*
  in die Länge ziehen *to drag on, spin out.*
langen *to suffice, last, be enough.*
  Lange mir den Hut! *Hand me my hat.*
Längengrad *degree of longitude.*
länger *longer.*
  Je länger, je lieber. *The longer, the better.*
  schon länger *for some time.*
Langeweile *f. boredom.*
langfristig *long-dated.*
LÄNGS *prep. (gen.) along.*
  Der Weg läuft längs des Stromes. *The road runs along the river.*

langsam *slow, tardy.*
  Langsam fahren! *Slow down!*
Langsamkeit *f. slowness.*
längst *long ago, long since.*
  schon längst *for a very long time.*
  am längsten *the longest.*
  längstens *at the latest, at the most.*
langweilen *to bore.*
  sich zu Tode langweilen *to be bored to death.*
langweilig *boring.*
Läm *m. noise, din, row.*
LASSEN *to let, allow, permit, suffer, omit, abandon.*
  aus dem Spiel lassen *to leave out of the question.*
  Das muss man ihm lassen. *One must credit him with that.*
  es beim alten lassen *to let things remain as they are.*
  Lassen Sie von sich hören! *Let us hear from you.*
  holen lassen *to send for.*
  Lass das! *Don't!*
  Lass nur! *Never mind!*
  Ich habe den Wagen waschen lassen. *I had the car washed.*
  machen (waschen, reinigen, richten, usw.) lassen *to have made (washed, cleaned, fixed, etc.).*
  mit sich reden lassen *to be reasonable.*
  sein Leben lassen *to lose one's life.*
  sich sagen lassen *to be told, take advice.*
  sich Zeit lassen *to take time.*
  warten lassen *to keep waiting.*
lässig *lazy, idle, indolent.*
Last *f. load, weight, burden, charge.*
lästig *troublesome, annoying, irksome.*
Lastwagen *m. cart, truck, van.*
Laterne *f. lantern, lamp.*
Laub *f. foliage, leaves.*
Laubwerk *n. foliage.*
Lauer *f. ambush.*
lauern *to wait for.*
Lauf *m. race, course, run, current.*
  in vollem lauf *at full gallop.*
  freien Lauf lassen *to give vent to.*
Laufbahn *f. career.*
LAUFEN *to run, flow, go on.*
  laufen lassen *to let things go.*
  auf dem laufenden sein *to be up to date, abreast.*
  Gefahr laufen *to run the risk.*
laufend *running.*
Laufjunge *m. errand-boy.*
Laune *f. mood, whim.*
  guter Laune sein *to be in good mood.*
launisch *moody.*
Laut *m. sound, tone.*

laut 1. *adj. loud, noisy, audible.*
  laut werden   *to become known, get about.*
  2. *prep. (gen.) according to, in accordance*
    with.
  lut Befehls   *by order.*
  laut Rechnung   *as per account.*
lauten *to sound.*
läuten *to ring, toll.*
lautlos *silent.*
Lautlosigkeit *f. silence.*
Lautsprecher *m. loudspeaker.*
lauwarm *lukewarm.*
LEBEN *n. life, lifetime, living.*
  am Leben bleiben   *to survive.*
  am Leben sein   *to be alive.*
  auf Leben und Tod   *a matter of life and*
    death.
  einem Kind das Leben schenken   *to give*
    birth to a child.
  ins Leben rufen   *to originate, start.*
  Lebenshaltung Kosten   *standard of living.*
LEBEN *to live, be alive, dwell, stay.*
lebendig *living, lively.*
Lebendigkeit *f. liveliness, animation.*
Lebensgefahr *f. danger, risk of one's life.*
lebensgefährlich *highly dangerous.*
Lebenslage *f. position.*
lebenslänglich *for life, perpetual.*
Lebenslauf *m. curriculum vitae, background.*
Lebensmittel *n. food, provisions.*
Lebensmittelgeschäft *food shop.*
lebensmüde *tired of life.*
Lebensraum *m. living space.*
Lebensunterhalt *m. livelihood, living.*
Lebensweise *f. mode of life.*
Leber *f. liver.*
lebhaft *lively, vivacious.*
Leck *n. leak.*
lecken *to lick.*
LEDER *n. leather*
LEER *empty, vacant, blank, idle.*
  mit leeren Händen   *with empty hands.*
Leere *f. emptiness, void, vacuum.*
  leerlauf   *m. neutral (gear).*
leeren *to empty.*
LEGEN *to put, lay, place.*
  sich legen   *to lie down, calm down,*
    subside.
Lehne *f. back of chair.*
lehnen *to lean against, rest upon.*
  sich lehnen   *to lean back.*
Lehnstuhl *m. armchair.*
Lehramt *n. teacher's post.*
Lehrberuf *m. teaching profession.*
Lehrbuch *n. text book.*
Lehre *f. instruction, precept, advice, lesson.*
LEHREN *to teach, instruct.*
LEHRER *m. (-in, f.) teacher.*
Lehrfach *n. subject.*

lehrhaft *didactic.*
Lehrjahre *pl. years of apprenticeship.*
lehrreich *instructive.*
Leib *m. body, belly, womb.*
Leibschmerzen *m. pl. stomach-ache, colic.*
Leiche *f. corpse.*
LEICHT *easy, light, slight, mild, careless,*
    frivolous; easy.
  etwas leicht nehmen   *to take it easy.*
  leicht möglich   *very probable.*
leichtfertig *thoughtless, frivolous.*
Leichtfertigkeit *f. thoughtlessness, frivolity.*
leichtgläubig *credulous.*
Leichtsinn *m. carelessness, thoughtlessness.*
leichtsinnig *careless, thoughtless.*
LEID *n. grief, sorrow, pain, harm.*
  Ihm tut mir leid.   *I am sorry for him.*
  Es tut mir leid.   *I am sorry about it.*
  zu meinem Leid   *to my regret.*
leiden *to suffer, bear, endure, stand.*
  leiden können, leiden mögen   *to like.*
  Sie leidet schwer darunter.   *It's making*
    her very miserable.
Leidenschaft *f. passion.*
leidenschaftlich *passionately.*
leidenschaftslos *dispassionate.*
leider *unfortunately.*
  leider nicht   *unfortunately not.*
Leihbibliothek *f. lending library.*
leihen *to lend.*
Leine *f. leash*
Leinwand *f. linen, screen.*
leise *soft, gentle, dim.*
  mit leiser Stimme   *in a low voice.*
Leiste *f. strip; ledge.*
leisten *to perform, carry out, accomplish.*
  es sich leisten können   *to be able to afford*
    something.
leistungsfähig *capable, fit, efficient.*
Leistungsfähigkeit *f. capacity for work,*
    efficiency, power.
leiten *to lead, conduct, manage, direct.*
Leiter *m. leader, manager, principal, head.*
Leitung *f. direction, management, guidance,*
    line, pipe.
Leitungswasser *tap water.*
Lektion *f. lesson (in a book).*
lenkbar *manageable, steerable.*
lenken *to direct, conduct, drive, steer.*
lernbegierig *anxious to learn.*
LERNEN *to learn, study.*
Lesebuch *reader (book).*
LESEN *to read, lecture.*
lesenswert *worth reading.*
Leser *m. reader (person).*
leserlich *legible.*
LETZT (er, -e, -es) *last, latest, final, extreme.*
  in letzter Zeit   *lately, recently.*
  letzte Neuheit   *latest novelty.*

letzten Endes   *after all.*
letzten Sonntag   *last Sunday.*
letztes hergeben   *to do one's utmost.*
letztens *lately, of late.*
Leuchte *f. lamp, light.*
leuchten *to light, shine, beam, glow.*
Leuchter *m. candlestick.*
Leuchtturm *m. lighthouse.*
Leuchtuhr *f. luminous clock or watch.*
Leuchtzifferblatt *m. luminous dial.*
leugnen *to deny, disavow.*
LEUTE *pl. people, persons, folk.*
Leutnant *m. second lieutenant.*
leutselig *affable.*
Lexikon *n. dictionary.*
LICHT *n. light, candle, illumination.*
Bitte, machen Sie das Licht an.   *Please turn on the light.*
Licht anzünden   *to turn on the light.*
Licht ausmachen   *to turn off the light.*
in ein falsches Licht setzen   *to misrepresent.*
Mir ging ein Licht auf.   *It dawned on me.*
licht
am lichten Tage   *in broad daylight.*
lichte Augenblicke   *sane moments.*
lichtempfindllch *sensitive to light.*
lichten *to thin out, clear (forest).*
Lichterglanz *m. brightness.*
Lichtreklame *f. luminous sign, illuminated advertisement.*
LIEB *dear, nice, beloved, agreeable.*
Es ist mir lieb.   *I am glad.*
es wäre mir lieb   *I should like.*
Liebchen *n. darling, love, sweetheart.*
LIEBE *f. love, affection, charity.*
aus Liebe   *for love.*
mir zu Liebe   *for my sake.*
LIEBEN *to love, like, be in love.*
liebenswürdig *amiable, kind.*
Liebenswürdigkeit *f. amiability, kindness.*
lieber *dearer, rather.*
Liebeserklärung *f. declaration of love.*
Liebesgedicht *n. love poem.*
Liebesgeschichte *f. love story.*
Liebespaar *n. lovers, couple.*
liebgewinnen *to grow fond of.*
liebhaben *to love.*
Liebhaber *m. (-in f.) lover; amateur.*
Liebhaberei *f. fancy, liking, hobby.*
liebkosen *to caress, fondle.*
Liebkosung *f. caress, petting.*
lieblich *lovely, charming.*
Liebling *m. darling, favorite.*
Lieblingsgericht *n. favorite dish.*
Liebreiz *m. charm, attraction.*
Liebschaft *f. love affair.*
Liebste *m. & f. dearest, beloved, lover, sweetheart.*

LIED *n. song, air.*
Liederbuch *n. song-book, hymn-book.*
liederlich *slovenly, immoral, dissolute.*
lieferbar *available.*
Lieferfrist *f. term of delivery.*
liefern *to deliver, yield, produce.*
Lieferung *f. delivery, supply.*
LIEGEN *to lie, rest, be situated, stand.*
Das liegt an mir.   *It is my fault.*
Mir liegt daran.   *I am interested in the matter.*
Mir liegt nichts daran.   *I don't care for it.*
liegenlassen *to leave behind; to neglect.*
Likör *m. liqueur, cordial.*
Limonade *f. lemonade.*
lindern *to soften, ease, soothe.*
Linderung *f. relief.*
Linie *f. line, descent, branch (of a family).*
in erster Linie   *first of all.*
LINK *left, wrong side of a cloth, reverse of a coin.*
linkisch *awkward, clumsy.*
LINKS *to the left, on the left.*
Gehen Sie nach links!   *Go to the left!*
Sie liess ihn ganz links liegen.   *She gave him the cold shoulder.*
linkshändig *left-handed.*
Linnen *n. linen.*
Linse *f. lentil.*
Lippe *f. lip.*
Lippenstift *m. lipstick.*
List *f. cunning, craft.*
Liste *f. list, roll, catalogue.*
listig *cunning, crafty, sly, astute.*
Liter *m. liter (1.056 quarts).*
literarisch *literary.*
Literatur *f. literature, letters.*
Litfasssäule *f. billboard.*
Lizenz *f. license, permit.*
Lob *n. praise.*
loben *to praise.*
lobenswert *praiseworthy.*
lobpreisen *to praise.*
Loch *n. hole, gap.*
Locke *f. lock, curl.*
locken *to entice, allure.*
Löffel *m. spoon.*
Essöffel   *m. tablespoon.*
Loge *f. box (theater).*
Logik *f. logic.*
logisch *logical.*
Lohn *m. compensation, reward, wages.*
Lohnempfänger *m. wage-earner.*
Lohnerhöhung *f. wage increase.*
lohnen *to reward.*
Es lohnt sich.   *It is worthwhile.*
Löhnung *f. pay.*
lokal *local, suburban.*
Lokomotive *f. engine (of a train).*

Los *n. lot, chance.*
LOS 1. *adv. loose, slack, free.*
  Hier ist viel los. *There's plenty going on here.*
  Mit ihm ist nicht viel los. *He is not up to much.*
  Was ist los? What's up?
  2. *separable prefix (implies the idea of separation or quick movement).*
  Du kannst die Hunde losmachen. *You can untie the dogs.*
  Eins, zwei, drei, los! *One, two, three, go!*
losbinden *to untie, unloosen.*
löschen *to put out, extinguish.*
losgehen *to set out, become loose, go off.*
loskommen *to get away.*
loswerden *to get rid of.*
Löwe *m. lion*
LUFT *f. air, breath, breeze.*
  aus der Luft greifen *to invent.*
  frische Luft schöpfen *to take the air.*
  in die Luft sprengen *to blow up.*
  keine Luft bekommen *not to be able to breathe.*
  luftdicht *air-tight.*
  in die Luft fliegen *to blow up.*
  Es liegt etwas in der Luft. *Something is in the wind.*
lüften *to air.*
luftig *airy, breezy.*
Luftkrankheit *f. airsickness.*
  luftkrank sein *to be airsick.*
Luftkurort *m. health resort.*
luftleer *airless.*
  lutleerer Raum *vacuum.*
Luftpost *f. air mail.*
Luftraum *m. atmosphere.*
Lüge *f. lie, untruth, falsehood.*
lügen *to lie (falsify).*
Lunge *f. lung.*
Lungenentzündung *f. pneumonia.*
Lupe *f. magnifying glass.*
Lust *f. pleasure, joy, delight, inclination, lust.*
  Lust haben *to be inclined to.*
  mit Lust und Liebe *with heart and soul.*
lustig *gay, funny, jolly.*
  sich lustig machen uber *to make fun of.*
Lustspiel *n. comedy.*
Luxus *m. luxury.*
Lyrik *f. lyrics.*

M

Machart *f. style, description, kind, sort.*
MACHEN *to make, do manufacture, cause, amount to.*
  Das lässt sich machen. *This is feasible.*
  Das macht nichts. *That does not matter.*

  Was macht Ihre Erkältung? *How is your cold?*
  Spass machen *to joke.*
  Anspruch machen auf *to claim.*
MACHT *f. strength, might, power, authority.*
mächtig *strong, mighty, powerful.*
machtlos *powerless.*
MÄDCHEN *n. girl, servant.*
  Mädchen für alles *general servant.*
mädchenhaft *girlish, maidenly.*
Mädchenname *m. maiden name.*
Magen *m. stomach.*
  Ich habe einen verdorbenen Magen. *I have an upset stomach.*
Magenverstimmung *f. stomach upset.*
mager *thin, scanty.*
Magerkeit *f. leanness, skimpiness.*
mähen *to mow, cut, reap.*
MAHL *n. meal.*
mahlen *to grind, mill.*
Mahnbrief *m. request to payment; demand notice.*
mahnen *to remind, admonish, exort.*
Mahnung *f. reminder, warning.*
MAI *m. May.*
Maiglöckchen *n. lily of the valley.*
Mais *m. corn, maize.*
Major *m. major.*
MAL *n.* 1. *landmark, monument, mark.*
     2. *time, turn.*
  dieses Mal *for once.*
  ein für alle Mal *once and for all.*
  mit einem Mal *suddenly.*
  zum ersten Mal *for the first time.*
mal *times, once, just.*
  Danke vielmals *thank you very much.*
  Viermal drei ist zwölf *Four times three is twelve.*
malen *to paint, portray, represent.*
  sich malen lassen *to have one's portrait made.*
Maler *m. painter.*
malerisch *pictorial, picturesque.*
MAN *one, they, people, you.*
  man hat mir gesagt, dass.... *I was told that....*
  Man spricht hier Deutsch. *They (We) speak German here.*
  Man sagt so. *So they say.*
MANCHE *many, some.*
manch(er,–e,–es) *many a.*
mancherlei *various, diverse.*
manchmal *sometimes*
Mangel *m. need, want, absence, lack.*
  aus Mangel an *for want of.*
mangelhaft *faulty, defective.*
mangeln *to want, be wanting.*
  es mangelt mir an *I am short of.*
Manier *f. manner, style.*

manierlich *polite, civil, mannerly.*

MANN *m. man; husband.*

  mit zweitausend Mann   *with 2,000 men (soldiers).*

  ein Mann ein Wort   *A man is as good as his word.*

  wenn Not am Mann ist   *if the worst comes to the worst.*

Mannesalter *n. manhood.*

mannhaft *manly.*

männlich *male, manly.*

Manschette *f. cuff.*

Manschettenknopf *m. sleeve link.*

MANTEL *m. coat.*

Mappe *f. document case, writing case.*

Märchen *n. fairy tale.*

märchenhaft *fabulous, legendary.*

Marine *f. navy.*

Mark *f. mark (currency).*

markant *characteristic, striking.*

Marke *f. mark, sign, postage stamp, token.*

MARKT *m. market, marketplace.*

Markthalle *f. market-hall.*

Marktplatz *m. marketplace.*

Marmelade *f. jam.*

Marmor *m. marble.*

Marmorplatte *f. marble slab.*

Marsch *m. march.*

marschieren *to march.*

MÄRZ *m. March.*

Marzipan *m. & n. marzipan.*

MASCHINE *f. machine, engine, typewriter.*

  auf der Maschine schreiben   *to typewrite.*

Maske *f. mask, disguise.*

Maskenball *m. fancy dress ball.*

Maskerade *f. masquerade.*

MASS *n. measure, dimension, size, degree, proportion, moderation.*

  in hohem Mass   *in a high degree.*

  Mass nehmen   *to measure.*

  Masse und Gewichte   *pl. weights and measurements.*

  nach Mass gemacht   *made to measure.*

Massarbeit *f. made to measure (to order).*

MASSE *f. crowd, mass, quantity.*

massenhaft *in large quantities, wholesale.*

massgebend *standard.*

massgeblich *standard.*

masshalten *to observe moderation, keep within limits.*

mässig *reasonable, moderate, poor, mediocre.*

mässigen *to observe moderation, restrain.*

Mässigkeit *f. moderation, frugality.*

masslos *boundless, without limit.*

Massregel *f. measure, step.*

Massstab *m. yard, measure, scale.*

Material *n. material, substance.*

materialisieren *to materialize.*

materialistisch *materialistic.*

Mathematik *f. mathematics.*

Matratze *f. mattress.*

Matrose *m. sailor.*

matt *weak, soft, dull; mate (chess).*

  mattsetzen   *to mate (chess).*

Matte *f. mat.*

Mauer *f. wall.*

mauern *to build with stones.*

Maultier *n. mule.*

Maurer *m. mason, bricklayer.*

Maus *f. mouse.*

Mechanik *f. mechanics.*

Mechaniker *m. mechanic.*

mechanisch *mechanical.*

Medikament *n. medicament.*

Medizin *f. medicine, remedy.*

Mediziner *m. medical student.*

MEER *n. sea, seashore.*

Meerenge *f. channel, straights, narrows.*

Meeresspiegel *m. sea-level.*

Mehl *n. flour.*

MEHR *more.*

  desto mehr   *all the more.*

  immer mehr   *more and more.*

  je mehr . . . desto   *the more . . . the more.*

  mehr als   *more than.*

  nicht mehr   *no more, any more, any longer.*

  nie mehr   *never again.*

  nur mehr   *only, nothing but.*

  um so mehr als . . .   *all the more as.*

Mehrbetrag *m. surplus.*

mehrere *several.*

mehreres *several things.*

mehrfach *manifold, numerous.*

Mehrheit *f. majority.*

mehrmals *several times, again and again.*

Mehrzahl *f. majority, plural.*

Meile *f. mile (1.609 kilometers).*

MEIN *poss. adj. my.*

MEIN(er, –e, –es) *poss. pron. mine.*

MEINEN *to mean, think, believe, suppose.*

  Was meinen Sie damit?   *What do you mean by that?*

  So war es nicht gemeint   *It wasn't meant that way.*

  Wie meinen Sie das?   *How do you mean that?*

meinerseits *for my part, as far as I am concerned.*

meinesgleichen *my equals, people like me.*

meinethalben *for my sake, for all I care.*

meinetwegen *for my sake, for me, on my account, as far as I am concerned.*

meinetwillen (um–) *for my sake.*

MEINUNG *f. meaning, opinion, view.*

  einem die Meinung sagen   *to give someone a piece of one's mind.*

meiner Meinung nach *to my mind, in my opinion.*
meist *most, mostly.*
  die meisten *most people.*
MEISTENS *mostly.*
MEISTER *m. master.*
  Übung macht den Meister. *Practice makes perfect.*
Meisterschaft *f. championship.*
Meistersinger *mastersinger.*
Meisterstück *n. masterpiece.*
Meisterwerk *n. masterpiece.*
Meldeamt *n. registration office.*
melden *to report, announce, inform, apply.*
Meldezettel *m. registration form.*
Meldung *f. news, announcement, advice, notification.*
melken *to milk.*
Melodie *f. melody, tune.*
Menge *f. quantity, amount, lots, multitude.*
  in Mengen *in abundance, plenty of*
mengen *to mix, meddle, interfere.*
MENSCH *m. man, human being, person.*
  Es kam kein Mensch. *Not a soul came.*
  seit Menschengedenken *within the memory of man; immemorial.*
  Was für ein Mensch ist er? *What sort of a person is he?*
Menschenalter *n. generation.*
menschenmöglich *humanly possible.*
Menschheit *f. human race.*
menschlich *human.*
Menschlichkeit *f. human nature.*
merkbar *noticeable.*
merken *to perceive, notice, observe, note.*
  sich merken *to keep in mind.*
  sich nichts merken lassen *to appear to know nothing.*
merklich *noticeable.*
Merkmal *n. characteristic, sign, mark.*
merkwürdig *characteristic, strange, peculiar, remarkable.*
merkwürdigerweise *strangely enough, strange to say.*
Merkwürdigkeit *f. strangeness, peculiarity.*
Messe *f. mass; fair; mess (officers').*
MESSEN *to measure, survey, take the temperature (of a patient).*
  Blicken messen *to eye.*
  messen mit *to compete with.*
  nicht messen können mit *to be no match*
MESSER *n. knife.*
Messergriff *m. knife handle.*
Messerstich *m. stab (with a knife).*
Messing *brass.*
Metall *n. metal.*
Meter *n. meter (39.37 inches).*
Metermass *n. tape-measure.*
Methode *f. method.*

Metzger *m. butcher.*
Metzgerei *n. butcher's shop.*
MICH *acc. of ich (pers. pron) me, myself.*
Miene *f. expression (facial), air, countenance.*
  gute Miene zum bösen Spiel machen *to put up a brave show.*
MIETE *f. rent, lease.*
  Die Miete ist fällig. *The rent is due.*
  zur Miete wohnen *to be a tenant, to rent.*
mieten *to rent.*
Mieter *m. tenant.*
mietefrei *rent free.*
Mietshaus *n. apartment house.*
Mietvertrag *m. lease.*
Mikrofon *n. microphone.*
Mikroskop *n. microscope.*
mikroskopisch *microscopic.*
MILCH *f. milk.*
Milchgeschäft *n. dairy.*
Milchgesicht *n. baby face.*
Milchglas *n. opalescent glass.*
Milchladen *n. dairy.*
Milchstrasse *f. Milky Way.*
Milchzahn *m. milk tooth.*
MILD *mild, soft, gentle, mellow, kind.*
MILDE *f. gentleness, kindness.*
mildern *to soften, extenuate.*
  Mildernde Umstände *extenuating circumstances.*
mildtätig *kind, generous.*
Militär *n. army, service.*
Militärdienst *m. active service.*
militärisch *military.*
Militarismus *m. militarism.*
MILLIARDE *f. billion.*
MILLION *f. million.*
Millionär *m. millionaire.*
MINDER *less, minor, inferior.*
minderbemittelt *of moderate means.*
Minderheit *f. minority.*
minderjährig *minor (age).*
  minderjährig sein *to be a minor.*
Minderjährigkeit *f. minority (age).*
minderwertig *inferior.*
Minderwertigkeitsgefühl *n. inferiority complex.*
MINDEST *least.*
  nicht im mindesten *not in the least, by no means.*
mindestens *at least.*
Mindestlohn *m. minimum wage.*
Mine *f. mine.*
Mineral *n. mineral.*
Minister *m. minister.*
Ministerium *n. ministry.*
Ministerpräsident *m. prime minister.*
MINUTE *f. minute.*
  minutenlang *for several minutes.*

MIR *dat. of ich (pers. pron.)* to me, me, myself.

mischen *to blend, mix, meddle, shuffle (cards).*

sich mischen *to interfere.*

Mischung *f. blend, mix.*

missachten *to disregard, disdain.*

Missachtung *f. disregard, disdain.*

missbilligen *to disapprove.*

Missbilligung *f. disapproval.*

missbrauchen *to misuse, abuse.*

missen *to do without.*

Misserfolg *m. failure.*

Missetat *f. misdeed, crime.*

Missetäter *m. criminal.*

missfallen *to displease.*

Missgeschick *n. bad luck, misfortune.*

missglücken *to fail.*

missgönnen *to grudge.*

missgünstig *envious, jealous.*

Misstrauen *n. distrust, mistrust.*

misstrauen *to distrust, mistrust.*

misstrauisch *suspicious.*

missvergnügt *displeased.*

missverstehen *to misunderstand.*

MIT *prep. (dat.)* with, at, by.

Der Patient hat mit gutem Appetit gegessen. *The patient has eaten with a good appetite.*

mit anderen Worten *in other words.*

mit der Post *by post.*

mit der Zeit *gradually.*

Die Kosten sind mitberechnet. *The costs are included.*

Mit fünf Jahren spielte er schon Klavier. *At the age of five, he already played the piano.*

Wir sind mit der Eisenbahn gereist. *We traveled by train.*

2. *separable prefix (implies accompaniment or participation).*

Kommen Sie mit? *Are you coming along?*

mitarbeiten *to collaborate, cooperate, contribute.*

Mitarbeiter *m. collaborator.*

Mitbesitzer *m. joint proprietor.*

mitbringen *to bring along.*

Mitbürger *m. fellow citizen.*

miteinander *with each other, together, jointly,*

mitempfinden *to sympathize with.*

Mitgefühl *n. sympathy.*

Mitgift *f. dowry.*

Mitglied *n. member.*

mitkommen *to accompany, come along, keep up.*

Mitleid *n. sympathy, pity, mercy.*

Mitleidenschaft *f. compassion.*

in Mitleidenschaft ziehen *to affect.*

mitleidig *compassionate.*

mitleidlos *pitiless.*

mitmachen *to take part in, go through.*

Sie hat sehr viel mitgemacht. *She went through a lot.*

mitnehmen *to take along, affect.*

Ihr Tod hat ihn sehr mitgenommen. *Her death affected him deeply.*

mitschuldig *implicated (in a crime).*

Mitschuldige *m. & f. accomplice.*

mitspielen *to join in a game; to accompany (music).*

MITTAG *m. noon, midday; south.*

zu Mittag essen *to have lunch.*

Mittagessen *n. lunch.*

mittags *at noon.*

Mittagspause *f. lunch hour.*

MITTE *f. middle, centre, mean, medium.*

Er ist Mitte dreissig. *He is in his middle thirties.*

goldene Mitte *golden mean.*

mitteilen *to impart, communicate.*

Mitteilung *f. information, communication, intelligence.*

Mittel *n. means; remedy, cure, medicine.*

Er ist ohne irgendwelche Mittel. *He is penniless.*

als Mittel zum Zweck *as a means to an end.*

Mittelalter *n. Middle Ages.*

Mitteleuropa *n. Central Europe.*

mittellos *without means.*

mittelmässig *average, mediocre.*

Mittelmeer *n. Mediterranean.*

Mittelstand *m. middle class.*

MITTEN *midway, in the middle of.*

mitten auf (in) *in the midst of.*

mittendrin *right in the middle of.*

mittendurch *right across, right through.*

mitten auf der Strasse *in/on the open street.*

mitten in der Nacht *in the middle of the night.*

MITTERNACHT *f. midnight.*

mitternachts *at midnight.*

mittlerweile *meanwhile, in the meantime.*

MITTWOCH *m. Wednesday.*

mitunter *sometimes, now and then.*

Mitwelt *f. our age, our generation.*

Mitwisser *m. confident, one in on the secret.*

MÖBEL *n. piece of furniture.*

Möbel *pl. furniture.*

Möbelhändler *m. furniture dealer.*

Möbelstück *n. piece of furniture.*

möblieren *to furnish.*

Mode *f. fashion.*

Modell *n. model, pattern, mold.*

modern *modern.*

Modenschau *f. fashion show.*
modisch *fashionable.*
MÖGEN *to want, wish, be able, be allowed;*
   to like, care for.
   Das mag ich nicht. *I don't like that.*
   Das mag sein *that may be so.*
   Er ist faul, er mag nicht lernen. *He is*
     lazy, he does not want to learn.
   Ich möchte nicht. *I don't want to.*
   Ich möchte wissen. *I'd like to know.*
   wie dern auch sein mag *be that as it*
     may.
   lieber mögen *to prefer.*
   Ich möchte lieber auf dem Land
     leben. *I'd rather live in the country.*
möglich *possible, practicable, feasible, likely.*
   alles mögliche *all sorts of things,*
     everything possible.
   möglichst wenig *as little as possible.*
   möglichst schnell *as quickly as possible.*
   Nicht möglich! *It can't be!*
   sein möglichstes tun *to do one's utmost.*
möglicherweise *possibly, perhaps.*
Möglichkeit *f. possibility, chance.*
Moment *m. moment.*
   Einen Moment! *One moment!*
Momentaufnahme *f. snapshot.*
Monarchie *f. monarchy.*
MONAT *m. month.*
monatelang *for months.*
monatlich *monthly.*
Mönch *m. monk.*
MOND *m. moon.*
Mondschein *m. moonlight.*
Monolog *m. monologue.*
MONTAG *m. Monday.*
Moor *n. swamp.*
Moos *n. moss.*
Mop *m. mop.*
moppen *to mop.*
Moral *f. morality, morals, moral.*
moralisch *moral.*
moralisieren *to moralize.*
Mord *m. murder.*
   Selbstmord *m. suicide.*
Mordanschlag *m. murderous attack.*
Mörder *m. murderer.*
MORGEN *m. morning, dawn, daybreak; the*
   following day.
   früh morgens *early in the morning.*
   Guten Morgen. *Good morning.*
   heute morgen *this morning.*
   morgens *in the morning.*
morgen *tomorrow.*
   morgen früh *tomorrow morning.*
   morgen in acht Tagen *a week from*
     tomorrow.
   Morgen ist auch ein Tag. *Tomorrow is*
     another day.

Morgengrauen *n. dawn of the day, break of*
   the day.
morgenländisch *eastern, oriental.*
Morgenrock *m. robe.*
Motor *m. motor, engine.*
Motorboot *n. motor boat.*
Motorpanne *f. engine trouble.*
Motorrad *n. motorcycle.*
Matte *f. moth.*
Mücke *f. mosquito (gnat).*
Mückenstich *m. mosquito bite.*
MÜDE *tired, weary.*
   müde werden *to get tired.*
Müdigkeit *f. weariness, fatigue.*
MÜHE *f. labor, toil, effort.*
   sich Mühe geben *to take pains.*
   der Mühe wert *worthwhile.*
   mit Müh und Not *only just, barely.*
   Mühe machen *to give troubles.*
   machen Sie sich Keine Mühe! *Don't*
     bother.
mühelos *easy, effortless.*
Mühevoll *laborious, difficult.*
Mühle *f. mill.*
Müller *m. miller.*
MUND *m. mouth.*
   den Mund halten *to keep one's mouth*
     shut.
   den Mund vollnehmen *to brag.*
   Er ist nicht auf den Mund gefallen. *He*
     has a ready tongue.
   nach dern Mund reden *to flatter.*
   Sie leben von der Hand in den
     Mund. *They live from hand to mouth.*
Mundwinkel *m. corner of the mouth.*
Munition *f. ammunition.*
munter *alive, wide-awake, gay.*
Münze *f. coin, medal.*
   Sie nimmt alles für bare Münze. *She*
     takes everything at its face value.
mürrisch *morose, sullen.*
Museum *n. museum.*
Musik *f. music.*
musikalisch *musical.*
Muskel *m. muscle.*
Muskelkater *m. stiffness and soreness.*
MÜSSEN *to have to, be obliged to, must,*
   ought to.
   Alle Menschen müssen sterben. *All*
     human beings must die.
   Man müsste es ihr eigentlich
     sagen. *Somebody really ought to tell*
     her.
   Sie müssen night, wenn Sie nicht
     wollen. *You don't have to if you*
     don't want to.
Muster *n. sample, model, design, pattern.*
musterhaft *exemplary, standard.*
mustern *to examine.*

Musterung *f. examination.*

MUT *m. courage, fortitude, state of mind.*

  jemandem den Mut nehmen   *to discourage*
    someone.

  Mut fassen   *to summon up courage.*

  Mut machen   *to encourage.*

  den Mut verlieren   *to lose one's courage.*

mutig *brave.*

mutlos *despondent, disheartened.*

MUTTER *f. mother.*

Muttermal *n. birthmark.*

Muttersprache *f. mother tongue.*

Mütze *f. cap.*

N

NACH 1. *prep. (with dat.) after, toward,*
according to, like, past, by, in.

  dern Namen nach kennen   *to know by*
    name.

  der Sage nach   *according to the legend.*

  Der Vater schickt die Kinder nach
    Hause.   *The father sends the children*
    home.

  einer nach dem anderen   *one after*
    another, one at a time.

  Es ist zehn nach fünf.   *It is ten after five.*

  Es sieht nach Schnee aus.   *It looks like*
    snow.

  Gehen Sie nach links!   *Turn left.*

  meiner Meinung nach   *in my opinion.*

  Nach dem Essen ruht er sich aus.   *He*
    rests after meals.

  nach und nach   *little by little*

  2. *adv. after, toward, according to.*

  3. *separable prefix (implies coming after,*
following, imitation).

  Der Schutzmann lief dem Dieb nach.   *The*
    policeman ran after the thief.

  Kannst du diese Arbeit nachmachen?   *Can*
    you copy this work?

nachahmen *to imitate.*

nachahmenswert *worthy of imitation.*

Nachahmung *f. imitation.*

Nachbar *m. neighbor.*

Nachbarschaft *f. neighborhood.*

nachdem *conj. after.*

  Nachdem er sie verlassen hatte, weinte
    sie.   *After he had left, she cried.*

nachdenken *to reflect, think.*

  nachdenken über   *to think over.*

nachdenklich *thoughtful.*

Nachdruck *m. stress, emphasis, reprint,*
reproduction.

  Nachdruck verboten.   *Reproduction*
    forbidden.

nachdrücklich *strong, emphatic.*

nacheifern *to emulate.*

nachforschen *to inquire into, investigate.*

Nachfrage *f. inquiry, demand.*

nachgeben *to yield, give way.*

nachgehen *to follow, investigate, inquire.*

Nachgeschmack *m. after-taste.*

nachher *afterwards, later.*

Nachhilfe *f. aid, help, coaching.*

nachkommen *to come later, follow on.*

Nachkriegszeit *f. postwar period.*

nachlässig *negligent, careless.*

Nachlässigkeit *f. negligence, carelessness.*

nachlaufen *to run after.*

nachlesen *to look up (in a book).*

nachmachen *to imitate, copy, counterfeit,*
duplicate.

NACHMITTAG *m. afternoon.*

nachmittags *afternoons, in the afternoon.*

Nachnahme *f. cash on delivery.*

Nachname *m. surname.*

nachprüfen *to test, check, verify.*

Nachricht *f. news, information, account,*
report, message.

  Ist eine Nachricht für mich da?   *Is there a*
    message for me?

nachsagen *to repeat after.*

nachsehen *to revise, check, examine.*

nachsenden *to send after.*

Nachsicht *f. indulgence.*

nachsichtig (–sichtsvoll) *indulgent, lenient.*

nächst *nearest, next, closest, following. prep.*
(dat.) next to, next after.

Nächstenliebe *f. love for one's fellow men;*
charity.

NACHT *f. night.*

  bei Nacht, des Nachts   *at night.*

  bis in die Nacht arbeiten   *to burn the*
    midnight oil.

  über Nacht   *during the night.*

  über Nacht bleiben   *to stay overnight.*

Nachteil *m. disadvantage, loss, damage,*
injury.

  im Nachteil sein   *to be at a*
    disadvantage.

Nachthemd *n. nightgown.*

Nachtigall *f. nightingale.*

Nachtisch *m. dessert.*

Nachtrag *m. supplement.*

nachtragen *to add.*

nachträglich *additional, further.*

Nachweis *m. proof, evidence.*

nachweisen *to prove.*

Nachwirkung *f. after-effect.*

Nachwuchs *m. after-crop, rising generation.*

Nacken *m. nape of the neck.*

nackt *naked, nude, bare, plain.*

Nadel *f. needle, pin.*

NAGEL *m. nail.*

  Es brennt mir auf den Nägeln.   *The matter*
    is urgent.

den Nagel auf den Kopf treffen   *to hit the nail on the head.*

Nagelfeile *f. nail file.*

Nähe *f. nearness, proximity, vicinity.*

in der Nähe   *near to, close at hand.*

NAHE *near, close to, imminent, approaching.*

nahe daran sein   *to be about.*

zu nahe treten   *to hurt one's feelings, offend.*

nahen *to draw near, approach.*

nähen *to sew, stitch.*

näher *nearer, closer, more intimate, further.*

Nähere *n. details, particulars.*

Näherin *f. seamstress.*

nähern *to bring near, place near.*

nahestehen *to be closely connected, be friends with.*

Nähgarn *n. sewing thread.*

Nähmaschine *f. sewing machine.*

Nähnadel *f. sewing needle.*

Nährboden *m. fertile soil.*

nähren *to feed, nurse, nourish.*

sich nähren von   *to live on.*

Nahrung *f. nourishment, food.*

Nahrungsmittel *pl. food, foodstuffs.*

NAME *m. name, appellation, character.*

dem Namen nach   *by name.*

im Namen   (*with gen.*) *on behalf of.*

namenlos *nameless.*

Namenstag *m. saint's day, name day.*

nämlich *namely, same, very.*

Narbe *f. scar.*

Narkose *f. anesthetic.*

Narr *m. fool, jester.*

zum Narren halten   *to make a fool of.*

narren *to fool.*

NASE *f. nose.*

Der Zug fuhr mir vor der Nase weg.   *I missed the train by a hair (nose).*

Sie schlug ihm die Tür vor der Nase zu.   *She slammed the door in his face.*

NASS *wet, damp.*

Die Strasse ist nass.   *The street is wet.*

Bei Nässe glatt.   *Slippery when wet.*

nass werden   *to get wet.*

Nation *f. nation.*

national *national.*

Nationalhymne *f. national anthem.*

NATUR *f. nature, disposition, constitution.*

Naturalismus *m. naturalism.*

naturalistisch *naturalistic.*

Naturgeschichte *f. natural science.*

natürlich *natural, unaffected.*

Natürlich!   *Of course!*

Natürlichkeit *f. naturalness, simplicity.*

Naturschutzgebiet *n. national park.*

naturtreu *lifelike.*

Nebel *m. fog, mist, haze.*

nebelhaft *nebulous.*

nebelig (neblig) *misty, foggy.*

Nebelregen *m. drizzle.*

Nebelwetter *n. foggy weather.*

NEBEN 1. *prep.* (*dat. when answering question, Wo?, acc. when answering question, Wohin?*). *next, next to, beside, among, besides.*

2. *adv. next to, beside, among.*

Setzen Sie sich neben mich!   *Sit down next to me!*

Er sass neben dem Mädchen.   *He was seated next to the girl.*

neben anderen Dingen   *among other things.*

nebenan *next door.*

Nebenanschluss *m. extension (telephone).*

Nebenbegriff *m. subordinate idea.*

nebenbei *on the side, by the way, adjoining.*

nebenbei bemerkt (gesagt)   *by the way, incidentally.*

Nebenberuf *m. additional occupation, side-line.*

nebeneinander *next to each other, side by side.*

Nebeneingang *m. side entrance.*

Nebeneinnahme *f. additional income.*

Nebenerzeugnis *n. by-product.*

Nebenfluss *m. tributary.*

Nebengebäude *n. additional building, annex.*

Nebengedanke *m. subordinate idea, mental reservation.*

nebenher (nebenhin) *by the side of.*

Nebenkosten *f. incidentals, extra.*

Nebenlinie *f. branch, secondary railroad line.*

Nebenmensch *m. fellow-creature.*

Nebenperson *f. secondary character (theater).*

Nebenrolle *f. secondary part (theater).*

Nebensache *f. matter of secondary importance.*

nebensächlich *unimportant, immaterial.*

Nebensatz *m. subordinate clause (grammar).*

Nebenstrasse *f. side-street.*

Nebenzimmer *n. next room.*

necken *to tease.*

Neffe *m. nephew.*

Neger *m. (–in, f.) black (person).*

negieren *to deny.*

NEHMEN *to take, accept, receive.*

Abschied nehmen   *to say good-bye.*

Anstoss nehmen   *to object.*

es sich nicht nehmen lassen   *to insist on something.*

es genau nehmen   *to be pedantic.*

etwas zu sich nehmen   *to eat something.*

genau genommen   *strictly speaking.*

Nehmen Sie Platz!   *Sit down!*

sich in Acht nehmen   *to be careful.*

ihm beim Worte nehmen   *to take him at his word.*

streng genommen   *strictly speaking.*

eine Stellung nehmen   *to express one's view about*

Neid *m. envy, jealousy.*

neidisch *jealous, envious.*

Neige *f. slope, decline.*

auf die Neige gehen   *to be on the decline, come to an end.*

neigen *to incline, bow.*

geneigt sein   *to be inclined.*

Neigung *f. slope, declivity, inclination, taste.*

NEIN *no.*

Nektar *m. nectar.*

Nelke *f. carnation.*

NENNEN *to name, call, mention.*

ein Ding beim rechten Namen nennen   *to call a spade a spade.*

nennenswert *worth mentioning.*

Nennwort *n. noun.*

Nerv *m. nerve.*

auf die Nerven fallen   *to get on one's nerves.*

Nervenheilanstalt *f. mental hospital.*

nervenkrank *neurotic, neurasthenic.*

Nervenschwäche *f. nervous debility, neurasthenia.*

nervös *nervous.*

Nervosität *f. nervousness.*

Nerz *m. mink.*

Nest *n. nest.*

NETT *nice, neat, pretty.*

Netz *n. net, network.*

NEU *new, fresh, recent, modern, latest.*

Was gibt's Neues?   *What's new?*

Neubau *m. new building, reconstruction.*

neuerdings *recently, lately.*

Neuerung *f. innovation, change.*

Neugier *f. curiosity.*

neugierig *curious.*

Neuheit *f. novelty.*

Neuhochdeutsch *n. modern high German.*

Neuigkeit *f. news.*

NEUJAHR *n. New Year.*

Glückliches Neujahr!   *Happy New Year!*

neulich *recently, the other day.*

NEUN *nine.*

NEUNTE *ninth.*

NEUNZEHN *nineteen.*

NEUNZEHNTE *nineteenth.*

NEUNZIG *ninety.*

NEUNZIGSTE *ninetieth.*

neutral *neutral.*

Neuzeit *f. modern times.*

neuzeitlich *modern.*

NICHT *not.*

auch nicht   *not even.*

ganz und gar nicht   *not in the least.*

gar nicht   *not at all.*

nicht einmal   *not even.*

nicht mehr   *no longer, no more.*

nicht wahr?   *isn't it?*

noch nicht   *not yet.*

Nichtachtung *f. disregard.*

Nichte *f. niece.*

NICHTS *nothing, not anything.*

gar nichts   *nothing at all.*

Es macht nichts.   *It doesn't matter.*

Ich will nichts mehr davon hören.   *I don't want to hear another word about that.*

mir nichts, dir nichts   *quite coolly.*

nichts als   *nothing but.*

nichts anderes   *nothing else.*

durchaus nicht   *not at all.*

nichtsdestoweniger *nevertheless.*

nichtssagend *meaningless, insignificant.*

Nichtstuer *m. idler.*

Nichtstun *n. idling.*

nie (mals) *never.*

fast nie   *hardly ever.*

NIEDER *down, low, mean.*

auf und nieder   *up and down.*

niedergeschlagen *downhearted, depressed.*

Niedergeschlagenheit *f. depression.*

Niederlage *f. defeat.*

niedertreten *to trample.*

niedrig *low, inferior, humble.*

NIEMAND *nobody.*

Niere *f. kidney.*

nimmer *never.*

nimmermehr *nevermore, by no means.*

nirgends *nowhere.*

nirgendwo *nowhere.*

NOCH *still, yet, besides.*

noch dazu   *in addition.*

noch ein   *another.*

noch einmal   *once more.*

noch einmal so   *twice as.*

noch etwas   *something else.*

noch immer   *still.*

noch nicht   *not yet.*

noch nie   *never before.*

weder ... noch   *neither ... nor.*

nochmals *once again.*

Norden *m. North.*

nach Norden   *in the direction of the North.*

nordisch *nordic, northern.*

nördlich *northern.*

nordöstlich *northeastern.*

Nordpol *m. North Pole.*

Nordsee *f. North Sea.*

Norm *f. standard, rule.*

normal *normal.*

NOT *f. distress, want.*

aus Not *from necessity.*
Not bricht Eisen. *Necessity is the mother of invention.*
ohne Not *without real cause.*
seine liebe Not haben mit *to have a hard time with.*
zur Not *if need be.*
Notar *m. notary.*
notariell *attested by a notary.*
Notausgang *m. emergency exit.*
Notbehelf *m. expedient.*
Notbremse *f. emergency brake.*
Note *f. note (music, bank, dipl.); mark (school); (–n, pl., music).*
Notfall *m. emergency.*
notgedrungen *compulsory, forced.*
nötig *necessary, needful.*
nötig haben *to need.*
nötigenfalls *if need be.*
notleidend *poor, distressed.*
Notlüge *f. white lie.*
notwendig *necessary.*
Notwendigkeit *f. necessity.*
Novelle *f. short story, short novel.*
NOVEMBER *m. November.*
nüchtern *empty, sober, insipid.*
Nüchternheit *f. emptiness, sobriety, insipidity.*
null *null.*
null und nichtig *null and void.*
Null *f. zero.*
numerieren *to number*
numerierter Platz *m. reserved seat.*
NUMMER *f. number, part, ticket, size, issue.*
Seine Nummer ist besetzt. *His line is busy.*
Welche Nummer tragen Sie? *What size do you wear?*
die letzte Nummer *the last issue (magazine).*
NUN *now, well, then.*
von nun an *henceforth, from now on.*
NUR *only, sole, merely, just, possibly.*
nur mehr *still more.*
Nur zu! *Go on!*
wenn nur *if only.*
wer nur immer *whoever.*
Lass mich nur machen! *Let me do it!*
nicht nur ... sondern auch *not only ... but also.*
Nuss *f. nut.*
Nussbaum *m. walnut tree.*
Nussknacker *m. nutcracker.*
nutzbar *useful, necessary.*
nutzbringend *profitable.*
Nutzen *m. profit, benefit.*
nützen *to be of use, be profitable, serve.*
Es nützt nichts! *It's no use!*
nützlich *useful.*

Nützlichkeit *f. usefulness, utility.*
nutzlos *useless.*
Nutzlosigkeit *f. uselessness, futility.*
Nylon *n. nylon.*

O

OB *whether, if.*
Wir möchten wissen, ob sie kommen. *We want to know whether they are coming.*
als ob *as if, as though.*
OBEN *above, up, upstairs, on top.*
auf ... oben *at the top of.*
dort oben *up there.*
nach oben *upwards.*
oben auf *on top of.*
von oben bis unten *from top to bottom.*
von oben herab behandeln *to treat in a condescending manner.*
obendrein *into the bargain, in addition.*
ober *upper, supreme, above.*
das obere Bett *the upper berth.*
Ober *m. waiter.*
Herr Ober! *Waiter!*
Oberbefehlshaber *m. commander-in-chief.*
Oberfläche *f. surface, area.*
oberflächlich *superficial, superficially.*
oberhalb *above.*
Oberhemd *n. shirt.*
Oberkellner *m. headwaiter.*
Oberkörper *m. upper part of the body.*
Oberlippe *f. upper lip.*
Oberschule *f. high school.*
Oberst *m. colonel.*
oberst *highest, uppermost.*
Oberstleutnant *m. lieutenant colonel.*
obgleich *although.*
Oboe *f. oboe.*
Obrigkeit *f. authority.*
obschon *although.*
Obst *n. fruit.*
Obstgarten *m. orchard.*
Ochs *m. ox.*
ochsen *to grind, cram, work hard (slang).*
öde *dull, empty.*
ODER *or.*
oder aber *instead.*
entweder oder *either or.*
Ofen *m. stove, furnace.*
offen *open, free, vacant, frank, sincere.*
auf offener Strecke *on the road.*
offen gestanden *frankly.*
offene Rechnung *current account.*
einen offenen Sinn für eine Sache haben *to be receptive to something.*
offenbar *obvious, evident.*
Offenbarung *f. disclosure, revelation.*

Offenheit f. frankness, sincerity.
offenherzig frank, sincere.
offensichtlich obvious, apparent.
öffentlich public.
Öffentlichkeit f. publicity.
offiziell official.
Offizier m. officer.
öffnen to open, dissect.
Öffnung f. opening, gap, dissection.
OFT often, frequently.
öfter more often
  je öfter . . . desto   the more . . . the more.
  des öfteren   frequently.
öfters quite often.
oftmals often, frequently.
OHNE prep. (acc.) without, but, for, except.
  Er ging ohne ein Wort zu sagen.   He left without saying a word.
  ohne Arbeit   out of work.
  ohne dass   without (conj.).
  ohne dass er mich angeredet hatte   without his having spoken to me.
  ohne weiteres   right off.
  ohne zu   without (before verb).
  ohne zu antworten   without answering.
  ohnehin   besides, apart.
Ohnmacht f. faintness, unconsciousness, faint.
ohnmächtig powerless, unconscious, helpless.
  ohnmächtig werden   to faint.
OHR n. ear, hearing.
  die Ohren steif halten   to keep one's courage.
  ganz Ohr sein   to be all ears.
Ohrring m. earring.
OKTOBER m. October.
ÖL n. oil.
Ölbaum m. olive tree.
Ölbild n. oil painting.
ölen to oil, lubricate.
Ölfarbe f. paint.
ölig oily.
Olive f. olive.
Omelett(e) n. omelet.
ONKEL m. uncle.
OPER f. opera, opera house.
Operation f. operation.
Operette f. operetta.
Opfer n. sacrifice, martyr, victim.
opfern to sacrifice.
Opferung f. sacrifice.
Optiker m. optician.
Optimismus m. optimism.
optimistisch optimistic.
Orange f. orange.
Orchester n. orchestra.
Orden m. order, decoration.
ordentlich in order, neat, tidy.
ordnen to put in order, arrange.

ORDNUNG f. order, arrangement.
  Das finde ich ganz in Ordnung.   I think it is quite all right.
  in Ordnung bringen   to settle, straighten out.
  Ist alles in Ordnung?   Is everything all right?
  nicht in Ordnung   out of order.
  zur Ordnung rufen   to call to order.
Organ n. organ (body).
organisieren to organize.
organisch organic.
Organist m. organist.
Orgel f. organ (music).
original original.
ORT m. place, spot, locality.
  Wir fanden alles wieder an Ort und Stelle.   We found everything back in place.
örtlich local.
Osten m. East, Orient.
  nach Osten   in the direction of the East.
Osterfest n. Easter.
Ostern n. East.
Österreicher m. Austrian.
österreichisch Austrian.
östlich eastern.
Ostsee f. Baltic sea.
ostwärts eastward.
Ozean m. ocean.

P

Paar n. pair, couple.
  mit ein Paar Worten   in a few words.
  ein Paar Strümpfe   a pair of socks.
paar few, some, even, matching.
  ein paar   a few, several.
  ein paarmal   several times.
paaren to pair, couple.
Pächter m. farmer, tenant, householder.
Päckchen n. small parcel.
packen to seize, grasp, pack.
packend thrilling, absorbing.
Packung f. package, packet.
Paddelboot n. canoe.
paddeln to paddle.
Paket n. parcel.
Paketannahme f. parcel-receiving office.
Pakt m. pact, agreement.
Palast m. palace.
Palme f. palm.
panieren to coat with breadcrumbs.
Panik f. panic.
Panne f. breakdown, trouble (motor).
Pantoffel m. slipper, mule.
Pantoffelheld m. henpecked husband.
Panzer m. armor, tank,

panzern *to armor, plate.*
Pagagei *m. parrot.*
PAPIER *n. paper, identification paper, document.*
  zu Papier bringen *to write down, put on paper.*
Papierbogen *m. sheet of paper.*
Papiergeld *n. paper money.*
Papierhandlung *f. stationery store.*
Papierkorb *m. wastepaper basket.*
Pappe *f. cardboard.*
Papst *m. Pope.*
Parade *f. parade, review.*
Paradies *n. paradise.*
paradiesisch *paradisiacal.*
parallel *parallel.*
Parfum or **Parfüm** *n. perfume.*
PARK *n. park, grounds.*
parken *to park.*
  Parkverbot! *No parking!*
Parkplatz *m. parking place.*
Parlament. *n. parliament.*
Parodie *f. parody.*
Partei *f. party, faction, tenant, side.*
  Partei nehmen für *to take the side of.*
Parterre *n. ground floor.*
Partie *f. part, section.*
  eine Partie Schach *a game of chess.*
Partner *m. partner.*
Partnerschaft *f. partnership.*
Pass *m. pass, passage, passport.*
Passagier *m. passenger.*
Passamt *n. passport division.*
Passant *m. passer-by.*
PASSEN *to fit, suit, be convenient, be suitable.*
  zu einander passen *to match, harmonize.*
PASSEND *suitable, convenient.*
passieren *to happen, go through, pass, cross.*
  Was ist passiert? *What happened?*
  (*What's the trouble?*)
passiv *passive.*
Passkontrolle *f. examination of passport.*
Pastete *f. pie, pastry.*
Pastor *m. pastor, minister, clergyman.*
Pate *m. godfather.*
Patenkind *n. godchild.*
Patent *n. (letters) patent.*
Patentamt *n. patent office.*
pathetisch *pathetic.*
Patient *m. patient.*
Patin *f. godmother.*
Patriot *m. patriot.*
patriotisch *patriotic.*
Pauke *f. kettledrum.*
Pause *f. pause, interval, break, rest (music).*
pausieren *to pause.*
Pech *n. bad luck, pitch.*
pechschwarz *pitch-black.*

Pechvogel *m. unlucky person.*
Pedal *n. pedal.*
Pedant *m. pedant.*
pedantisch *pedantic.*
Pein *f. pain, agony, torture.*
peinigen *to torment, harass.*
Peiniger *m. tormentor.*
Peinigung *f. torment, torture.*
peinlich *painful, embarrassing.*
Peinlichkeit *f. painfulness; carefulness, embarrassment.*
Peitsche *f. whip, lash.*
Pelikartoffeln *pl. potatoes in their jackets.*
PELZ *m. fur, pelt, skin, hide, fur coat.*
Pelzhändler *m. furrier.*
Pelzmantel *m. fur coat.*
Pension *f. pension; boarding-house.*
  Er erhält eine Pension. *He receives a pension.*
  in Pension sein *to board.*
Pensionat *n. boarding-school.*
pensionieren *to pension off.*
per *per.*
  per Post *by post.*
  per Adresse (*in) care of.*
Periode *f. period.*
Perle *f. pearl, bead.*
perlen *to sparkle, glisten.*
Perlenkette *f. pearl necklace, string of pearls.*
PERSON *f. person, personage, character (theater).*
  in Person *in person.*
Personal *n. staff, employees, personnel.*
Personalbeschreibung *f. personal description of a person.*
Personalien *pl. particulars about a person, data.*
Personenaufzug *m. passenger elevator.*
Personenkraftwagen *m. motor-car.*
Personenzug *m. passenger train.*
persönlich *personal; personally.*
Persönlichkeit *f. personality.*
Perücke *f. wig.*
pessimistisch *pessimistic.*
Pest *f. plague, pestilence, epidemic.*
Petersilie *f. parsley.*
Pfad *m. path.*
Pfadfinder *m. (–in, f.) boy (girl) scout.*
Pfahl *m. pole, stake, pile, post.*
Pfand *m. pledge, security, forfeit.*
pfänden *to seize, take in pledge.*
Pfandhaus *n. pawnshop.*
Pfandleiher *m. pawnbroker.*
Pfandschein *m. pawn ticket.*
Pfanne *f. pan.*
Pfannkuchen *m. pancake.*
Pfarrer *m. priest, pastor, minister.*
Pfarrgemeinde *f. parish.*

Pfau *m. peacock.*
PFEFFER *m. pepper*
Pfefferkuchen *m. spiced cakes, gingerbread.*
Pfefferminz *n. & f. peppermint.*
pfeffern *to season with pepper.*
Pfeife *f. pipe, whistle.*
pfeifen *to whistle, pipe.*
Pfeil *m. arrow.*
Pfeiler *m. pillar, post.*
PFERD *n. horse.*
Pfiff *m. whistle, whistling, trick.*
Pfingsten *n. & f. Pentecost, Whitsuntide.*
Pfirsich *m. peach.*
PFLANZE *f. plant.*
pflanzen *to plant.*
Pflanzenkunde *f. botany.*
Pflaster *n. plaster, pavement.*
Pflasterstein *m. paving-stone.*
PFLAUME *f. plum.*
    gedörrte Pflaume   *f. prune.*
Pflaumenmus *n. plum jam.*
PFLEGE *f. care, attention, nursing.*
Pflegeeltern *pl. foster parents.*
Pflegekind *n. foster child.*
pflegen *to care for, cherish, nurse, cultivate.*
PFLICHT *f. duty, obligation.*
Pflichteifer *m. zeal.*
Pflichtgefühl *n. sense of duty.*
pflichtgemäss *obligatory.*
pflücken *to pick, gather, pluck.*
Pflug *m. plough.*
pflügen *to plough.*
Pförtner *m. gatekeeper.*
Pfote *f. paw.*
Pfui! *Shame!*
Pfund *n. pound.*
Pfütze *f. puddle.*
Phänomen *n. phenomenon.*
Phantasie *f. imagination, fancy.*
phantasieren *to daydream, imagine.*
Phantast *m. dreamer, visionary.*
phantastisch *fantastic, fanciful.*
Philosoph *m. philosopher.*
Philosophie *f. philosophy.*
philosophieren *to philosophize.*
Photoapparat *m. camera.*
Photograph *m. photographer.*
Photographie *f. photography.*
photographieren *to photograph.*
Physik *f. physics.*
Pianist *m. pianist.*
Piano *n. piano.*
Picknick *n. picnic.*
Pietät *f. reverence, piety.*
pietätlos *irreverent.*
Pikkolöflöte *f. piccolo.*
Pilger *m. pilgrim.*
pilgern *to go on a pilgrimage.*
Pille *f. pill.*

Pilot *m. pilot.*
Pilz *m. mushroom.*
    Giftpilz   *m. poisonous mushroom.*
Pinsel *m. brush, paintbrush.*
pinseln *to paint (art).*
Pirat *m. pirate.*
Pistole *f. pistol.*
Plage *f. plague.*
plagen *to plague, torment.*
    sich plagen   *to struggle, overwork oneself.*
Plakat *placard, poster.*
    Keine Plakate.   *Post no bills.*
Plakatsäule *f. sign post.*
Plan *m. plan, map, design; intention.*
planen *to plan, scheme.*
Planet *m. planet.*
planlos *without any fixed plan.*
planmässig *according to plan; methodical.*
Planung *f. planning, plan.*
Planwirtschaft *f. economic planning.*
Plastik *f. plastic art, sculpture.*
plastisch *plastic.*
Platin *n. platinum.*
plätschern *to splash.*
PLATT *flat, level, insipid, dull.*
Plattdeutsch *n. Low German.*
Platte *f. plate, tray; record (phonograph)*
    kalte Platte   *cold meats.*
PLATZ *m. place, spot, room, seat; square
    (street).*
    Platz machen   *to make room.*
    Bitte, nehmen Sie Platz.   *Please have a
    seat.*
    am Platz sein   *to be opportune.*
Platzanweiser *m. (–in, f.) usher.*
Plätzchen *n. little place; cookie.*
platzen *to burst, explode, crack.*
Platzmangel *m. lack of space.*
Plauderei *f. chat, small talk, conversation.*
PLAUDERN *to chat, talk, gossip.*
PLÖTZLICH *sudden; suddenly.*
plump *heavy, shapeless, tactless, clumsy.*
Plumpheit *f. shapelessness, heaviness,
    clumsiness.*
plumpsen *to plump down.*
plündern *to plunder, pillage.*
Plünderung *f. plundering, sack.*
Plural *m. plural.*
Pöbel *m. mob, populace.*
pöbelhaft *vulgar, low.*
pochen *to knock, beat, throb.*
Pocken *f. pl. smallpox.*
Pockenimpfung *f. smallpox vaccination.*
Podium *n. platform, rostrum.*
Poesie *f. poetry.*
Poet *m. poet.*
poetisch *poetical.*
Pol *m. pole.*
polar *polar, arctic.*

Polarforscher m. polar explorer.
Pole m. Pole (native of Poland).
polieren to polish.
Poliermittel n. polish.
Politik f. politics, policy.
Politiker m. politician.
politisch political.
politisieren to talk politics.
Politur f. polish, gloss, refinement.
POLIZEI f. police.
    Rufen Sie die Polizei! Call the police!
    Polizeibehörde police authorities.
Polizeiamt n. police-station.
Polizeiaufsicht f. police control.
polizeilich of the police.
Polizeistreife f. police raid.
Polizeistunde f. curfew.
polizeiwidrig contrary to police regulations.
Polizist m. policeman, constable.
polnisch Polish.
Polster n. cushion, pillow, bolster, pad.
Polstermöbel pl. upholstered furniture.
Polstersessel m. easy chair.
Polsterung f. upholstery, padding, stuffing.
Pomade f. pomade, hair gel.
Pomp m. pomp.
pomphaft pompous, magnificent.
pompös pompous, magnificent.
populär popular
Pore f. pore.
porös porous.
Portemonnaie n. purse.
Portion f. portion, helping, ration, order.
Porto n. postage.
portofrei postfree, prepaid.
portopflichtig liable to postage fee.
Porträt n. portrait, likeness.
porträtieren to portray, paint a portrait.
Porträtmaler m. portrait painter.
Porzellan n. porcelain, china.
Porzellanservice n. set of china.
positiv positive.
POST f. post, mail, post office.
Postfach n. post-office box.
Postamt n. post office.
Postanweisung f. money order.
Postbeamte m. post-office clerk.
Postbote m. postman.
Posten m. post, situation.
    auf dem Posten sein to feel well.
Postkarte f. postcard.
postlagernd general delivery (USA).
postlich postal.
Postschliessfach n. post-office box.
postwendend by return mail.
Pracht f. splendor.
Prachtausgabe f. deluxe edition.
prächtig magnificent, splendid, lovely.
prachtvoll splendid, gorgeous, magnificent.

prahlen to brag, boast.
Prahlerei f. boasting, bragging.
prahlerisch boastful, ostentatious.
praktisch clever, handy, useful.
    praktischer Arzt general practitioner.
praktizieren to practice (a profession).
prall blazing, tight, tense.
    in der prallen Sonne in the full glare of
    the sun.
Prämie f. premium.
prämieren to award a prize to.
Präposition f. preposition.
präsentieren to present.
Präsident m. president.
Präsidium n. chair, presidency.
prassen to feast, revel.
präzis precise, exact, punctual.
Präzision f. precision.
predigen to preach.
Prediger m. preacher, minister.
Predigt f. sermon, lecture.
PREIS m. price, cost, rate, praise.
    um jeden Preis at any cost.
    um keinen Preis not at any price.
    zum festem Preis at fixed price.
    den Preis davontragen to take the prize.
Preisangabe f. quotation of prices.
Preisausschreiben n. prize competition.
Preisbewerber m. competitor.
Preiselbeere f. cranberry.
preisen to praise, extol, glorify.
Preiserhöhung f. rise in prices.
Preisgabe f. surrender, abandonment.
preisgeben to surrender, give up, abandon,
    sacrifice.
Preislage f. price range.
Preisrichter m. arbiter, judge.
Preissturz m. fall in prices.
Preisträger m. prize-winner.
Preistreiberei f. forcing up of prices.
preiswert reasonable, cheap.
Premiere f. first night.
Presse f. press.
Pressestimme f. press comment, review.
Priester m. priest.
Prima f. highest class of secondary school.
prima prime, first-rate, great.
primitiv primitive.
Prinz m. (–essin, f.) prince(ss).
Prinzip n. principle.
    aus Prinzip as a matter of principle.
prinzipiell on principle.
PRIVAT private, privately.
Privatrecht n. civil law.
Probe f. trial, experiment, test, probation;
    rehearsal (theater).
    auf die Probe stellen to put to the test.
    Probe ablegen to give proof of.
    die Probe bestehen to pass the test.

zur Probe *as a sample; on approval.*
Proben halten *to have a rehearsal.*
Probeabzug *m. proof.*
proben *to rehearse.*
probeweise *on approval, on trial.*
Probezeit *f. time of probation.*
probieren *to try, taste.*
Darf ich das anprobieren? *May I try this on?*
Er probiert die Suppe *He tastes the soup.*
Problem *n. problem.*
problematisch *problematic.*
Produkt *n. product.*
Produktion *f. production.*
Produzent *m. producer, manufacturer.*
produzieren *to produce, show off, exhibit.*
Professor *m. professor.*
Prognose *f. forecast, prognosis.*
Programm *n. program.*
Projekt *n. project.*
Projektionsapparat *m. projector.*
Proklamation *f. proclamation.*
Prokura *f. procuration, power of attorney.*
prolongieren *to prolong.*
Promenade *f. promenade.*
Propaganda *f. propaganda.*
Prophet *m. prophet.*
prophetisch *prophetic.*
prophezeien *to prophesy.*
Prophezeiung *f. prophecy.*
Proportion *f. proportion.*
Prosa *f. prose.*
Prosit! *To your health!*
Prospekt *m. prospect.*
Protest *m. protest.*
Protest erheben *to protest.*
Protestant *m. Protestant.*
protestantisch *Protestant.*
Protestantismus *m. Protestantism.*
protestieren *to protest.*
Protokoll *n. protocol; proceedings.*
Proviant *m. provisions (mil.)*
Provinz *f. province.*
provinziell *provincial.*
Provision *f. brokerage.*
Prozent *n. per cent.*
Prozentsatz *m. percentage.*
prozentual *expressed as percentage.*
PROZESS *m. lawsuit, process, proceedings, trial.*
im Prozess liegen *to be involved in a law suit.*
kurzen Prozess machen mit *to dispose of quickly.*
prozessieren *to be involved in a lawsuit.*
Prozession *f. procession.*
PRÜFEN *to test, investigate, inspect, examine.*
Prüfer *m. examiner.*

Prüfling *m. examinee.*
PRÜFUNG *f. investigation, examination.*
eine Prüfung ablegen *to take an examination.*
Prunk *m. splendor, ostentation.*
prunkvoll *gorgeous, splendid.*
Psychiater *m. psychiatrist.*
Psychiatrie *f. psychiatry.*
psychisch *psychic.*
Psychologe *m. psychologist.*
Psychologie *f. psychology.*
psychologisch *psychological.*
Psychopath *m. psychopath.*
Publikum *n. public.*
Pudel *m. poodle.*
pudelnass *drenched, soaked.*
Puder *m. toilet powder.*
pudern *to powder.*
Puls *m. pulse.*
Pulsschlag *m. pulse-beat.*
Pult *n. desk.*
Pulver *n. powder, gunpowder.*
Pulverfass *n. powder barrel.*
auf dem Pulverfass sitzen *to sit on top of a volcano.*
PUNKT *m. point, dot, spot.*
der springende Punkt *the salient point.*
Punkt ein Uhr *at one o'clock sharp.*
Ausgangspunkt *point of departure.*
pünktlich *on time, punctual, prompt.*
Pünktlichkeit *f. punctuality.*
Puppe *f. doll, puppet.*
Putz *m. trimming, ornament, dress.*
putzen *to clean, polish.*
Putzfrau *f. charwoman, cleaning lady.*
Putzlappen *m. duster, flannel, polishing cloth.*
Pyjama *n. & m. pajamas*

Quadrat *n. square.*
Quäker *m. Quaker.*
Qual *f. torment, torture, pain.*
Quälen *to torment, worry, torture, bother.*
Quäler *m. tormentor.*
Quälerei *f. tormenting, torture.*
Quälgeist *m. nuisance (person).*
qualifizieren *to qualify.*
Qualität *f. quality.*
qualitativ *qualitative.*
Qualitätsware *f. high-class article.*
Qualm *m. dense smoke.*
qualmen *to smoke (chimney).*
qualmig *smoky.*
qualvoll *very painful, agonizing.*
Quarantäne *f. quarantine.*
unter Quarantäne stellen *to quarantine.*

Quecksilber *n. mercury.*
Quelle *f. spring, fountain.*
quellen *to gush, well, flow.*
Quellwasser *n. spring water.*
quer *cross, lateral, oblique; across, obliquely.*
  kreuz under quer *all over.*
querfeldein *across country.*
Querschnitt *m. cross-section.*
Querstrasse *f. crossroad.*
quetschen *to squeeze, smash.*
Quetschung *f. contusion.*
Quetschwunde *f. bruise.*
quietschen *to scream, squeal.*
quittieren *to receipt.*
Quittung *f. receipt.*
Quote *f. quota, share.*

R

Rabatt *m. discount.*
Rabbiner *m. rabbi.*
Rache *f. revenge.*
rächen *to revenge, avenge.*
  sich rächen *take revenge, get revenge.*
  Deine Faulheit wird sich an dir
    rächen. *You will have to suffer for your laziness.*
Rachsucht *f. thirst for revenge.*
rachsüchtig *revengeful.*
RAD *n. wheel, bicycle.*
radfahren *to cycle.*
Radfahrer *m. cyclist.*
Radfahrweg *m. cycle track.*
Radiergummi *m. eraser.*
Radierung *f. etching.*
Radio *n. radio.*
Radreifen *m. bicycle tire.*
raffiniert *refined, cunning.*
Rahm *m. cream.*
Rahmen *m. frame.*
Rakete *f. rocket.*
Rampe *f. ramp, platform; limelight.*
RAND *m. edge, brim, border, margin.*
  ausser Rand und Band sein *to be out of hand.*
  Schreiben Sie es an den Rand! *Write it in the margin!*
Randbemerkung *f. marginal note.*
Rang *m. rank, order, quality, class.*
  den Rang ablaufen *to get the better of.*
  ersten Ranges *first class, first rate.*
  erster Rang *first balcony, dress circle.*
  zweiter Rang *second balcony, upper circle.*
Rangabzeichen *n. badge of rank.*
Rangordnung *f. order of precedence.*
Rangstufe *f. degree.*

rar *rare, scarce.*
Rarität *f. rarity, curiosity.*
rasch *quick, swift, speedy.*
rascheln *to rustle.*
rasen *to rave, rage, speed (coll.)*
rasend *raving, raging, frantic.*
  rasend machen *to make mad, enrage.*
Raserei *f. raving, fury; rage.*
Rasierapparat *m. safety razor.*
  elektrischer Rasierapparat *electric razor.*
rasieren *to shave.*
  sich rasieren *to shave (oneself).*
  sich rasieren lassen *to get shaved.*
Rasierklinge *f. razor blade.*
Rasiermesser *n. razor.*
Rasierpinsel *m. shaving brush.*
Rasierzeug *n. shaving things.*
Rasse *f. race, breed.*
rassig *thoroughbred.*
rassisch *racial.*
Rast *f. resting, recreation, rest, repose.*
rasten *to rest.*
rastlos *restless, indefatigable.*
Rastlosigkeit *f. restlessness.*
RAT *m. counsel, advice, consultation, remedy.*
  Rat schaffen *to devise means.*
  um Rat fragen *to ask advice.*
  zu Rat ziehen *to consult.*
  etwas zu Rate halten *to economize.*
  mit Rat und Tat *by word and deed.*
  ihm Rat erteilen *to give him advice.*
Rate *f. installment.*
raten *to advise, guess, solve.*
ratenweise *by installments.*
Ratgeber *m. adviser.*
Ration *f. ration.*
rationell *rational; economical.*
ratlos *at a loss, helpless.*
Ratlosigkeit *f. helplessness, perplexity.*
Ratschläge *m. counsel, advice.*
Rätsel *n. riddle, enigma, puzzle.*
  Es ist mir ein Rätsel. *It puzzles me.*
rätselhaft *mysterious, enigmatic.*
Ratte *f. rat.*
Raub *m. robbery, plundering.*
  auf Raub ausgehen *to go on the prowl.*
rauben *to rob, plunder.*
Räuber *m. robber, thief.*
Raubmord *m. murder and robbery.*
Raubtier *n. beast of prey.*
Raubvogel *m. bird of prey.*
Rauch *m. smoke.*
RAUCHEN *to smoke.*
  Rauchen Verboten! *No Smoking!*
Raucher *m. smoker.*
räuchern *to smoke, cure, fumigate.*
Räucherwaren *pl. smoked meats and fish.*
Rauchtabak *m. tobacco.*

Rauchzimmer n. smoking room.
RAUH uneven, rough, raw, hoarse, harsh.
Rauheit f. roughness, harshness.
RAUM m. place, room, space.
   Raum geben   to give way, indulge.
räumen to clear away, remove, clean,
   evacuate.
Rauminhalt m. volume, capacity.
räumlich relating to space, spatial.
Räumlichkeit f. room, premises, space.
Raummangel m. lack of room.
Räumung f. removal, evacuation.
Raupe f. caterpillar.
Raupenschlepper m. caterpillar tractor.
Rausch m. intoxication, frenzy, drunkenness.
rauschen to rustle, rush, roar.
Rauschgift n. narcotic, drug.
Reaktion f. reaction.
Rebe f. grape, vine.
Rebell m. rebel.
rebellieren to rebel.
Rechen m. rake.
Rechenmaschine f. calculating machine.
RECHNEN to count, reckon, calculate.
RECHNUNG f. sum, account, bill,
   calculation.
   auf eigene Rechnung   at one's own risk.
   auf Rechnung setzen   to charge, put to
      one's account.
   in Rechnung ziehen   to take into account.
   laut Rechnung   as per invoice.
   Die Rechnung, bitte.   Please bring me the
      check.
   Sind Sie auf Ihre Rechnung
      gekommen?   Did you get your
      money's worth? (Was it worth while?)
   die Rechnung führen   to keep accounts.
Rechnungsprüfer m. auditor.
RECHT n. right, privilege, title, claim, law.
   alle Rechte vorbehalten   all rights
      reserved.
   an den Rechten kommen   to meet one's
      match.
   mit vollem Recht   for good reasons.
   nach dem Rechten sehen   to see to things.
   Recht behalten   to be right in the end.
   Recht geben   to agree with.
   Recht haben   to be right.
   Recht sprechen   to administer justice.
   von Rechts wegen   by rights, according to
      the law.
   zu Recht bestehen   to be valid.
RECHT right, all right, right-hand, correct,
   proper, genuine, lawful.
   Das ist mir recht.   That's all right with
      me.
   Das ist nur recht und billig.   That's only
      fair.
   die rechte Hand   the right hand.

erst recht   all the more now, now more
   than ever.
Es geschieht ihm recht.   It serves him
   right.
es recht machen   to suit, please.
Man kann es nicht allen recht
   machen.   You cannot please
   everybody.
schlecht und recht   not bad.
zur rechten Zeit   in time.
rechtzeitig   on time.
bürgerliches Recht   civil law.
wenn es Ihnen recht ist . . .   if it's
   agreeable to you . . .
Rechteck n. rectangle.
rechteckig rectangular.
rechterhand on the right hand.
rechtfertigen to justify, to exculpate.
   sich rechtfertigen   to justify oneself.
Rechtfertigung f. justification.
rechthaberisch dogmatic, obstinate.
rechtlich just, lawful, legitimate.
Rechtlichkeit f. integrity, honesty.
rechtmässig lawful, legitimate.
RECHTS to the right, on the right.
   Biegen Sie rechts ab!   Turn to the right!
   nach rechts   to the right.
   Nehmen Sie die erste Strasse rechts.   Take
      the first turn to your right.
   Rechts halten!   Keep to the right!
   Rechts um!   Right turn!
Rechtsanspruch m. legal claim.
Rechtsanwalt m. lawyer, counsel.
rechtschaffen honest, upright; very,
   extremely, thoroughly.
Rechtschreibung f. spelling.
Rechtsfall m. lawsuit.
Rechtsgelehrte m. jurist.
rechtsgültig legal, valid.
Rechtsspruch m. verdict.
rechtsungültig illegal, invalid.
rechtsverbindlich legally, binding.
Rechtsweg m. legal proceedings, law.
rechtswidrig illegal.
Rechtswissenschaft f. jurisprudence.
rechtzeitig in good time.
recken to stretch, extend.
   die Glieder recken   to stretch one's limbs.
Redakteur m. editor.
Redaktion f. editors, editorial staff; wording.
redaktionell editorial.
REDE f. talk, discourse, speech,
   conversation, rumor.
   Davon ist keine Rede!   That's out of the
      question!
   Davon ist nicht dir Rede!   That's not the
      point!
   eine Rede halten   to make a speech.
   in die Rede fallen   to interrupt.

nicht der Rede wert   *not worth mentioning.*
Rede stehen   *to answer for.*
Wovon ist die Rede?   *What is it all about?*
zur Rede stellen   *to call to account, to take to task.*
Redefreiheit *f. freedom of speech.*
redegewandt *fluent, eloquent.*
REDEN *to talk, speak, converse, make a speech.*
begeistert reden   *to rave, enthuse.*
mit sich reden lassen   *to listen to reason.*
nicht zu reden von   *to say nothing of.*
von sich reden machen   *to cause a stir.*
Redensart *f. phrase, idiom, nonsense.*
Redner *m. orator, speaker.*
reduzieren *to reduce.*
Reederei *f. steamship company.*
Referenz *f. reference.*
reformieren *to reform.*
Regal *n. shelf.*
rege *active, brisk.*
Regel *f. rule, regulation, principle.*
in der Regel   *as a rule.*
regelmässig *regular, proportional.*
regeln *to arrange, regulate.*
geregelt   *regular, well ordered.*
regelrecht *regular, correct, proper.*
REGEN *m. rain, precipitation.*
Auf Regen folgt Sonnenschein.   *The calm follows the storm. ("After rain follows sunshine.")*
Regenbogen *m. rainbow.*
regendicht *waterproof.*
Regenmantel *m. raincoat.*
Regenschirm *m. umbrella.*
Regenzeit *f. rainy season.*
Regie *f. production (theater); administration, management.*
regieren *to rule, govern, reign.*
Regierung *f. government, reign, rule.*
Regierungsbeamte *n. government official.*
Regiment *n. regiment, government.*
Regisseur *m. stage manager.*
Register *n. register, index, table of contents.*
registrieren *to register.*
REGNEN *to rain*
Es regnet in Strömen.   *It's raining cats and dogs.*
regnerisch *rainy.*
regsam *active, agile, quick.*
Regsamkeit *f. agility, activity, quickness.*
Regung *f. movement.*
Reh *n. deer.*
Rehbraten *m. roast venison.*
Reibeisen *n. grater.*
Reiben *to rub, grate, grind.*
sich wundreiben   *to chafe oneself.*

REICH *rich, wealthy, well off, plentiful, abundant.*
Reich *n. empire, kingdom.*
Deutsches Reich   *n. Germany.*
Österreich   *n. Austria.*
reichen *to give, present, hand.*
reichhaltig *full, rich, abundant.*
Reichhaltigkeit *f. fullness, richness.*
reichlich *plentiful, abundant, copious.*
Reichsautobahn *f. state road.*
Reichtum *m. wealth, abundance.*
Reichweite *f. range, reach.*
Reif *m. frost.*
REIF *ripe, mature, mellow.*
Reifen *m. tire.*
reifen *to ripen, mature.*
Reifenpanne *f. flat tire, blowout.*
Reifenschaden *m. flat tire, blowout.*
Reifeprüfung *f. final comprehensive examination.*
Reifezeugnis *n. final certificate, diploma.*
reiflich *maturely, carefully.*
REIHE *f. row, range, series, sequence.*
ausser der Reihe   *out of one's mind.*
der Reihe nach   *successively, in rotation.*
Er ist an der Reihe.   *It is his turn.*
Reihenfolge *f. succession, sequence.*
reihenweise *in rows.*
Reim *m. rhyme.*
reimen *to rhyme.*
REIN *clean, plain, sheer, pure, genuine, tidy.*
aus reinem Trotz   *out of sheer obstinacy.*
reine Bahn machen   *to clear the way.*
reiner Gewinn   *net profit.*
reiner Zufall   *sheer luck, pure chance.*
aus reinem Mitleid   *out of sheer compassion.*
Reingewinn *m. net profit.*
Reinheit *f. purity, pureness.*
REINIGEN *to clean, cleanse, purify.*
Reinigung *f. cleaning, cleansing, cleaners.*
reinlich *clean, neat, tidy.*
Reinlichkeit *f. cleanliness, neatness, tidiness.*
Reis *m. rice.*
REISE *f. trip, journey, voyage.*
Glückliche Reise!   *Have a nice trip!*
eine Reise machen   *to take a trip.*
Reiseandenken   *n. souvenir (from a trip).*
Reisebüro *n. tourist office.*
Reiseführer *m. guidebook.*
REISEN *to travel.*
REISENDE *m. passenger, traveler.*
Reisescheck *m. traveler's check.*
reissen *to tear, pull, drag.*
an sich reissen   *to seize, hold up, snatch up.*
in Stücke reissen   *to tear to pieces.*
sich reissen um   *to fight for.*
reissend *ravenous, rapid, torrential.*

der reissende Strom   *m. torrent.*
Reissverschluss *m. zipper.*
reiten *to ride a horse.*
Reiter *m. horseman, cavalryman.*
Reithose *f. riding pants.*
Reitschule *f. riding school.*
REIZ *m. charm, attraction; irritation; incentive.*
reizbar *sensitive, irritable, excitable.*
reizen *to irritate, excite, provoke, tempt.*
reizend *charming.*
reizlos *unattractive.*
reizvoll *charming, attractive.*
REKLAME *f. publicity, advertisement.*
  Reklame machen   *to advertise.*
rekonstruieren *to reconstruct.*
Rekord *m. record, competition.*
Rektor *m. university president.*
relativ *relative, relating to.*
Religion *f. religion.*
religiös *religious.*
Rennbahn *f. racecourse.*
RENNEN *to run, race.*
Rennfahrer *m. racing cyclist.*
Rennstall *m. racing stable.*
renovieren *to renovate, redecorate.*
Rentamt *n. revenue office.*
Rente *f. pension, revenue.*
Reparation *f. reparation.*
Reparatur *f. repair.*
  Wegen Reparatur geschlossen.   *Closed for repairs.*
Reparaturwerkstätte *f. repair shop.*
Reportage *f. commentary, eye-witness account.*
repräsentieren *to represent.*
Republik *f. republic.*
Republikaner *m. Republican.*
republikanisch *republican.*
Reserve *f. reserve.*
Reserverad *n. spare wheel.*
reservieren *to reserve.*
Respekt *m. respect.*
respektabel *respectable.*
respektieren *to respect.*
respektlos *without respect, irreverent.*
respektvoll *respectful.*
Rest *m. rest, remains, remnant.*
restaurieren *to repair, restore (work of art).*
Restbestand *m. remainder, residue.*
restlos *complete, without anything left over.*
Resultat *n. result, answer.*
retten *to save, preserve, rescue, deliver.*
Rettung *f. rescue, saving, escape.*
Rettungsboot *n. lifeboat.*
Rettungsgürtel *m. lifebelt.*
Reue *f. repentance.*
reuen *to repent, regret.*
  Es reut mich.   *I regret.*

reumütig *repentant, penitent.*
Revier *n. hunting ground, district.*
  Polizeirevier   *n. district police station.*
Revolte *f. revolt, insurrection.*
Revolution *f. revolution.*
revolutionär *revolutionary.*
Revolver *m. revolver.*
Rezept *n. recipe, prescription.*
rezitieren *to recite.*
Rheumatismus *m. rheumatism.*
rhythmisch *rhythmical.*
Richter *m. judge.*
RICHTIG *right, correct, true, real, straight.*
  Das ist nicht sein richtiger Name.   *That's not his real name.*
  Meine Uhr geht richtig.   *My watch is right.*
  Richtig!   *Quite right!*
Richtigstellung *f. rectification.*
Richtlinie *f. guiding principle, rule.*
Richtung *f. direction, line, course, tendency.*
riechen *to smell.*
Riemen *m. strap.*
Riese *m. giant.*
riesenhaft *gigantic, colossal.*
Rind *n. ox, cow, cattle.*
Rinde *f. bark, rind of cheese, crust.*
Rinderbraten *m. roast beef.*
Rindfleisch *n. beef.*
Ring *m. ring, circle.*
ringen *to struggle, wrestle.*
Ringkampf *m. wrestling match.*
Ringkämpfer *m. wrestler.*
Ringrichter *m. umpire, referee.*
rings *round, around.*
ringsum *(–her) all around.*
Rinne *f. gutter, channel.*
rinnen *to flow, run.*
Rinnstein *m. gutter.*
Rippe *f. rib.*
riskant *risky.*
riskieren *to risk.*
Riss *m. tear, hole, gap, crack.*
Ritter *m. knight, cavalier.*
Rittergut *n. estate, manor.*
ritterlich *chivalrous, gallant.*
Rivale *m. rival.*
Rock *m. coat (man's); skirt.*
rodeln *to sled.*
Rodelschlitten *m. sled.*
roden *to root out, clear (forest, garden).*
ROH *raw, crude, coarse, rare (steak).*
Rohmaterial *n. raw material.*
Rohr *n. pipe, oven.*
Röhre *f. tube, valve.*
Rolle *f. roll, cylinder; part (theater).*
  aus der Rolle fallen   *to misbehave.*
  die Rollen verteilen   *to cast (a play).*
  eine Rolle spielen   *to be important.*

Rollenbesetzung *f. cast.*
Rollmops *m. pickled herring.*
Rollschuh *m. rollerskate.*
  Rollschuh laufen   *to rollerskate.*
Rollstuhl *m. wheelchair.*
Rolltreppe *f. escalator.*
Roman *m. novel.*
Romanschriftsteller *m. novelist.*
Romantik *f. Romanticism.*
Romantiker *m. romanticist.*
romantisch *romantic.*
röntgen *to x-ray.*
Röntgenaufnahme *f. X-ray photograph.*
Röntgenbild *n. X-ray photograph.*
Röntgenstrahlen *pl. X-rays.*
rosa *pink, rose-colored.*
Rose *f. rose.*
Rosenkohl *m. Brussels spouts.*
Rosine *f. raisin*
Rost *m.* 1. *rust.*
  2. *grate.*
Rostbraten *m. roast beef.*
Röstbrot *toast.*
rösten *to roast, grill, toast.*
Rostfleck *m. ironmold.*
rostfrei *stainless*
  rostfreier Stahl   *stainless steel.*
rostig *rusty.*
ROT *red, ruddy.*
  rot werden   *to blush.*
rotblond *auburn.*
Röte *f. red, redness, blush.*
Rotkohl *m. red cabbage.*
Rotstift *m. red pencil.*
Rotwein *m. red wine.*
Rübe *f. sugar beet.*
  weisse Rübe   *turnip.*
  gelbe Rübe   *carrot*
Rubin *m. ruby.*
Rückantwort *f. reply.*
Rückblick *m. glance back, retrospect.*
RÜCKEN *m. back, rear.*
  den Rücken kehren   *to turn one's back.*
  in dem Rücken fallen   *to attack from the rear.*
  Rücken gegen Rücken   *back to back.*
  Es läuft mir kalt über den Rücken.   *A shiver runs down my spine.*
rücken *to move, push, move away.*
Rückendeckung *f. rear, cover, protection.*
rückerstatten *to refund, reimburse.*
Rückfahrkarte *f. return ticket.*
Rückfahrt *f. return trip.*
Rückfall *m. relapse.*
rückfällig *relapsing.*
Rückflug *m. return flight.*
Rückfrage *f. query, search back; further inquiry.*
Rückgabe *f. return.*

Rückgang *m. decline, falling off.*
rückgängig *retrogressive.*
  rückgängig machen   *to cancel.*
Rückgrat *spine, backbone.*
rückhaltlos *unreserved, without reserve.*
Rückkehr *f. return.*
Rücklehne *f. back (of chair).*
Rückmarsch *m. retreat.*
Rückporto *n. return postage.*
Rückreise *f. return trip.*
Rückschlag *m. reverse, setback, reaction, recoil (of a gun).*
Rückschritt *m. step back, relapse.*
Rückseite *f. back, reverse side.*
Rücksicht *f. regard, consideration.*
  Rücksicht nehmen auf   *to be considerate of.*
rücksichtslos *inconsiderate, reckless.*
rücksichtsvoll *considerate.*
Rücksitz *m. back seat.*
Rücksprache *f. discussion, consultation.*
  Rücksprache nehmen   *to discuss, talk over.*
Rückstand *m. arrears, residue.*
rückständig *backward, old-fashioned.*
Rückstelltaste *back-spacer (on a typewriter).*
Rücktritt *m. retirement, resignation.*
Rückwand *f. back wall.*
rückwärts *backwards; back.*
Rückwärtsgang *m. reverse gear.*
Rückweg *m. way back, return.*
rückwirkend *retroactive, retrospective.*
Rückwirkung *f. reaction, retroaction.*
Rückzahlung *f. repayment.*
Rückzug *m. withdrawal, retreat.*
Ruder *n. oar, rudder, helm.*
  ans Ruder kommen   *to come into power.*
Ruderboot *n. rowboat.*
rudern *to row.*
Ruf *m. reputation, cry, call.*
  in gutem Rufe stehen mit   *to have a good reputation with.*
RUFEN *to call, shout.*
  Soll ich Sie rufen lassen?   *Shall I send for her?*
  wie gerufen kommen   *to come at the right moment.*
Rufname *m. Christian name.*
RUHE *f. rest, repose, calm.*
  Angenehme Ruhe!   *Sleep well!*
  in aller Ruhe   *very calmly.*
  Lassen Sie mich in Ruhe!   *Leave me alone!*
  Nichts bringt ihn aus der Ruhe.   *Nothing upsets him.*
  Ruhe!   *Silence! Quiet!*
  sich zur Ruhe setzen   *to retire.*
  keine Ruhe haben   *to have no peace.*
ruhelos *restless.*

RUHEN *to rest, sleep, stand still.*
  ruhen auf *to rest on, be based on.*
Ruhestätte *f. resting-place.*
Ruhestellung *f. at-ease position (standing).*
Ruhestörer *m. brawler, rioter.*
RUHIG *still, quiet, silent, calm, composed.*
  Bleiben Sie ruhig sitzen! *Don't get up!*
  Seien Sie ruhig! *Be quiet!*
Ruhm *m. fame, glory.*
rühmen *to praise.*
  sich rühmen *to boast, brag.*
rühmlich *glorious, praiseworthy.*
ruhmlos *inglorious, obscure.*
Rührei *n. scrambled egg.*
rühren *to move, stir.*
  sich rühren *to touch, move.*
  zu Tränen rühren *to move to tears.*
rührend *touching, moving, pathetic.*
rührig *active, quick.*
Rührung *f. emotion, feeling.*
Ruine *f. ruin.*
ruinieren *to ruin.*
RUND *round, circular, plump.*
  rund heraus *flatly.*
  rund (her)um *all around.*
Rundblick *m. panorama.*
RUNDE *f. circle, lap, beat.*
  die Runde machen *to be passed around.*
runden *to make round, round.*
Rundfahrt *f. circular tour.*
Rundfrage *f. inquiry, questionnaire.*
RUNDFUNK *m. radio, wireless,*
  broadcasting.
  im Rundfunk gehört *heard over the*
  radio.
Rundfunkgerät *n. wireless set.*
Rundfunkhörer *m. listener (radio).*
Rundgang *m. stroll, round (military).*
rundlich *round, rounded.*
Rundschreiben *n. circular letter.*
Russe *m. (**Russin** f.) Russian (person).*
russig *sooty.*
russisch *Russian.*
Russische *n. Russian (language).*
rüsten *to arm, prepare for war.*
rüstig *strong, robust, vigorous.*
Rüstung *f. preparation, equipment, armor.*
Rutsch *m. slide, glide, landslip.*
rutschen *to slide, slip, skid.*
rutschig *slippery.*

S

Saal *m. large room, hall.*
Saat *f. seed.*
Säbel *m. saber.*
sabotieren *to sabotage.*
Sachbearbeiter *m. expert.*

sachdienlich *relevant, pertinent.*
SACHE *f. thing, subject, business, case,*
  circumstances, cause, point, subject.
  bie der Sache sein *to pay attention.*
  gemeinsame Sache machen *to make*
  common cause with.
  zur Sache *to the point.*
Sachen *pl. things, clothes.*
  seine sieben Sachen *all one's belongings.*
sachgemäss *appropriate, suitable.*
Sachkunde *f. expert knowledge.*
sachkundig *expert, competent.*
Sachlage *f. state of affairs.*
sachlich *factual, essential, objective.*
Sachlichkeit *f. reality, objectivity.*
Sachschaden *m. damage to property.*
sachte *soft, gentle.*
Sachverhalt *m. facts of the case.*
Sack *m. sack, bag, pocket, purse.*
Sackgasse *f. blind alley, dead end.*
säen *to sow.*
Saft *m. juice, liquid, sap.*
  Apfelsinensaft *m. orange juice.*
saftig *juicy, succulent.*
saftlos *dry, sapless.*
Sage *f. legend, tale.*
Säge *f. saw.*
SAGEN *to say, tell, mean.*
  Das hat nichts zu sagen. *That does not*
  matter.
  Das ist leichter gesagt als getan. *That's*
  easier said than done.
  Er hat es mir ins Ohr gesagt. *He*
  whispered it in my ear.
  Gesagt, getan. *No sooner said than done.*
  man sagt *they say.*
  sagen lassen *to send word.*
  sage und schreibe *precisely.*
  sich etwas gesagt sein lassen *to be*
  warned.
  unter uns gesagt *between you and me.*
  ihm gehörig die Meinung sagen *to give*
  him a piece of one's mind.
  er lässt sich nichts sagen *he won't listen*
  to reason.
  auf alles etwas zu sagen wissen. *to have*
  an answer for everything.
  ihr sagen lassen *to let her know.*
  Dank sagen *to express thanks.*
  Was sagen Sie dazu? *What do you say to*
  that?
  Was wollen Sie damit sagen? *What do*
  you mean by that?
sagenhaft *legendary, fabulous, mythical.*
Sägewerk *n. sawmill.*
Sahne *f. cream.*
Saison *f. season.*
Saisonausverkauf *m. clearance sale.*
Saite *f. string, chord.*

Saiteninstrument n. stringed instrument.
Salat m. salad.
   grüner Salat lettuce.
Salbe f. salve, ointment.
salben to anoint.
Salon m. drawing room, parlor.
salutieren to salute.
SALZ n. salt.
salzen to salt, season.
Salzgurke f. pickled cucumber.
salzhaltig containing salt.
salzig salted, salty.
Same m. seed.
SAMMELN to collect, gather, accumulate.
Sammelplatz m. assembly point, meeting
    place.
Sammelstelle f. assembly point, meeting
    place.
Sammler m. collector.
Sammlung f. collection.
SAMSTAG m. Saturday.
Samt m. velvet.
samt together with.
   samt und sonders one and all.
sämtlich altogether, complete.
Sanatorium n. sanatorium.
SAND m. sand.
Sandale f. sandal.
Sandboden m. sandy soil.
sandig sandy.
SANFT soft, tender, delicate, gentle, smooth.
Sanftheit f. softness.
sänftigen to soften, appease.
Sanftmut f. gentleness.
sanftmütig gentle, meek.
Sänger m. (–in, f.) singer.
Sanitäter m. medical aid (person).
Sardelle f. anchovy.
Sardine f. sardine.
Sarg m. coffin.
sarkastisch sarcastic.
Satiriker m. satirist.
satirisch satirical.
SATT full, satisfied, saturated.
   Ich habe es satt. I've enough of it, I'm fed
    up with it.
Sattel m. saddle.
   in allen Sätteln gerecht sein to be good at
    everything.
satteln to saddle.
sättigen to satisfy.
Satz m. set, clause, sentence (grammar);
   proposition (philo.); phrase (music);
   sediment.
Satzbau m. sentence structure.
Satzzeichen n. punctuation mark.
sauber clean, neat, tidy.
Sauberkeit f. tidiness, cleanliness.
säuberlich clean, neat.

säubern to clean, clear.
Säuberung f. cleaning.
Sauce f. sauce, gravy.
SAUER sour, acid, pickled.
Sauerbraten m. sauerbraten.
Sauerkraut n. sauerkraut.
säuerlich acid, acidulous.
säuern to make sour.
Sauerstoff m. oxygen.
Sauerstoffgerät n. oxygen apparatus.
saugen to suck, absorb.
säugen to suckle, nurse.
Säugling m. infant, baby.
Säule f. pillar, column.
Saum m. edge, border, hem.
Säure f. acid, sourness, tartness, acidity.
säurehaltig containing acid.
Saxophon n. saxophone.
schäbig shabby, worn out.
Schäbigkeit f. shabbiness.
Schach n. chess.
   Schach bieten to defy.
Schachbrett n. chessboard.
Schachfeld n. square of a chessboard.
schachmatt checkmate.
Schachpartie f. chess game.
Schachtel f. box.
SCHADE too bad.
   Es ist schade! It is a pity!
   Wie schade! What a pity!
   zu schade für too good to.
Schaden m. damage, harm, injury, bias.
   Durch Schaden wird man klug. You learn
    by your mistakes.
   zu Schaden kommen to suffer damage.
   Schaden anrichten to do damage.
   zu Schaden Kommen to come to harm.
   Durch Schaden wird man klug. Once
    bitten, twice shy.
SCHADEN to hurt, damage, injure,
   prejudice.
   Es schadet nichts. It doesn't matter.
Schadenersatz m. compensation.
Schadenfreude f. malicious joy.
schadenfroh rejoicing over another's
   misfortune.
schadhaft damaged, defective, dilapidated.
   sich schadlos halten to get even with.
schädlich harmful, bad.
Schaf n. sheep.
Schäfchen n. lamb.
   sein Schäfchen ins Trockene bringen to
    feather one's nest.
Schäfer m. shepherd.
Schäferhund m. sheep-dog.
schaffen to create, produce, accomplish,
   make, do.
   sich zu schaffen machen to be busy.
   wie geschaffen für as though cut out for.

schaffend *creative, working.*

Schaffner *m. conductor, (train) guard.*

Schal *m. shawl, scarf.*

Schale *f. skin, peel, rind, shell; bowl.*

schälen *to peel, shell, bark, skin.*

Schall *m. sound.*

schalldicht *soundproof.*

Schalleffekt *m. sound effect.*

schallen *to sound, resound.*

Schallplatte *f. record (phonograph).*

Schaltanlage *f. switch, gear.*

schalten *to deal with, use, direct, change gears.*

Schalter *m. switch, ticket-window.*

Schaltjahr *n. leap year.*

Schaltung *f. gear change, connection.*

Scham *f. shame, modesty.*

(sich) schämen *to be ashamed.*

Schamgefühl *n. sense of shame.*

schamhaft *modest, bashful.*

schamlos *shameless, impudent.*

Schamlosigkeit *f. shamelessness, impudence.*

schamrot *blushing red.*

Schamröte *f. blush.*

schandbar *infamous.*

Schande *f. shame, disgrace.*

schänden *to spoil, disfigure, dishonor, rape.*

schändlich *shameful, disgraceful.*

Schändlichkeit *f. infamy.*

Schandtat *f. crime, misdeed.*

SCHARF *sharp, keen, harsh, pointed, piercing, acute, strong, quick.*

   Behalten Sie ihn scharf im Auge! *Keep a sharp eye on him!*

   Ich bin nicht so scharf darauf. *I am not so keen on that.*

Scharfblick *m. penetrating glance.*

Schärfe *f. sharpness, rigor, acuteness.*

schärfen *to sharpen.*

scharfkantig *sharp-edged.*

Scharfsicht *f. keenness of sight, perspicacity.*

scharfsichtig *keen-sighted, penetrating.*

Scharlach *m. scarlet fever.*

SCHATTEN *m. shadow, shade, spirit, phantom.*

   in den Schatten stellen *to overshadow.*

   Sie folgt mir wie ein Schatten. *She follows me like a shadow.*

Schattenseite *f. shady side.*

schattieren *to shade.*

schattig *shady.*

Schatz *m. treasure.*

Schatzamt *n. treasury.*

Schatzanweisungen *f. treasury bonds.*

schätzen *to value, estimate, judge.*

schätzenswert *estimable.*

Schatzmeister *m. treasurer.*

Schätzung *f. estimate, taxation.*

schätzungsweise *approximately.*

SCHAU *f. sight, view, show, exhibition.*

   zur Schau stellen *to exhibit, display.*

Schauder *m. shudder, shivering, horror, terror, fright.*

schauen *to see, behold, gaze, view.*

Schauer *m. horror, terror, awe, thrill.*

schauerlich *awful.*

schauern *to shudder, shiver.*

   mich schaudert bei *I shudder at.*

Schauerroman *m. thriller.*

Schaufel *f. shovel, scoop.*

schaufeln *to shovel.*

Schaufenster *n. show-window.*

Schaukasten *m. show case.*

Schaukel *f. swing.*

schaukeln *to swing, rock.*

Schaukelstuhl *m. rocking chair.*

schaulustig *curious.*

SCHAUSPIEL *n. spectacle, scene, play, drama.*

Schauspieler *m (–in, f.) actor (actress).*

Schauspielkunst *f. dramatic art.*

Schaustellung *f. exhibition.*

Schaustück *n. specimen; showpiece.*

Schaum *m. foam.*

   zu Schaum schlagen *to beat up (food).*

schäumen *to foam.*

schaumig *foamy, frothy.*

Scheck *m. check.*

Scheckbuch *n. check book.*

Scheckformular *n. blank check.*

Scheckinhaber *m. bearer.*

Scheibe *f. (window) pane, disk, slice, target.*

Scheibenwischer *m. window-wiper.*

scheiden *to separate, divide, part, divorce.*

   sich scheiden lassen *to get a divorce.*

Scheidewand *f. partition.*

Scheidung *f. separation, divorce.*

Scheidungsklage *f. divorce suit.*

SCHEIN *m. appearance, air, look; shine; ticket, receipt.*

   Der Schein trügt. *Appearances are deceiving.*

scheinbar *apparent(ly).*

Scheinbild *n. phantom, illusion.*

SCHEINEN *to shine; seem; look.*

scheinheilig *hypocritical, sanctimonious.*

Scheintod *m. suspended animation, trance.*

Scheinwerfer *m. reflector, search light, headlight (car).*

Scheitel *m. top, crown, summit; parting of the hair.*

scheitern *to fail.*

Schelle *f. door bell, little bell.*

Schema *n. order, arrangement, model.*

schematisch *systematic, mechanical.*

Schenkel *m. thigh.*

schenken *to give, present with, grant.*

   geschenkt bekommen *to get as a present.*

Schenker *m. donor.*
Schenkung *f. donation, gift.*
Schere *f. scissors.*
Scherz *m. joke, jest, pleasantry.*
scherzen *to joke.*
scherzhaft *joking.*
SCHEU *shy, timid.*
  scheu werden *to become shy, to take fright.*
scheuen *to avoid, shun.*
  sich scheuen *to shy away.*
scheuern *to scrub, rub, clean, chafe.*
Schicht *f. layer, bed, coat, shift, stratum.*
Schichtwechsel *m. change of shift.*
Schick *m. elegance, smartness, chic.*
SCHICKEN *to send, dispatch.*
  schicken nach *to send for.*
  sich schicken in *conform, adapt oneself to.*
  Waren ins Haus schicken. *to deliver goods to the door.*
  zuschicken *to send by mail.*
schicklich *proper, decent.*
Schicksal *n. fate, destiny, lot.*
SCHIEBEN *to move, push, shove.*
  schieben auf *to lay the blame on.*
  etwas auf die lange Bank schieben *to postpone a thing.*
Schiebetür *f. sliding door.*
Schiebung *f. profiteering, graft.*
Schiedsrichter *m. umpire.*
schief *oblique, crooked, askance.*
Schiefer *m. slate, splinter.*
Schieferdach *n. slate roof.*
Schiene *f. rail, track, splint.*
schiessen *to shoot, flash, fire.*
  einen Blick schiessen auf *to shoot a glance at.*
  ein Tor schiessen *to score a goal.*
SCHIFF *n. boat, ship, vessel.*
  zu Schiff *on board, by boat.*
schiffbar *navigable.*
Schiffbruch *m. shipwreck.*
Schiffchen *n. small boat, shuttle.*
schiffen *to ship, sail.*
Schiffer *m. sailor.*
Schiffsbesatzung *f. crew.*
Schiffskörper *m. hull.*
Schiffsladung *f. cargo, freight.*
Schiffswerft *m. wharf, dock.*
Schild *m. shield, coat of arms, sign.*
  im Schilde führen *to have something up one's sleeve.*
schildern *to relate, describe.*
Schilderung *f. description.*
Schimmel *m. mold, mildew.*
schimmelig *moldy.*
Schimmer *m. glitter.*
schimmern *to glitter, gleam.*

Schimpf *m. disgrace, insult.*
schimpfen *to kick, gripe, scold.*
  schimpfen mit *to scold.*
schimpflich *disgraceful.*
Schimpfwort *n. rude name; term of abuse.*
SCHINKEN *m. ham.*
  Eier mit Schinken *ham and eggs.*
Schirm *m. umbrella, shelter, lampshade.*
Schlacht *f. combat, battle.*
schlachten *to slaughter, kill, butcher.*
Schlächter *m. butcher.*
Schlachtfeld *n. battlefield.*
Schlachthaus *n. slaughterhouse.*
Schlachtschiff *n. battleship.*
SCHLAF *m. sleep.*
  im Schlaf liegen *to be asleep.*
Schlafanzug *m. pajamas.*
Schläfchen *n. nap.*
SCHLAFEN *to sleep.*
  schlafen gehen *to go to bed.*
Schlafenszeit *m. bedtime.*
schlaff *slack, loose, relaxed.*
Schlaffheit *f. laxity.*
Schlafkrankheit *f. sleeping sickness.*
schlaflos *sleepless.*
Schlaflosigkeit *f. insomnia.*
Schlafmittel *m. narcotic.*
schläfrig *sleepy.*
Schlafsaal *m. dormitory.*
Schlafwagen *m. sleeping-car.*
Schlafwandler *m. sleepwalker.*
Schlafzimmer *n. bedroom.*
SCHLAG *m. blow, stroke, striking (clock).*
  zwei Fliegen auf einen Schlag treffen *to kill two birds with one stone.*
Schlagader *f. artery.*
Schlaganfall *m. stroke, fit.*
SCHLAGEN *to beat, knock, hit, strike, throb.*
  sich schlagen *to fight.*
  sich geschlagen geben *to give up.*
  schlagen nach *to take after.*
  eine geschlagene Stunde *a whole hour.*
  etwas aus dem Kopfe schlagen *to dismiss something from one's thoughts.*
  die Schanze schlagen *to risk one's life.*
  einen Rekord schlagen *to set a record.*
  Die Uhr schlägt zehn. *The clock strikes ten.*
  seine Unkosten auf die Ware schlagen *to add one's expenses to the price of the goods.*
schlagfertig *quick at repartee.*
Schlagfertigkeit *f. quickness at repartee.*
Schlagsahne *f. whipped cream.*
Schlagwort *n. slogan.*
Schlagzeile *f. headline.*
Schlagzeug *n. percussion instrument.*
Schlamm *m. mud, ooze.*

schlammig *muddy, oozy.*
Schlange *f. snake.*
    Schlange stehen   *to stand in line; to make a line.*
Schlangenbiss *m. snake bite.*
schlank *slim, slender.*
Schlankheit *f. slimness, slenderness.*
schlapp *weak, tired, limp, flabby.*
    schlapp machen   *to collapse.*
schlau *sly, cunning.*
Schlauberger *m. sly fox.*
Schlauch *m. hose, tube.*
Schlauheit *f. slyness, cunning.*
Schlaukopf *m. sly fox.*
SCHLECHT *bad, poor, inferior, ill, wicked.*
    mir ist schlecht   *I feel sick.*
    schlecht machen   *to run down.*
    schlecht und recht   *somehow.*
    schlecht werden   *to spoil (food).*
schlechtgelaunt *in a bad temper.*
Schlechtigkeit *f. badness, wickedness.*
schleichen *to creep, drag, sneak.*
    sich davon schleichen   *to steal away.*
    wie die Katze um den heissen Brei schleichen   *to beat around the bush* (*"to creep like the car around the hot roast"*)
schlicht *simple, plain, even.*
schlichten *to make simple, smooth.*
Schlichtheit *f. simplicity.*
Schliesse *f. clasp, fastening.*
SCHLIESSEN *to close, lock, shut, break up.*
    in die Arme schliessen   *to embrace.*
    geschlossen   *enclosed.*
    die Ehe schliessen   *to get married.*
Schliessfach *n. locker.*
schliesslich *final, finally, after all.*
Schliessung *f. closing.*
schlimm *bad, sore.*
    schlimmstenfalls   *if the worst comes to the worst.*
Schlips *m. necktie (coll.).*
Schlitten *m. sled, sleigh.*
Schlittenfahrt *f. sleigh driving.*
Schlittschuh *m. skate.*
    Schlittschuh laufen   *to skate.*
Schlittschuhläufer *m. skater.*
SCHLOSS *n. castle, lock.*
Schlosser *m. locksmith.*
Schluck *m. gulp, draught.*
Schluckauf *m. hiccup.*
schlucken *to gulp, swallow.*
Schlucker *m. hiccup.*
    armer Schlucker   *poor wretch.*
Schlummer *m. slumber.*
schlummern *to slumber.*
Schlüpfer *m. panties.*
SCHLUSS *m. closing, shutting, conclusion.*
Schlüssel *m. key, code.*

Schlüsselbund *m. bunch of keys.*
Schlüsselloch *m. keyhole.*
Schlusslicht *n. tail light.*
Schlusswort *n. summary, last word.*
Schmach *f. disgrace, dishonor, humiliation.*
schmachten *to languish.*
schmachvoll *disgraceful, humiliating.*
schmackhaft *tasty, savory.*
schmähen *to abuse.*
schmählich *disgraceful.*
SCHMAL *narrow, thin, slender, poor.*
schmälern *to diminish, lessen.*
Schmalz *n. drippings.*
SCHMECKEN *to taste, try.*
    Es schmeckt gut.   *It tastes good.*
    Es schmeckt mir nicht.   *I don't like it.*
    schmecken nach   *to taste of.*
    Wie schmeckt's?   *How do you like it?*
Schmeichelei *f. flattery.*
schmeichelhaft *flattering.*
Schmeichelkatze *f. wheedler, flatterer.*
schmeicheln *to flatter.*
Schmeichler *m. flatterer.*
schmeichlerisch *flattering.*
schmelzen *to melt.*
SCHMERZ *m. pain, ache, hurt, sorrow.*
SCHMERZEN *to hurt, pain, grieve.*
Schmerzensgeld *n. smart money, compensation.*
schmerzerfüllt *deeply affected.*
schmerzhaft *painful.*
schmerzlich *grievous, sad.*
schmerzlos *painless.*
schmerzstillend *soothing.*
Schmetterling *m. butterfly.*
Schmied *m. blacksmith.*
Schmiede *f. forge.*
schmieden *to forge, hammer.*
    Pläne schmieden   *to devise plans.*
schmiegen *to bend.*
schmiegsam *flexible, supple.*
Schmiegsamkeit *f. flexibility.*
schmieren *to spread, grease, smear.*
Schminke *f. rouge, paint, make up.*
schminken *to make up, paint the face.*
Schmorbraten *stewed steak.*
SCHMUCK *m. jewelry, ornament, decoration.*
schmücken *to decorate, adorn.*
Schmuckstück *n. piece of jewelry.*
Schmuggel *m. smuggling.*
schmuggeln *to smuggle.*
schmunzeln *to grin, to smirk.*
Schmutz *m. dirt, mud.*
schmutzen *to dirty.*
Schmutzfleck *m. stain, spot.*
schmutzig *dirty.*
Schnabel *m. beak, bill.*
schnarchen *to snore.*

schnaufen *to breathe heavily, pant.*
Schnecke *f. snail.*
  wie eine Schnecke kriechen *to go at a snail's pace.*
SCHNEE *m. snow.*
Schneeball *m. snowball.*
Schneedecke *f. blanket of snow.*
Schneefall *m. snowfall.*
Schneeflocke *f. snowflake.*
Schneekette *f. non-skid chain (automobile).*
Schneeschuh *m. snow shoe, ski.*
Schneetreiben *n. blizzard.*
schneeweiss *snow-white.*
SCHNEIDEN *to cut, carve.*
  sich schneiden *to cut oneself.*
schneidend *sharp, bitter.*
Schneider *m. tailor.*
schneien *to snow.*
SCHNELL *quick, fast, swift, prompt, speedy.*
Schnelligkeit *f. rapidity, velocity.*
Schnellzug *m. express train.*
(sich) schneuzen *to blow one's nose.*
Schnippchen *n. snap of the fingers.*
  ein Schnippchen schlagen *to play a trick.*
Schnitt *m. cut, cutting, incision.*
Schnittblumen *pl. cut flowers.*
Schnittmuster *n. cut pattern.*
Schnittwunde *f. cut.*
schnitzen *to carve, cut.*
Schnupfen *m. (head) cold.*
  sich einen Schnupfen holen *to get a (head) cold.*
schnupfen *to sniff.*
Schnur *f. string, cord.*
  Ober die Schnur hauen *to kick over the traces.*
Schnurrbart *m. moustache.*
schnurren *to hum, buzz, purr.*
Schnürsenkel *m. shoelaces.*
Schock *m. shock.*
Schokolade *f. chocolate.*
SCHON *already, all right, very, yet, even, indeed, certainly.*
  Schon gut! *All right!*
  Wenn schon! *So what!*
  Haben Sie es schon einmal gesehen? *Did you ever see it before?*
SCHÖN *beautiful, handsome, fine, nice, fair, noble.*
  Danke schön (Schönen Dank). *Thanks.*
  Das wäre noch schöner! *That's all we need!*
  die Schönen Künste *the fine arts.*
  schön tun *to flatter.*
  Schönen Gruss an Ihre Frau. *Best regards to your wife.*
  Schönsten Dank. *Many thanks.*
  sich schön machen. *to smarten oneself.*
schonen *to spare, save, look after, preserve.*

schonend *careful, considerate.*
Schöngeist *m. wit; esthete.*
schöngeistig *esthetical.*
Schönheit *f. beauty.*
Schönheitsmittel *n. cosmetic.*
Schönheitspflege *f. beauty treatment.*
Schonung *f. indulgence.*
schonungslos *pitiless.*
schöpfen *to draw, create.*
Schöpferkraft *f. power, creative.*
Schöpflöffel *m. scoop, dipper.*
Schornstein *m. chimney.*
Schoss *m. lap.*
Schotte *m. Scotsman.*
schottisch *Scottish.*
schräg *diagonally.*
Schräge *f. slant, slope.*
Schramme *f. scratch, scar.*
schrammen *to scratch.*
Schrank *m. wardrobe.*
Schranke *f. fencing, enclosure, gate.*
  sich in Schranken halten *to keep within bounds.*
schrankenlos *boundless, without limits.*
Schrankkoffer *m. wardrobe trunk.*
Schraube *f. screw, propeller, bolt.*
schrauben *to screw, turn, wheel.*
Schraubenschlüssel *m. wrench.*
Schraubenzieher *m. screwdriver.*
SCHRECK (EN) *m. scare, fright, fear, dread, horror.*
  in Schrecken setzen *to terrify.*
schrecken *to frighten.*
Schreckgespenst *n. terrible vision.*
schreckhaft *timid, easily frightened.*
schrecklich *terrible, awful.*
Schreckschuss *m. warning shot.*
Schrei *m. scream, cry.*
SCHREIBEN *to write, spell.*
  auf der Maschine schreiben *to type.*
  die Zeitung schreibt *the paper says.*
  Schreiben Sie sich das hinter die Ohren. *to make a special note of it; to take it to heart.*
Schreiberei *f. writing, correspondence.*
Schreibfehler *m. slip of the pen.*
Schreibmappe *f. writing case, portfolio, blotter.*
Schreibmaschine *f. typewriter.*
Schreibpapier *n. note paper.*
Schreibstube *f. office.*
Schreibwaren *pl. stationery.*
Schreibwarengeschäft *n. stationery store.*
Schreibwarenhändler *m. stationer.*
Schreibwarenhandlung *f. stationery store.*
SCHREIEN *to scream, shout, yell.*
schreiend *loud, gaudy.*
Schreier *m. shouter, bawler.*
Schreiner *m. carpenter, cabinetmaker.*

Schreinerei *f. cabinetmaker's shop.*
SCHRIFT *f. writing, handwriting, script.*
schriftlich *in writing, written.*
Schriftführer *m. secretary (association or politics).*
Schriftsteller *m. writer (author).*
SCHRITT *m. step, stride.*
    auf Schritt und Tritt *everywhere, all the time.*
    Schritt fahren! *Drive slowly!*
    Schritt für Schritt *step by step.*
    Schritt halten *to keep pace with.*
schroff *rugged, rough, uncouth.*
schrubben *to scrub.*
Schrubber *m. scrubber.*
schrumpfen *to shrink, contract.*
Schrumpfung *f. shrinking, contraction.*
Schublade *f. drawer.*
schüchtern *bashful, timid.*
Schüchternheit *f. bashfulness, timidity.*
Schuft *m. scoundrel.*
SCHUH *m. shoe.*
    einem etwas in die Schuhe schieben *to put the blame on someone.*
Schuhanzieher *m. shoehorn.*
Schuhkrem *f. shoe-polish.*
Schuhmacher *m. shoemaker.*
Schuhputzer *m. bootblack.*
Schuhriemen *m. shoelace.*
Schuhsohle *f. sole of a shoe.*
Schularbeit *f. lesson, homework.*
Schulbesuch *m. attendance at school.*
Schulbildung *f. schooling, education.*
SCHULD *f. obligation, debt, cause, blame.*
    in jemandes Schuld stehen *to have an obligation.*
    Schuld sein an *to be guilty of.*
    Schulden machen *to incur debts.*
    Schuld geben *to accuse.*
schuldbewusst *guilt-conscious.*
schulden *to owe.*
Schuldenmacher *m. contractor of debts.*
schuldig *owing, due, obliged, guilty.*
    schuldig sein *to be indebted.*
    Geld schuldig sein *to owe money.*
    keine Antwort schuldig bleiben *never to be at a loss for an answer.*
Schuldigkeit *f. duty, obligation.*
schuldlos *innocent.*
Schuldner *m. debtor.*
Schuldschein *m. bond, promissory note.*
SCHULE *f. school, academy, courses.*
    die Schule schwänzen *to cut classes.*
    Schule machen *to find followers.*
schulen *to school, train, teach.*
Schüler *m. student, pupil.*
Schulferien *pl. m. school holidays.*
schulfrei *having a holiday, off from school.*
Schulfreund *m. school friend.*

Schulgeld *n. school fees.*
Schulmappe *f. schoolbag, satchel.*
Schulmeister *m. schoolmaster, teacher.*
schulmeistern *to censure, to be pedantic.*
Schulstunde *f. school lesson.*
Schulter *f. shoulder.*
Schulung *f. school training.*
Schulzeugnis *n. school certificates, report card*
Schuppe *f. scale (fish).*
Schürze *f. apron.*
Schuss *m. shot, report, round.*
schussbereit *ready to shoot.*
Schusswaffe *f. firearm.*
Schussweite *f. range.*
Schusswunde *f. bullet wound.*
schütteln *to shake.*
schütten *to pour in, to spill, to shed.*
SCHUTZ *m. shelter, protection, refuge.*
    im Schutz der Nacht *under cover of the night.*
    in Schutz nehmen *to defend.*
    Schutz suchen *to take shelter.*
Schutzbrille *f. safety goggles.*
Schützen *to protect.*
    sich schützen *to protect oneself.*
Schutzengel *m. guardian angel.*
Schutzhaft *f. protective custody.*
Schutzimpfung *f. vaccination.*
schutzlos *defenseless, unprotected.*
Schutzmann *n. policeman.*
Schutzpockenimpfung *f. vaccination against smallpox.*
SCHWACH *weak, frail, faint, feeble.*
Schwäche *f. weakness, debility, frailty.*
schwächen *to weaken.*
    schwachen Besuch *poor attendance.*
Schwächheit *f. weakness, feebleness.*
schwächlich *weak, delicate.*
Schwächlichkeit *f. delicacy, infirmity.*
Schwachsinn *m. imbecility.*
schwachsinnig *imbecile.*
Schwager *m. brother-in-law.*
Schwägerin *f. sister-in-law.*
Schwalbe *f. swallow.*
Schwamm *m. sponge, mushroom.*
Schwan *m. swan.*
schwanger *pregnant.*
schwanken *to rock, toss, sway.*
Schwankung *f. variation.*
Schwanz *m. tail, end.*
Schwarm *m. crowd, multitude.*
schwärmen *to swarm, riot.*
Schwärmer *m. enthusiast, fanatic.*
Schwärmerei *f. enthusiasm.*
schwärmerisch *enthusiastic, fanatic.*
Schwarte *f. rind, skin.*
SCHWARZ *black, dark, dirty, gloomy.*
    ins Schwarze treffen *to hit the bull's eye.*

schwarz auf weiss *in black and white.*
Sie sieht immer alles schwarz *She always sees the dark side of things.*
Schwarzbrot *n. black bread.*
Schwarze *m. black (person).*
Schwarzhandel *m. black market.*
Schwarzwald *m. Black Forest.*
Schwatz *m. chat, talk.*
Schwatzbase *f. chatterbox.*
schwatzen, schwätzen *to chatter, gossip.*
Schwätzer *m (–in, f.) gossip.*
schwatzhaft *talkative.*
Schwatzhaftigkeit *f. loquacity.*
Schwebe *f. state of suspense.*
in der Schwebe sein *to be undecided, to be pending.*
Schwebebahn *f. suspension railway.*
schweben *to be suspended, pending.*
auf der Zunge schweben *to have on the tip of the tongue.*
in Gefahr schweben *to be in danger.*
Schwede *m. Swede.*
schwedisch *Swedish.*
Schwefel *m. sulphur.*
schweigen *n. silence.*
schweigsam *silent, taciturn.*
Schweigsamkeit *f. taciturnity.*
Schwein *n. pig, hog.*
Schweinebraten *m. roast pork.*
Schweinefleisch *n. pork.*
Schweiss *m. sweat, perspiration.*
Schweisstropfen *m. bead of perspiration.*
Schweizer *m. Swiss.*
schweizerisch *Swiss.*
schweigen *to keep silent.*
Schwelle *f. threshold.*
schwellen *to swell, rise, grow.*
Schwellung *f. swelling, tumor, growth.*
SCHWER *heavy, hard, difficult, serious, strong; heavily, seriously, strongly.*
etwas schwer nehmen *to take something to heart.*
schwer fallen (halten) *to be difficult.*
ein schweres Geld kosten *to cost a lot of money.*
schweren Herzens *with a heavy heart.*
schwer beleidigen *to deeply offend.*
schwerblütig *melancholy.*
schwerfällig *phlegmatic*
Schwerfälligkeit *f. heaviness, clumsiness.*
Schwergewicht *n. heavyweight.*
schwerhörig *hard of hearing.*
Schwerhörigkeit *f. deafness.*
Schwerkraft *f. force of gravity.*
Schwerkriegsbeschädigte *m. disabled soldier.*
schwerlich *hardly, scarcely, with difficulty.*
Schwermut *f. melancholy, sadness.*
schwermütig *melancholy, sad.*

Schwerpunkt *m. center of gravity.*
Schwert *n. sword.*
Schwerverbrecher *m. criminal, gangster.*
schwerwiegend *serious, grave.*
SCHWESTER *f. sister, hospital nurse.*
schwesterlich *sisterly.*
Schwiegereltern *pl. parents-in-law.*
Schwiegermutter *f. mother-in-law.*
Schwiegersohn *m. son-in-law.*
Schwiegertochter *f. daughter-in-law.*
Schwiegervater *m. father-in-law.*
schwierig *difficult.*
Schwierigkeit *f. difficulty.*
Schwimmanstalt *f. swimming-pool.*
SCHWIMMEN *to swim, float, sail.*
Schwimmhose *f. swimming trunks.*
Schwimmweste *f. life jacket.*
Schwindel *m. swindle; fraud; dizziness.*
Schwindelanfall *m. fit of dizziness.*
schwindeln *to swindle, cheat; be dizzy, to tell a lie.*
Mir schwindelt. *I feel dizzy.*
Schwindler *m. swindler.*
schwindlig *dizzy.*
schwingen *to swing, sway, oscillate, vibrate.*
Schwingung *f. oscillation.*
Schwips *m. Smack! Slap!*
einen Schwips haben *to be tipsy.*
schwören *to swear, take an oath.*
schwül *sultry, muggy.*
Schwung *f. swing (push), vault.*
in Schwung bringen *to set going.*
im Schwung sein *to be in full swing.*
schwungvoll *energetic.*
Schwur *m. oath.*
Schwur leisten *to take an oath.*
SECHS *six.*
SECHSTE *sixth.*
SECHZEHN *sixteen.*
SECHZEHNTE *sixteenth.*
SECHZIG *sixty.*
SECHZIGSTE *sixtieth.*
See *m. lake.*
SEE *f. sea, seaside.*
an die See gehen *to go to the seaside.*
in See stechen *or* gehen *to set sail; to put to sea.*
Seebad *n. seaside resort.*
seefest *seaworthy.*
seefest sein *to be a good sailor.*
Seehund *m. seal.*
seekrank *seasick.*
seekrank sein *to be seasick.*
Seekrankheit *f. seasickness.*
SEELE *f. soul, mind, spirit.*
jemandem aus der Seele sprechen *to express a person's thoughts.*
Sie sind mit Leib und Seele dabei. *They are in it with heart and soul.*

seelisch *spiritual, mental, emotional.*
Seemann *m. sailor.*
Seemeile *f. nautical mile (1.852 kilometers).*
Seenot *f. distress (at sea).*
Seewasser *n. sea-water.*
Segel *n. sail, canvas.*
Segelboot *n. sailboat.*
Segelflugzeug *n. glider.*
segeln *to sail.*
Segelschiff *n. sailboat.*
Segen *m. blessing.*
segnen *to bless.*
SEHEN *to see, look, behold, contemplate.*
  darauf sehen *to watch carefully.*
  gut sehen *to have good eyesight.*
  Ich kenne sie nur vom Sehen. *I know her only by sight.*
  schlecht sehen *to have poor eyesight.*
  sehen nach *to look after.*
  sich sehen lassen *to appear.*
  Ich kann sie nicht sehen. *I can't stand the sight of her.*
  ihm auf die Finger sehen *to watch him closely.*
  nach der Uhr sehen *to look at the clock.*
  sehen auf *to look at, to look over, to face, to see it.*
sehenswert *worth seeing, remarkable.*
Sehenswürdigkeit *f. point of interest.*
Sehkraft *f. eyesight.*
Sehne *f. sinew, ligament.*
SEHNEN *to long, yearn for.*
  sich sehnen nach *to yearn for.*
sehnlich *ardent, longing.*
Sehnsucht *f. longing, yearning.*
sehnsüchtig *longing, yearning.*
SEHR *very; very much.*
  Bitte sehr. *You are quite welcome.*
seicht *shallow.*
SEIDE *f. silk.*
Seidenpapier *n. tissue paper.*
Seidenraupe *f. silkworm.*
seidig *silky.*
Seife *f. soap.*
Seifenflocken *pl. soapflakes.*
Seifenpulver *n. soap powder.*
Seil *n. rope, line.*
Seilbahn *f. cable.*
Sein *n. being.*
SEIN *to be, exist.*
  es sei denn, dass . . . *unless.*
SEIN *poss. adj. his, her, its.*
SEIN(ER, –E, –ES) *poss. pron. his, hers.*
  die Seinen *one's own people.*
seinetwegen *because of him, for his sake.*
SEIT *prep. (with dat.) since, for.*
  Ich warte seit einer Stunde. *I have been waiting for an hour.*
  seit kurzer Zeit *lately.*

  seit meiner Ankunft *since my return.*
  Seit Wann? *Since when?*
Seitdem *conj. since, since that time.*
SEITE *f. side, page, party, member.*
  auf die Seite *aside, away.*
  auf die Seite gehen *to step aside.*
  Schwache Seite *weakness.*
  Seite an Seite *side by side.*
  zur Seite stehen *to stand by, help.*
  auf dieser Seite *on this side.*
  auf meiner Seite stehen *to be on my side.*
  nach allen Seiten *in all directions.*
Seitenflügel *m. side, aisle, wing.*
Seitenstrasse *f. side street.*
Seitenzahl *f. number of pages.*
seither *since then.*
seitlich *lateral, collateral.*
seitwärts *sideways, aside.*
Sekt *m. champagne.*
Sekretär *m. (–in, f.) secretary.*
SEKUNDE *f. second (time, music, fencing).*
Sekundenzeiger *m. second hand (on clocks).*
selbe (der, die, das) *same.*
selber *self.*
  ich selber *myself.*
SELBST 1. *adj. or pron. self.*
  Ich habe es selbst getan. *I did it myself.*
  Das versteht sich von selbst. *That goes without saying.*
  2. *adv. even.*
  Ich habe alles zu Hause gelassen, selbst mein Geld. *I left everything at home, even my money.*
selbständig *independent.*
Selbstbeherrschung *f. self-control.*
selbstbewusst *self-assured.*
Selbstbewusstsein *n. self-assurance.*
Selbsterhaltung *f. self-preservation.*
Selbsterkenntnis *f. self-knowledge.*
selbstgefällig *self-satisfied, complacent.*
Selbstgefühl *n. self-respect.*
Selbstgespräch *m. monologue, soliloquy.*
selbstherrlich *autocratic.*
Selbstkostenpreis *m. cost price.*
selbstlos *unselfish, disinterested.*
Selbstlosigkeit *f. unselfishness.*
Selbstmörder *m. suicide.*
selbstredend *self-evident, obvious.*
Selbstsucht *f. selfishness, egoism.*
selbstsüchtig *selfish, egoistic.*
SELBSTVERSTÄNDLICH *evident.*
Selbstvertrauen *n. self-confidence.*
selbstzufrieden *self-satisfied.*
selig *blessed.*
Seligkeit *f. happiness, bliss.*
Sellerie *f. celery.*
SELTEN *rare, unusual.*
Seltenheit *f. rarity, scarcity.*
SELTSAM *strange, unusual, odd.*

Selterwasser *n. soda-water.*
Semester *n. term, session.*
Seminar *n. training college.*
Senat *m. senate.*
senden *to send, broadcast, transmit.*
Sender *m. transmitter.*
Senderaum *m. studio.*
Sendung *f. mission, transmission.*
Senf *m. mustard.*
Senkel *m. lace (shoe).*
senken *to lower, dip, sink.*
  sich senken *to settle.*
sensationell *sensational.*
Sensationslust *f. desire to cause a sensation.*
Sentimentalität *f. sentimentality.*
SEPTEMBER *m. September.*
Serie *f. series, issue.*
Service *n. service set, attendance.*
Servierbrett *n. tray.*
servieren *to serve, wait at a table.*
Serviette *f. table napkin.*
Sessel *m. armchair.*
sesshaft *settled, established.*
SETZEN *to put, set, place, fix, erect.*
  sich setzen *to sit down.*
  alles daran setzen *to risk everything.*
  gesetzt den Fall, dass *suppose that.*
  in Frieheit setzen *to set free.*
  Setzen Sie sich! *Sit down!*
  sich etwas in den Kopf setzen *to get an idea into one's head.*
  sich in Verbindung setzen mit *to get in touch with.*
  unter Druck setzen *to put pressure on.*
  ausser Gebrauch setzen *to supersede, discard.*
  ausser Kraft setzen *to invalidate.*
  in Bewegung setzen *to set into motion.*
  in die Zeitung setzen *to advertise in the newspapers.*
  übers Wasser setzen *to ferry across.*
  sich zur Ruhe setzen *to retire.*
Seuche *f. epidemic, pestilence.*
seufzen *to sigh.*
sezieren *to dissect.*
SICH *oneself, himself, herself, itself, yourself, yourselves, themselves, each other, one another.*
  sich selbst *itself, oneself, etc.*
SICHER *secure, safe, certain, positive, surely.*
  aus sicherer Hand *on good authority.*
  seiner Sache sicher sein *to be certain of a thing.*
  sicher gehen *to be on the safe side.*
  sicher rechnen auf *to have complete confidence in.*
  sicher stellen *to put in safe keeping.*
  sicher wissen *to know for certain.*

Sicherheit *f. safety, security.*
  in Sicherheit bringen *to secure.*
  Sicherheit leisten *to give security.*
sicherheitshalber *for safety's sake.*
Sicherheitsnadel *f. safety-pin.*
Sicherheitsschloss *n. safety-lock.*
sicherlich *surely, certainly.*
sichern *to protect.*
Sicherung *f. protection.*
SICHT *f. sight, visibility.*
  sichtbar *visible, apparent.*
sichten *to sight; to sift, sort.*
SIE (sie) *pers. pron. 3rd pers. sing. (fem. nom. & acc.); 3rd pers. pl. (m., f., n., nom. & acc.) she, her, it; they, them.*
Sieb *n. colander, strainer.*
sieben *to sift, strain.*
SIEBEN *seven.*
SIEBENTE *seventh.*
SIEBZEHNTE *seventeenth.*
SIEBZIG *seventy.*
siebzigst *seventieth.*
siech *sickly, ailing, infirm.*
siedeln *to settle, colonize.*
SIEG *m. victory, triumph.*
Siegel *n. seal.*
Sieger *m. victor, winner.*
siegesgewiss *certain or confident of victory.*
siegreich *victorious.*
Signal *n. signal.*
Signalanlage *f. signaling system.*
Signalhupe *f. siren.*
signalisieren *to signal.*
Signatur *f. mark, sign, characteristic, stamp.*
Silbe *f. syllable.*
Silber *n. silver.*
Silbergeschirr *n. silver plate, silverware.*
Silberpapier *n. silver paper, tin foil.*
Silvesterabend *m. New Year's Eve.*
SINGEN *to sing.*
Singstimme *f. singing voice, vocal part.*
sinken *to sink, drop, fall.*
SINN *m. sense, faculty, mind, understanding, intellect.*
  anderen Sinnes werden *to change one's mind.*
  in gewissem Sinn *in a way, in a sense.*
  im Sinn haben *to intend.*
  sich etwas aus dem Sinn schlagen *to dismiss a thing from one's mind.*
Sinnbild *n. symbol, emblem, allegory.*
sinnbildlich *symbolic.*
sinnen *to think, reflect, meditate.*
  sinnen auf *to plot, devise.*
sinnlich *sensual, sensuous, material.*
sinnlos *senseless, absurd.*
Sinnlosigkeit *f. senselessness, foolishness.*
sinnreich *sensible, clever.*
Sirene *f. siren.*

Sitte *f. custom, habit.*

Sittengesetz *n. moral law, moral code.*

Sittenlehre *f. moral, philosophy, ethics.*

sittenlos *immoral, dissolute.*

sittlich *moral.*

sittsam *modest.*

Sittsamkeit *f. modesty, decency.*

SITZ *m. seat, residence.*

SITZEN *to sit, fit, adhere.*

   etwas auf sich sitzen lassen *to put up with.*

   sitzen bleiben *to remain seated; to be left back (school).*

   sitzen lassen *to leave.*

   im Gefängnis sitzen *to be in jail.*

Sitzgelegenheit *f. seating accommodation.*

Sitzplatz *m. seat.*

Skandal *m. scandal.*

Skelett *n. skeleton.*

skeptisch *sceptical.*

Ski *m. ski.*

   skilaufen *to ski.*

Skiläufer *m. skier.*

Skispringen *n. ski-jumping.*

Skizze *f. sketch.*

skizzieren *to sketch.*

Sklave *m. slave.*

sklavisch *slavish, servile.*

Skrupel *m. scruple.*

SO *so, thus, in this way, like that, anyhow.*

   Ach so! *Oh, I see!*

   So? *Is that so? Indeed? Really?*

   so ... auch, *however.*

   so bald als *as soon as.*

   so ... doch *yet, nevertheless.*

   so ein *such a.*

   so etwas *a thing like that.*

   so gut wie *as if, practically.*

   so oder so *this way or that way.*

   so ... so *though ... yet.*

   so wie *as, the way*

Socke *f. sock.*

sodann *then.*

sodass *so that.*

soeben *just, just now.*

sofern *so far as.*

sofort *immediately, at once.*

sogar *even.*

sogenannt *so-called.*

sogleich *at once, immediately.*

Sohle *f. sole.*

sohlen *to resole.*

SOHN *m. son.*

solange *so, as long as.*

SOLCH *such, the same.*

   solch ein *such a.*

Soldat *m. soldier.*

Solist (–in) *m. soloist. (female)*

SOLLEN *ought, shall, to have to, must, be*

supposed to, be said to.

   Du sollst nicht töten. *Thou shalt not kill.*

   Die Schüler sollen fleissig sein. *Students must be industrious.*

   Er soll ein Millionär sein. *They say he is a millionaire.*

   Sollte er nicht zu Hause sein? *Is it possible that he is not at home?*

   Sollte er telefonieren? *Should he telephone?*

   Was soll das heissen? *What is the meaning of that?*

   Was soll es bedeuten? *What does that mean?*

   Was sollte ich dagegen machen? *How could I help it?*

somit *consequently.*

SOMMER *m. summer.*

   Sommernachtstraum *m. Midsummer Night's Dream*

Sommerfrische *f. health-resort.*

Sommersprosse *f. freckle.*

Sommerzeit *f. summertime.*

Sondereausgabe *f. special edition.*

SONDERBAR *strange, peculiar.*

sonderbarenweise *strange to say.*

sondergleichen *unequaled, unique.*

Sonderling *m. strange character.*

Sondermeldung *f. special announcement.*

SONDERN *but (in a negative sentence).*

   Ich wollte niche ausgehen, sondern zu Hause bleiben. *I did not want to go out but to stay home.*

   nicht nur ... sondern auch *not only ... but also.*

   Sie war nicht nur schön, sondem auch gut. *She was not only beautiful but kind as well.*

SONNABEND *m. Saturday.*

SONNE *f. sun.*

(sich) sonnen *to sun oneself, bask.*

Sonnenaufgang *m. sunrise.*

Sonnenblume *f. sunflower.*

Sonnenbrand *m. sunburn.*

Sonnenbrille *f. sunglasses.*

Sonnenstrahl *m. sunbeam.*

Sonnenuntergang *m. sunset.*

sonnig *sunny.*

SONNTAG *m. Sunday.*

sonntags *on Sunday.*

SONST *else, moreover, besides, otherwise, formerly.*

   Sonst noch etwas? *Anything else?*

   sonst jemand *anybody else.*

   sonst nichts *nothing else.*

   Sonst niemand? *No one else?*

   sonst und jetzt *formerly and now.*

   Was konnte ich sonst tun? *What else could I do?*

Wenn es sonst nichts wäre! *If that were all it was!*

wie sonst *as usual.*

sonstwie *in some other way.*

sonstwo *elsewhere.*

Sopran *m. soprano.*

Sopranistin *f. soprano singer.*

SORGE *f. grief, sorrow, anxiety, worry, trouble, care.*

einem Sorgen machen *to worry someone.*

sich Sorgen machen *to worry.*

Sorge tragen *to see about something.*

SORGEN *to care for, look after, take care of, provide.*

sich sorgen um *to be concerned about; to see to, to take responsibility.*

sorgen für *to look after.*

Sorgenkind *n. problem child.*

sorgenvoll *worried.*

Sorgfalt *f. carefulness, care, accuracy.*

sorgfältig *careful, painstaking.*

sorglich *thoughtful.*

sorglos *carefree, careless.*

Sorglosigkeit *f. lightheartedness, thoughtlessness.*

SORTE *f. kind, sort, brand, grade.*

sortieren *to sort, arrange.*

SOVIEL *as much as, so far as.*

soweit *as far as.*

sowenig *as little as.*

sowie *as soon as.*

sowieso *anyway, anyhow.*

sozial *social.*

Sozialismus *m. Socialism.*

Sozialist *m. Socialist.*

sozialistisch *socialistic.*

Sozialwissenschaft *f. sociology.*

Sozius *m. partner.*

spähen *to be on the look out, patrol.*

Spalier bilden/stehen *to form an honor guard; to line.*

Spalt *m. crack, slot, gap.*

spalten *to split, divide.*

sich spalten *to split.*

Spaltholz *n. firewood sticks.*

Spange *f. buckle, brooch.*

Spanier *m (–in, f.) Spaniard*

spanisch *Spanish.*

Spanisch *n. Spanish (language).*

Spanne *f. short space of time, margin.*

SPANNEN *to put up, stretch, pull, tighten, grip, clamp.*

gespannt sein *to be anxious, curious.*

Ich bin auf die Antwort gespannt. *I am curious to know the answer.*

das Pferd hinter den Wagen spannen. *to put the cart before the horse.*

spannend *fascinating, absorbing, thrilling.*

Spannung *f. tension, strain, suspense, voltage.*

Sparbüchse *f. money-box (piggy bank).*

Spareinlage *f. savings deposit.*

Spargel *m. asparagus.*

Sparkasse *f. savings bank.*

spärlich *scarce, frugal, thin, scanty.*

Spärlichkeit *f. scarcity.*

SPARSAM *economical, thrifty.*

Sparsamkeit *f. economy, thrift.*

Spass *m. joke, fun.*

zum Spass *for fun.*

spassen *to joke.*

Spassmacher *m. joker.*

SPÄT *late, belated, backward.*

Besser spät als nie. *Better late than never.*

zu spät kommen *to be late.*

Wie spät ist es? *What time is it?*

Spaten *m. spade.*

später *later, afterwards.*

späterhin *later on.*

spätestens *at the latest.*

Spatz *m. sparrow.*

SPAZIEREN *to walk about, stroll.*

spazieren gehen *to go for a walk.*

Spazierfahrt *f. drive, pleasure trip*

Spaziergang *m. walk.*

Spaziergänger *m. walker, stroller.*

Speck *m. bacon.*

Speckschwarte *f. rind of bacon.*

Spediteur *m. mover, shipper, forwarding agent.*

Speicher *m. silo, granary, warehouse.*

speichern *to store.*

SPEISE *f. food, meal.*

Speiseeis *n. ice cream.*

Speisekarte *f. menu.*

Speisesaal *m. dining room.*

Speisewagen *m. dining car.*

Spekulant *m. speculator.*

spekulieren *to speculate.*

Spende *f. gift, present, donation.*

spenden *to dispense, bestow, administer.*

Spender *m. giver, donor, benefactor.*

spendieren *to give freely, lavishly.*

Sperre *f. gate, closing, barrier.*

sperrangelweit *wide open.*

sperren *to close, shut, block, barricade.*

ins Gefängnis sperren *to put in prison.*

Sperrklinke *f. safety catch.*

Sperrholz *n. plywood.*

Spesen *f. pl. charges, expenses.*

Spezialarzt *n. specialist.*

spezialisieren *to specialize.*

speziell *special, particular.*

spezifisch *specific.*

spezifizieren *to specify.*

Spiegel *m. mirror.*

Spiegelbild n. reflected image.
spiegelglatt smooth as a mirror.
spiegeln to shine, glitter.
  sich spiegeln to be reflected.
SPIEL n. game, deck of cards, playing, play,
    sport, touch (music).
  auf dem Spiel stehen to be at stake.
  aufs Spiel setzen to risk.
  Lassen Sie mich aus dem Spiel. Leave me
    out of this.
  leichtes Spiel haben to have no
    difficulties.
  seine Hand im Spiel haben to have a
    finger in the pie.
  sein Spiel treiben mit to make game of.
  Ich bin am Spiel. It's my turn.
  ihm freies Spiel lassen to give him a
    (free) hand.
Spielautomat m. gambling machine.
Spielbank f. gambling casino.
Spielergebnis n. score (result of play).
Spieldose f. musical box.
SPIELEN to play, act, perform, gamble,
    pretend.
  Was spielt man heute abend? What's
    playing tonight?
Spielerei f. trifle.
Spielplan m. program, repertory.
Spielsachen pl. toys.
Spielverderber m. kill-joy.
Spielzeug n. toy.
Spiess m. lance, spear, pike.
Spiessbürger m. bourgeois, narrow minded,
    commonplace.
Spinat m. spinach.
Spinne f. spider.
spinnen to spin.
Spinngewebe n. cobweb.
Spinnrad n. spinning wheel.
Spion m. spy.
Spionage f. spying, espionage.
Spionageabwehr f. counterespionage.
spionieren to spy.
Spiritus m. spirits, alcohol.
Spital n. hospital.
SPITZ pointed, sharp, acute, caustic.
Spitze f. point, tip (tongue), top, head, lace,
    sarcasm.
  etwas auf die Spitze treiben to carry to
    extremes.
SPITZEN to sharpen, point.
  seine Ohren spitzen to prick one's ears.
Spitzenleistung f. record, maximum.
Spitzenlohn m. maximum pay.
spitzfindig pointed, sharp, sarcastic, subtle.
Spitzfindigkeit f. subtlety.
spitzig pointed, sharp, sarcastic.
Spitzname m. nickname.
Splitter m. splinter, chip, fragment.

splittern to splinter, split.
spontan spontaneous.
Sporn m. spur.
Sport m. sport
  Sport treiben to go in for sports.
Sportfunk m. radio sports news.
Sportler (–in) m. sportsman (woman).
sportlich sporting, athletic.
Sportname m. nickname.
Spott m. mockery, ridicule.
spotten to mock, make fun, defy.
spöttisch mocking, scoffing, sarcastic.
SPRACHE f. language, speech, talk.
  zur Sprache bringen to bring up a
    subject.
  zur Sprache kommen to be mentioned.
  gehobene Sprache elevated diction.
Sprachfertigkeit f. fluency (of speech).
sprachgewandt fluent
sprachkundig proficient in languages.
Sprachlehre f. grammar.
sprachlich linguistic.
sprachlos speechless.
Sprachschatz m. vocabulary.
Sprachschnitzer m. grammatical blunder,
    mistake.
Sprachstörung f. speech defect.
SPRECHEN to speak, talk, say, converse,
    discuss.
  Der Herr Doktor ist nicht zu
    sprechen. The doctor is busy.
  gut zu sprechen sein auf to be kindly
    disposed to.
  Ich bin für niemanden zu sprechen. I am
    in to no one.
  sich herumsprechen to be whispered
    about town.
  Sie sprechen nicht miteinander. They are
    not on speaking terms.
  Sprechen Sie Deutsch? Do you speak
    German?
  Sprechen Sie langsam, bitte. Please speak
    slowly.
  unter uns gesprochen between us.
  das Urteil sprechen to pronounce
    judgment.
  zu sprechen kommen auf to come to
    speak of.
  Wen wünschen Sie zu sprechen? Whom
    do you want to see?
Sprecher m. speaker.
Sprechstunde f. office hours, office (doctor).
Sprechstundenhilfe f. doctor's receptionist.
Sprechweise f. diction.
Sprechzimmer n. consulting room.
sprengen to burst, blow up, blast, spray.
Sprengung f. blowing up, explosion.
Sprichwort n. proverb.
Springbrunnen m. fountain.

SPRINGEN *to jump, skip, spring, play.*
> Das ist der springende Punkt. *That is the crucial point.*
> in die Augen springen *to be obvious.*

spritzen *to spray, splash, sprinkle.*

spröde *brittle, hard, inflexible.*

Sprosse *f. sprout, sprig, offspring.*

Sprössling *m. sprout, shoot, offshoot, son (heir).*

Spruch *m. aphorism, saying.*

spruchreif *ripe for decision.*

sprudeln *to bubble up.*

sprühen *to spark.*

Sprühregen *m. drizzle, drizzling rain.*

SPRUNG *m. leap, jump, crack.*
> Es ist nur ein Sprung von meinem Haus. *It is only a stone's throw from my house.*
> Ich war auf dem Sprung auszugehen. *I was just going to leave.*

Sprungschanze *f. ski-jump.*

spucken *to spit.*
> Spucken Verboten! *No spitting!*

Spülbecken *n. washtub.*

spülen *to rinse.*

Spülwasser *n. dishwater.*

SPUR *f. trace, trail, track, footprint.*
> einem auf die Spur kommen *to be on a person's tracks.*
> Keine Spur! *Not in the least!*
> keine Spur von *no trace of.*

spüren *to feel, sense, experience.*
> spüren nach *to track, follow.*

spurlos *trackless.*

Spürsinn haben *to have a flair.*

(sich) sputen *to hurry up.*

STAAT *m. state, government, pomp, parade, show.*
> in vollem Staat *in full dress.*
> Staat machen *to show off.*

staatlich *public, political.*

Staatsaktion *f. government undertaking.*

Staatsangehörige *m. & f. subject, national.*

Staatsangehörigkeit *f. nationality, citizenship.*

Staatsanwalt *m. public prosecutor.*

Staatsbeamte(r) *m. civil servant.*

Staatsbesitz *m. state/public property.*

Staatsgebäude *n. public building.*

Staatsdienst *m. civil service.*

Staatsmann *m. statesman, politician.*

staatsmännisch *statesmanlike.*

Stab *m. stick, rod, bat, condemn.*
> den Stab brechen über *to condemn.*

stabil *stable.*

stabilisieren *to stabilize.*

Stachel *m. thorn, prickle, sting, spur.*

Stachelbeere *f. gooseberry.*

Stacheldraht *m. barbed wire.*

Stadion *n. stadium, arena.*

Stadium *n. phase, stage.*

STADT *f. town, city.*

Stadtbahn *f. city railway.*

stadtbekannt *known all over town.*

Städter (–in) *m. townsman (woman)*

Stadtgespräch *n. local call.*

städtisch *municipal, urban.*

Stadtteil *m. quarter (of a town).*

Stahl *m. steel.*

stählern *of steel.*

Stahlguss *m. steel.*

Stall *m. stable.*

Stamm *m. stem, root, trunk.*

Stammbaum *m. genealogical tree.*

stammeln *to stammer.*

stammen *to spring from, come from.*

Stammgast *m. regular customer.*

Stammhalter *m. eldest son and heir.*

stämmig *sturdy, strong, vigorous.*

stampfen *to stamp, mash, crush.*

Stand *m. standing position.*
> einen schweren Stand haben *to have a tough job.*
> einen guten Stand haben *to be well thought of.*
> Stand der Dinge *State of affairs.*

Standbild *n. statute.*

Ständchen *n. serenade.*

Standesamt *n. registrar's office.*

Standesbeamte *m. registrar.*

Standesehe *f. marriage for position or rank.*

standesgemäss *in accordance with one's rank.*

Standesgericht *n. court martial.*

Standesunterschied *m. difference of class.*

standhaft *steady, constant.*

standhalten *to hold firm.*

ständig *permanent.*

Standort *m. station, position.*

Standpunkt *m. point of view.*

Standuhr *f. grandfather's clock.*

Stange *f. pole, bar, perch.*
> eine Stange Gold *a bar of gold.*
> von der Stange *ready-made.*
> ein Anzug von der Stange *a suit off the rack.*

Stanze *f. stanza.*

stanzen *to stamp.*

STARK *strong, stout, considerable, hard.*
> Das ist denn doch zu stark! *That is too much!*
> stark auftragen *to exaggerate, boast.*
> starke Erkältung *bad cold.*
> starkes Gedächtnis *good memory.*
> starker Regen *heavy rain.*
> stark besetzt *well attended.*
> stark übertrieben *grossly exaggerated.*

Stärke *f. strength, force, vigor, intensity, energy, violence.*
stärken *to strengthen, fortify, starch, confirm.*
Starkstrom *m. power current.*
Starkstromleitung *f. power-circuit.*
starr *stiff, hard, paralyzed.*
  starren vor Staunen *to be dumbfounded.*
starren *to stare, be, numb.*
starrköpfig *stubborn.*
Starrsinn *m. obstinacy.*
Start *m. start.*
Startbahn *f. runway.*
starten *to start.*
Station *f. station, stop, ward.*
  freie Station *free board and lodging.*
Stationsarzt *m. resident physician.*
Stationsvorsteher *m. station master.*
Statistik *f. statistics.*
statistisch *statistical.*
STÄTTE *f. place, spot.*
STATT (anstatt) *prep. (gen.) instead of.*
stattfinden *to take place.*
stattgeben *to permit, allow.*
statthaft *admissible, legal.*
stattlich *stately, magnificent, imposing.*
Stattlichkeit *f. dignity, magnificence.*
Statue *f. statute.*
Staub *m. dust, powder.*
  in den Staub ziehen *to depreciate.*
  Staub wischen *to dust.*
staubig *dusty.*
Staublappen *m. duster.*
Staubsauger *m. vacuum-cleaner.*
staunen *to be surprised.*
STECHEN *to stick, bite, sting.*
  sich stechen *to prick oneself.*
  in die Augen stechen *to take one's fancy.*
Stechfliege *f. horse-fly.*
Steckdose *f. wall-plug, socket.*
STECKEN *to stick, pin up, fasten, fix, plant, stuff.*
  Dahinter steckt etwas. *There is something behind this.*
  in Brand stecken *to set fire.*
steckenbleiben *to be stuck.*
Steckenpferd *n. hobby, pet project.*
Stecker *m. plug.*
Stecknadel *f. pin.*
STEHEN *to stand, stop, be, suit, become.*
  gut stehen *to be becoming.* (Rot steht ihr. *Red is becoming to her.*)
  gut stehen mit *to be on good terms with*
  geschrieben stehen *to be written.*
  Das Thermometer steht auf Null. *The thermometer reads zero.*
  Es steht bei ihr. *It's up to her.*
  im Verdacht stehen *to be under suspicion.*
  in einem Amte stehen *to hold an office.*

stehenbleiben *to stop, remain standing.*
stehend *standing, stationary, permanent.*
  stehenden Fusses *at once.*
stehenlassen *to leave (standing).*
Stehlampe *f. floor lamp.*
STEHLEN *to steal, rob, take away.*
steif *stiff.*
Steig *m. path.*
STEIGEN *to climb, go up, ascend, rise, increase.*
  zu Kopf steigen *to go to one's head.*
steigend *growing, increasing.*
steigern *to raise, increase, intensify.*
  sich steigern in *to intensify, work up.*
Steigerung *f. raising, increase, gradation, climax.*
steil *steep, precipitous.*
Steilhang *m. steep slope.*
STEIN *m. stone, rock, jewel.*
  Das hat den Stein ins Rollen gebracht. *That started the ball rolling.*
  Das ist nur ein Tropfen auf den heissen Stein. *That's only a drop in the bucket.*
  einen Stein im Brett haben bei *to be in favor with.*
  Mit fällt ein Stein vom Herzen! *I feel so relieved!*
  Stein des Anstosses *stumbling block.*
  Stein und Bein schwören *to swear by all the gods.*
Steinbruch *m. quarry.*
steinern *of stone.*
steinhart *as hard as stone.*
steinig *stony, rocky.*
steinreich *very wealthy.*
Steinzeit *f. Stone Age.*
STELLE *f. spot, place, position, situation, passage.*
  auf der Stelle *on the spot.*
  offene Stelle *vacancy.*
  von der Stelle kommen *to make progress.*
  zur Stelle sein *to be present.*
  an Stelle von *instead of.*
STELLEN *to put, place, set, arrange, regulate, provide, furnish.*
  auf den Kopf stellen *to turn upside down.*
  auf sich selbst gestellt sein *to be dependent on oneself.*
  eine Bedingung stellen *to make a condition.*
  eine Frage stellen *to ask a question.*
  Er ist sehr gut gestellt. *He is very well off.*
  Antrag stellen auf *to apply for.*
  in Dienst stellen *to put into service.*
  auf die Probe stellen *to put to the test.*

etwas in Aussicht stellen *to hold out the prospect of something.*
sich stellen gegen *to oppose.*
sich stellen *to stand.*
kalt stellen *to put in a cool place.*
sich gut stellen mit *to be on good terms with.*
sich stellen zu *to behave toward.*
zur Verfügung stellen *to place at one's disposal.*
Stellenangebot n. *job offer; vacancy.*
Stellengesuch n. *application for a position, situations wanted.*
stellenlos *unemployed.*
Stellennachweis m. *employment reference.*
Stellenvermittlung f. *employment agency.*
STELLUNG f. *position, situation, stand, job.*
Stellung nehmen zu *to express one's opinion.*
Stellungnahme f. *opinion, comment, point of view.*
Stellungsgesuch n. *application for a position.*
stellungslos *unemployed.*
Stellungswechsel m. *change of position.*
Stellvertreter m. *representative.*
Stempel m. *stamp, postmark.*
Stempelkissen n. *ink-pad.*
stempeln *to stamp, mark.*
stenografieren *to write in shorthand.*
stenografisch *stenographic.*
Stenogramm n. *shorthand.*
Stenogramm aufnehmen *to take down in shorthand.*
Stenotypist m. (**–in,** f.) *stenotypist.*
Steppdecke f. *quilt.*
Sterbebett n. *deathbed.*
Sterben n. *death.*
im Sterben liegen *to be dying.*
STERBEN *to die.*
sterblich *mortal.*
sterblich verliebt *madly in love.*
Sterblichkeit f. *death rate.*
steril *sterile.*
sterilisieren *to sterilize.*
Stern m. *star.*
Sternbild n. *constellation.*
Sterndeuter m. *astrologer.*
Sternhimmel m. *starry sky.*
stets *always, forever.*
Steuer n. *rudder, helm, steering wheel.*
Steuer f. *tax.*
Steueraufschlag m. *supplementary tax.*
steuerfrei *tax-free.*
steuern *to steer, pilot, drive.*
steuerpflichtig *subject to taxation.*
Steuerrad n. *steering wheel.*
Steuerzahler m. *taxpayer.*
Stich m. *sting, prick, stitch.*
im Stich lassen *to forsake.*

einen Stich haben *to have a screw loose* (*coll.*).
Stichtag m. *fixed day.*
Stichwort n. *catchword, cue.*
Stiefbruder m. *stepbrother.*
Stiefmutter f. *stepmother.*
Stiefmütterchen n. *pansy.*
Stiefschwester f. *stepsister.*
Stiefsohn m. *stepson.*
Stieftochter f. *stepdaughter.*
Stiefvater m. *stepfather.*
Stier m. *bull.*
Stierkämpfer m. *bullfighter.*
Stift m. *pencil, crayon; charitable institution.*
stiften *to donate; to found, establish.*
Stifter m. *founder; donor.*
Stiftung f. *foundation.*
Stil m. *style, manner.*
Stilgefühl n. *stylish sense.*
STILL *still, quiet, silent, secret.*
Seien Sie still! *Be quiet!*
stille Jahreszeit *off-season, slow season.*
stille Liebe *secret love.*
bei stiller Nacht *in the dead of the night.*
sich still verhalten *to keep still/quiet.*
STILLE f. *silence, calm, quietude, peace.*
im Stillen *secretly.*
in aller Stille *privately, secretly.*
stillen *to quiet, appease, satisfy, quench, nurse.*
stillhalten *to keep still.*
Stilleben n. *still life* (*art*).
stilllegen *to shut down, close, discontinue.*
stillschweigen *to be silent.*
stillschweigend *silent.*
Stillstand m. *standstill, stop.*
stillstehen *to stand still, stop.*
Still gestanden! *Attention!*
stilvoll *in good style, taste.*
Stimmabgabe f. *vote, voting.*
stimmberechtigt *entitled to vote.*
STIMME f. *voice, part, comment, vote.*
Stimme abgeben *to vote.*
STIMMEN *to tune, vote, be correct, impress someone, influence someone's mood.*
Das stimmt! *That is correct!*
Werden Sie dafür oder dagegen stimmen? *Are you going to vote for or against?*
Stimmrecht n. *right to vote.*
STIMMUNG f. *tuning, pitch, key, mood, humor, impression, atmosphere.*
Stimmung machen für *to create a mood for, to make propaganda for.*
Stimmungsmensch m. *moody person.*
stimmungsvoll *impressive, appealing.*
Stimmzettel m. *ballot.*
Stirn f. *forehead, front, imprudence.*
die Stirn runzeln *to frown.*

einem die Stirne bieten *to show a bold front.*

Stock *m. stick, rod, cane, floor (story).*
über Stock und Stein *up hill and down dale.*
Welcher Stock? *What floor?*
stockdumm *utterly stupid.*
stocken *to stop, stand still.*
ins Stocken geraten *to get tied up.*
im Reden stocken *to break down, hesitate.*
stock dunkel *pitch dark.*
stockfinster *pitch-dark.*
Stockfisch *m. dried cod.*
Stockwerk *n. story, floor.*
Stoff *m. matter, substance.*
stöhnen *to groan.*
stolpern *to stumble, trip over.*
stolz *proud.*
stolz sein auf *to be proud of.*
stopfen *to darn, fill, stuff.*
Stopfgarn *n. darning thread.*
Stopfnadel *f. darning needle.*
stoppen *to stop.*
Stoppuhr *f. stop-watch.*
Stöpsel *m. stopper, cork.*
stöpseln *to cork.*
Storch *m. stork.*
STÖREN *to disturb, trouble, inconvenience.*
Nicht stören! *Do not disturb!*
gestörte Leitung *faulty electrical line.*
störrisch *stubborn.*
Störung *f. disturbance, upset.*
geistige Störung *mental disorder.*
Stoss *m. push, poke, pile, jerk, shock.*
stossen *to push, shove, hit, kick, knock.*
stossen auf *to run into.*
Stossstange *f. bumper (on a car).*
stottern *to shutter, stammer.*
Strafanstalt *f. penitentiary.*
strafbar *liable to punishment.*
Strafe *f. punishment, penalty, fine.*
bei Strafe von *on pain of.*
strafen *to punish.*
Straferlass *m. amnesty.*
straff *stretched, tense, tight, strict.*
straffällig *punishable.*
straffen *to tighten.*
straffrei *exempt from punishment, unpunished.*
Strafgefangene *m. convict.*
Strafgericht *n. criminal court.*
sträflich *criminal, punishable.*
Strafmassnahme *f. sanction.*
Strafporto *n. extra postage, surcharge.*
Strafprozess *m. criminal case.*
strafwürdig *punishable.*
STRAHL *m. ray, beam, stream.*
strahlen *to radiate, beam, shine.*

stramm *tight, close.*
stramm stehen *to stand at attention.*
STRAND *m. seashore, beach, strand.*
Strandbad *n. seaside, resort.*
stranden *to run around or ashore.*
Strandschuhe *pl. beach shoes.*
STRANG *m. rope, cord, line.*
am gleichen Strang ziehen *to act in concert.*
an einem Strang ziehen *to act together.*
über die Stränge schlagen *to kick over the traces.*
wenn alle Stränge reissen *if the worst comes to the worst.*
Strapaze *f. fatigue.*
strapazieren *to tire, exhaust.*
STRASSE *f. street, highway, road.*
an der Strasse *by the wayside.*
auf der Strasse *in the street.*
Strassenarbeiter *m. roadman.*
Strassenbahn *f. tram, streetcar.*
Strassenfeger *m. street cleaner.*
Strassenübergang *m. pedestrian crossing.*
Strassenverstopfung *f. traffic congestion, traffic jam.*
sträuben *to ruffle up, bristle.*
Strauch *m. shrub, bush.*
streben *to endeavor, aspire, aim at.*
Streber *m. climber, careerist.*
Strecke *f. distance, way, route, tract.*
auf freier Strecke *on the road.*
strecken *to stretch, extend, stretch out.*
die Waffen strecken *to lay down arms.*
sich strecken *to stretch.*
Streich *m. stroke, blow.*
einem einen Streich spielen *to play a trick on a person.*
streichen *to spread, rub, strike, erase, cancel, paint, wander, stroll, migrate.*
Frisch gestrichen! *Wet paint!*
Streichholz *n. match.*
Streichmusik *f. string music.*
Streichquartett *n. string quartet.*
Streifen *m. stripe, marking.*
streifen *to touch lightly, stripe, brush, wander.*
Streik *m. strike.*
in den Streik treten *to go on strike.*
streiken *to strike.*
STREIT *m. fight, quarrel, dispute.*
streiten *to fight.*
sich streiten *to quarrel.*
Streitfall *m. quarrel, controversy.*
Streitfrage *f. matter in dispute.*
einem etwas streitig machen *to contest a person's right to a thing.*
STRENG *strict, stern, severe.*
streng genommen *strictly speaking.*
Strenge *f. severity, strictness.*

strengläubig *orthodox.*

streuen *to strew, scatter, spread.*

Strich *m. dash, stroke, line, compass point.*

    gegen den Strich   *against the grain.*

    Machen wir einen Strich darunter! *Let's put an end to that.*

    nach Strich und Faden   *thoroughly.*

Strichpunkt *m. semicolon.*

Strick *m. cord, rope.*

    wenn alle Stricke reissen   *if everything else fails.*

stricken *to knit.*

Stroh *n. straw.*

Strohhalm *m. straw (for drinking).*

STROM *m. large river, stream, current.*

    Es regnet in Strömen.   *It's pouring.*

stromabwärts *downstream.*

stromaufwärts *upstream.*

strömen *to stream, flow, pour.*

Strömung *f. current, stream.*

Stromzähler *electric meter.*

Strudel *m. whirlpool; type of pastry.*

Strumpf *m. stocking, sock.*

Strumpfband *n. garter.*

Strumpfhalter *m. garter (woman's).*

struppig *bristly, unkempt.*

STUBE *f. room, chamber, living room.*

Stubenhocker *m. stay-at-home.*

stubenrein *housebroken (of dogs).*

STÜCK *n. piece, play, extract, morsel.*

    aus einem Stück   *all of a piece.*

    aus freien Stücken   *of one's own free will.*

    ein starkes Stück   *a bit stiff.*

    ein Stück Arbeit   *a stiff job.*

    ein Stück mitnehmen   *to give a lift.*

    Er hält grosse Stücke auf ihn.   *He thinks a lot of him.*

    in allen Stücken   *in every respect.*

    zwanzig Stück Vieh   *twenty head of cattle.*

stückweise *piece by piece, by the piece.*

Student *m. (–in, f.) student.*

Studie *f. study, sketch (art).*

studieren *to study.*

Studium *n. study, university education.*

Stufe *f. step, stair, level.*

    auf gleicher Stufe mit   *on a level with.*

stufenweise *by degrees, gradually.*

STUHL *m. chair, seat.*

stumm *dumb, silent, mute.*

Stummheit *f. dumbness.*

stumpf *blunt, obtuse, dull.*

    mit Stumpf und Stiehl   *root and branch.*

Stumpfsinn *m. stupidity.*

stumpfsinning *stupid, dull.*

STUNDE *f. hour; lesson, period.*

stundenlang *for hours.*

Stundenplan *m. timetable.*

Stundenzeiger *m. hour-hand.*

stündlich *hourly.*

STURM *m. storm, gale.*

stürmen *to take by storm.*

stürmisch *stormy, impetuous.*

Sturz *m. fall, crash, tumble, overthrow, collapse.*

    zum Sturz bringen   *to overthrow.*

stürzen *to overthrown, throw down, fall down, plunge into, crash.*

    Nicht stürzen!   *Handle with care!*

Stütze *f. stay, support, help.*

stutzen *to trim, cut short, stop short.*

stützen *to support, base, prop up.*

Stutzer *m. dandy, fop.*

Stützpfeiler *m. pillar, support.*

Stützpunkt *m. base, strong point.*

Subjekt *n. subject.*

Substantiv *n. substantive, noun.*

Substanz *f. substance.*

substrahieren *to subtract.*

Suche *f. search, quest.*

    auf die Suche gehen   *to go in search of.*

    auf der Suche sein nach   *in search of.*

SUCHEN *to look for, try, seek.*

    das Weite suchen   *to run away.*

    nach Worten suchen   *to be at a loss for words.*

    Sie hat hier nichts zu suchen.   *She has no business here.*

Sucht *f. passion, rage.*

Süden *m. south.*

Südfrüchte *pl. tropical fruits.*

südlich *southern, (to the) south.*

Südpol *m. south pole.*

Sühne *f. expiation, atonement.*

sühnen *to expiate, atone.*

Summe *f. sum, amount.*

summieren *to add up.*

Sumpf *m. swamp, marsh.*

Sünde *f. sin.*

Sünder *m (–in. f.) sinner.*

sündhaft *sinful.*

sündigen *to sin.*

Suppe *f. soup, broth.*

Suppenanlage *f. things (that are) added to the soup.*

suspendieren *to suspend.*

SÜSS *sweet, fresh, lovely.*

Süsse *f. sweetness.*

Süssigkeit *f. sweetness, sweets.*

süsslich *sweetish, mawkish.*

Symbol *n. symbol.*

symbolisch *symbolical.*

Sympathie *f. sympathy.*

sympathisch *nice, likable, congenial.*

Symphonie *f. symphony.*

Symptom *n. symptom.*

Synagoge *f. synagogue.*

System *n. system.*

Szene *f. scene.*
Szenerie *f. scenery, settings.*

T

Tabak *m. tobacco.*
Tabelle *f. table, index, schedule.*
Tablett *n. tray.*
Tablette *f. tablet.*
Tadel *m. reprimand, blame.*
tadellos *excellent, perfect.*
tadeln *to blame, find fault.*
TAFEL *f. board, blackboard, bar, plate, table.*
    sich von der Tafel aufheben *to rise from the table.*
TAG *m. day, daylight, life (one's days).*
    alle acht Tage *every week.*
    alle Tage *every day.*
    am Tag *during the day, in the daytime.*
    an den Tag bringen *to bring to light.*
    auf ein paar Tage *for a few days.*
    auf seine alten Tage *in his old age.*
    bei Tage *in the daytime.*
    den ganzen Tag *all day long.*
    dieser Tage *one of these days.*
    eines Tages *some day.*
    Er lebt in den Tag hinein. *He lives from hand to mouth.*
    Guten Tag! *Good morning!*
    in acht Tagen *in a week.*
    Tag aus, Tag ein *day in, day out.*
    Tag für Tag *day by day.*
    einen Tag um den andern *every other day.*
    Man soll den Tag nicht von dem Abend loben. *Don't count your chickens before they hatch.*
    vierzehn Tage *two weeks.*
    vor acht Tagen *a week ago.*
Tagebuch *n. diary.*
tagelang *for days on end.*
Tagesbericht *m. daily report, bulletin.*
Tageseinnahme *f. day's earnings.*
Tagesgespräch *n. topic of the day.*
Tageswerk *n. day's work.*
Tageszeit *f. time of day.*
Tageszeitung *f. daily paper.*
taghell *as light as day.*
täglich *daily.*
tagsüber *during the day.*
Tagung *f. conference, meeting.*
Taille *f. waist.*
Takt *m. time measure (music).*
Taktgefühl *n. tact.*
Taktik *f. tactics.*
taktisch *tactical.*
taktlos *tactless.*

Taktlosigkeit *f. tactlessness, indiscretion.*
taktvoll *tactful, discreet.*
Tal *n. valley.*
Talent *n. talent, ability.*
talentiert *talented.*
Talk *m. talcum powder.*
Talsperre *f. river dam.*
talwärts *downhill.*
Tank *m. tank (car).*
tanken *to fill up (car).*
Tanne *f. fir tree.*
Tannenadeln *pl. fir needles.*
Tannenbaum *m. fir tree.*
Tannenzapfen *m. fir cone.*
Tante *f. aunt.*
Tanz *m. dance, ball.*
    Darf ich um den nächsten Tanz bitten? *May I have the next dance?*
TANZEN *to dance.*
Tänzer *m. (–in, f.) dance partner.*
Tapete *f. wallpaper.*
Tapezier *m. paperhanger, upholsterer.*
tapezieren *to paper.*
tapfer *brave, gallant.*
Tapferkeit *f. bravery, gallantry.*
Tarif *m. rate, tariff.*
tarifmässig *in accordance with the tariff.*
tarnen *to camouflage, disguise.*
Tarnung *f. camouflage.*
TASCHE *f. pocket, bag, purse.*
    jemandem auf der Tasche liegen *to be a financial drain to a person.*
Taschenausgabe *f. pocket book edition.*
Taschengeld *n. change.*
Taschenbuch *n. pocketbook.*
Taschendieb *m. pickpocket.*
Taschenlampe *f. flashlight.*
Taschenmesser *n. pocket knife.*
Taschentuch *n. handkerchief.*
Taschenuhr *f. pocket-watch.*
TASSE *f. cup.*
    eine Tasse Kaffee *a cup of coffee.*
Taste *f. key (music and typewriter).*
tasten *to touch, feel.*
TAT *f. deed, act, fact, achievement, feat.*
    auf frischer Tat *in the very act.*
    in der Tat *indeed, as a matter of fact.*
tatenlos *inactive, idle.*
Täter *m. perpetrator, doer.*
tätig *active.*
    tätig sein *to be active, hard at work.*
Tätigkeit *f. activity, job.*
tatkräftig *energetic, active.*
Tatsache *f. fact.*
tatsächlich *real, actual.*
Tau *m. dew.*
Tau *n. rope.*
taub *deaf, empty, hollow.*
Taube *f. pigeon.*

Taubheit f. deafness.
taubstumm deaf and dumb.
Taubstumme(r) m. deaf-mute.
tauchen to dive, dip, plunge.
Taucher m. diver.
tauen to thaw.
Taufe f. baptism, christening.
  aus der Taufe heben   to be godfather (or godmother).
taufen to baptize.
Taufnahme m. Christian name.
taugen to be of use.
Taugenichts m. good-for-nothing.
Tauglichkeit f. fitness, suitability.
Tausch m. exchange.
tauschen to exchange, swap.
täuschen to delude, deceive, disappoint.
  Mich können Sie nicht täuschen.   You can't fool me.
  Der Schein täuscht
  sich täuschen lassen   to let oneself be fooled.
Täuschung f. deception.
TAUSEND thousand.
tausendmal a thousand times.
Tauwetter n. thaw.
Taxe f. tax, rate, duty.
Taxi n. taxi.
  ein Taxi holen   to call a cab.
taxieren to appraise, value.
Technik f. technology.
Techniker m. technician.
technisch technical.
Tee m. tea.
Teelöffel m. teaspoon.
Teer n. tar.
Teich m. pond.
Teig m. dough.
TEIL m. & n. part, share, portion.
  ich für mein Teil   as for me.
  sich sein Teil denken   to have one's own ideas.
  zum Teil   partly.
  zum grössten Teil   for the most part.
teilbar divisible.
Teilbeschäftigung f. part-time work.
Teilchen n. particle.
TEILEN to divide, share, distribute, deal out.
  geteilte Gefühle   mixed feelings.
  geteilter Meinung sein   to be of a different opinion.
  sich teilenlassen durch   to be divisible by
Teilhaber m. partner, participant.
Teilhaberschaft f. partnership.
Teilnahme f. participation, condolences.
  Meine aufrichtige Teilnahme   my sincere condolences.
teilnahmslos indifferent.

teilnahmsvoll sympathetic.
teilnehmen to take part in.
Teilnehmer m. participant, subscriber.
teilweise partial.
Teilzahlung f. part-payment, installment.
Telekopierer m. fax
telekopieren to fax.
Telefax m. facsimile, fax.
  einen Telefax übersenden   to send a fax.
  Ich möchte etwas faxen (colloq.).   I'd like to fax (something).
TELEFON n. telephone.
Telefonanruf m. telephone call.
Telefonbuch n. telephone directory.
TELEFONIEREN to telephone.
telefonisch telephonic, by telephone.
Telefonist m. (-in, f.) telephone operator.
Telefonnummer f. telephone number.
Telefonzelle f. telephone booth.
Telefonzentrale f. telephone exchange.
Telegrafie f. telegraphy.
TELEGRAFIEREN to telegraph.
telegrafisch by telegram.
TELEGRAMM n. telegram.
Telegrammformular n. telegraph form.
Teller m. plate.
Temperament n. temperament, character, disposition.
temperamentvoll high spirited, impetuous.
Temperatur f. temperature.
Temperaturanstieg m. rise in temperature
Temperaturschwankungen pl. variations in temperature.
Temperatursturz m. fall/drop in temperature.
Tempo n. time, measure, speed.
Tendenz f. tendency, inclination.
Tennis n. tennis.
Tennisplatz m. tennis court.
Tennisschläger m. tennis racket.
Tenor m. tenor.
Teppich m. carpet.
Termin m. deadline.
Terrasse f. terrace.
Territorium n. territory.
Testament n. testament.
TEUER expensive, high, costly.
Teuerung f. dearness, scarcity, high cost of living.
Teufel m. devil.
  den Teufel an die Wand malen.   speak of the devil.
teuflisch devilish, diabolical.
Text m. text, libretto.
  aus dem Text kommen   to lose the thread.
Textbuch n. words, libretto.
Textilien pl. textiles.
Textilwaren pl. textiles.
THEATER n. theater, stage.

Theaterbesuch m. playgoing.
Theaterbesucher m. theatergoer.
Theaterdirektor m. manager of a theater.
Theaterkasse f. box office.
theatralisch theatrical.
Theke f. counter, bar.
Thema n. theme, subject.
Theologe m. theologian.
Theoretiker m. theoretician.
Thermometer n. thermometer.
Thermometerstand m. thermometer reading.
Thron m. throne.
Thronbesteigung f. accession to the throne.
TIEF deep, low, deeply, far.
   Das lässt tief blicken.   That gives food for
     thought.
   in tiefer Nacht   late at night.
   aus tiefstem Herzen   from the bottom of
     my heart.
   tiefe Einsicht   profound insight.
   im tiefsten Winter   in the dead of winter.
Tiefe f. depth, profundity.
tiefgründig deep, profound.
tiefliegend sunken.
Tiefsee f. deep sea.
tiefsinnig profound, pensive, melancholy.
Tiefstand m. lowness, low level.
TIER n. animal, beast.
Tierarzt m. veterinarian.
Tiergarten m. zoo.
Tiger m. tiger.
Tinte f. ink.
   in der Tinte sitzen   to be in a mess.
Tintenfass n. inkwell.
Tintenfleck m. blot, ink spot.
TISCH m. table.
   bei Tisch   during the meal.
   Bitte, zu Tisch!   Dinner is ready!
   Er ist gerarde zu Tisch gegangen.   He has
     just gone out to lunch.
   reinen Tisch machen   to make a clean
     sweep.
   unter den Tisch fallen   to be ignored.
Tischdecke f. tablecloth.
Tischler m. cabinet-maker.
Tischplatte f. table top.
Tischrede f. after-dinner talk.
Tischtennis n. table tennis, ping-pong.
Tischtuch n. tablecloth.
Tischzeit f. dinner-time.
Titel m. title, claim.
Titelbild n. frontispiece.
Titelblatt n. title page.
Titelhalter m. title-holder.
Toast m. toast.
toasten to drink toasts.
toben to rage, rave.
Tobsucht f. raving madness.
tobsüchtig raving mad.

TOCHTER f. daughter.
TOD m. death, decease.
   des Todes sein   to be doomed.
   sich den Tod holen   to catch one's death
     of a cold.
   Es geht um Leben und Tod.   It's a matter
     of life and death.
Todesanzeige f. death notice.
Todeskampf m. death agony.
Todesstrafe f. capital punishment, death
   penalty.
Todestag m. death anniversary.
todkrank very ill.
tödlich fatal, deadly, mortal.
todmüde dead tired.
Toilette f. toilet, dress, dressing table,
   lavatory.
   Toilette machen   to dress, get dressed.
tolerant tolerant.
toll mad, insane, raving, awful.
tölpisch clumsy.
Ton m. sound, note, stress, accent.
tönen to sound, resound.
Tonfall m. musical intonation, cadence.
Tonfilm m. sound film.
tonlos soundless, voiceless.
Tonne f. barrel, ton.
Tönung f. shading.
Topf m. pot.
Tor n. gate.
Tor m. fool.
Torheit f. foolishness, folly.
töricht foolish, silly.
Torte f. layer cake.
tosen to rage, roar.
TOT dead, dull.
   tote Zeit   dead season.
   toter Punkt   deadlock.
(sich) totarbeiten to kill oneself with work.
Tote(r) m. dead person, deceased.
TÖTEN to kill.
   sich töten   to commit suicide.
   sich totlachen   to die laughing.
Totenbett n. deathbead.
totenbleich deadly pale.
totenstill still as death.
Tötung f. killing, slaying.
Tour f. tour, excursion.
   in einer Tour   without stopping.
Tournee f. tour (theater).
Trab m. trot.
   im Trab   quickly.
Tracht f. dress, costume.
trachten to strive, seek after.
traditionell traditional.
TRAGEN to carry, bear, wear, take, endure,
   suffer, produce.
   die Schuld tragen an   to carry the blame
     for.

Sie trägt Trauer. *She is in mourning.*
TRÄGER *m. porter.*
Tragfähigkeit *f. capacity.*
Tragflügel *m. wing of aircraft.*
tragisch *tragic.*
Tragödie *f. tragedy.*
trainieren *to train.*
Träne *f. tear.*
Trank *m. drink.*
tränken *to water, soak.*
transpirieren *to perspire.*
Transport *m. transport.*
Traube *f. grape, bunch of grapes.*
Traubenlese *f. grape harvest.*
Traubenmost *m. grape juice.*
trauen *to marry, give in marriage, join, trust, rely.*
 Ich traue ihm alles zu. *I trust him completely.*
 sich trauen lassen *to get married.*
Trauer *f. sorrow, grief, affliction.*
Traueranzeige *f. announcement of a death.*
Trauermarsch *m. funeral march.*
trauern *to mourn, grieve.*
Trauerspiel *n. tragedy.*
träufeln *to drop.*
traulich *intimate, cosy.*
TRAUM *m. dream, fancy, illusion.*
 Träume sind Schäume. *All dreams are lies.*
träumen *to dream.*
Träumer *m. dreamer.*
träumerisch *dreamy.*
traumhaft *dreamlike.*
TRAURIG *sad, sorrowful, mournful.*
Traurigkeit *f. sadness.*
Trauschein *m. marriage certificate.*
Trauung *f. marriage ceremony.*
Trauzeuge *m. witness to a marriage.*
TREFFEN *to meet, hit, strike, affect, touch, fall upon.*
 Alle nötigen Vorbereitungen sind getroffen worden. *All the necessary arrangements have been made.*
 sich getroffen fühlen *to feel hurt.*
 sich gut treffen *to be lucky.*
 sich treffen *to meet.*
 Vorsichtsmassregeln treffen *to take all the necessary precautions.*
 Wen trifft die Schuld? *Who is to blame?*
treffend *to the point.*
Treffer *m. target, luck, winning ticket, prize.*
trefflich *excellent, admirable.*
Trefflichkeit *f. excellence.*
treiben *to drive, set in motion, float, drift.*
 Wintersport treiben *to practice winter sports.*
Treibhaus *n. conservatory, hothouse.*
trennbar *separable, divisible.*

TRENNEN *to separate, divide, dissolve.*
 getrennt leben *to live separately.*
 sich trennen *to part.*
 sich trennen von *to part from.*
Trennung *f. separation.*
Treppe *f. stairway, stairs.*
Treppenabsatz *m. landing.*
Treppengeländer *n. banisters, railing.*
Tresor *m. treasury.*
TRETEN *to step, tread, walk, go.*
 in jemandes Fusstapfen treten *to follow one's footsteps.*
 aus dem Dienste treten *to retire from active service.*
 in Erscheinung treten *to appear.*
 in Kraft treten *to go into effect.*
 mit Füssen treten *to trample under foot.*
 zu nahe treten *to hurt one's feelings.*
TREU *faithful, true, loyal.*
treubrüchig *faithless, perfidious.*
Treue *f. fidelity, faithfulness, loyalty.*
treuherzig *frank, naive.*
treulich *faithfully.*
treulos *unfaithful.*
Treulosigkeit *f. faithlessness.*
Tribüne *f. tribune.*
Trieb *m. sprout, shoot, driving force, motive power.*
trinkbar *drinkable.*
TRINKEN *to drink, absorb.*
Trinker *m. drunkard.*
Trinkgeld *n. tip.*
Trinkspruch *n. toast.*
Tritt *m. step, footstep.*
Trittbrett *n. running board.*
Triumph *m. triumph, victory.*
triumphieren *to triumph.*
trocken *dry, arid, dull.*
 trockener Empfang *cool reception.*
Trockenmilch *f. dry milk.*
trocknen *to dry up.*
Trommel *f. drum.*
trommeln *to beat the drum.*
Trompete *f. trumpet.*
Trompeter *m. trumpeter.*
Tropen *pl. tropics.*
tropfen *to drop, drip.*
tropfenweise *by drops, drop by drop.*
TROST *m. comfort.*
trostbedürftig *in need of consolation.*
trösten *to comfort, console, cheer up.*
 sich trösten *to cheer up.*
tröstlich *consoling, comforting.*
trostlos *discouraged.*
Trostlosigkeit *f. despair, hopelessness.*
trostreich *comforting, consoling.*
Trottoir *m. pavement, sidewalk.*
TROTZ *prep. (gen.) in spite of.*
 Trotz der Kälte ging ich jeden Tag

spazieren. *In spite of the cold, I took a walk every day.*

Trotz *m. obstinacy, stubbornness, defiance.*

jemandem zum Trotz *in defiance of someone.*

Trotz bieten *to defy.*

trotzdem *nevertheless, anyway, although.*

Trotzdem es sehr kalt ist, werde ich spazieren gehen. *Although it is very cold, I shall take a walk.*

trotzen *to defy, be obstinate.*

trotzig *defiant.*

trüb(e) *dark, sad, gloomy.*

trüben *to dim, trouble, spoil.*

Der Himmel trübt sich. *The sky is clouding over.*

Trübsal *f. affliction, misery; sorrow.*

trübselig *sad, gloomy, dreary, troubled.*

trübsinnig *melancholy, dejected.*

trügen *to deceive.*

trügerisch *deceitful.*

Truhe *f. chest, trunk.*

Trümmer *f. ruins, debris.*

in Trümmer gehen *to be shattered.*

Trumpf *m. trump.*

trumpfen *to trump.*

Trunk *m. drink.*

Trunkenheit *f. drunkenness.*

Truppe *f. troop, company.*

Truthahn *m. turkey.*

Tube *f. tube.*

Tuberkulose *f. tuberculosis.*

TUCH *n. cloth, fabric, shawl.*

tüchtig *good, able, fit, qualified, competent, efficient.*

Tüchtigkeit *f. fitness, ability, efficiency.*

Tücke *f. malice, spite.*

tückisch *malicious, spiteful.*

TUGEND *f. virtue.*

tugendhaft *virtuous.*

Tulpe *f. tulip.*

Tumult *m. tumult, commotion.*

TUN *to do, make, act, perform, execute.*

Das tut nichts. *That does not matter.*

des Guten zu viel tun *to overdo something.*

Er tut nur so. *He is only pretending.*

Es tut mir leid. *I am sorry.*

es zu tun bekommen mit *to have trouble with.*

Haben Sie sich weh getan? *Did you hurt yourself?*

Mir ist daran zu tun. *It is very important for me.*

tun als ob *to pretend.*

Tun Sie als ob Sie zu Hause wären! *Make yourself at home.*

Wir haben viel zu tun. *We are very busy.*

Das lässt sich tun. *That can be done.*

in die Schule tun *to send to school.*

Tue ihm nichts! *Don't do anything to him (Don't hurt him)!*

tunlich *feasible, practicable.*

Tunnel *m. tunnel.*

tupfen *to dot, touch lightly, dab.*

TÜR *f. door, doorway.*

ihn vor die Tür setzen *to show him to the door; to throw him out of the house.*

Er wohnt zwei Türen von hier. *He lives next door (one or two houses).*

Türgriff *m. doorknob.*

Türklinke *f. door latch (handle).*

Turm *m. tower, steeple.*

Turmuhr *f. church clock, tower clock.*

Turnen *n. gymnastics.*

turnen *to do gymnastics.*

Turnhalle *f. gymnasium.*

Turnier *n. tournament.*

Tusche *f. watercolor.*

Tüte *f. paper bag.*

typisch *typical.*

Tyrann *m. tyrant.*

tyrannisieren *to tyrannize.*

U

Übel *n. evil, ailment, misfortune, inconvenience.*

ÜBEL *evil, wrong, bad, ill.*

Das ist nicht übel. *That is not bad.*

Mir ist übel. *I feel sick.*

übel daran sein *to be in a bad way.*

auf ihn übel zu sprechen sein *not to have a good word to say about him.*

übel zumute *ill at ease, uncomfortable.*

übelgelaunt *cross, grumpy.*

übelgesinnt *evil-minded.*

Übelkeit *f. nausea.*

übelnehmen *to take offense.*

übelnehmerisch *touchy, susceptible.*

Übeltäter *m. evil-doer, criminal.*

üben *to exercise, practise.*

ÜBER 1. *prep (dat. when answering question, Wo?; acc. when answering question Wohin?, and depending on the idiom) higher, while, concerning, via.*

den Winter über *the whole winter long.*

Er schwamm über den See. *He swam across the lake.*

Er zog sich die Decke über den Kopf. *He pulled the blanket over his head.*

Ich wundere mich über ihre Einstellung. *I am surprised at her attitude.*

Sie sprach über ihre Sorgen. *She spoke about her sorrows.*

über Bord *overboard.*

Über der Erde ziehen Wolken. *Clouds are floating above the earth.*

über kurz oder lang   *sooner or later.*

über und über   *over and over.*

Seine Liebe geht ihr über alles. *She places his love above everything.*

überall   *all over.*

von Berlin über Strassburg nach Paris   *from Berlin to Paris via Strassburg.*

über dem Essen.   *during the meal.*

über den Sommer   *during the course of the summer.*

2. *adv. wholly, completely, in excess.*

3. *prefix* a) *separable* (*when meaning above*).

Das Flugzeug fliegt über dem Ozean. *The airplane flies above the ocean.*

b) *inseparable* (*in all uses where it does not mean above*).

Er übersetzt ein Gedicht von Schiller. *He translates a poem by Schiller.*

überaltert *too old.*

überanstrengen *to overwork, overstrain.*

überarbeiten *to review, go over.*

sich überarbeiten   *to overwork oneself.*

überbelichten *to overexpose* (*photo*).

überbieten *to excel, surpass.*

Überblick *m. perspective, summary, survey.*

überblicken *to survey, sum up.*

überdauern *to outlast.*

überdies *besides, moreover.*

Überdruss *m. boredom, satiety, disgust.*

überdrüssig *tired of, sick of, bored with.*

Übereifer *m. excess zeal.*

übereignen *to transfer, assign, convey.*

übereilen *to rush, hurry, precipitate.*

sich übereilen   *to be in a great hurry.*

Übereilen Sie sich nicht!   *Don't rush!*

Übereilung *f. hastiness, rush.*

übereinkommen *to agree.*

Übereinkunft *f. agreement, arrangement.*

übereinstimmen *to agree, coincide.*

Übereinstimmung *f. agreement, conformity.*

überessen *to overeat.*

überfahren *to overrun* (*signal*) *run over.*

Überfahrt *f. crossing.*

Überfall *m. holdup, attack.*

überfallen *to hold up, attack.*

überfällig *overdue.*

überfliegen *to fly over, skim through.*

überfliessen *to overflow, run over.*

Überfluss *m. abundance, profusion.*

im Überfluss   *abundantly.*

zum Überfluss   *unnecessarily.*

überflüssig *superfluous, unnecessary.*

überfordern *to overcharge.*

Überfracht *f. excess freight, overweight.*

überführen *to convey, transport.*

Überführung *f. conveying, transfer.*

überfüllen *to overload, crowd.*

Überfüllung *f. overloading.*

Übergabe *f. delivery, surrender.*

Übergang *m. passage, crossing.*

übergeben *to hand over, deliver.*

übergehen (*separable prefix*) *to cross, pass over.*

übergehen (*separable prefix*) *to transfer.*

Das Geschäft ist in andere Hände übergegangen. *This store has changed hands.*

übergehen (*inseparable*) *to pass over, to omit.*

Er übergeht diese Frage im Kapital. *He passes over this question in the chapter* (*but will get back to it*).

Übergewicht *n. overweight, excess weight.*

das Übergewicht bekommen   *to lose one's balance.*

übergiessen *to spill.*

Überhandnahme *f. increase.*

überhandnehmen *to increase, spread.*

Überhang *m. curtain, hangings.*

überhangen *to hang over.*

ÜBERHAUPT *in general, altogether.*

überhaupt nicht   *not at all.*

überheben *to save, spare, exempt.*

überheblich *presumptuous.*

Überheblichkeit *f. presumption, arrogance.*

überholen *to pass* (*car*), *surpass, overhaul.*

überholt *outdated.*

überhören *to miss, ignore.*

Überkleid *n. overdress, overall.*

überkochen *to boil over.*

überladen *to overload*

überlassen *to leave, give up, relinquish.*

überlasten *to overload.*

überlaufen *to run over, boil over, desert.*

Überläufer *m. deserter.*

überleben *to survive, outlive.*

sich überlebt haben   *to be outdated.*

Er hat sie überlebt. *He outlived her.*

Überlebende *m. survivor.*

überlegen *to reflect, consider.*

sich überlegen   *to think over, consider.*

Ich habe es mir anders überlegt. *I've changed my mind.*

überlegen *adj. superior.*

überlegen sein   *to feel superior to.*

Überlegenheit *f. superiority.*

Überlegung *f. consideration, thought, deliberation.*

überliefern *to deliver, transmit.*

Überlieferung *f. delivery, tradition, surrender.*

ÜBERMACHT *f. superiority, predominance.*

Übermass *n. excess.*

im Übermass   *to excess, excessive.*

übermässig *excessive, immoderate.*

Übermensch *m. superman.*

übermenschlich *superhuman.*

übermitteln *to transmit, convey.*

Übermittlung *f. transmission, conveyance.*

ÜBERMORGEN *the day after tomorrow.*

übermüden *to overtire.*

Übermüdung *f. over-fatigue.*

Übermut *m. high spirits, bravado.*

übermütig *to be in high spirits.*

übernachten *to stay overnight, spend the night.*

Übernahme *f. taking over, take-over.*

übernatürlich *supernatural.*

übernehmen *to take over, seize.*
   sich übernehmen *to overstrain oneself.*

überraschen *to surprise.*

Überraschung *f. surprise.*

überreden *to persuade.*

überreichen *to hand over, present.*

überreif *overripe.*

Überrest *m. remainder.*

überschätzen *to overrate, overestimate.*

überschauen *to overlook, survey.*

überschneiden *to intersect, overlap.*

überschreiten *to cross, exceed, overstep.*

Überschreitung *f. crossing, excess, transgression.*

Überschrift *f. heading, title.*

Überschuh *m. overshoe, galosh.*

Überschuss *m. surplus, excess.*

überschüssig *in excess.*

überschwemmen *to inundate.*

Überschwemmung *f. inundation, flood.*

Übersee *f. overseas.*

übersehen *to survey, overlook.*

übersenden *to send, transmit, forward.*
   einen Telefax übersenden *to send a fax.*

Übersendung *f. transmission.*

übersetzen *to pass across.*

ÜBERSETZEN *to translate.*

Übersetzer *m. translator.*

Übersetzung *f. translation.*

Übersicht *f. view, review, summary.*

übersichtlich *clear, visible.*

Übersichtlichkeit *f. clearness, lucidity.*

übersinnlich *transcendental.*

überspannen *to stretch over, span.*

überspannt *eccentric.*

überspringen *to jump across.*

überstehen *to endure, come through.*

überströmen *to overflow.*

Überstunden *pl. overtime.*
   Überstunden machen *to work overtime.*

ÜBERSTÜRZEN *to rush, hurry, act hastily.*
   Überstürzen Sie sich nicht! *Don't rush yourself!*

übertragbar *transferable.*

übertragen *to transfer, give up, entrust with, transmit, broadcast.*

Übertragung *f. transfer, transcription, transmission.*

übertreffen *to excel, surpass.*

übertreiben *to exaggerate.*

Übertreibung *f. exaggeration.*

übertreten *to go over, change over, violate.*

Übertretung *f. violation, transgression.*

übervölkert *overpopulated.*

überwachen *to watch over, supervise.*

Überwachung *f. observation, surprise.*

überwältigen *to overwhelm.*

Überwältigung *f. overwhelming.*

überweisen *to transfer, remit.*
   telegraphisch überweisen *to send a cable.*

Überweisung *f. transfer, remittance.*

überwiegen *to outweigh.*

überwiegend *preponderant, predominant.*

überwinden *to overcome.*

Überwindung *f. overcoming, conquest.*

Überzahl *f. numerical superiority, majority.*

überzählig *surplus.*

überzeugen *to convince.*

Überzeugung *f. conviction, belief.*
   der Überzeugung sein *to be convinced.*

überziehen *to cover, re-cover; to overdraw (bank account).*
   das Bett überziehen *to change the sheets.*

üblich *usual, customary.*

U-Boot *n. submarine.*

ÜBRIG *left over, remaining, other.*
   das Übrige *the rest.*
   ein übriges tun *to do more than necessary.*
   Haben Sie ein paar Minuten für uns übrig? *Can you spare us a few minutes?*
   im Übrigen *otherwise.*
   nichts übrig haben für *to care little for.*
   übrig bleiben *to be left over.*
   übrig lassen *to leave (over).*
   zu wünschen übrig lassen *to leave much to be desired.*

ÜBRIGENS *besides, by the way.*

ÜBUNG *f. exercise, practice, drill.*

UFER *n. shore, bank (river).*

UHR *f. hour, clock, watch.*
   nach der Uhr sehen *to look at the time.*
   um halb fünf Uhr *at half past five.*
   Um wieviel Uhr? *At what time?*
   Wieviel Uhr ist es? *What time is it?*

Uhrmacher *m. watchmaker.*

Uhrzeiger *m. clock hand.*

UM 1. *prep. (acc.), at, about, around, because of, for the sake of, for, up.*
   Der Zug verlässt Düsseldorf um drei Uhr. *The train leaves Düsseldorf at three o'clock.*

Ihre Zeit ist um. *Your time is up.*

Tag um Tag *every day, day after day.*

Wir ängstigen uns um sie. *We worry about her.*

Wir sitzen um den Tisch. *We sit around the table.*

Um Himmels willen! *For God's sake!*

um jeden Preis *not at any cost.*

um keinen Preis *not at any price.*

um so besser *all the better.*

um zwei Jahre älter *two years older.*

2. *Adv. around.*

um und um *around.*

um herum *all around.*

3. *Conj.* (um . . . zu), *in order to.*

Um den Frieden zu erhalten, dankt der Prinz ab. *The prince abdicates in order to preserve peace.*

4. *Prefix.* 1) *inseparable* (*implies the meaning of around*).

Gärten umgeben das Schloss. *The castle is surrounded by gardens.*

b) *separable* (*implies the meaning of to upset, to transform*).

Er warf den Stuhl um. *He overturned the chair.*

umändern *to change, alter.*

Umänderung *f. change, alteration.*

umarbeiten *to remodel.*

Umarbeitung *f. remodeling.*

umarmen *to embrace, hug.*

Umarmung *f. embrace, hug.*

Umbau *m. rebuilding, reconstruction.*

umbinden *to tie around, put on.*

umblättern *to turn over.*

umblicken *to look about.*

umdrehen *to turn, turn round.*

Umdrehung *f. turning round.*

umfahren *to drive around, make a detour.*

Umfahrt *f. circular tour.*

umfallen *to topple over.*

Umfang *m. circumference, extent, size.*

umfangreich *comprehensive, extensive.*

umfassen *to clasp, embrace, enclose.*

umfassend *comprehensive, extensive, complete, full.*

umformen *to transform, remodel.*

Umfrage *f. inquiry.*

Umgang *m. association, relations.*

umgänglich *sociable.*

Umgangssprache *f. colloquial speech.*

umgeben *to surround.*

Umgebung *f. surroundings, environs.*

Umgegend *f. neighborhood, vicinity.*

UMGEHEN *to go around, circulate, haunt, evade.*

umgehend antworten *to answer by return.*

umgekehrt *opposite, reverse, contrary.*

umgestalten *to alter, transform, reform.*

umgraben *to dig up.*

UMHER *around, about, here and there.*

umherblicken *to glance around, look around.*

umhin *about.*

Ich kann nicht umhin. *I can't help* (*refrain from*).

umhüllen *to wrap, cover, veil, envelope.*

Umkehr *f. return, change.*

UMKEHREN *to turn back, turn around, turn upside down, invert, reverse.*

Umkehrung *f. inversion, reversal.*

umkleiden *to change clothes.*

umkommen *to perish, die*

Umkreis *m. circle, circuit, periphery.*

umkreisen *to revolve, circle around.*

Umkreisung *f. encirclement.*

Umlauf *m. rotation, revolution, circulation.*

in Umlauf setzen *to circulate.*

umleiten *to divert* (*traffic*).

Umleitung *f. detour.*

Strassenbau! Umleitung! *Road under repair! Detour!*

umliegend *surrounding, neighboring.*

umpflanzen *to transplant.*

umreissen *to knock down, to pull, to blow down* (*trees*).

Umriss *m. sketch, outline, contour.*

Umsatz *m. sale, turnover.*

umschalten *to switch over.*

Umschalter *m. switch, commutator.*

UMSCHLAG *m. envelope, cover, wrapper, hem, compress, change.*

umschlagen *to fell, knock down, put on, change.*

umschliessen *to enclose.*

umschwärmen *to swarm around.*

Umschwung *m. change, revolution.*

umsehen *to look back, round.*

Sie sehen sich nach einer neuen Wohnung um. *They are looking for a new apartment.*

Umsicht *f. circumspection, prudence, caution.*

umsichtig *cautious, prudent.*

umsonst *gratis, for nothing; in vain.*

UMSTAND *m. circumstances, fact.*

ohne Umstände *without ceremony.*

mildernde Umstände *extenuating circumstances.*

sich Umstände machen *to put oneself out.*

Sie ist in anderen Umständen. *She is expecting a baby.*

Umstände machen *to make a fuss.*

unter allen Umständen *in any case, by all means.*

unter keinen Umständen *on no account.*

unter gewissen Umständen *in certain circumstances.*

in anderen Umständen sein   *to be pregnant, expecting a child.*
umständlich *laborious.*
Umsteigefahrschein *m. transfer-ticket.*
  einen Umsteigefahrschein verlangen   *to ask for a transfer (ticket).*
umsteigen *to change trains.*
umstritten *disputed, controversial.*
Umsturz *m. downfall, revolution.*
umstürzen *to throw down, overturn.*
Umtausch *m. exchange, conversion of money.*
umtauschen *to change for.*
umtun *to drape around.*
umwechseln *to exchange, change (money).*
Umweg *m. detour.*
Umwelt *f. surroundings, environment.*
umwenden *to turn, turn over.*
umwickeln *to wrap up.*
umziehen *to change clothes.*
Umzug *m. procession, change of residence, move.*
unabhängig *independent.*
Unabhängigkeit *f. independence.*
unabkömmlich *indispensable, essential.*
unablässig *incessant.*
unabsehbar *incalculable.*
unabsichtlich *unintentional.*
unabwendbar *inevitable.*
unachtsam *careless, negligent.*
unangebracht *out of place.*
unangemessen *inadequate, improper.*
unangenehm *unpleasant, disagreeable.*
unannehmbar *unacceptable.*
Unannehmlichkeit *f. inconvenience, trouble.*
Unansehnlichkeit *f. annoyance.*
unanständig *improper, indecent.*
unappetitlich *unappetizing, uninviting.*
Unart *f. bad behavior, rudeness.*
unartig *naughty, uncivil.*
unauffindbar *undiscoverable.*
unaufgefordert *unasked.*
unaufhaltsam *inevitable, impetuous.*
unaufhörlich *incessant, incessantly.*
unaufmerksam *inattentive.*
unaufrichtig *insincere.*
unausbleiblich *unfailing, certain.*
unausführbar *impracticable, not feasible.*
unaussprechlich *inexpressible.*
unausstehlich *intolerable, unbearable.*
unbarmherzig *unmerciful, pitiless, brutally.*
Unbarmherzigkeit *f. harshness, mercilessness.*
unbeabsichtigt *unintentional, inadvertent.*
unbeachtet *unnoticed.*
unbeanstandet *not objected to, unopposed.*
unbeantwortet *unanswered.*
unbedachtsam *inconsiderate, thoughtless.*
unbedenklich *harmless.*

unbedeutend *insignificant, trifling.*
unbedingt *unconditional, absolute.*
  Sie müssen unbedingt dabei sein.   *You must be there whatever may happen.*
unbeeinflusst *unprejudiced.*
unbefangen *impartial, unprejudiced.*
Unbefangenheit *f. impartiality; facility.*
unbefriedigend *unsatisfactory, unsatisfactorily.*
unbefriedigt *unsatisfied.*
unbefugt *unauthorized, incompetent.*
unbegabt *not gifted, not clever.*
unbegreiflich *inconceivable.*
unbegrenzt *unbounded, unlimited.*
unbegründet *unfounded, groundless.*
Unbehagen *n. discomfort.*
unbehaglich *uncomfortable.*
unbehilflich *helpless.*
unbehindert *unrestrained.*
unbeholfen *clumsy.*
UNBEKANNT *unknown.*
  Er ist hier unbekannt.   *He is a stranger here.*
unbekümmert *unconcerned.*
unbeliebt *unpopular.*
unbemerkt *unnoticed.*
UNBEQUEM *uncomfortable, inconvenient.*
Unbequemlichkeit *f. discomfort.*
unberechenbar *incalculable.*
unberechtigt *unauthorized, unjustified.*
unberührt *untouched, intact, innocent.*
unbeschädigt *undamaged, uninjured.*
unbescheiden *immodest, insolent.*
unbeschreiblich *indescribable.*
unbeschwert *unburdened.*
unbesehen *without inspection, hesitation.*
unbesiegbar *invincible.*
Unbesonnenheit *f. indiscretion, imprudence.*
unbesorgt *unconcerned.*
  Seien Sie unbesorgt!   *Don't worry.*
unbeständig *unstable, unsteady.*
unbestechlich *incorruptible.*
unbestimmt *undetermined, undefined, indefinite.*
unbestreitbar *indisputable.*
unbeträchtlich *trivial.*
unbeugsam *inflexible, stubborn.*
unbeweglich *immovable, fixed.*
unbewohnt *uninhabited.*
unbewusst *unconscious.*
unbezahlbar *priceless, invaluable.*
unbezwingbar *invincible.*
unbrauchbar *useless, of no use.*
UND *and*
  und so weiter   *and so forth.*
Undank *m. ingratitude.*
undankbar *ungrateful.*
Undankbarkeit *f. ingratitude.*
undenkbar *unconceivable.*

undeutlich *indistinct, vague.*
Unding *n. absurdity, monstrosity.*
unduldsam *intolerant.*
undurchdringlich *impenetrable.*
uneben *uneven, rough.*
unecht *not genuine, false, improper, artificial.*
unehelich *illegitimate.*
unehrbar *indecent, immodest.*
unehrenhaft *dishonorable, discreditable.*
unehrlich *dishonest.*
uneigennützig *unselfish, disinterested.*
uneinig *disunited.*
Uneinigkeit *f. discord, disagreement.*
unempfindlich *insensible.*
UNENDLICH *infinite, endless, infinitely.*
    unendlich klein *infinitesimal.*
unentbehrlich *indispensable.*
unentgeltlich *free of charge.*
unentschieden *undecided.*
unentschlossen *irresolute.*
unentschuldbar *inexcusable.*
unentwickelt *undeveloped.*
unerbittlich *inexorable.*
unerfahren *inexperienced.*
unerforschlich *impenetrable.*
unerfreulich *unpleasant, unsatisfactory.*
unerfüllbar *unrealizable.*
unerhört *unheard of, insolent.*
unerklärlich *inexplicable.*
unerlaubt *illicit, unlawful.*
unermesslich *boundless, infinite.*
unermüdlich *untiring.*
unerreichbar *inaccessible.*
unerreicht *unequaled.*
unerschrocken *fearless.*
unerschütterlich *imperturbable.*
unersetzlich *irreplaceable.*
unerträglich *unbearable, intolerable.*
unerwartet *unexpected.*
unerwünscht *undesired, unwelcome.*
unerzogen *uneducated, ill-bred.*
UNFÄHIG *incapable, unable.*
Unfähigkeit *f. inefficiency.*
Unfall *m. accident.*
Unfallversicherung *f. insurance against accidents.*
unfehlbar *certainly, unfailing.*
unfreiwillig *involuntary.*
unfreundlich *unfriendly, unpleasant.*
unfruchtbar *unproductive, sterile.*
Unfug *m. wrong, mischief, nonsense.*
ungeachtet *not esteemed; notwithstanding.*
ungebildet *uneducated.*
ungebührlich *excessive, undue.*
ungebunden *unbound, unrestrained.*
ungedeckt *uncovered (also for a check).*
ungeduldig *impatient, impatiently.*
ungeeignet *unsuitable, unfit.*

UNGEFÄHR *approximately, about, nearly.*
    von ungefähr *from about.*
ungefährlich *harmless.*
ungehalten *angry.*
Ungeheuer *monster.*
ungeheuer *huge, enormous, vast, monstrous.*
ungehorsam *disobedient.*
ungelegen *inconvenient.*
ungelernt *unskilled.*
ungemein *unusual, extremely.*
ungemütlich *uncomfortable.*
ungeniessbar *inedible, unpalatable.*
ungenügend *insufficient.*
ungepflegt *neglected, untidy.*
UNGERECHT *unjust.*
ungerechtfertigt *unjustified.*
Ungerechtigkeit *f. injustice.*
UNGERN *unwillingly, reluctant.*
ungeschehen *undone, remedied.*
Ungeschick *n. misfortune.*
Ungeschicklichkeit *f. awkwardness.*
ungeschickt *awkward, clumsy.*
ungesetzlich *illegal.*
ungestört *undisturbed.*
ungestüm *impetuous, vehement.*
ungesund *unhealthy.*
ungetreu *faithless.*
ungewiss *uncertain.*
Ungewissheit *f. uncertainty.*
ungewöhnlich *unusual, strange.*
ungewohnt *unaccustomed, unfamiliar.*
ungezogen *ill-bred, naughty.*
Unglaube *m. disbelief.*
ungläubig *incredulous, skeptical.*
unglaublich *incredible.*
ungleich *unequal, unlike.*
UNGLÜCK *n. misfortune, bad luck, accident.*
unglücklich *unfortunate, unlucky.*
unglücklickerweise *unfortunately.*
Unglücksvogel *m. unlucky person.*
Ungnade *f. disgrace, displeasure.*
    in Ungnade fallen bei *to displease someone, to fall into disgrace.*
ungültig *void, invalid.*
    für ungültig erkären *to annul.*
ungut
    Nichts für ungut. *No harm meant.*
Unheil *n. mischief, harm, disaster, calamity.*
unheilbar *incurable, irreparable.*
unheilvoll *disastrous.*
unheimlich *sinister.*
unhöflich *impolite, rude.*
Uniform *f. uniform.*
UNIVERSITÄT *f. university, college.*
unkenntlich *unrecognizable.*
Unkenntnis *f. ignorance, unawareness.*
unklar *not clear.*
unklug *imprudent, unwise.*

Unkosten *pl. expenses.*

Unkraut *n. weeds.*

unleserlich *illegible.*

unliebenswürdig *unamiable, unkind.*

unlogisch *illogical.*

unmässig *immoderate, inordinate.*

unmenschlich *inhuman.*

Unmenschlichkeit *f. inhumanity, cruelty.*

unmerklich *imperceptible.*

unmittelbar *immediate, direct.*

UNMÖBLIERT *unfurnished.*

unmodern *old-fashioned, antiquated.*

UNMÖGLICH *impossible.*

Unmöglichkeit *f. impossibility.*

unmoralisch *immoral.*

unmündig *under age, minor*

    unmündig sein *to be a minor.*

unnachgiebig *unyielding, inflexible.*

unnachsichtig *strict, severe.*

unnahbar *unapproachable, inaccessible.*

unnatürlich *unnatural, affected.*

UNNÖTIG *unnecessary, needless.*

unordentlich *disorderly, untidy.*

UNORDNUNG *f. disorder.*

    in Unordnung bringen *to mess up.*

unparteiisch *impartial.*

unpassend *inappropriate.*

unpersönlich *impersonal.*

unpraktisch *impractical.*

unpünktlich *unpunctual.*

Unrecht *n. injustice.*

    im Unrecht *in the wrong.*

    Unrecht haben *to be wrong.*

UNRECHT *wrong, unjust, unfair.*

unredlich *dishonest.*

unregelmässig *irregular.*

unreif *unripe.*

unrein *unclean.*

    ins Unreine schreiben *to make a rough copy.*

Unruhe *f. uneasiness.*

Unruhen *pl. riots.*

unruhig *restless, uneasy.*

Unruhstifter *m. agitator* (*pol.*) *troublemaker*

UNS *acc. and dat. of the pers. pron. wir; reflexive and reciprocal pron.: us, to us, ourselves, each other.*

unsachlich *subjective, personal.*

unsagbar *unspeakable.*

unsauber *dirty, filthy.*

Unsauberkeit *f. dirt, filth.*

unschädlich *harmless.*

    unschädlich machen *to render harmless, neutralize, disarm.*

unschätzbar *invaluable.*

unscheinbar *insignificant, plain, homely.*

unschlüssig *wavering, irresolute.*

UNSCHULDIG *innocent.*

unselbständig *helpless, dependent.*

UNSER *Poss. adj. our.*

UNSER (**er, –e –es**) *Poss. pron. ours.*

unsereins *people like us.*

unsererseits *as for us, for our part.*

unseresgleichen *people like us.*

unserethalben *for our sakes, on our behalf.*

unseretwegen *for our sake.*

unseretwillen *for our sake.*

UNSICHER *unsafe, uncertain, unsteady.*

Unsicherheit *f. insecurity, uncertainty.*

Unsinn *m. nonsense.*

Unsitte *f. bad habit, abuse.*

unsterblich *immortal.*

unstet *changeable, unsteady, variable.*

unsympathisch *unpleasant.*

untätig *inactive.*

UNTEN *below, beneath, underneath.*

    von oben bis unten *from top to bottom, from head to foot.*

    nach unten *downwards.*

    von unten auf *right from the bottom.*

UNTER 1. *Prep.* (*dat. when answering question, Wo?; acc. when answering question, Wohin?, and depending on the idiom*): *under, underneath, below, beneath, among, during, by.*

    Ich habe meine Schuhe unter das Bett gestellt. *I put my shoes under the bed.*

    Ich sass unter den Zuschauern. *I sat among the spectators.*

    Unter anderem hat sie mir gesagt . . . *Among other things, she told me . . .*

    unter freiem Himmel *in the open air.*

    unter uns gesagt *between us.*

    unter vier Augen *privately ("under four eyes").*

    unter Vorbehalt aller Rechte *all rights reserved.*

    jemandem etwas unter die Nase reiben *to rub one's nose in something.*

    unter diesen Umständen *under these circumstances.*

    2. *Prefix.* a) *separable* (*when meaning under*).

    Die Sonne geht im Westen unter. *The sun sets in the West.*

    b) *inseparable when not meaning under.*

    Wir unterhielten uns über die Ferien. *We talked about the holidays.*

unterbauen *to lay a foundation.*

unterbelichten *to underexpose* (*photo*).

Unterbewusstsein *n. subconsciousness.*

unterbieten *to undersell.*

UNTERBRECHEN *to interrupt, disconnect, cut off.*

    Fräulein, wir sind unterbrochen worden. *Operator, we have been cut off.*

Unterbrechung f. interruption.
unterbringen to put up, accommodate, place.
unterdessen meanwhile, in the meantime.
unterdrücken to oppress, suppress.
Unterdrückung f. repression, oppression.
untereinander among ourselves, reciprocally.
Unterernährung f. malnutrition.
Unterführung f. underpass.
Untergang m. setting, going down, destruction, fall; decline.
   der Sonnenuntergang   the sunset.
UNTERGEHEN to go down, set, sink.
Untergrundbahn f. subway.
unterhalb below.
Unterhalt m. maintenance, living.
UNTERHALTEN to support, maintain, keep up.
   sich gut unterhalten   to have a good time.
   sich unterhalten   to converse, talk.
unterhandeln to negotiate, to confer.
Unterhemd n. undershirt, vest.
Unterhosen pl. shorts, drawers.
unterirdisch underground.
Unterkleidung f. underwear.
unterkommen to find accommodation, find employment.
Unterkunft f. accommodation.
Unterlage f. foundation, support, base (plate), evidence, pad.
Unterlass m. stopping
   ohne Unterlass   incessantly.
unterlassen to discontinue, neglect, fail to.
unterlegen to lay under, put under.
unterliegen to be defeated, to be subject to.
Unterlippe f. lower lip.
Untermieter m. subtenant.
UNTERNEHMEN to undertake, attempt.
unternehmend enterprising.
Unternehmer m. contractor.
Unternehmung f. enterprise, undertaking.
unterordnen to subordinate, submit.
Unterordnung f. subordination.
unterreden to converse, confer with.
Unterredung f. talk, conference (press).
UNTERRICHT m. instruction, teaching, education, lesson.
unterrichten to teach, instruct.
Unterrock m. slip, petticoat.
unterschätzen to underestimate, underrate.
unterscheiden to distinguish, differentiate, discriminate.
   sich unterscheiden   to differ.
Unterscheidung f. distinction, discrimination.
UNTERSCHIED m. difference.
   ohne Unterschied   alike.
unterschiedlich different, distinct.
unterschiedslos indiscriminately.
unterschlagen to embezzle, to suppress.

Unterschlagung f. embezzlement, suppression.
unterschreiben to sign.
Unterschrift f. signature.
Unterseeboot n. submarine.
unterstehen to stand under, be subordinate.
   sich unterstehen   to dare.
unterstützen to support, aid, assist.
Unterstützung f. support, aid, relief.
untersuchen to examine, investigate.
Untersuchung f. examination, investigation.
Untertasse f. saucer.
Untertitel m. subtitle (movie).
Unterwäsche f. underwear.
unterwegs on the way.
Unterweisung f. instruction.
Unterwelt f. underworld.
unterwerfen to subjugate.
unterwürfig submissive.
unterzeichnen to sign, ratify.
Unterzeichner m. signatory.
Unterzeichnung f. signature, ratification.
untragbar not transferable, not negotiable; unbearable.
untrennbar inseparable.
UNTREU untrue, unfaithful.
untröstlich disconsolate.
unübersehbar immense, vast.
unübertrefflich unequaled.
ununterbrochen continuously.
unverantwortlich irresponsible.
unverbesserlich incorrigible.
unverbindlich not obligatory, without obligation.
unverdient undeserved.
unverdorben unspoiled, pure.
unvergänglich imperishable, immortal.
unvergleichlich incomparable.
unverheiratet unmarried.
unverhofft unexpected.
unverkennbar unmistakable.
unverletzt unhurt, uninjured.
unvermeidlich inevitable.
Unvermögen n. inability, incapacity, powerlessness.
unvermutet unexpected.
unvernünftig unreasonable.
unverrichtet unperformed, unaccomplished.
   unverrichteter Sache   unsuccessfully.
unverschämt impudent, fresh.
unversehens unexpectedly.
unversehrt intact, safe, undamaged.
unverständlich unintelligible, incomprehensible.
unverwandt fixed, resolute, steadfast.
unverwüstlich indestructible, inexhaustible.
unverzeihlich unpardonable.
unverzollt duty unpaid.
unverzüglich immediate, instant, prompt.

unvollkommen *imperfect.*
unvollständig *incomplete, defective.*
unvorhergesehen *unforeseen.*
UNVORSICHTIG *careless.*
unvorteilhaft *unprofitable, unbecoming.*
unweiblich *unwomanly.*
unweit *not far off, near.*
Unwesen *n. mischief, abuse.*
   sein Unwesen treiben   *to be up to mischief.*
unwesentlich *unessential, immaterial.*
   Das ist ganz unwesentlich.   *That does not
    matter.*
Unwetter *n. violent, stormy weather, storm.*
unwiderruflich *irrevocable.*
unwiderstehlich *irresistible.*
Unwille *m. indignation.*
unwillkommen *unwelcome.*
unwillkürlich *instinctively, involuntarily.*
unwirksam *ineffective, inefficient.*
unwirtlich *inhospitable, dreary.*
unwirtschaftlich *uneconomic.*
unwissend *ignorant, unaware.*
UNWOHL *not well, indisposed.*
Unwohlsein *n. indisposition.*
unwürdig *unworthy.*
Unzahl *f. endless number.*
unzählig *countless.*
unzeitgemäss *old-fashioned.*
unzerbrechlich *unbreakable.*
unzivilisiert *uncivilized, barbarian.*
unzufrieden *dissatisfied.*
unzulänglich *inaccessible.*
unzulässig *inadmissible.*
unzureichend *insufficient.*
unzuverlässig *unreliable.*
unzweideutig *unequivocal, explicit.*
unzweifelhaft *undoubted, indubitable.*
üppig *luxuriant, abundant, voluptuous.*
Üppigkeit *f. luxury.*
uralt *very old, ancient, primeval.*
Uraufführung *f. first performance, opening
   night.*
Ureinwohner *m. original inhabitant.*
Urgrosseltern *pl. great-grandparents.*
Urkunde *f. deed, document, record.*
Urkundenfälscher *m. forger of documents.*
urkundlich *documentary, authentic.*
Urlaub *m. leave, furlough, vacation.*
   der bezahlte Urlaub   *the paid vacation.*
Urquell *m. primary source.*
URSACHE *f. cause, reason.*
   Keine Ursache!   *Don't mention it!*
Ursprung *m. source, origin, beginning.*
ursprünglich *original.*
URTEIL *n. judgment, decision, sentence,
   opinion.*
   ein Urteil fällen über   *to sentence.*
urteilen *to judge, pass a sentence, give an
   opinion.*

urteilsfähig *competent to judge.*
urteilslos *without judgment.*
Urteilsspruch *m. sentence, verdict.*

V

Vagabund *m. vagabond.*
Vanille *f. vanilla.*
Variante *f. variant.*
Variation *f. variation.*
variieren *to vary.*
Vase *f. vase.*
VATER *m. father.*
Vaterhaus *n. home (of one's childhood).*
Vaterland *n. native land, fatherland.*
vaterländisch *national, patriotic.*
väterlicherseits *on the father's side.*
vaterlos *fatherless.*
Vaterstadt *f. native town.*
vegetarisch *vegetarian.*
Veilchen *n. violet.*
Vene *f. vein.*
Ventil *n. valve, air valve, vent.*
verabreden *to agree upon, make an
   agreement.*
   verabredet sein   *to have a date or
    appointment.*
Verabredung *f. agreement, engagement;
   appointment.*
verabscheuen *to detest.*
verabschieden *to dismiss, discharge.*
   sich verabschieden   *to say good-bye.*
verachten *to despise, scorn, disdain.*
verächtlich *contemptuous, disdainful.*
Verachtung *f. contempt, scorn, disdain.*
verallgemeinern *to generalize.*
veraltet *old, obsolete.*
veränderlich *variable, unstable.*
VERÄNDERN *to change, alter, vary.*
Veränderung *f. change, alteration, variation.*
verängstigt *intimidated.*
Veranlagung *f. talent.*
veranlassen *to cause.*
Veranlassung *f. reason, suggestion.*
veranschlagen *to estimate.*
   zu hoch veranschlagen   *to overrate.*
veranstalten *to arrange, organize, set up.*
Veranstaltung *f. arrangement, performance,
   event.*
verantworten *to answer for, account for.*
verantwortlich *responsible.*
VERANTWORTUNG *f. responsibility.*
   auf seine Verantwortung   *at his own risk.*
   zur Verantwortung ziehen   *to call to
    account.*
verantwortungslos *irresponsible.*
verarbeiten *to process, work up,
   manufacture, to treat.*

Verarbeitung *f. workmanship, manufacturing.*
Verband *m. bandage, association.*
verbannen *to banish, exile.*
Verbannung *f. banishment, exile.*
verbergen *to hide.*
VERBESSERN *to improve, correct.*
Verbesserung *f. improvement, correction.*
verbeugen *to bow.*
Verbeugung *f. bow, reverence.*
verbiegen *to bend, twist.*
verbieten *to forbid.*
  Rauchen verboten! *No smoking!*
  Strengstens verboten! *Strictly forbidden!*
verbinden *to tie, bind, bandage, connect, combine, join.*
  Fräulein, Sie haben mich falsch verbunden! *Operator, you gave me the wrong number!*
  sich verbinden *to unite.*
  sich zu Dank verbunden fühlen *to feel indebted to.*
verbindlich *obligatory, courteous.*
Verbindlichkeit *f. obligation.*
VERBINDUNG *f. union, combination.*
  sich in Verbindung setzen mit *to get in touch with.*
Verbindugsstrasse *f. connecting road, feeder road.*
verblüffen *to disconcert, perplex.*
verblüffend *amazing.*
Verblüffung *f. stupefaction, amazement.*
verbluten *to bleed to death.*
verborgen *hidden, concealed, secret.*
Verborgenheit *f. concealment, retirement, seclusion.*
Verbot *n. prohibition, ban.*
verboten *prohibited, forbidden.*
Verbrauch *m. consumption.*
verbrauchen *to consume, use.*
Verbraucher *m. consumer.*
Verbrechen *n. crime.*
Verbrecher *m. criminal.*
verbrecherisch *criminal.*
verbreiten *to spread, diffuse.*
verbrennen *to burn, cremate.*
  sich verbrennen *to burn oneself.*
Verbrennung *f. burning, combustion.*
verbringen *to spend, pass time.*
verbunden *connected.*
verbürgen *to guarantee, vouch for.*
Verdacht *m. suspicion.*
verdächtig *suspicious.*
verdächtigen *to distrust.*
verdammen *to condemn.*
verdammenswert *damnable.*
Verdammnis *f. damnation, perdition.*
Verdammung *f. condemnation.*
verdanken *to owe something.*

Verdauung *f. digestion*
Verdeck *n. covering, awning*
Verderb *m. ruin.*
Verderben *n. ruin, destruction.*
  jemanden ins Verderben stürzen *to ruin a person.*
VERDERBEN *to spoil, ruin.*
  Ich möchte es mir nicht mit ihm verderben. *I don't want to displease him.*
  sich den Magen verderben *to upset one's stomach.*
Verderber *m. corrupter.*
verderblich *perishable, pernicious.*
verdienen *to earn, gain, deserve, merit.*
Verdienst *m. gain, profit, earnings.*
Verdienst *n. merit.*
verdienstvoll *deserving.*
verdient *deserving.*
  sich verdient machen um *to deserve well of.*
Verdikt *n. verdict.*
verdolmetschen *to interpret, translate.*
verdoppeln *to double.*
verdorben *spoiled.*
verdrängen *to displace, push aside.*
verdrehen *to twist, sprain.*
  einem den Kopf verdrehen *to turn one's head, to drive someone crazy.*
verdriessen *to annoy, displease.*
verdummen *to grow stupid.*
verdünnen *to thin, dilute.*
Verdünnung *f. attenuation, rarefaction, dilution.*
verdunsten *to evaporate.*
Verdunstung *f. evaporation.*
verdursten *to die of thirst.*
veredeln *to ennoble, improve, refine, finish.*
verehren *to respect, worship, adore.*
Verehrer *m. worshipper.*
Verehrung *f. respect, veneration.*
vereidigen *to swear in, put on oath.*
Vereidigung *f. swearing in, taking of an oath.*
Verein *m. union, association.*
vereinbar *compatible, consistent.*
Vereinbarung *f. agreement, arrangement.*
vereinfachen *to simplify.*
vereinigen *to join, unite, reconcile.*
  die Vereinigten Staaten von Amerika. *The United States of America.*
vereisen *to turn to ice.*
vereiteln *to frustrate, thwart.*
verelenden *to sink into poverty.*
vererben *to bequeath, transmit, hand down.*
verewigen *to perpetuate, immortalize.*
verfahren *to act, behave.*
Verfall *m. decay, ruin.*
  im Verfall geraten *to go to ruin, decay.*

verfallen *to decline, go to ruin, grow weaker, expire.*
  verfallen lassen *to let go to waste.*
  verfallene Züge *sunken features.*
verfassen *to compose, write.*
Verfasser *m. author, writer.*
Verfassung *f. state, condition.*
verfaulen *to decay.*
verfliegen *to fly away, disappear, vanish.*
verfolgen *to follow, pursue, prosecute.*
  heimlich verfolgen *to shadow.*
  gerichtlich verfolgen *to prosecute.*
Verfolgung *f. pursuit, prosecution.*
verfügbar *available.*
verfügen *to arrange, decree, obtain.*
  verfügen über *to dispose of, have at one's disposal.*
  zur Verfügung stellen *to place at one's disposal.*
verführen *prevail upon, seduce, to lead astray.*
Verführer *m. tempter, seducer.*
verführerisch *tempting, seductive.*
Verführung *f. temptation.*
Vergangenheit *f. past; past tense (grammar).*
vergänglich *transitory, perishable.*
Vergaser *m. carburetor.*
vergeben *to give away, dispose of, confer, forgive.*
vergebens *in vain, vainly.*
Vergebung *f. pardon, forgiveness, bestowal.*
vergelten *to pay back, repay, retaliate.*
Vergeltung *f. recompense, reprisal.*
VERGESSEN *to forget, neglect.*
vergesslich *forgetful.*
Vergesslichkeit *f. forgetfulness.*
vergiften *to poison.*
Vergiftung *f. poisoning.*
Vergleich *m. comparison, agreement, arrangement.*
VERGLEICHEN *to compare, check, settle.*
VERGNÜGEN *n. pleasure, joy, fun.*
vergnügen (sich) *to amuse, enjoy oneself.*
VERGNÜGT *pleased, glad.*
  Ich komme mit Vergnügen. *I'll be delighted to come.*
  Viel Vergnügen! *Have a good time!*
  Vergnügungsreise *f. pleasure trip.*
vergnügungssüchtig *pleasure-seeking.*
vergraben *to bury, hide in the ground.*
vergriffen *out of print.*
vergrössern *to enlarge, magnify.*
Vergrösserung *f. enlargement.*
Vergünstigung *f. privilege, favor.*
Verhältnis *n. relation, ratio, love-affair.*
verhältnismässig *relative, proportional.*
verhasst *hated, hateful, odious.*
verheimlichen *to conceal, keep secret.*

verheiraten *to marry off.*
  sich verheiraten *to get married.*
verherrlichen *to glorify.*
Verherrlichung *f. glorification.*
verhindern *to hinder, prevent.*
Verhinderung *f. hindrance, draw-back.*
Verhör *n. examination, trial.*
verhören *to examine, interrogate.*
verhungern *to die of hunger.*
verirren *to lose one's way, go astray.*
VERKAUF *m. sale.*
VERKAUFEN *to sell.*
  billiger verkaufen *to undersell.*
  zu verkaufen *for sale.*
VERKÄUFER m. (–in, *f.) sales person, vendor.*
verkäuflich *saleable.*
VERKEHR *m. traffic, circulation, communication, trade.*
Verkehrschild *n. traffic sign, road sign.*
Verkehrsmittel *n. means of communication or transport, passenger vehicle.*
Verkehrsordnung *f. traffic regulations*
Verkehrsstauung *f. traffic jam, congestion.*
Verkehrszeichen *n. traffic sign, road sign.*
verkehren *to associate, transform, to reverse. convert, change, run (buses).*
  verkehren mit *to associate with, see a great deal of.*
Verkehrsampel *f. traffic light.*
Verkehrsschutzmann *m. traffic policeman.*
Verkehrsunfall *m. traffic-accident.*
verkehrt *wrong, backwards, upside down, absurd.*
  verkehrt gehen *to go the wrong way.*
verkennen *to fail to recognize, mistake, misunderstand, undervalue.*
verkleiden *to disguise, camouflage.*
Verkleidung *f. disguise, camouflage.*
verkommen *to be ruined, become bad, degenerate.*
Verkommenheit *f. depravity, degeneracy.*
verkörpern *to personify, incarnate, embody.*
Verlag *m. publication (Austria), publishing firm.*
verlangen *to demand, desire, require.*
  auf Verlangen *by request, on demand.*
  verlangen nach *to long for, to desire.*
verlängern *to extend, prolong.*
Verlängerung *f. extension, prolonging.*
Verlass *m. trustworthiness.*
  Auf ihn ist kein Verlass. *He cannot be relied on.*
VERLASSEN *to leave, abandon, desert.*
Verlauf *m. lapse, development*
verlaufen *to elapse, to take its course*
  sich verlaufen *to get lost*
verlegen *embarrassed, self-conscious, confused.*

um etwas verlegen sein *to be at a loss for.*

um Geld verlegen sein *to be short of money.*

Verlegenheit *f. embarrassment, difficulty.*

Verleger *m. publisher.*

verleihen *to lend out, confer, bestow, grant.*

verletzbar *vulnerable, susceptible.*

verletzen *to hurt, injure, offend.*

Verletzung *f. injury, offense, violation.*

verleugnen *to deny, injure, offend.*

Verleugnung *f. denial, denunciation.*

verleumden *to calumniate, slander.*

Verleumder *m. slanderer.*

verleumderisch *slanderous.*

Verleumdung *f. slander, defamation, libel.*

(sich) VERLIEBEN *to fall in love.*

verliebt *in love.*

Sie ist verliebt bis über die Ohren. *She is head over heels in love.*

VERLIEREN *to lose, waste, disappear.*

An ihm ist nicht viel verloren. *He's no great loss.*

Ich habe keinen einzigen Augenblick zu verlieren. *I don't have a single moment to lose.*

(sich) verloben *to get engaged.*

Verlobte *m. & f. fiancé(e).*

Verlobung *f. engagement.*

Verlust *m. loss, waste, escape.*

vermehren *to increase.*

Vermehrung *f. increase.*

vermieten *to rent, let, hire out.*

Vermieter *m. landlord.*

vermissen *to miss.*

vermuten *to suppose, presume, suspect.*

vermutlich *presumable, probable.*

vernachlässigen *to neglect.*

Vernachlässigung *f. neglect.*

verneigen *to bow.*

Verneigung *f. bow.*

vernichten *to annihilate, destroy.*

Vernichtung *f. annihilation, destruction.*

VERNUNFT *f. reason, understanding, intelligence, good sense, judgment.*

Vernunft annehmen *to listen to reason.*

zur Vernunft bringen *to bring to one's senses.*

vernünftig *reasonable, sensible.*

veröffentlichen *to publish.*

Veröffentlichung *f. publication.*

verordnen *to order, decree.*

Verordnung *f. order, decree, prescription.*

verpacken *to pack up, wrap up.*

Verpackung *f. packing up, wrapping up.*

verpfänden *to pawn, mortgage.*

verpflegen *to board, to provide for.*

Verpflegung *f. feeding, board, food.*

Zimmer mit Verpflegung. *Room and board.*

verpflichten *to oblige, bind, engage.*

sich verpflichten *to commit (bind) oneself.*

verpflichtet sein *to be under obligation.*

Verpflichtung *f. obligation, duty, engagement.*

Verrat *m. treason, betrayal.*

verraten *to betray, disclose, reveal.*

Verräter *m. traitor.*

verräterisch *treacherous.*

verrechnen *to reckon up, charge, account; miscalculate.*

Verrechnung *f. settling of an account, reckoning.*

verreisen *to go away.*

verreist sein *to be away.*

verrichten *to execute, perform, accomplish.*

die Hausarbeit verrichten *to do the housework.*

Verrichtung *f. execution, performance, function, work.*

VERRÜCKT *crazy, mad.*

Vers *m. verse, stanza.*

versagen *to deny, refuse; fail, miss.*

VERSAMMELN *to assemble, bring together, gather.*

sich versammeln *to gather.*

Versammlung *f. gathering, assembly, meeting.*

versäumen *to neglect, omit, miss.*

verschaffen *to get, obtain, secure, procure.*

verschenken *to give away.*

verschicken *to send away, dispatch, evacuate.*

Verschickung *f. dispatch, transportation, evacuation.*

VERSCHIEDEN *different from, distinct, various.*

verschlafen *to oversleep, sleepy.*

verschlimmern *to aggravate, to make worse.*

Verschlimmerung *f. deterioration.*

verschlucken *to swallow the wrong way.*

Verschluss *m. lock, fastener, clasp, seal, plug, zipper.*

verschmachten *to languish.*

verschonen *to spare, exempt from.*

verschönern *to beautify, embellish, adorn.*

Verschönerung *f. embellishment.*

verschreiben *to prescribe, order in writing, write for.*

sich verschreiben *to make a mistake in writing.*

verschwenden *to waste, lavish.*

Verschwender *m. spendthrift, extravagant person.*

verschwenderisch *wasteful, extravagant.*

verschwiegen *discreet, close.*

Verschwiegenheit f. secrecy, discretion.
verschwistert like brothers and sisters,
    closely united.
Versehen n. mistake, oversight.
VERSEHEN to provide, furnish, supply with;
    to overlook.
    aus Versehen   by mistake.
    ehe man sich's versieht   unexpectedly,
      suddenly.
    den Dienst eines andern versehen   to stand
      in for someone
    sich versehen   to make a mistake.
VERSETZEN to displace, transfer, pledge,
    pawn.
    den Verstand verlieren   to go out of one's
      mind. Just put yourself in my place.
Versetzung f. transfer, moving up.
VERSICHERN to insure, affirm.
Versicherung f. insurance.
versinnbildlichen to symbolize, represent.
versöhnen to reconcile, conciliate.
Versöhnung f. reconciliation.
versorgen to provide, supply.
Versorger m. support, breadwinner.
Versorgung f. maintenance, providing (for)
verspätet late.
Verspätung f. delay, lateness.
    Verspätung haben   to be late.
verspielen to lose, gamble away.
VERSPRECHEN to promise.
    Ich habe mich nur versprochen.   It was
      only a slip of the tongue.
    sich etwas versprechen von   to expect
      much of.
Versprechung f. promise.
VERSTAND m. mind, sense, brain,
    intellect.
    den Verstand verlieren   to go out of one's
      mind.
    zu Verstand kommen   to arrive at the age
      of discretion.
verständig intelligent, sensible, wise.
verständigen to inform, notify.
    sich verständigen   to come to an
      understanding with.
Verständigung f. understanding.
verständlich understandable, clear,
    comprehensible.
    sich verständlich machen   to make oneself
      understood.
Verständlichkeit f. intelligibility, clearness.
Verständnis comprehension, understanding.
    Verständnis haben für   to appreciate.
verständnislos unappreciative, stupid.
verständnisvoll understanding, appreciative.
Versteck n. hiding place.
verstecken to hide, conceal.
versteckt hidden, concealed.
    versteckte Absichten   ulterior motives.

VERSTEHEN to understand, comprehend,
    know.
    falsch verstehen   to misunderstand.
    Ich verstehe nicht!   I don't understand!
    sich verstehen   to understand each other.
    sich von selbst verstehen   to go without
      saying.
    Was verstehen Sie darunter?   What do you
      understand by that?
    zu verstehen geben   to give to
      understand.
versteifen to stiffen.
versteigern to sell at auction.
Versteigerung f. auction.
verstellbar adjustable.
verstellen to change order or position, shift,
    block, disguise.
Verstellung f. dissimulation, disguise,
    hypocrisy.
versteuern to pay duty on.
verstimmen to annoy, upset.
Verstimmung f. ill humor, bad temper.
Versuch m. experiment, trial, attempt.
VERSUCHEN to try, attempt, taste,
    endeavor.
    es versuchen mit   to give a trial to, put to
      the test.
Versuchung f. temptation.
vertagen to adjourn.
vertauschen to exchange, substitute.
verteidigen to defend.
Verteidiger m. defender, advocate, attorney.
Verteidigung f. defense.
verteilen to distribute, dispense, assign.
Verteiler m. distributor, retailer.
Verteilung f. distribution.
Vertrag m. contract, treaty, agreement.
VERTRAGEN to carry away, bear, stand,
    endure, tolerate, digest.
    ich kann diese Speise nicht
      vertragen.   This food does not agree
      with me.
    sich vertragen   to get along.
    sich wieder vertragen   to settle one's
      differences, to be reconciled.
    einen Spass vertragen   to take a joke.
Vertrauen n. confidence.
vertrauen to trust.
vertrauensvoll trusting.
vertrauenswürdig trustworthy.
vertraulich confidential.
Vertraulichkeit f. confidence.
vertraut familiar,
    im Vertrauen   in confidence,
      confidentially.
    im Vertrauen auf   relying on, trusting to.
    sich vertraut machen   to become familiar.
Vertraute(r) m. f. intimate friend.
vertreiben to drive away, expel, scatter.

vertreten *to represent, substitute for; to sprain.*
Vertreter *m. representative, substitute.*
VERTRETUNG *f. representation, replacement.*
  eine Vertretung übernehmen   *to take the place of, represent.*
vertrösten *to console, put off.*
verunglücken *to have an accident.*
verursachen *to cause.*
verurteilen *to sentence, condemn.*
Verurteilung *f. sentence, condemnation.*
vervielfältigen *to multiply, duplicate, reproduce.*
verwachsen *overgrown, deformed.*
verwahren *to keep, put away.*
verwaisen *to become an orphan.*
verwaist *orphaned, deserted.*
verwandeln *to transform.*
verwandt *related, similar, allied.*
Verwandte *m. f. relation, relative.*
Verwandtschaft *f. relationship, relations.*
verwechseln *to take for, mistake for.*
Verwechslung *f. mistake, confusion.*
verweigern *to deny, refuse.*
Verweigerung *f. denial, refusal.*
Verweis *m. reproof, reprimand, reference.*
Verweisung *f. exile, banishment.*
verwendbar *applicable.*
VERWENDEN *to use, utilize, employ, expend.*
  sich verwenden für   *to put in a good word for.*
  verwenden auf   *to put in on, spend on.*
  Zeit verwenden auf   *to devote time to.*
Verwendung *f. use, utilization, application.*
verwirklichen *to realize, materialize.*
Verwirklichung *f. realization, materialization.*
Verwöhnung *f. spoiling, pampering.*
verwundern *to surprise.*
Verwunderung *f. surprise, astonishment.*
verzagen *to lose heart, despair.*
VERZEIHEN *to pardon, forgive, excuse.*
  Verzeihen Sie!   *Excuse me!*
verzeihlich *excusable.*
VERZEIHUNG *f. pardon, excuse.*
  Ich bitte Sie um Verzeihung!   *Please excuse me!*
Verzicht *m. resignation, renunciation.*
verzichten *to renounce, resign, forgo.*
verzinsen *to pay interest on.*
verzögern *to delay.*
verzollen *to pay duty on.*
  Haben Sie etwas zu verzollen?   *Have you anything to declare?*
Verzollung *f. payment of duty, clearance.*
verzweifeln *to despair*
verzweifelt *desperate, despairing.*

Verzweiflung *f. despair, desperation.*
  zur Verzweiflung bringen   *to drive one mad.*
Veto *n. veto.*
  Veto einlegen   *to veto a thing.*
VETTER *m. cousin.*
Vieh *n. cattle.*
Viehhändler *m. cattle dealer.*
VIEL *much, a great deal, a lot of.*
  ein bisschen viel   *a little too much.*
  sehr viel   *a great many.*
  in vielem   *in many respects.*
  noch einmal so viel   *as much again.*
  viele   *many.*
  zu viel   *far too much.*
  Viel Glück!   *Lots of luck!*
  Viel Vergnügen!   *Have a good time!*
vielgerühmt *much-praised.*
VIELLEICHT *perhaps.*
vielmalig *frequent, repeated.*
vielseitig *versatile; many-sided.*
vielumstritten *widely discussed/disputed.*
VIER *four.*
  zu vieren, zu viert   *four of us.*
Viereck *n. square.*
viereckig *square, quadrangular.*
VIERTE *fourth.*
VIERTEL *n. quarter, fourth.*
  Es ist Viertel vor zwei.   *It is a quarter to two.*
vierteljährlich *quarterly.*
Viertelstunde *f. a quarter of an hour.*
viertelstündlich *every quarter of an hour.*
VIERZEHN *fourteen.*
  vierzehn Tage   *two weeks.*
VIERZEHNTE *fourteenth.*
VIERZIG *forty.*
VIERZIGSTE *fortieth.*
Violine *f. violin.*
virtuos *masterly.*
Virtuose(–sin) *m. (f.) virtuoso.*
Virtuosität *f. virtuosity.*
Vision *f. vision.*
Visite *f. visit.*
Visitenkarte *f. visiting-card.*
Vitrine *f. showcase.*
VOGEL *m. bird.*
  den Vogel abschiessen   *to carry off the prize, to steal the show.*
Vogelscheuche *f. scarecrow.*
Vokabel *f. word.*
Vokabelschatz *m. vocabulary (range).*
VOLK *n. people, nation, crowd.*
  das arbeitende Volk   *the working classes.*
  der Mann aus dem Volk   *the man in the street.*
Volksabstimmung *f. plebiscite.*
Volkslied *n. folk song.*
Volksschule *f. elementary or primary school.*

volkstümlich *national, popular.*

Volksversammlung *f. public meeting.*

VOLL 1. *adj. & adv. full, filled, complete, whole, entire; fully, completely.*

aus vollem Herzen *from the bottom of the heart.*

aus voller Kehle *at the top of one's voice.*

den Mund voll nehmen *to boast.*

Die Rechnung ist voll bezahlt. *The bill is paid in full.*

in voller Fahrt *at full speed.*

Man cannot take him too seriously.

2. *Prefix.* a) *separable (meaning to fill)*

Sie giesst die Gläser voll. *She fills up the glasses.*

b) *inseparable (meaning to accomplish, finish).*

Er vollführte eine gute Leistung. *He executed a good performance.*

Vollbart *m. beard.*

vollblutig *full-blooded.*

vollbringen *to finish, accomplish, complete.*

Volldampf *m. full steam.*

vollenden *to complete, to bring to a close.*

Vollendung *f. completion, perfecting.*

volles Vertrauen *complete confidence.*

völlig *complete, entire, quite.*

volljährig *of age.*

Volljährigkeit *f. majority (of age).*

VOLLKOMMEN *perfect, complete.*

Vollkommenheit *f. perfection.*

Vollkraft *f. full vigor.*

Vollmacht *f. full power, power of attorney.*

Vollmilch *f. unskimmed milk.*

Vollmond *m. full moon.*

vollständig *complete.*

vollzählig *complete, full, completely, absolutely.*

VON 1. *pret. (dat.). from, by, with, of, on, upon, about.*

Amerika wurde von Kolumbus entdeckt. *America was discovered by Columbus.*

Der Platz war voll von Menschen. *The place was full of people.*

ein Gedicht von Heine *a poem by Heine.*

eine Feder von Gold *a gold pen.*

von heute ab *from today on.*

Von meinem Fenster sehe ich auf den Garten. *From my window I see the garden.*

2. *adv.: apart, separate.*

von einander *apart.*

von klein auf *from childhood (on).*

von mir aus *as far as I am concerned.*

von selbst *by itself, automatically.*

von Nutzen sein *to be needful, necessary.*

VOR 1. *prep. (dat. when answering question, Wo?; acc. when answering question, Wohin?, and depending on the idiom), before, in front of, ahead of, for, with, against, from.*

Das Bild ist vor mir. *The picture is in front of me.*

Es ist ein Viertel vor elf. *It is a quarter to eleven.*

Ich werde sie vor ihm warnen. *I will warn her against him.*

nach wie vor *as usual.*

nicht vor *not until.*

vor acht Tagen *a week ago.*

vor allem *above all, first of all.*

vor der Klasse *before class.*

vor Hunger sterben *to die of hunger.*

Vor ihm müssen Sie sich in Acht nehmen. *With him, you must be on your guard.*

vorzeiten *formerly*

vorab *above all.*

2. *separable prefix (implies movement forward, presentation, demonstration).*

Der Lehrer las ein Gedicht vor. *The teacher read a poem aloud.*

Die Soldaten rückten vor. *The soldiers moved forward.*

Wir bereiten uns auf die Prüfung vor. *We prepare ourselves for the examination.*

Vorabend *m. evening before.*

vorahnen *to have a presentiment.*

Vorahnung *f. presentiment.*

voran *ahead, before.*

vorangehen *to precede.*

mit gutem Beispiel vorangehen *to set a good example.*

Voranschlag *m. estimate.*

Voranzeige *f. preliminary advertisement.*

Vorarbeit *f. preliminary work.*

Vorarbeiter *m. foreman.*

VORAUS *in front of, ahead of.*

etwas voraus haben vor *to have an advantage over a person.*

im Voraus *in advance.*

weit voraus *way ahead.*

vorausgehen *to lead the way, precede.*

Voraussage *f. prediction, prophecy.*

voraussetzen *to presuppose, assume.*

Voraussetzung *f. supposition, assumption.*

voraussichtlich *presumable, probable.*

Vorbehalt *m. reservation, proviso.*

ohne Vorbehalt *unconditionally.*

unter Vorbehalt aller Rechte *all rights reserved.*

vorbehalten *to keep in reserve, withhold.*

sich vorbehalten *to reserve to oneself.*

vorbehaltlos *unconditional.*

vorbei *by, along, past, over, gone.*

vorbereiten *to prepare, make ready.*

Vorbereitung *f. preparation.*

Vorbeugungsmassregel *m. preventive measure.*

Vorbild *n. model, standard.*

vorbildlich *model, ideal.*

Vorbildung *f. preparatory training, education.*

vorder *fore, forward, anterior.*

Vordergrund *m. foreground.*

Vorderhaus *n. front part of the house.*

vordringlich *urgent.*

voreilig *hasty, rash.*

Voreiligkeit *f. precipitation, rashness.*

voreingenommen *prejudiced.*

Voreingenommenheit *f. prejudice.*

vorenthalten *to keep back, withhold.*

Vorfall *m. occurrence, event.*

vorfallen *to occur, happen, take place.*

Vorfreude *f. joy of anticipation.*

vorführen *to demonstrate, produce.*

Vorführung *f. demonstration.*

Vorgang *m. occurrence.*

Vorgänger *m. predecessor.*

VORGEHEN *to go on, go forward, go first, lead, take place, occur, act, be of special importance.*

    Gehen Sie vor! *Go right ahead!*

Vorgeschichte *f. prehistory.*

Vorgeschmack *m. foretaste.*

Vorgesetzte *m. & f. chief, boss*

VORGESTERN *the day before yesterday.*

vorhaben *to have on, wear, to intend, plan.*

    Haben Sie morgen etwas vor? *Do you have any plans for tomorrow?*

vorhalten *to hold up, to hold out.*

Vorhang *m. curtain.*

vorher *before, beforehand, in advance, previously.*

vorherrschen *to predominate, prevail.*

vorherrschend *predominant, prevailing.*

Vorkenntnis *f. previous knowledge.*

vorkommen *to come forward, occur, happen.*

    Es kommt Ihnen nur so vor. *You are just imagining that.*

Vorkommnis *n. occurrence, event.*

Vorlage *f. presentation of documents.*

vorlassen *to give precedence to.*

vorläufig *preliminary.*

Vorleger *m. mat, rug.*

vorlesen *to read aloud.*

Vorlesung *f. lecture.*

vorletzt *one before the last.*

Vorliebe *f. predilection, preference.*

vormachen *to put, place before, impose on someone, fool.*

vormerken *to make a note of, put down.*

Vormittag *m. morning ("before noon").*

Vormund *m. guardian.*

Vormundschaft *f. guardianship.*

VORN *in front, in front of.*

    nach vorn *forward.*

    nach vorne heraus wohnen *to live in the front part of a house.*

    von vorn *from the front.*

    von vorn anfangen *to start afresh.*

    vor vorn herein *from the first.*

Vorname *m. Christian name, first name.*

vornehm *of high rank, noble, distinguished.*

Vornehmheit *f. distinction, high rank.*

vornehmlich *principally, chiefly, especially.*

Vorort *m. suburb.*

Vorplatz *m. court, hall, vestibule.*

Vorrang *m. precedence, priority.*

Vorrat *m. store, stock, provision.*

vorrätig *in stock, on hand.*

    nicht mehr vorrätig *out of stock.*

Vorratskammer *f. storeroom, pantry.*

Vorrede *f. words of introduction; opening speech.*

vorsagen *to dictate, say, prompt.*

Vorsatz *m. purpose.*

Vorschlag *m. proposal, proposition.*

vorschlagen *to propose, offer.*

vorschreiben *to set a copy.*

Vorschrift *f. copy, direction.*

vorschriftmässig *according to instructions.*

vorsehen *to provide for, consider, take care.*

Vorsehung *f. providence.*

VORSICHT *f. foresight, caution, prudence.*

    Vorsicht! *Take care! Beware!*

    Vorsicht Stufe! *Mind the step!*

vorsichtig *cautious, prudent.*

vorsichtshalber *as a precaution.*

Vorsichtsmassregel *f. precautionary measure.*

Vorsitz *m. presidency, chairman.*

    den Vorsitz führen *to preside in the chair.*

Vorspeise *f. hors d'oeuvre.*

vorsprechen *to pronounce, recite.*

Vorsprung *m. projection, projecting part.*

Vorstadt *f. suburb.*

Vorstand *m. board of directors.*

vorstellen *to place before, put in front of, demonstrate, introduce, represent, act.*

    sich etwas vorstellen *to imagine something.*

    sich vorstellen *to introduce oneself.*

VORSTELLUNG *f. introduction, presentation, performance, picture.*

    Wann fängt die Vorstellung an? *When does the performance start?*

Vorstellungsvermögen *n. imagination.*

Vorteil *m. advantage, profit.*

VORTEILHAFT *advantageous, favorable.*

    vorteilhaft aussehen *to look one's best.*

Vortrag *m. reciting, delivery, execution, lecture.*

vortragen *to carry forward, recite, declaim, exclaim, perform.*
vortrefflich *excellent, admirable, splendid.*
Vortrefflichkeit *f. excellence.*
vorüber *past, over, by, along.*
vorübergehen *to go by, pass.*
Vorurteil *n. prejudice.*
vorurteilslos *unprejudiced.*
Vorverkauf *m. booking in advance (theater); advance sale.*
vorvorgestern *three days ago.*
Vorwahl *f. primary election.*
Vorwand *m. pretext, pretense, excuse.*
VORWÄRTS *forward, onward, on.*
   Vorwärts! *Go on! Go ahead!*
vorwärtsgehen *to go on, advance, progress.*
vorwärtskommen *to get on, advance, prosper.*
vorwärtskommend *predominant.*
Vorwurf *m. reproach.*
   Vorwürfe machen *to blame.*
vorwurfsvoll *reproachful.*
vorzeigen *to show, produce, exhibit, display.*
vorzeitig *premature, precocious.*
vorziehen *to draw forward, prefer.*
Vorzimmer *n. antechamber.*
Vorzug *m. preference, superiority.*
vorzüglich *excellent, superior, first-choice.*
Vorzüglichkeit *f. excellency, superiority.*
Vorzugspreis *m. special price.*
Vorzugsrecht *n. privilege.*

W

WAAGE *f. balance, scales.*
   einem die Waage halten *to be a match for.*
   sich die Waage halten *to counterbalance each other.*
   wagerecht *horizontal level.*
WACH *awake, alive, brisk.*
Wachdienst *m. guard duty.*
Wache *f. guard, watch, sentry.*
WACHEN *to be awake, remain awake.*
   wachen über *to watch over.*
Wachs *n. wax.*
wachsam *vigilant, watchful.*
Wachsamkeit *f. vigilance.*
WACHSEN *to grow, increase, extend.*
   ans Herz wachsen *to grow fond of.*
   einem gewachsen sein *to be a match for one.*
   einer Sache gewachsen sein *to be equal to a task.*
Wachstum *n. growth, increase.*
Wacht *f. guard, watch.*
Wächter *m. watchman, guard.*
wack(e)lig *shaky, unsteady.*

Waffe *f. weapon, arm.*
Waffel *f. wafer, waffle.*
Waffeleisen *n. waffle-iron.*
Waffenschein *m. gun-license.*
Waffenstillstand *m. armistice.*
WAGEN *m. car, automobile, railroad car, cab, wagon.*
Wagen *to venture, risk, dare.*
   gewagt *daring, risky, perilous.*
Wagnis *n. risk.*
WAHL *f. choice, selection, election.*
   seine Wahl treffen *to make one's choice.*
   vor die Wahl stellen *to let one choose.*
wahlberechtigt *entitled to vote.*
WÄHLEN *to choose, select, pick out, elect, dial.*
   Wählen abhalten *to hold elections.*
Wähler *m. elector, selector.*
wählerisch *particular, fastidious.*
Wahlkampf *m. election, contest.*
wahllos *indiscriminately.*
Wahlstimme *f. vote.*
Wahn *m. delusion, illusion.*
Wahnsinn *m. insanity, madness, craziness.*
wahnsinnig *insane, mad.*
WAHR *true, sincere, genuine, real, proper, veritable.*
   etwas nicht wahr haben wollen *not to admit a thing.*
   Nicht wahr? *Isn't it? Don't you think so?*
   so wahr ich lebe *as sure as I live.*
   wahr werden *to come true.*
WÄHREND 1. *prep. (gen.): during, for, in the course of.*
   Während des Winters verbringen wir unsere Ferien in den Bergen. *During the winter we spend our vacations in the mountains.*
   2. *conj. while.*
   Sie kam, während Sie weg waren. *She came while you were out.*
WAHRHEIT *f. truth.*
   Ich habe ihm gehörig die Wahrheit gesagt. *I really gave him a piece of my mind.*
wahrheitsgetreu *truthful, true.*
wahrnehmbar *perceptible, noticeable.*
wahrsagen *to foretell, to predict.*
Wahrsagerin *f. fortune teller.*
WAHRSCHEINLICH *probable, likely.*
Wahrscheinlichkeit *f. probability.*
Währung *f. standard, currency.*
Waise *f. & m. orphan.*
Waisenhaus *m. orphanage.*
Wal *m. whale.*
WALD *m. forest, woodland.*
waldig *wooded.*
Waldung *f. woodland, wood.*
Wall *m. rampart, dike.*

Walnuss *f. walnut.*
walzen *to waltz.*
Walzer *m. waltz.*
WAND *f. wall, partition.*
Wandel *m. change, alteration.*
   Handel und Wandel *trade, commerce.*
wandelbar *perishable, changeable, fickle.*
wandern *to wander, to hike.*
Wanderschaft *f. trip, tour, travels.*
Wanderung *f. traveling, migration.*
Wandgemälde *n. mural painting, fresco.*
Wandschrank *m. cupboard.*
Wandteppich *m. tapestry, wall hanging.*
Wankelmut *m. inconsistency, fickleness.*
WANN *when*
   wann immer *whenever.*
   dann und wann *now and then.*
Wanne *f. tub, bath.*
WARE *f. article, goods, merchandise.*
Warenhaus *n. department store.*
WARM *warm.*
   Ist es Ihnen warm genug? *Are you warm*
     enough?
   warm stellen *to keep hot.*
Wärme *f. heat, warmth.*
WÄRMEN *to warm, heat.*
Wärmflasche *f. hot-water bottle.*
warnen *to warn, caution.*
Warnung *f. warning.*
Warnungssignal *n. danger signal.*
WARTEN *to wait, attend to, nurse.*
   warten auf *to wait for.*
   warten lassen *to keep waiting.*
Wärter *m. attendant, caretaker.*
Wartesaal *m. waiting-room.*
Wartezimmer *n. doctor's waiting room.*
WARUM *why, for what reason.*
WAS *what, whatever, that which, which,*
   that.
   Ach was! *Nonsense!*
   Nein so was! *Well, I never!*
   was ... auch immer *no matter what,*
     whatever.
   was für ein *what sort of, what a.*
   was mich betrifft *as for me.*
   Ich will dir was sagen. *I'll tell you*
     something.
Waschbecken *n. wash basin.*
WÄSCHE *f. wash; linen, underclothing.*
   in die Wäsche geben *to send to the*
     laundry.
   schmutzige Wäsche *soiled linen, dirty*
     clothes.
Wäschegeschäft *n. haberdashery, lingerie*
   store.
Wäscheklammer *f. clothespin.*
Wäscheleine *f. clothesline.*
waschen *to wash.*
Wäscherei *f. laundry.*

Waschmaschine *f. washing machine.*
WASSER *n. water.*
   fliessendes Wasser *running water.*
   mit allen Wassern gewaschen sein *to be*
     cunning.
   sich über Wasser halten *to keep one's*
     head above water.
   zu Wasser und zu Lande *by land and sea.*
Wasserabbluss *m. drain.*
Wasserball *m. water polo.*
Wasserbehälter *m. reservoir, tank.*
wasserdicht *waterproof.*
Wasserfall *m. waterfall.*
Wasserfarbe *f. water-color.*
Wasserflugzeug *n. sea plane.*
Wasserglas *n. glass, tumbler.*
wasserhältig *containing water.*
wässerig *watery.*
   einem den Mund wässerig machen *to*
     make a person's mouth water.
Wasserkanne *f. watering-can.*
Wasserleitung *f. water supply, water pipes,*
   faucet.
Wasserspiegel *m. water-surface.*
Wasserstiefel *pl. rubber boots.*
Wasserstoffbombe *f. hydrogen bomb*
   (H-bomb).
Wasserstrasse *f. waterway.*
Watte *f. wadding, cotton-wool.*
weben *to weave.*
Weber *m. weaver.*
Wechsel *m. change, alteration, succession,*
   turn.
   gezogener Wechsel *draft.*
Wechselgeld *n. change (money).*
   Bitte, zahlen Sie ihr Wechselgeld
     nach. *Please count your change.*
Wechselkurs *m. rate of exchange.*
WECHSELN *to change, exchange, alternate,*
   shift.
   seinen Wohnort wechseln *to move; to*
     change one's residence.
   den Besitzer wechseln *to change*
     ownership.
wechselseitig *reciprocal, mutual, alternate.*
WECKEN *to wake, awaken.*
Wecker *m. alarm-clock.*
weder *neither.*
   weder ... noch *neither ... nor.*
WEG *m. way, path, road, street, walk.*
   am Weg *by the roadside.*
   auf halbem Weg *halfway.*
   aus dem Weg gehen *to make way for,*
     stand aside.
   in die Wege leiten *to prepare for.*
   seiner Wege gehen *to go one's way.*
   sich auf den Weg machen *to set out.*
   in den Weg kommen *to get into the way.*
   in Wege stehen *to stand in the way.*

auf dem Wege   *on the way.*

WEG 1. *adv. away, off, gone, lost, disappeared.*

Hände weg!   *Hands off!*

Ich muss weg.   *I must go.*

2. *separable prefix (implies a motion away from the speaker).*

Er warf das alte Buch weg.   *He threw the old book away.*

Geh weg!   *Go away!*

wegbleiben *to stay away, be omitted.*

wegbringen *to take away, remove.*

WEGEN *prep. (gen.): because of, for the sake of, owing to.*

Wegen des Krieges konnte ich nicht von Europa zurückkommen.   *Because of the war, I could not come back from Europe.*

wegfahren *to drive off, away.*

weggehen *to go away, depart, leave.*

wegiegen *to put away.*

wegnehmen *to take away, carry off, confiscate, occupy.*

Wegweiser *m. signpost, roadsign.*

wegwerfen *to throw away.*

wegwerfend *disparaging, contemptuous.*

WEH *sore, aching, painful.*

weh tun   *to ache, to hurt.*

wehleidig *plaintive.*

Wehmut *f. sadness, melancholy.*

wehmütig *sad, melancholy.*

Wehrdienst *m. military service.*

wehren *to hinder, forbid, arrest, defend.*

wehrfähig *able-bodied.*

wehrlos *unarmed, defenseless, weak.*

Wehrmacht *f. armed forces.*

Wehrpflicht *f. conscription.*

wehrpflichtig *liable to military service.*

Weib *n. woman.*

weiblich *female, feminine, womanly.*

Weiblichkeit *f. womanhood, feminine nature.*

WEICH *soft, mold, mellow, tender, smooth.*

weiches Ei   *soft-boiled egg.*

weichen *to retreat, give in, yield; soften, soak.*

weichherzig *soft-hearted.*

weichlich *soft, flabby, weak.*

weigern *to refuse.*

Weigerung *f. refusal.*

Weihe *f. consecration, initiation, inauguration.*

weihen *to consecrate, dedicate, devote.*

WEIHNACHTEN *pl. Christmas.*

weihnachtlich *of Christmas.*

Weihnachtsabend *m. Christmas Eve.*

Weihnachtsbaum *m. Christmas tree.*

Weihnachtslied *n. Christmas carol.*

WEIL *because, since.*

WEILE *f. while, space of time.*

Damit hat es gute Weile.   *There is no hurry.*

Eile mit Weile.   *Haste makes waste.*

WEIN *m. wine, vine.*

Weinberg *m. vineyard.*

WEINEN *to weep, cry.*

Weinessig *m. wine vinegar.*

Weinfass *n. wine cask.*

Weinkarte *f. winelist.*

Weinlese *f. vintage.*

Weinprobe *f. wine-tasting.*

Weinrebe *f. vine.*

Weinstock *m. vine.*

Weinstube *f. tavern.*

Weintraube *f. grape.*

WEISE *f. manner, way, tune.*

auf diese Weise   *in this way.*

in der Weise, dass   *in such a way that, so that.*

WEISEN *to show, refer, direct, point out, point at.*

Weisheit *f. wisdom, prudence.*

weismachen *to make one believe, hoax.*

WEISS *white, blank, clean.*

Weisser Sonntag   *Sunday after Easter.*

weissagen *to predict, prophesy.*

Weissager *m. (–in, f.) prophet.*

WEIT *distant, far, vast, loose, wide, big.*

bei weitem   *by far, by much.*

bei weitem nicht   *by no means.*

es weit bringen   *to get on well, be successful.*

nicht weither sein   *not to be worth much.*

von weitem   *from a distance.*

weit gefehlt   *quite wrong.*

weit und breit   *far and wide.*

weit voraus   *way ahead.*

weit weg   *far away.*

wenn alles so weit ist   *when everything is ready.*

weitab *far away.*

weitaus *by far.*

Weite *f. width, size, extent, distance, length.*

WEITER *further, farther, more, else, additional.*

bis auf weiteres   *until further notice.*

des weiteren   *furthermore.*

nichts weiter   *nothing more.*

niemand weiter   *no one else.*

Nur weiter!   *Go on!*

ohne weiteres   *immediately.*

und so weiter   *and so on.*

was weiter   *what else.*

wenn's weiter nichts ist   *if that's all there is to it.*

Weitere *n. rest, remaining part.*

weiterführen *to continue, carry on.*

weitergeben *to pass on to.*

weiterhin *furthermore, moreover.*

Weiterreise f. *continuation of a trip.*
weitgehend *far-reaching, full, much.*
weither *from afar.*
weitläufig *distant, wide, extensive, roomy.*
weitschweifig *detailed, tedious.*
weitsichtig *far-sighted.*
Weizen m. *wheat, corn.*
WELCH (ein) *what (a)*
  Welch ein Zufall! *What a coincidence!*
WELCH(–ER, –E, –ES) 1. *inter. pron. &*
    adj. what, who, whom, which.
  2. *rel. pron. what, which, that, who,*
    whom.
Welle f. *wave, surge.*
  Wellen schlagen *to rise in waves.*
Wellenlinie f. *wavy line.*
Wellenreiter m. *surf-rider.*
WELT f. *world, universe, people.*
  alle Welt *everybody, everyone in the*
    world.
  auf der Welt *on earth.*
  auf die Welt kommen *to come into the*
    world, be born.
  aus der Welt schaffen *to put out of the*
    way.
  in der ganzen Welt *on earth.*
  in die Welt setzen (zur Welt bringen)
    to give birth to.
Weltall n. *universe.*
Weltanschauung f. *world outlook.*
weltbekannt *world-famous.*
weltfremd *secluded, solitary.*
Weltmacht f. *world power.*
Weltmann m. *man of the world.*
Weltmeister m. *world champion.*
Weltraum m. *space, universe.*
Weltuntergang m. *end of the world.*
WEM dat. *of wer. to whom.*
WEN acc. *of wer. whom.*
Wende f. *turn, turning point.*
wenden *to turn, turn around.*
  Bitte wenden! *Please turn over!*
  sich wenden an *to return to (someone).*
Wendepunkt m. *turning point.*
WENIG *little, few, a few.*
  ein wenig *a little, a bit.*
WENIGER *less, fewer, minus.*
  immer weniger *less and less.*
  nichts weniger als *anything but.*
  vier weniger eins *four minus one.*
wenigst (er,–e,–es) *least.*
wenigstens *at least.*
WENN *if, in case of, when.*
  auch wenn *even if.*
  immer wenn *whenever.*
  Rufen Sie mich an, wenn Sie kommen
    wollen! *Call me when you want to*
    come.
  selbst wenn *even if, supposing that.*

  wenn auch (wenn gleich, wenn
    schon) *although.*
  Wenn das nur wahr wäre! *If it were only*
    true!
  wenn nur *provided that.*
  wenn schon! *What of it!*
  wenn Sie kommen könnten *If you could*
    come.
WER inter. pron. *who, what.*
  wer anders *who else.*
  wer auch immer *whoever.*
  Wer (ist) da? *Who is it?*
werben *to recruit, to win, to advertise.*
Werbung f. *advertising.*
WERDEN 1. *to become, turn out, prove,*
  happen.
  Was soll aus ihr werden? *What's to*
    become of her?
  2. *aux, verb to form future and passive.*
    shall, will, is, are.
werfen *to throw, cast, toss.*
WERK n. *work, labor, production, doing,*
  performance, deed.
  ans Werk! *Go to it! Begin!*
  ins Werk setzen *to set going.*
  Das ist sein Werk. *That's his doing.*
Werkstatt f. *workshop.*
Werkstelle f. *place of work.*
Werktag m. *working day.*
werktags *on weekdays.*
werktätig *active*
  die werktätige Bevolkerung *working*
    classes.
Werkzeug m. *utensil.*
WERT *worth, valuable, worthy, honored,*
  esteemed.
  im Werte von *at a price of.*
  nichts wert sein *to be no good.*
Wertangabe f. *declaration of value.*
Wertgegenstand pl. *valuables.*
wertlos *worthless.*
Wertpapier n. *security, bond.*
Wertsachen pl. *valuables.*
Wertung f. *evaluation, appraisal.*
wertvoll *valuable, precious.*
Wesen n. *creature, soul, personality.*
wesentlich *essential, substantial.*
WESSEN gen. *of wer. whose?*
Weste f. *waistcoat, vest.*
Westen m. *the West, Occident.*
  nach Westen *west (direction).*
westlich *western, occidental.*
Wettbewerb n. *contest.*
Wette f. *bet, wager.*
  eine Wette machen *to make a bet.*
  um die Wette laufen *to race someone.*
wetteifern *to emulate; to vie.*
wetten *to bet, wager.*
WETTER n. *weather.*

Alle Wetter! *My word!*

Heute ist das Wetter wunderschön! *The weather is wonderful today!*

Wetterbericht *m. meteorological report.*

Wetterlage *f. weather conditions.*

Wettkampf *m. match, contest, prize fighting.*

Wettrennen *n. race, racing.*

WICHTIG *important.*

  sich wichtig machen   *to act important.*

WIDER 1. *prep. (acc.). against, contrary to, versus.*

  Wider meinen Willen   *against my will.*

  2. *inseparable prefix. (con–, re–, anti–, contra–)*

widerhallen *to echo, resound.*

widerlegen *to refute.*

Widerlegung *f. refutation.*

widerlich *repulsive, disgusting.*

Widerrede *f. contradiction.*

widerrufen *to revoke, withdraw, retract, cancel.*

widersetzen (sich) *to oppose, resist.*

widerspiegeln *to reflect, mirror.*

Widersprechen *to contradict, to talk back to.*

Widerspruch *m. contradiction, disagreement.*

Widerstand *m. resistance, opposition.*

Widerwille *m. repugnance, disgust.*

widerwillig *reluctant, unwilling.*

widmen *to dedicate.*

Widmung *f. dedication.*

WIE *how, as, such, like.*

  so ... wie   *as ... as.*

  wie auch immer   *however.*

  Wie bitte?   *What did you say?*

  wie dem auch sei   *be that as it may.*

  Wie geht es Ihnen?   *How are you?*

  wie gesagt   *as has been said.*

WIEDER 1. *adv. again, anew, back, in return for.*

  hin und wieder   *now and then.*

  immer wieder   *again and again.*

  2. *prefix.* a) *inseparable. In verb wiederholen (to repeat).* b) *separable (implies the idea of repetition or opposition).*

wiederbekommen *to get back, recover.*

wiederbeleben *to revive, reanimate.*

Wiederbelebungsversuch *m. attempt at resuscitation.*

wiederfinden *to find, recover.*

wiedererkennen *to recognize.*

wiedererlangen *to get back.*

wiedererobern *to reconquer.*

Wiedergabe *f. return; reproduction, recital (work of art).*

wiedergeben *to give back, return.*

wiedergewinnen *to recover, regain, reclaim.*

Wiedergutmachung *f. reparation.*

WIEDERHOLEN *to repeat, renew, reiterate, fetch, bring back.*

Wiederholung *f. repetition, reiteration.*

  im Wiederholungsfalle   *if it should happen again.*

wiederhören *to hear again.*

  auf Wiederhören!   *Good-bye! (radio, tel.).*

WIEDERSEHEN *to see again, meet again.*

  auf Wiedersehen!   *Good-bye! So long!*

Wiege *f. cradle.*

wiegen *to weigh, to rock, move to, shake, sway.*

Wiese *f. meadow.*

wieso *why.*

WIEVIEL *how much.*

  Der wievielte ist heute?   *What date is today?*

wieviele *how many.*

WILD *wild, rough, angry, furious, savage, untidy.*

Wild *n. game (hunting).*

Wildbraten *m. venison.*

Wilddieb *m. poacher.*

Wildente *f. wild duck.*

Wildleder *n. deerskin, suede.*

Wildnis *f. wilderness, desert.*

WILLE *m. will, say, determination, purpose.*

  aus freiem Willen   *voluntarily.*

  guter Wille   *kind intention.*

  letzter Wille   *last will.*

willenlos *lacking will power, irresolute.*

Willenlosigkeit *f. lack of will power.*

Willenskraft *f. will power.*

Willkommen *n. welcome, reception.*

Willkür *f. discretion, arbitrariness.*

willkürlich *arbitrary, despotic.*

WIND *m. wind, breeze.*

  bei Wind und Wetter   *in storm and rain (all types of bad weather).*

  guter Wind   *fair wind.*

  in den Wind reden   *to talk in vain.*

  in den Wind schlagen   *to disregard.*

  vor dem Wind segeln   *to run before the rain.*

Windel *f. baby's diaper.*

windeln *to swaddle.*

winden *to wind.*

windig *windy, breezy.*

Windstille *f. calm.*

Wink *m. sign, nod, wink.*

Winkel *m. corner, angle, secret spot.*

winken *to wave, nod, wink, wave.*

WINTER *m. winter.*

  im Winter   *in winter.*

Winterschlaf *m. hibernation.*

Wintersport *m. winter sports.*

Wintersportplatz *m. winter resort.*

winzig *tiny, diminutive.*

Winzigkeit *f. tininess.*

Wirbel *m. whirlpool, eddy.*

Wirbelknochen *m. vertebra.*

wirbeln *to whirl.*

Wirbelsäule *f. spine.*

Wirbelsturm *m. tornado, hurricane.*

wirken *to act, do, work, produce.*

WIRKLICH *real, actual, true, genuine.*

Wirklichkeit *f. reality, actuality.*

wirksam *active, effective.*

Wirkung *f. action, working, operation.*

wirkungslos *ineffectual, inefficient.*

wirkungsvoll *effective, striking.*

Wirt *m. host, proprietor, landlord.*

wirtlich *hospitable.*

Wirtschaft *f. housekeeping, economy, tavern, public house.*

   die Wirtschaft führen   *to keep house, to manage things.*

wirtschaften *to manage, run the business.*

Wirtschaftsgeld *n. housekeeping money.*

Wirtschaftslage *f. economic situation.*

Wirtshaus *n. inn, public house.*

WISSEN *n. knowledge, learning.*

   meines Wissens   *as far as I know.*

   wider besseres Wissen   *against one's better judgment.*

WISSEN *to know, be aware of, understand, be acquainted with.*

   Ich weiss nicht.   *I don't know.*

   nicht dass ich wüsste   *not that I am aware of.*

   Bescheid wissen über   *to be well informed about.*

   wissen um   *to know of or about.*

   wissen von   *to be informed or aware of.*

   Ihnen wissen lassen   *to let you know.*

Wissenschaft *f. science, knowledge.*

Wissenschaftler (–in) *m. (f.) scientist, scholar.*

wissenswert *worth knowing, interesting.*

Witwe *f. widow.*

Witwer *m. widower.*

Witz *m. wittiness, witticism, wit, joke, pun.*

witzig *witty.*

WO *where, in which; when.*

   wo auch immer   *wherever.*

woanders *elsewhere.*

wobei *in the course of which, whereby, in which, upon which.*

WOCHE *f. week.*

   diese Woche   *this week.*

   heute in einer Woche   *a week from today.*

Wochenende *n. weekend.*

wochenlang *for weeks.*

wochentags *on weekdays.*

Wochenschau *newsreel; weekly publication.*

wöchentlich *weekly.*

wodurch *by which, whereby, how.*

wofür *for which, for what.*

WOHER *from where, from what place?*

   Woher wissen Sie das?   *How do you know that?*

WOHIN *to where, to what place?*

WOHL *n. welfare, prosperity, good health.*

   sich wohl fühlen   *to feel well.*

WOHL *well, all right, probably, presumably, very likely, indeed.*

   Er wird wohl noch kommen.   *He may yet come.*

   Ich verstehe wohl.   *I can well understand.*

   Leben Sie wohl!   *Good-bye!*

   wohl oder übel   *willy nilly.*

   Zum Wohl!   *To you! (a toast)*

Wohlbehagen *n. comfort, ease.*

wohlbekannt *well-known, familiar.*

Wohlfahrt *f. welfare.*

wohlgefällig *pleasant, agreeable.*

Wohlgefühl *f. pleasant feeling, sense of well-being.*

wohlhabend *well-to-do, wealthy.*

Wohlklang *m. harmony, melody.*

wohlschmeckend *tasty, palatable.*

Wohlstand *m. well-being, wealth, fortune.*

wohltuend *comforting, pleasant.*

wohlverdient *well-deserved, merited.*

WOHNEN *to live, dwell, reside, stay.*

   zur Miete wohnen   *to live as a tenant, rent-payer.*

wohnhaft *living, dwelling.*

wohnlich *comfortable, cozy.*

WOHNUNG *f. house, dwelling, residence, flat.*

Wohnviertel *n. residential district.*

Wohnzimmer *n. living room*

Wolf *m. wolf.*

Wolke *f. cloud.*

   aus allen Wolken fallen   *to be thunderstruck.*

Wolkenbruch *m. cloudburst.*

Wolkenkratzer *m. skyscraper.*

WOLLE *f. wool.*

WOLLEN *to want, wish, will, desire, like, mean.*

   Das will etwas heissen.   *That means something.*

   Das will was heissen.   *That's really something.*

   Er mag wollen oder nicht.   *Whether he likes it or not.*

   Wie Sie wollen.   *As you like.*

WOMIT *with what, by which, with which.*

   Womit kann ich dienen?   *What can I do for you?*

womöglich *if possible.*

WORAN *whereon, by what.*

   woran liegt es?   *how is it that? what is the reason for it?*

WORAUF *on what, upon which.*

WORAUS *of what, out of which.*
WORIN *in which, in what.*
WORT *n. word, expression, saying, promise.*
  aufs Wort gehorchen *to obey implicitly.*
  das grosse Wort führen *to brag.*
  das Wort ergreifen *to begin to speak.*
  das Wort führen *to be spokesman.*
  einen beim Wort nehmen *to take one at one's word.*
  Er hat sein Wort gebrochen. *He broke his promise.*
  Ich habe kein Wort davon gewusst. *I did not know a thing about it.*
  ins Wort fallen *to interrupt, cut short.*
  mit anderen Worten *in other words.*
  Sie macht viele Worte. *She talks too much.*
  ums Wort bitten *to ask for the floor.*
  zu Wort kommen lassen *to let one speak.*
  geflügelte Worte *familiar quotations.*
Wörterbuch *n. dictionary.*
Wortschatz *m. vocabulary.*
wortwörtlich *word for word.*
WORÜBER *of what, about which, whereof.*
WORUNTER *among what, which.*
WOVON *about what, which.*
WOVOR *of what, for what, before what, which.*
WOZU *to which end, of what, for what, which.*
wund *sore, wounded.*
Wunde *f. wound.*
Wunder *n. wonder, miracle.*
  sein blaues Wunder erleben *to be amazed.*
  Wunder verrichten *to perform miracles.*
WUNDERBAR *wonderful, marvelous.*
  Wunderbar! *Wonderful! Splendid!*
wunderbarerweise *strange to say.*
Wunderkind *n. child prodigy.*
wunderlich *strange, odd.*
WUNDERN *to astonish, surprise.*
  sich wundern *to be surprised, wonder.*
wunderschön *beautiful, lovely, exquisite.*
WUNSCH *m. wish, desire, request.*
  auf Wunsch *by request, if desired.*
  Hätten Sie noch einen Wunsch? *Is there anything else you'd like?*
  nach Wunsch *as one desires.*
WÜNSCHEN *to wish, desire, long for.*
  Glück wünschen *to congratulate (wish luck).*
  Was wünschen Sie? *May I help you?*
  Ich wünsche Ihnen alles Gute. *I wish you all the best.*
Würde *f. dignity, honor, title, rank.*
  in Amt und Würden *holding a high office.*
würdelos *undignified.*

würdevoll *dignified.*
würdig *worthy, deserving of, respectable.*
würdigen *to value, appreciate.*
  jemanden keines Blickes würdigen *to ignore someone completely.*
Würfel *m. die, cube.*
  Der Würfel ist gefallen. *The die is cast.*
würfeln *to play dice.*
Würfelspiel *n. dice game.*
Würfelzucker *m. lump of sugar.*
würgen *to choke, strangle.*
Wurm *m. worm.*
Wurst *f. sausage.*
Würze *f. seasoning, spice, condiment.*
Wurzel *f. root.*
würzen *to season.*
würzig *spicy.*
wüst *waste, deserted, desolate, wild, dissolute.*
Wüste *f. desert.*
WUT *f. rage, fury.*
  in Wut geraten *to fly into a rage.*
  vor Wut kochen *to boil, fume with rage.*
wüten *to rage, be furious.*
wütend *enranged, furious.*

X

x-beliebig *at random.*
x-mal *every so often, any number of times.*

Y

Y *the twenty-fifth letter of the alphabet.*
Y-Achse *f. (math) y-axis.*
Yacht (*or* **Jacht**) *f. yacht.*
Yard *n. yard.*
Yen *m. yen.*

Z

zagen *to be afraid, hesitate.*
zähe *tough, tenacious, stubborn, stingy.*
ZAHL *f. figure, number, numeral.*
zahlbar *payable, due.*
zahlen *to pay.*
ZÄHLEN *to count, number, calculate.*
  gezahlt *numbered.*
Zahlkarte *f. money-order form.*
zahllos *countless, innumerable.*
zahlreich *numerous.*
Zahltag *m. pay-day.*
Zahlung *f. payment.*
Zahlungsanweisung *f. postal or money order.*

zahlungsfähig solvent (financially).
zahm tame, domestic.
zähmen to tame, break in.
ZAHN m. tooth.
  ein schlechter Zahn a bad tooth.
  sich die Zähne putzen to brush one's
    teeth.
  einem auf den Zahn fühlen to sound out
    a person.
  falsche Zähne artificial teeth.
Zahnarzt (–in) m. (f.) dentist.
Zahnbürste f. toothbrush.
Zahnfleisch n. gum(s).
Zahnfüllung f. filling.
zahnlos toothless.
Zahnpasta f. toothpaste.
Zahnschmerzen pl. toothache.
Zahnstein m. tartar.
Zahnstocher m. toothpick.
Zahnweh n. toothache.
Zange f. pincers, tongs, pliers.
Zank m. quarrel.
zanken to quarrel.
zanksüchtig quarrelsome.
ZART tender, soft, delicate, fragile, frail.
zartfühlend tactful, sensitive.
Zartgefühl n. delicacy of feeling.
Zartheit f. tenderness, delicacy.
Zauber m. magic, charm, spell.
Zauberei f. magic, witchcraft.
Zauberflöte f. magic flute.
zauberhaft magical, enchanting.
zauberkünstler m. illusionist.
zaubern to practice magic, conjure.
zaudern to hesitate, delay.
Zaun m. hedge, fence.
  Streit von Zaune brechen to pick a
    quarrel.
Zebra n. zebra.
Zehe f. toe.
Zehenspitze f. point of the toe.
  auf Zehenspitzen gehen to tiptoe.
ZEHN ten.
zehnfach tenfold.
ZEHNT tenth.
Zeichen n. sign, signal, token, brand.
  zum Zeichen dass as a proof that.
Zeichensetzung f. punctuation.
Zeichensprache f. sign language.
ZEICHNEN to draw, design, mark.
ZEICHNUNG f. drawing, sketch, design.
Zeigefinger m. forefinger, index.
ZEIGEN to show, point at, point out, exhibit,
  display.
Zeiger m. hand of the clock, pointer.
ZEIT f. time, duration, period, epoch,
  season.
  Damit hat es Zeit. There is no hurry.
  die freie Zeit leisure, spare time.

Es ist an der Zeit. It is high time.
  höchste Zeit high time.
  in der letzten Zeit lately.
  in jüngster Zeit quite recently.
  Lassen Sie sich Zeit! Take your time!
  mit der Zeit gradually, in the course of
    time.
  Zeit seines Lebens during life.
  zu gleicher Zeit at the same time.
  zur rechten Zeit in the nick of time.
  zur Zeit at present.
Zeitablauf m. lapse of time.
Zeitalter n. age, generation.
zeitgemäss timely, seasonable.
Zeitgenosse m. contemporary.
zeitgenössisch contemporary.
ZEITIG early, timely, mature, ripe.
Zeitmangel m. lack of time.
Zeitrechnung f. chronology.
Zeitpunkt m. time, moment.
Zeitschrift f. journal, periodical, magazine.
ZEITUNG f. newspaper, paper.
Zeitungsausschnitt m. press cutting.
Zeitungskiosk m. newsstand.
Zeitungsnotiz f. notice, item, paragraph.
Zeitungsstand m. newsstand.
Zeitungsinserat n. newspaper advertisement,
  notice.
Zeitungsverkäufer m. news vendor.
Zeitverschwendung f. loss of time.
Zeitvertreib m. pastime, amusement.
Zeitwort n. verb.
Zelle f. cell, booth.
Zelt n. tent, canopy.
Zement m. cement.
Zentimeter m. & n. centimeter (.3937 inch).
Zentrale f. central office, station, telephone
  exchange.
Zentralheizung f. central heating.
ZENTRUM n. center.
zerbrechen to break, smash.
  sich den Kopf zerbrechen to rack one's
    brains.
zerbrechlich fragile.
Zerbrechlichkeit f. fragility, brittleness.
Zeremonie f. ceremony.
zerreissbar tearable.
zerreissen to tear, rip up.
zerren to drag, pull.
  eine Muskel zerren to strain a muscle.
zerschmettern to crush, destroy.
zerstören to destroy, demolish, devastate,
  ruin.
Zerstörer m. destroyer, devastator.
Zerstörung f. devastation, demolition,
  destruction.
zerstreuen to disperse, scatter, dissipate,
  divert.
zerstreut absent-minded.

Zerstreuung f. dispersion, distraction.

Zerwürfnis n. disagreement, quarrel, strife.

Zettel m. slip, note, label, ticket, poster, bill.

Zeug n. stuff, material, cloth, fabric, utensils, things.

Zeuge m. witness.

zeugen to testify, bear witness, give evidence.

Zeugenaussage f. evidence, deposition.

Zeugenvernehmung f. hearing of witnesses.

Ziege f. goat.

Ziegel m. brick, tile.

Ziegelstein m. brick.

ZIEHEN to pull, draw, haul, tug, tow, extract, move, migrate, weigh.

den Kürzeren ziehen   to get the worst of it.

nach sich ziehen   to have consequences.

Er zieht den Hut.   He tips his hat.

zur Rechenschaft ziehen   to call to account.

ein Gesicht ziehen   to make faces.

in Betracht ziehen   to take into consideration.

Ziehung f. drawing of lottery.

Ziel n. goal.

sich ein Ziel setzen   to aim at.

zielbewusst systematic, methodical.

zielen to aim.

ziellos aimless.

Zielscheibe f. target.

Zielscheibe des Spottes sein   to be a laughing stock.

ziemen to become, be suitable.

ZIEMLICH rather, pretty, fairly, quite, considerable.

so ziemlich   about, pretty much.

ziemlich viele   quite a few.

Zierde f. ornament, decoration.

zieren to decorate, adorn, embellish.

zierlich elegant, graceful, delicate.

Ziffer f. figure, cipher.

Zifferblatt n. dial, face.

ZIGARETTE f. cigarette.

Zigarettenetui n. cigarette-case.

Zigarettenspitze f. cigarette-holder.

Zigarre f. cigar.

Zigarrenkiste f. cigar-box.

Zigeuner m. gypsy.

ZIMMER n. room, apartment, chamber.

Zimmerdecke f. ceiling.

Zimmermädchen n. chambermaid.

Zimmermann m. carpenter.

zimperlich supersensitive, prudish, affected.

Zimt m. cinnamon.

Zinn n. tin, pewter.

Zins m. tax, duty, rent; interest.

auf Zinsen ausleihen   to lend money at interest.

mit Zins und Zinseszins   in full measure.

Zinseszins m. compound interest.

Zinsfuss m. rate of interest.

Zirkel m. compasses.

Zirkus m. circus.

Zitat n. quotation.

Zitrone f. lemon.

Zitronenlimonade f. lemonade.

Zitronensaft m. lemon juice.

zittern to tremble, shake, quiver, shiver.

zivil civil, reasonable, moderate.

in Zivil   in plain clothes.

Zivilbevölkerung f. civilian population.

Zivilisation f. civilization.

zivilisieren to civilize.

zögern to hesitate, delay, linger.

ZOLL m. duty, toll, tariff, customs.

Zoll m. inch.

Zollabfertigung f. customs inspection, clearance.

ZOLLAMT n. customhouse.

Zollbeamte m. customhouse officer.

zollfrei free of duty.

Zollgebühr f. duty.

Zöllner m. customs collector.

zollpflichtig subject to customs.

Zollstock m. yardstick.

Zone f. zone.

Zopf m. braid, pigtail.

Zorn m. anger, rage, wrath.

zornig angry.

ZU 1. prep. (dat.). to, at, by, near, beside, for, with, in front of, on.

Die Deutschen essen gern Kartoffeln zum Fleisch.   Germans like to eat potatoes with meat.

Et war nicht zu Hause.   He was not at home.

Ich gehe zu meiner Tante.   I am going to my aunt's house.

Setzen Sie sich zu mir!   Sit down by me.

Wenn es friert, wird das Wasser zu Eis.   When it freezes, water turns to ice.

Wit essen Eier zum Frhustück.   We eat eggs for breakfast.

zu Fuss/zu Pferd   on foot, on horseback.

zu meinem Erstaunen   to my surprise.

zum König gekrönt werden   to become a king.

zum Teil   partly.

zum "Weisses Rössi"   at the "White Horse" (inn).

2. adv. too (more than enough), toward.

zu viel   too much.

3. before infinitive to.

Sie wussten nicht was tun.   They did not know what to do.

4. Separable prefix (implies direction

toward the speaker, increase,
continuation, closing, confession).

Sie liefen dem Walde zu.They ran toward
the forest.

Der Verbrecher gab es zu. *The criminal
confessed.*

Ich darf nicht mehr zunehmen. *I must not
gain more weight.*

Mach die Tür zu! *Close the door!*

Zubehör m. & n. accessories, trimmings,
belongings.

zubereiten to prepare, cook, mix.

Zubereitung f. preparation.

Zucht f. breeding, training, education; breed,
race, stock.

züchten to breed, grow, cultivate, train.

züchtig chaste, modest.

züchtigen to punish, correct, chastise.

zucken to jerk, twitch.

mit den Achseln zucken *to shrug one's
shoulders.*

ZUCKER m. sugar.

Zuckerguss m. icing.

zuckerhältig containing sugar.

zuckerkrank diabetic.

zuckern to sugar, sweeten.

Zuckerwerk n. confectionery, sweets.

zudem besides, moreover.

zudrücken to shut, close.

ein Auge zudrücken *to turn a blind eye,
to overlook.*

zuerst at first, in the first place.

Zufahrt f. driveway, approach.

Zufall m. chance, accident, occurrence.

durch Zufall *by accident.*

zufällig casual, by accident, by chance.

zufällig tun to happen to do.

zufälligerweise by chance.

Zuflucht f. refuge, shelter.

sine Zuflucht nehmen zu *to take refuge
with.*

ZUFRIEDEN satisfied, content.

sich zufrieden geben *to rest content with.*

zufrieden lassen *to let alone, leave in
peace.*

Zufriedenheit f. contentment, satisfaction.

zufriedenstellen to content, satisfy.

zufriedenstellend satisfactory.

ZUG m. train; drawing, draft; procession,
march, impulse; feature,
characteristic.

Er liegt in den letzten Zügen. *He is
breathing his last.*

Zug um Zug *without delay,
uninterruptedly.*

Wann kommt der Schnellzug aus Berlin
an? *When does the express train
from Berlin arrive?*

Das ist ein Zug seines Charakters. *This is*

a feature of his character.

Zugabe f. extra, addition, encore, confession.

Zugang m. entrance, door, access.

zugänglich accessible, open to.

zugeben to add, allow, permit, admit.

Zügel m. bridle, rein.

zügellos unbridled, unrestrained.

Zugeständnis n. concession, admission.

Zugluft f. draught, current of air.

zugunsten in favor of, for the benefit of.

zugute (halten) to allow for, take into
consideration, give credit for.

zugute kommen *to come in handy, be an
advantage to.*

Zuhilfenahme f. (unter Zuhilfenahme von)
with the help of.

zuhören to listen to.

Zuhörer m. hearer, listener.

Zuhörerschaft f. audience.

ZUKUNFT f. future.

zukünftig future.

zulächeln to smile at.

Zulage f. addition, raise.

zulangen to hand, give.

zulässig admissible, permissible.

Zulassung f. admission, permission.

zulegen to add something to.

ZULETZT finally, ultimately,

zuletzt kommen *to arrive last.*

zuliebe (tun) to do for someone's sake.

einem zuliebe tun *to please someone.*

zumachen to close, shut, fasten; to hurry.

zumal especially, particularly.

zumindest at least.

zumuten to expect of.

sich zu viel zumuten *to attempt too much.*

Zumutung f. unreasonable demand.

zunächst first, first of all, above all.

zünden to catch fire, inflame, arouse
enthusiasm.

zunehmen to grow, increase, get fuller.

zuneigen to lean forward, incline.

Zuneigung f. liking, affection, sympathy,
inclination.

ZUNGE f. tongue.

Das Wort liegt mir auf der Zunge. *I have
the word on the tip of my tongue.*

eine belegte Zunge *a coated tongue.*

eine feine Zunge haben *to be a gourmet.*

zurechnungsfähig responsible, of sound
mind.

Zurechnungsfähigkeit f. accountability,
responsibility before the law.

zurecht right, in order, in time.

zurechtfinden to find one's way about.

**zurechtsetzen (einem den Kopf
zurechtsetzen)** to bring one to
reason.

ZURÜCK 1. adv. back, backwards, late,

behind. 2. *separable prefix (implies the idea of a return motion; back).*
Wir kamen erst um elf Uhr zurück. *We only came back at eleven.*

zurückbeben *to start back, recoil.*

zurückbehalten *to keep back, retain.*

zurückbekommen *to get back, recover.*

zurückbleiben *to stay behind.*

zurückbringen *to bring back.*

zurückfahren *to drive back, return.*

zurückfordern *to demand back.*

zurückgehen *to go back, return, retreat, decrease, decline.*

zurückgezogen *retired, secluded, lonely.*

Zurückgezogenheit *f. retirement, seclusion.*

zurückhalten *to hold back, delay, detain.*

zurückhaltend *reserved.*

zurückkehren *to return, go back, come back.*

zurücklassen *to leave behind.*

zurücknehmen *to take back.*

zurücksetzen *to put back, replace, reduce, neglect.*

Zurücksetzung *f. reduction (in price).*

zurückstellen *to put back, replace, reserve, put aside.*

zurücktreten *to step back, withdraw, resign.*

zurückversetzen *to put back, restore.*
sich in eine Zeit zurückversetzen *to go back (in imagination) to a time.*

zurückweisen *to send away, to turn back, send back, repulse.*

zurückzahlen *to pay back, repay.*

Zurückzahlung *f. repayment.*

zurückziehen *to draw back, take back.*

Zuruf *m. acclamation, shout, call.*

zurufen *to call to, shout to.*

Zusage *f. acceptance, promise.*

ZUSAGEN *to promise, please, appeal.*
einem etwas auf den Kopf zusagen *to tell a person plainly.*

ZUSAMMEN *together, altogether.*

zusammenfassen *to sum up, summarize.*

zusammenfassend *comprehensive.*

zusammengehören *to belong together, match, be correlated.*

Zusammenhalt *m. holding together, cohesion, solidarity.*

Zusammenhang *m. connection, relationship.*

zusammenhangslos *disconnected.*

Zusammenkunft *f. meeting, reunion, assembly.*

Zusammenstoss *m. collision, clash, crash.*

zusammenstossen *to smash, collide.*

zusammentreffen *to meet each other, coincide.*

zusammenzählen *to count up, add up.*

Zusatz *m. addition.*

zusätzlich *additional.*

ZUSCHAUER *m. spectator.*

Zuschauerraum *m. theater auditorium.*

Zuschlag *m. addition, increase in price.*

zuschlagpflichtig *liable to additional payment.*

zuschliessen *to lock, lock up.*

Zuschrift *f. letter, communication.*

zuschulden *adv. guilty.*
sich etwas zuschulden kommen lassen *to be guilty of doing something.*

zusehen *to look on, watch for, wait.*

zusichern *to assure of, promise.*

Zusicherung *f. insurance.*

zusprechen *to encourage.*
Trost zusprechen *to comfort, console.*

Zuspruch *m. consolation, exhortation, encouragement, pep talk.*

ZUSTAND *m. state, condition, position, situation.*
zustande bringen *to do, get done, achieve.*

zuständig *belonging to, responsible, authorized, competent.*

Zuständigkeit *f. competence, power, jurisdiction.*

zustimmen *to consent, agree.*

Zustimmung *f. consent.*

Zustrom *m. influx, crowd, multitude.*

zutrauen *to believe (one) capable of.*

zutraulich *confiding, trusting.*

zutreffend *correct, right, applicable.*

ZUTRITT *m. admission, entrance.*
Zutritt verboten! *No admittance!*

zuverlässig *reliable, trustworthy.*

Zuversicht *f. confidence, trust.*

zuversichtlich *confident.*

ZUVIEL *too much.*

zuvor *before, previously, formerly.*

zuvorkommen *to come first.*

zuvorkommend *obliging.*

Zuvorkommenheit *f. politeness, kindness.*

ZUWEILEN *sometimes, now and then, occasionally.*

zuwider (sein) *to be repugnant.*
Das ist mir zuwider. *I hate it.*

zuzahlen *to pay extra.*

zuziehen *to draw together, call, invite, consult.*

Zwang *m. compulsion, constraint, force, pressure.*
Zwang antun *to do violence to*
sich keinen Zwang antun *not to stand on ceremony.*

zwanglos *free and easy.*

Zwanglosigkeit *f. freedom, ease.*

Zwangslage *f. condition of constraint, quandary, "jam."*
sich in einer Zwangslage befinden *to be under compulsion.*

zwangsläufig *necessarily, inevitably.*

ZWANZIG *twenty.*

Zwanziger *m. figure 20, a 20-year old.*
  in den Zwanzigern sein *to be in one's twenties.*
ZWANZIGSTE *twentieth.*
ZWAR *indeed, although.*
  und zwar *in fact, namely.*
ZWECK *m. purpose, design, aim, object, end, goal.*
  keinen Zweck haben *to be of no use.*
  Zu welchem Zweck? *Why? For what purpose?*
zwecklos *useless, purposeless.*
Zwecklosigkeit *f. uselessness, aimlessness.*
zweckmässig *expedient.*
ZWEI *two.* **zwo** *two (coll.)*
  zu zweien *by pairs, two by two.*
zweideutig *ambiguous.*
zweifach *twofold, double.*
ZWEIFEL *m. doubt, suspicion.*
zweifelhaft *doubtful.*
zweifellos *indubitable.*
zweifeln *to doubt, question, suspect.*
Zweifelsfall *m.*
  im Zweifelsfall *in case of a doubt.*
Zweig *m. branch.*
Zweiggeschäft *n. branch (office).*
Zweikampf *m. duel.*
zweimal *twice.*
zweireihig *having two rows, columns; double-breasted.*
Zweisitzer *two-seater.*
ZWEITE *second, next.*
  zu zweit *two by two.*
zweitens *secondly, in the second place.*
Zwerg *m. dwarf.*
Zwieback *m. rusk, biscuit.*
Zwiebel *f. onion, bulb (plant).*

Zwielicht *n. twilight, dusk.*
Zwilling *m. twin.*
zwingen *to compel, force, get through, finish.*
zwingend *forcible.*
zwinkern *to blink, wink.*
Zwirn *m. thread, sewing-cotton.*
ZWISCHEN *prep. (dat. when answering question, Wo?; acc. when answering question, Wohin?, and depending on the idiom). among, between.*
  Zwischen den Städten Duisburg und Köln liegt Düsseldorf. *Between the cities of Duisburg and Cologne lies Düsseldorf.*
  zwischen drei und vier *between three and four.*
  Er läuft zwischen die Wagen. *He walks between the cars.*
Zwischenbemerkung *f. incidental remark, verbal aside.*
Zwischendeck *n. lower deck.*
zwischendurch *through, in the midst of.*
Zwischenfall *m. incident, episode.*
Zwischenlandung *f. intermediate landing or stop (flight).*
Zwischenpause *f. interval, break.*
Zwischenraum *m. space, gap, interval.*
Zwischenzeit *f. interval.*
  in der Zwischenzeit *in the meantime.*
zwitschern *to twitter, chirp.*
ZWÖLF *twelve.*
ZWÖLFTE *twelfth.*
Zyklus *m. cycle, course, series.*
Zylinder *m. cylinder.*
Zyniker *m. cynic.*
zynisch *cynical.*
Zynismus *m. cynicism.*

GLOSSARY OF
PROPER NAMES

Albrecht *Albert.*
Alfred *Alfred.*
Andress *Andrew.*
Anne *Ann.*
Anton *Anthony.*
August *August.*
Barbara *Barbara.*
Bernhard *Bernard.*
Bertha *Bertha.*
Eduard *Edward.*
Elisabeth (Else) *Elizabeth.*
Emilie *Emily.*
Emma *Emma.*
Erich *Eric.*
Ernst *Ernest.*
Eugen *Eugene.*
Franz *Frank.*
Franziska *Frances.*
Friederich *Frederick.*
Fritz *Fred.*
Genoveva *Genevieve.*
Georg *George.*
Gertrud (Trudchen) *Gertrude.*
Gretchen *Margaret.*
Gustav *Gustave.*
Heinrich *Henry.*
Helene *Helen.*
Ilse *Elsie.*
Jakob *James, Jacob.*
Johann *John.*
Johanna *Jane, Joan.*
Josef *Joseph.*
Karl *Charles.*
Katharina (Kätchen) (Käthe)
          Katherine (Kate).
Klaus *Nicholas.*
Lotte *Charlotte.*
Ludwig *Lewis.*
Luise *Louise.*
Maria *Mary.*
Mark *Mark.*
Martha *Martha.*
Michael *Michael.*
Minna *Wilhelmina.*
Moritz *Maurice.*
Otto *Otto.*
Paul *Paul.*
Paula *Paula.*
Peter *Peter.*
Richard *Richard.*
Robert *Robert.*
Rosa *Rose.*
Rüdiger *Roger.*
Rudolph *Ralph.*

Susanne *Susan.*
Theodor *Theodore.*
Therese *Theresa.*
Thomas *Thomas.*
Walter *Walter.*
Wilhelme *William.*

GLOSSARY OF
GEOGRAPHICAL NAMES

Aachen *n. Aix-la-Chapelle.*
Afrika *n. Africa.*
Ägypten *n. Egypt.*
die Alpen *pl. Alps.*
Amerika *n. America*
  die Vereinigten Staaten *pl. the United
          States (of America).*
  Nord-Amerika *n. North America.*
  Süd-Amerika *n. South America.*
  Mittel-Amerika *n. Central America.*
Antwerpen *n. Antwerp.*
Asien n. Asia.
Atlantik *m. (der Atlantische Ozean)
          Atlantic (the Atlantic Ocean).*
Australien *n. Australia.*
Belgien *n. Belgium.*
Berlin *n. Berlin.*
Bonn *n. Bonn.*
Brasilien *n. Brazil.*
Brüssel *n. Brussels.*
Commonwealth Unabhängiger Nationen
          *n. Commonwealth of Independent States
          (formerly the U.S.S.R.)*
Dänemark *n. Denmark.*
Deutschland *n. Germany.*
England *n. England.*
Europa *n. Europe.*
Frankfurt a.M. *n. Frankfurt on the Main.*
Frankreich *n. France.*
Griechenland *n. Greece.*
Haag (den) *The Hague.*
Hamburg *n. Hamburg.*
Holland *n. Holland.*
Indien *n. India.*
Irland *n. Ireland.*
Israel *n. Israel.*
Italien *n. Italy.*
Japan *n. Japan.*
Kanada *n. Canada.*
Köln *n. Cologne.*
London *n. London.*
Madrid *n. Madrid.*
Mexico *n. Mexico.*
Moskau *n. Moscow.*
München *n. Munich.*

Norwegen   *n. Norway.*
Nürnberg   *n. Nuremberg.*
Österreich   *n. Austria.*
Paris   *n. Paris.*
Polen   *n. Poland.*
Portugal   *n. Portugal.*
Preussen   *n. Prussia.*
Rhein   *m. Rhine.*
Rheinland   *n. Rhineland.*
Rom   *n. Rome.*
Rumänien   *n. Rumania.*
Russland   *n. Russia.*

Saar   *f. Saar*
Sachsen   *n. Saxony.*
Schlesien   *n. Silesia.*
Schottland   *n. Scotland.*
Schweden   *n. Sweden.*
Schweiz   *f. Switzerland.*
Spanien   *n. Spain.*
Stille Ozean (der)   *Pacific Ocean.*
Tschechoslovakei   *f. Czechoslovakia.*
Türkei   *f. Turkey.*
Ungarn   *n. Hungary.*
Wien   *n. Vienna.*

English-German

A

a (an) *ein, eine.*
abandon (to) *verlassen.*
abbreviate (to) *abkürzen.*
abbreviation *Abkürzung, f.*
ability *Fähigkeit, f.*
able *fähig.*
able (to be) *können.*
abolish (to) *abschaffen.*
about *ungefähr, um* (acc.) (around).
above *über, oberhalb.*
abroad *im Ausland.*
absence *Abwesenheit, f.*
absent *abwesend.*
absolute *unbedingt, völlig.*
absorb (to) *aufsaugen.*
abstain (to) *sich enthalten.*
abstract *abstrakt.*
absurd *unvernünftig, sinnlos.*
abundant *reichlich.*
abuse *Missbrauch, m.*
academy *Akademie, f.*
accent *Akzent, m.*
accent (to) *betonen.*
accept (to) *annehmen.*
acceptance *Annahme, f.*
accident *Unfall, m.; Zufall, m.* (chance).
accidental *zufällig.*
accidentally *nebenbei.*
accommodate (to) *unterbringen, sich an
    passen.*
accommodation *Unterkunft, f.*
accompany (to) *begleiten.*
accomplish (to) *vollführen.*
accord *Übereinstimmung, f.*
according to *zu* (dat.); *zufolge dem.*
account *Rechung, f.; Konto, n.* (balance).
    on no account   *auf keinen Fall.*
    to pay the account   *die Rechnung bezahlen.*
accuracy *Genauigkeit, f.*
accurate *genau, richtig, akkurat.*
accuse (to) *anklagen, beschuldigen.*
accustom (to) *gewöhnen.*
ace *Ass, n.*
ache *Schmerz, m.*
ache (to) *schmerzen.*
achieve (to) *vollbringen, leisten.*
achievement *Vollbringung, f.; Leistung*
    (result).
acid *sauer* (adj.), *Säure* (noun), *f.*
acknowledge (to) *anerkennen.*
acknowledgment *Anerkennung, f.*
acquaintance *Bekannte, m. & f.*
acquire (to) *erwerben.*
across *gegenüber.*
act *Handlung, f.; Akt, m.* (of a play); *Gesetz,
    n.* (law).

active *tätig.*
activity *Tätigkeit, f.*
actor *Schauspieler, m.*
actress *Schauspielerin, f.*
actual *wirklich.*
acute *akut.*
adopt (to) *anpassen.*
add (to) *zufügen.*
addition *Zusatz, m.; Addition, f.* (math).
    in addition to *zusätzlich zu* (dat.).
address *Adresse, f.; Anschrift, f.; Ansprache,
    f.; Anrede, f.* (speech).
address (to) *adressieren; anreden,
    ansprechen, sich wenden an* (speech).
adequate *ausreichend, genügend.*
adjective *Eigenschaftswort, Adjektiv, n.*
adjoining *angrenzend, anstossend.*
administer (to) *verwalten.*
admiral *Admiral, m.*
admiration *Bewunderung, f.*
admire (to) *bewundern.*
admission *Eintritt, m.*
admit (to) *einlassen; zugeben* (concede).
admittance *Zutritt, m.*
    no admittance   *Zutritt verboten.*
adopt (to) *adoptieren* (child); *annehmen*
    (idea).
adult *Erwachsene(r)* (noun), *m. & f.;
    erwachsen* (adj.).
advance (to) *vorangehen* (lead); *steigen*
    (price).
    in advance   *im Voraus.*
advantage *Vorteil, m.*
adventure *Abenteuer, n.*
adverb *Adverb, n.*
advertise (to) *anzeigen; Reklame machen.*
advertisement *Anzeige, f.; Reklame, f.*
advice *Rat, m.*
advise (to) *raten.*
affair *Sache, f.* (thing); *Angelegenheit, f.;
    Veranstaltung* (party, meeting) *f.*
affect (to) *betreffen.*
affected *geziert, affektiert* (pretentious);
    gerührt (moved).
affection *Zuneigung, f.*
affectionate *herzlich, zärtlich, liebevoll.*
affirm (to) *bestätigen, bekräftigen.*
affirmation *Bestätigung, f.; Bekräftigung, f.*
afloat *schwimmend, auf dem Meere.*
afraid *ängstlich.*
after *nach* (dat.).
afternoon *Nachmittag, m.*
afterward *nachher.*
again *wieder.*
against *gegen* (acc.); *wider* (acc.).
age *Alter, n.* (also old age); *Epoche, f.*
    (history).
agency *Vertretung, f.*
agent *Agent, m.*

aggravate (to) *verschlimmern; ärgern*
    (annoy), *reizen.*
ago *vor* (dat.).
    three days ago   *vor drei Tagen.*
agree (to) *übereinstimmen.*
agreeable *angenehm.*
agreed *abgemacht.*
agreement *Übereinstimmung, f.; Vertrag, m.*
    (contract).
    to be in agreement with   *einverstanden sein*
agricultural *landwirtschaftlich.*
agriculture *Landwirtschaft, f.*
ahead *voran, voraus.*
aid *Hilfe, f.*
    first aid   *Erste Hilfe.*
aid (to) *helfen.*
aim *Ziel, n.; Zweck, m.*
aim (to) *erreichen; zielen* (shooting)
    to aim at   *richten gegen*
air *Luft, f.*
air force *Luftwaffe, f.*
air mail *Luftpost, f.*
airfield *Flugplatz, m*
airplane *Flugzeug, n.*
airport *Flughafen, m.*
aisle *Seitenschiff, n.* (church); *gang, m.*
    (hall).
alarm *Alarm, m.*
alarm clock *Wecker, m.*
alcohol *Alkohol, m.*
alike *gleich, ähnlich.*
all *ganz, alles.*
    all right   *in Ordnung, bestimmt.*
    not at all   *keineswegs überhaupt micht.*
alliance *Verbindung f.; Allianz, f.* (pact).
allow (to) *erlauben, gestatten.*
allowed *gestattet*
ally *Verbündete, m.*
almost *fast, beinahe.*
alone *allein.*
along *entlang.*
already *schon, bereits.*
also *auch.*
altar *Altar, m.*
alter (to) *ändern, verwandeln.*
alternate *abwechselnd.*
alternate (to) *abwechseln.*
although *obwohl, obgleich.*
altitude *Höhe, f.*
altogether *zusammen; gänzlich* (wholly).
always *immer*
amaze (to) *erstaunen.*
amazement *Verwunderung, f.*
ambassador *Botschafter, m.*
ambassadress *Botschafterin, f.*
ambitious *ehrgeizig.*
amend (to) *berichtigen, (ab)ändern,*
    verbessern.

American *Amerikaner* (noun, m.);
    amerikanisch (adj.); *Amerikanerin*
    (f.).
among *mitten; unter* (dat. or acc.).
amount *Betrag, m.*
ample *geräumig, umfassend.*
amuse (to) *amüsieren.*
amusement *Unterhaltung, f.*
amusing *amüsant.*
analyze (to) *analysieren.*
ancestors *Vorfahren, pl.*
anchor *Anker, m.*
ancient, *uralt, alt, aus alten Zeiten.*
and *und.*
anecdote *Anekdote, f.*
angel *Engel, m.*
anger *Ärger, m.*
angry *ärgerlich, bös.*
animal *Tier, n.*
animate (to) *beleben.*
annex *Nebengebäude, n.*
annihilate (to) *vernichten.*
anniversary *Hochzeitstag, m.*
announce (to) *ansagen.*
announcement *Anzeige, f.*
annoy (to) *ärgern, belästigen.*
annual *jährlich.*
annul (to) *annulieren; ungültig machen.*
anonymous *anonym.*
another *ein anderer.*
answer *Antwort, f.*
answer (to) *antworten.*
answering machine *Anrufbeanworter, m.*
anterior *vorhergehend.*
anticipate (to) *vorhersehen* (foresee).
    erwarten (expect).
antique *altertümlich, antik.*
anxiety *Unruhe, f.; Ängstlichkeit f.*
anxious *unruhig, ängstlich, bekümmert.*
any *etwas* (some); *irgend ein; irgend welche*
    (whatever).
anybody *irgendjemand.*
anyhow *sowieso.*
    anyway   *sowieso.*
anything *irgendetwas.*
anywhere *irgendwo.*
apart *abseits, getrennt.*
apartment *Wohnung, f.*
apiece *pro Stück.*
apologize (to) *sich entschuldigen.*
apparent *scheinbar, anscheinend.*
appeal (to) *gefallen.*
appear (to) *erscheinen.*
appearance *Erscheinung, f.*
appease (to) *besänftigen.*
appendix *Anhang, m.*
appetite *Appetit, m.*
applaud (to) *applaudieren; klatschen.*
applause *Applaus, m.*

apple *Apfel, m.*
application *Antrag, m.* (request);
   Gewissenhaftigkeit, f. (diligence).
application form *Anmeldungs–*
   Antragsformular.
apply (to) *sich bewerben um* (for a job);
   auftragen (use).
appoint (to) *emennen.*
appointment *Verbredung, f.*
appreciate (to) *schätzen.*
appreciation *Anerkennung, f.*
appropriate *angemessen.*
approve (to) *genehmigen.*
April *April, m.*
apron *Schürze, f.*
arbitrary *eigenwillig, beliebig.*
arcade *Arkade, f.*
architect *Architekt, m.; Baumeister, m.*
architecture *Architektur, f.*
ardent *feurig, glühend.*
area *Gebiet, n.*
argue (to) *verhandeln, diskutieren.*
argument *Wortwechsel, m.*
arise (to) *aufsteigen; auftauchen* (emerge);
   aufstehen (get up).
arm *Arm, m.*
   firearms *Waffen, pl.*
arm (to) *bewaffnen.*
arms control *Abrustung, f.*
army *Heer, n.; Armee, f.*
around *herum, um* (acc.).
arouse (to) *erregen* (revolt); *erwecken*
   (suspicion); *aufwecken* (wake up).
arrange (to) *ordnen, arrangieren.*
arrangement *Ordnung, f.* (order);
   Anordnung, f. (preparation).
arrest *Verhaftung, f.*
arrest (to) *verhaften.*
arrival *Ankunft, f.*
arrive (to) *ankommen.*
art *Kunst, f.*
article *Artikel, m.*
artificial *künstlich.*
artificial intelligence kunstliche Intelligenz
   (computer), *f.*
artist *Künstler, m.*
artistic *künstlerisch, kunstvoll.*
as *als* (when); *so* (as much); *da* (because).
   as . . . as   *so . . . wie.*
   as long as   *so lange wie.*
   as soon as   *sobald.*
   as to   *mit Bezug auf* (business); *was . . .
   anbetrifft.*
   as well   *sowohl, auch.*
   as yet   *bis jetzt.*
ascertain (to) *feststellen.*
ash *Asche, f.*
ashamed *beschämt, verschämt* (shy).
aside *beiseite, abseits.*

ask (to) *fragen, bitten* (um).
asleep *schlafend.*
aspire (to) *streben nach.*
aspirin *Aspirin, n.*
assault *Angriff, m.*
assemble (to) *sich versammeln.*
assembly *Versammlung, f.* (congress);
   Gesellschaft, f.
assign (to) *zuteilen, aufgeben.*
assist (to) *beistehen,* (aus) *helfen.*
assistant *Gehilfe, m., Gehilfin, f.;
   Assistent(in) m. (f.).*
associate (to) *anschliessen, verbinden.*
assume (to) *annehmen.*
assurance *Versicherung, f.*
assure (to) *versichern.*
astonish (to) *erstaunen.*
astound (to) *verblüffen.*
astronaut *astronaut(in, f.) m.*
asylum *Asyl, n.*
at an *in* (dat. or acc.); *beim, zu* (dat.).
   at home   *zu Hause* (heim)
   at first   *zuerst.*
   at last   *endlich.*
   at once   *sofort.*
   at times   *zuweillen, manchmal*
   (sometimes).
athlete *Athlet, m.*
athletics, *Gymnastik, f.*
atmosphere *Atmosphäre, f.*
attach (to) *anhängen.*
attain (to) *erreichen.*
attempt (to) *versuchen.*
attend (to) *beiwohnen, besuchen* (school).
attendant *Gehilfe, m.*
attention *Aufmerksamkeit, f.*
attic *Dachkammer, f., Dachstube f.*
attitude *Haltung, f.; Einstellung, f.*
   (mental).
attorney *Anwalt, m.*
attract (to) *anziehen.*
attraction *Anziehung, f.*
attractive *schön, anziehend, reizend.*
audience *Zuhörer, pl, Zuhörerschaft f.;
   Audienz, f.; Publikum n.*
August *August, m.*
aunt *Tante, f.*
author *Autor, m.*
authority *Autorität, f.*
authorize (to) *ermächtigen.*
automatic *automatisch.*
automobile *Auto, n.*
autumn *Herbst, m.*
available *vorhanden, verfügbar, erhältlich.*
average *Durchschnitt, m.*
avoid (to) *vermeiden.*
awake *wach.*
awake (to) *wecken; erwachen* (oneself).
award *Belohnung, f.*

award (to) *zuerkennen, zusprechen, verleihen.*
aware *gewahr, bewusst.*
  I'm fully aware that ... *Es ist mir völlig bewusst (klar), dass ...*
away *fort, weg.*
  to go away *weggehen.*
awful *furchtbar.*
awkward *ungeschickt.*

B

baby *Kind, n.*
back *Rücken* (noun, *m.*) (body); *zurück* (adv.).
background *Hintergrund, m.*
backwards *rückwärts.*
bacon *Speck, m.*
bad *schlecht.*
badge *Marke, f., Abzeichen, n.* (Verdienst); *Medaille f.* (military).
bag *Beutel, m., Tüte, f.* (paper bag).
baggage *Gepäck, n.*
baker *Bäcker, m.*
bakery *Bäckerei, f.*
balance *Gleichgewicht, n.*
balcony *Balkon, m.*
ball *Ball, m.*
balloon *Ballon, m.*
banana *Banane, f.*
band *Band, n.; Musikkapelle, f.*
bandage *Verband, m.*
banister *Treppengeländer, n.*
bank *Bank, f., Ufer, n.* (of a river).
bank note *Banknote, f.*
bankruptcy *Bankrott, m.; Konkurs, m.*
banquet *Bankett, n.; Festessen, n.*
bar *Bar, f.* (for drinks).
barber *Frisör, m.*
bare *bloss, bar, unbekleidet.*
barefoot *barfuss.*
barge *Barke, f. Lastschiff, n.*
barn *Scheune, f.*
barrel *Fass, n.*
barren *unfruchtbar.*
basin *Becken, n.*
basis *Grundlage, f.*
basket *Korb, n.*
bath *Bad, n.*
bathroom *Badezimmer, n.*
bathe (to) *baden.*
battle *Schlacht, f.; Kampf, m.*
bay *Bucht, f.*
be (to) *sein.*
  to be hungry *hungrig sein, Hunger haben.*
  to be right *Recht haben.*
  to be thirsty *Durst haben, durstig sein.*
  to be tired *müde sein.*

  to be wrong *Unrecht haben, im Unrecht sein.*
beach *Strand, m.*
bean *Bohne, f.*
bear (to) *aushalten.*
beard *Bart, m.*
beat (to) *schlagen.*
beautiful *schön, wunderschön.*
beauty *Schönheit, f.*
beauty parlor *Schönheitssalon, m.*
because *weil, denn* (for).
become (to) *werden.*
becoming *passend, vorteilhaft.*
bed *Bett, n.*
beef *Rindfleisch, n.*
beer *Bier, n.*
beet *Rübe, f.*
before *vor* (dat. or acc.); *bevor* (conj.).
beg (to) *betteln.*
beggar *Bettler, m.*
begin (to) *beginnen, anfangen.*
beginning *Anfang, f.*
behave (to) *sich betragen, sich benehmen.*
behavior *Verhalten, n.; Behnehmen, n.*
behind *hinter* (dat. or acc.).
belief *Glaube, m.*
believe (to) *glauben.*
bell *Glocke, f.*
belong (to) *gehören.*
below *unter* (dat. or acc.).
belt *Gürtel, m.*
bench *Bank, f.*
bend (to) *biegen.*
beneath *unten; unter* (dat. or acc.).
benefit *Vorteil, m.*
beside *neben* (dat. or acc.).
besides *ausserdem.*
best *beste (der, die, das)* (adj.); *am besten* (adv.).
bet *Wette, f.*
bet (to) *wetten.*
betray (to) *verraten.*
better *besser.*
between *zwischen* (dat. or acc.).
beware (to) *sich hüten.*
  Beware! *Achtung!*
beyond *jenseits* (gen.).
bicycle *Fahrrad, n.*
bid (to) *bieten; befehlen* (order).
big *gross.*
bill *Rechnung, f.*
  bill of fare *Speisekarte, f.*
billion *Milliarde* (Am.), *Billion.*
bind (to) *binden.*
bird *Vogel, m.*
birth *Geburt, f.*
birthday *Geburtstag, m.*
biscuit *Zwieback, m., Keks, m.*
bishop *Bischof, m.*

bit *Stück, n. Gibiss, n.* (horse).
bite *Biss, m.*
bite (to) *beissen.*
bitter *bitter.*
bitterness *Bitterkeit, f.*
black *schwarz, Schwarz* (person) *m. & f.*
blade *Klinge, f.* (razor); *Blatt, n.* (grass).
blame *Schuld, f.; Tadel, m.*
blame (to) *tadeln, rügen.*
blank *unbeschrieben* (page); *verwundert* (expression).
blanket *Decke, f.*
bleed (to) *bluten.*
bless (to) *segnen.*
blessing *Segnung, f.; Segen, m.*
blind *blind.*
block *Block, m.*
block (to) *versperren.*
blood *Blut, n.*
blotter *Löschpapier, n.*
blouse *Bluse, f.*
blow *Schlag, m.*
blow (to) *blasen; putzen* (nose).
blue *blau.*
blush (to) *erröten.*
board *Brett, n.* (plank); *Verpflegung, f.* (food).
boarding house *Pension, f.*
boarding pass *Bordkarte, f., Einsteigarte, f.*
boast (to) *prahlen.*
boat *Boot, n.*
body *Körper, m.*
boil (to) *kochen, sieden.*
boiler *Kessel, m., Heisswasserspeicher, m.*
bold *kühn.*
bomb *Bombe, f.*
      atom bomb. *Atombombe, f.*
bond *Aktie, f.* (stock).
bone *Knochen, m.*
book *Buch, n.*
bookseller *Buchhändler, m.*
bookstore *Buchhandlung, f.*
border *Grenze, f.*
boring *langweilig.*
born *geboren.*
borrow (to) *borgen, leihen.*
boss *Boss, m., Chef, m.*
both *beide.*
bother (to) *ärgern, plagen, bemühen.*
      Don't bother! *Bemühen Sie sich nicht!*
bottle *Flasche, f.*
bottle opener *Flaschenöffner, m.*
bottom *Boden, m.*
bounce (to) *aufspringen.*
bowl *Schale, f.*
box *Schachtel, f.*
boy *Junge, m.*
bracelet *Armband, n.*
braid *Borte, f.; Zopf, m.* (hair), *Haarflechte, f.*

brain *Gehirn, n.*
brake *Bremse, f.*
branch *Ast, m.* (tree); *Filiale, f.* (business).
brave *tapfer.*
brassiere *Büstenhalter, m.*
bread *Brot, n.*
break (to) *brechen; lösen* (engagement).
breakfast *Frühstück, n.*
      have breakfast *frühstücken.*
breath *Atem, m.*
breathe (to) *atmen.*
breeze *Wind, m.; Brise, f.*
bribe (to) *bestechen.*
brick *Backstein, m.*
bride *Braut, f.*
      bridegroom *Bräutigam, m.*
bridge *Brücke, f.*
brief *kurz.*
bright *hell, klar.*
brighten (to) *erheitern; sich aufklären* (weather).
brilliant *glänzend.*
bring (to) *bringen.*
bring up (to) *erziehen* (a person).
British *britisch.*
broad *weit, breit.*
broil (to) *braten.*
broken *zerbrochen.*
brook *Bach, m.*
broom *Besen, m.*
brother *Bruder, m.*
brother-in-law *Schwager, m.*
brown *braun.*
bruise (to) *quetschen, zerstossen.*
brush *Bürste, f.*
bubble *Blase, f.*
bucket *Eimer m.*
buckle *Schnalle, f.*
bud *Knospe, f.*
budget *Budget, n; Wirtschaft, f.* (house).
build (to) *bauen.*
building *Gebäude, n.*
bulletin *Bulletin, n., Bekanntmachung, f.; Ansage, f.*
bundle *Bündel, n.*
burn (to) *(ver)brennen.*
burst (to) *bersten; platzen.*
bus *Autobus, m. Omnibus, m.*
bush *Busch, m.*
business *Geschäft, n.*
businessman *Geschäftsmann, m.; Kaufmann, m.; businesswoman Geschäftsfrau, f.*
busy *beschäftigt.*
but *aber; sondern* (neg.).
butcher *Metzger, m.; Fleischer, m.*
butcher shop *Metzgerei, f.; Fleischerei, f.*
butter *Butter, f.*
button *Knopf, m.*
buy (to) *kaufen.*

buyer *Käufer, m.*
by *von* (dat.)*; durch* (acc.)*; neben* (dat. & acc.) (close to)*; um* (acc.) (time).
byte *Byte, m.*

C

cab *Taxi, n.*
cabbage *Kohl, m.; Kraut, n.*
cable *Kabel, n.*
cage *Käfig, m.*
cake *Kuchen, m.*
calendar *Kalender, m.*
calf *Kalb, n.*
call *Ruf, m.; Anruf* (telephone) *m.*
call (to) *rufen; anrufen; telefonieren* (telephone)*; heissen* (name).
calm *ruhig.*
camera *Kamera, f.; Fotoapparat m.*
camp *Lager, n.*
camp (to) *lagern, zelten.*
can *Büchse, f.; Dose, f.*
can (to be able) *können.*
can opener *Büchsenöffner, m.*
cancel (to) *rückgängig machen, absagen, annulieren* (annul)*, durchstreichen.*
candidate *Kandidat, m.*
candle *Kerze, f.*
candy *Bonbons, pl.*
cap *Mütze, f.*
capital *Hauptstadt, f.* (city)*; Kapital, n.* (finance).
capital punishment *Toddesstrafe* (death penalty)*, f.*
capricious *launisch; eigensinnig* (temperamental).
captain *Hauptmann, n.* (army)*; Kapitän, m.* (navy).
captive *Gefangene, m.*
capture (to) *fangen; einnehmen.*
car *Wagen, m., Auto, n.*
carbon paper *Durchschlagpapier, n.*
card *Karte, f.; Ausweis* (I.D.) *m.*
care *Sorge, f.* (anxiety)*; Sorgfalt, f.* (caution).
   care of *per Adresse*
   take care of *pflegen*
care (to) *sich sorgen.*
   care about *sich kümmern um*
   care for (to like) *gern haben.*
   I don't care. *Das ist mir gleich.*
career *Laufbahn, f.*
careful *vorsichtig, sorgfältig.*
careless *nachlässig, sorglos.*
caress *Liebkosung, f.*
carpenter *Zimmermann, m.*
carpet *Teppich, m.*
carry (to) *tragen.*

carve (to) *schnitzen.*
case *Fall, m.; Aktentasche, f.*
   in case *im Falle, falls*
cash *Bargeld, n.*
   to pay cash *bar zahlen.*
cash (to) *einlösen, kassieren.*
cashier *Kassierer, m.*
cassette *Kassette, f.*
   cassette tape deck *Kassettendeck, n.*
castle *Schloss, n.*
cat *Katze, f.*
catch (to) *fangen.*
category *Kategorie, f.*
cathedral *Dom, m.*
Catholic *katholisch.*
cattle *Vieh, n.*
cause *Grund, m.; Ursache, f.*
cause (to) *verursachen.*
cease (to) *aufhören.*
ceiling *Decke, f.*
celebrate (to) *feiern.*
cellar *Keller, m.*
cement *Zement, m.*
cemetery *Friedhof, m.*
censorship *Zensur, f.*
center *Zentrum, n.; Mittelpunkt, m.*
central *zentral.*
central heating *Zentralheizung, f.*
century *Jahrhundert, n.*
cereal *Getreide, n.* (grain)*; Mehlspeise, f.* (prepared).
ceremony *Zeremonie, f.*
certain *gewiss, sicher.*
certainty *Gewissheit, f.; Sicherheit, f.*
certificate *Zeugnis, n.; Zertifikat, n.*
chain *Kette, f.*
chair *Stuhl, m.*
chairman (-woman) *Vorsitzende, m.* (f) *Präsident, m.*
chalk *Kreide, f.*
challenge *Herausforderung, f.; Aufforderung, f.*
challenge (to) *herausfordern.*
champion *Meister, m.*
   world champion *Weltmeister, m.*
chance *Zufall, m.*
change *Veränderung, f.; Kleingeld, n.* (money).
change (to) *ändern; wechseln* (money).
chapel *Kapelle, f.*
chapter *Kapitel, n.*
character *Charakter, m.*
characteristic *charakteristisch.*
charge (to) *beladen; berechnen* (price)*; anklagen* (law).
charitable *wohltätig.*
charity *Wohltätigkeit, f. Nächstenliebe, f.*
charming *reizend.*
chase (to) *jagen.*

chat (to) *plaudern.*
cheap *billig.*
cheat (to) *betrügen.*
check *Scheck, m.; Rechnung, f.* (in a restaurant).
check (to) *knotrolliern; aufgeben, nachprüfen* (baggage).
cheek *Wange, f.*
cheer (to) *aufheitern.*
cheerful *heiter, freudig, fröhlich.*
cheese *Käse, m.*
chemical *chemisch.*
cherish (to) *schätzen.*
cherry *Kirsche, f.*
chest *Brust, f.; Kiste, f.* (box).
    chest of drawers *Kommode, f.*
chestnut *Kastanie, f.*
chew (to) *kauen.*
chicken *Huhn, n.; Hühnchen, n., Huhn, n.*
chief *Leiter, m., Vorgesetzte(r), m.; chef, m.*
chief (adj.) *haupt-.*
chime *Glockenspiel,n.*
chimney *Schornstein, m.*
chin *Kinn, n.*
china *Porzellan, n.*
chip *Span, m.; Splitter, m.*
chocolate *Schokolade, f.*
choice *Wahl, f.*
choir *Chor, m.*
choke (to) *ersticken.*
choose (to) *auswählen.*
chop *Kotelett, n.*
Christian *Christ* (noun) *m.; christlich* (adj.).
Christmas *Weihnachten, f. pl.*
church *Kirche, f.*
cigar *Zigarre, f.*
cigarette *Zigarette, f.*
circle *Kreis, m.*
circular *rund.*
circulate (to) *kreisen, umlaufen.*
circumstances *Umstände, pl.*
citizen *Bürger, m.*
city *Stadt, f.*
city hall *Rathaus, m.*
civil *zivil, bürgerlich.*
civilization *Zivilisation, f.*
civilize (to) *zivilisieren.*
claim *Forderung, f; Rechtsanspruch, m.*
claim (to) *fordern.*
clamor *Geschrei, n.*
clap (to) *klatschen.*
class *Klasse, f.; Kategorie, f.*
classify (to) *klassifizieren.*
clause *Klausel, f.; Satzglied, m.*
clean *rein, sauber.*
clean (to) *reinigen.*
cleaners *Reinigungsanstalt, f.*
cleanliness *Reinlichkeit, f.; Sauberkeit, f.*
clear *klar.*

clerk *Angestellte, m.*
clever *klug, schlau.*
climate *Klima, n.*
climb (to) *steigen* (stairway)*; besteigen* (mountain).
clip *Klammer, f.*
clip (to) *beschneiden* (cut)*; scheren zusammenfügen* (attach)*; festhalten.*
clock *Uhr, f.*
close *nahe.*
close (to) *zumachen, schliessen.*
closed *geschlossen.*
closet *Schrank, m.*
cloth *Tuch, n.*
clothes *Kleider, pl.*
cloud *Wolke, f.*
cloudy *bewölkt.*
clover *Klee, m.*
club *Klub, m.; Kreuz* (cards).
coal *Kohle, f.*
coarse *roh.*
coast *Küste, f.*
coat *Mantel, m.* (overcoat)*; Anzug, m.* (suit).
code *Gesetzbuch, n.* (law)*; Kodex, m.*
coffee *Kaffee, m.*
coffin *Sarg, m.*
coin *Münze, f.*
cold *kalt.*
coldness *Kälte, f.*
collaborate (to) *zusammenarbeiten.*
collar *Kragen, m.; Halsband, n.* (dog).
collect (to) *sammeln.*
collection *Sammlung, f.*
collective *gesamt.*
college *Universität, f.*
colonial *kolonial.*
colony *Kolonie, f.*
color *Farbe, f.*
color (to) *färben.*
column *Spalte, fl., Kollonne, f.* (military)*; Säule, f.* (arch).
comb *Kamm, m.*
comb (to) *kämmen.*
combination *Verbindung, f.; Zusammenstellung, f.; Verknüpfung, f.*
combine (to) *verbinden, zusammenstellen.*
come (to) *kommen.*
    come back *zurückkommen.*
comedy *Komödie, f.*
comet *Komet, m., Schweifstern, m.*
comfort *Behaglichkeit, f.; Trost, m.* (moral).
comfort (to) *trösten.*
comfortable *bequem.*
comma *Komma, n.*
command *Befehl, m.*
command (to) *befehlen*
commander *Befehlshaber, m.*
commercial *geschäftsmässig, handelsüblich; Fernsehwerbung, f.* (TV commercial).

commission *Kommission, f.*
commit (to) *begehen.*
common *gemein, gewöhnlich.*
Commonwealth of Independent States *das Commonwealth Unabhängiger Nationen, n.*
communicate (to) *mitteilen.*
communication *Mitteilung, f.*
community *Gemeinde, f.*
compact disc (CD) *Compact Disc, f.; Kompaktplatte, f.*
companion *Genosse, m.*
company *Gesellschaft, f.* (social); *Kompanie, f.* (military).
compare (to) *vergleichen.*
comparison *Vergleich, m.*
compel *zwingen, nötigen.*
compete (to) *konkurrieren.*
competition *Konkurrenz, f.; Tournier, n.* (sports), *Wettbewerb, n.* (sports).
complain (to) *sich beklagen.*
complaint *Klage, f.*
complete *vollenden.*
complex *Komplex,* (noun) *m.; verwickelt* (adj.); *kompliziert* (adj.).
complexion *Gesichtsfarbe, f.*
complicate (to) *verwickeln, komplizieren.*
complicated *verwickelt, kompliziert.*
compliment *Kompliment, n.*
compose (to) *komponieren.*
composer *Komponist, m.*
composition *Komposition, f.*
compromise *Kompromiss, m.; Vergleich, m.*
compromise (to) *einen Kompromiss machen, kompromittieren.*
computer *Computer, m.*
conceit *Einbildung, f.*
conceited *eingebildet.*
conceive (to) *ersinnen, ausdenken, schwanger werden* (med.).
concentrate (to) *konzentrieren.*
concern *Angelegenheit, f.* (matter); *Sorge, f.* (anxiety); *Geschäft, n.* (business).
concern (to) *betreffen.*
concert *Konzert, n.*
concrete *konkret, wesenhaft.*
condemn (to) *verurteilen, verdammen.*
condense (to) *kondensieren.*
condition *Zustand, m.*
conduct *Benehmen, n.*
conduct (to) *führen; dirigieren* (music).
conductor *Führer, m.* (guide); *Schaffner, m.* (vehicle); *Dirigent, m.* (music).
confess (to) *gestehen; beichten* (church).
confession *Geständnis, n.; Beichte, f.* (church).
confidence *Vertrauen, n.*
confident *vertrauend, vertrauensvoll.*
confidential *vertraulich, geheim.*
confirm (to) *bestätigen.*

confirmation *Bestätigung, f.*
congratulate (to) *gratulieren.*
congratulations *Glückwunsch, m.*
connect (to) *verbinden.*
connection *Verbindung, f.*
conquer (to) *erobern, besiegen.*
conquest *Eroberung, f.; Sieg, m.*
conscience *Gewissen, n.*
conscientious *gewissenhaft.*
conscious *bewusst.*
consent *Einwilligung, f.; Genehmigung, f.*
conservative *konservativ.*
consider (to) *betrachten* (look); *bedenken* (think).
considerable *beträchtlich, bedeutend.*
consideration *Betrachtung, f.*
consist of (to) *bestehen aus* (dat.).
consistent *übereinstimmend, fest, dicht.*
constant *beständig.*
constitution *Verfassung, f.; Gesundheit, f.* (health).
constitutional *verfassungsmässig.*
consul *Konsul, m.*
contagious *ansteckend.*
contain (to) *enthalten.*
container *Behälter, m.*
contemporary *Zeitgenosse* (noun) *m.; zeitgenössisch* (adj.).
content *zufrieden.*
content (to) *befriedigen.*
contents *Inhalt, m.; Gehalt, m.*
continent *Kontinent, m.*
continual *fortwährend.*
continue (to) *fortfahren.*
contract *Vertrag, m.*
contractor *Unternehmer, m.*
contradict (to) *widersprechen.*
contradiction *Widerspruch, m.*
contradictory *widersprechend.*
contrary *Gegenteil* (noun) *n.; entgegengesetzt* (adj.).
on the contrary *im Gegenteil.*
contrast *Gegensatz, m.*
contrast (to) *vergleichen, gegenüberstellen*
contribute (to) *beitragen.*
contribution *Beitrag, m.*
control *Kontrolle, f.*
control (to) *kontrollieren.*
controversy *Meinungsverschiedenheit, f.; Kontroverse, f.; Angemessenheit, f.*
convenience *Bequemlichkeit, f.*
convenient *passend; bequem* (practical).
convent *Kloster, n.*
convention *Versammlung, f.*
conversation *Gespräch, n.; Unterhaltung, f.*
converse (to) *sich unterhalten.*
convert (to) *umwandeln einlösen* (bonds).
convict (to) *verurteilen.*
conviction *Verurteilung, f.*

convince (to) *überzeugen.*
cook *Koch, m.; Köchin, f.*
cook (to) *kochen.*
cool *kühl.*
cool (to) *kühlen.*
copy *Kopie, f.*
cork *Kork(en) m.; Stöpsel, m.*
corkscrew *Korkenzieher, m.*
corn *Mais, m.*
corner *Ecke, f.*
corporation *Körperschaft, f., Korporation, f.*
correct *richtig.*
correct (to) *berichtigen, korrigieren.*
correction *Verbesserung, f., Berichtigung, f.*
correspond (to) *korrespondieren.*
correspondence *Briefwechsel, m.*
correspondent *Korrespondent, m.*
corresponding *entsprechend.*
corrupt (to) *verderben.*
corruption *Verdorbenheit, f.*
cost *Kosten, f.*
costume *Kostüm, n.*
cottage *Häuschen, n.*
cotton *Baumwolle, f.; Watte, f.* (pharmacy).
couch *Sofa, n., Couch, f.*
cough *Husten, m.*
count *Graf, m.* (nobility); *Zählung, f.*
count (to) *zählen.*
counter *Ladentisch, m.*
countess *Gräfin, f.*
countless *zahllos.*
country *Land, n.; Vaterland, n.* (fatherland).
countryman *Landsmann, m.*
couple *Paar, n.*
coupon *Coupon, Kupon, m.*
courage *Mut, m.*
course *Lauf, m.* (direction); *Kursus, m.*
(studies), *Verlauf, m.* (illness).
court *Gericht, n.*
courteous *zuvorkommend.*
courtesy *Höflichkeit, f.*
courtyard *Hof, m., Spielplatz, m.*
cousin *Vetter, m.; Cousine, f.*
cover *Decke, f.*
cow *Kuh, f.*
crack *Riss, m.*
crack (to) *knacken.*
cradle *Wiege, f.*
crash *Zusammenbruch, m., Absturz, m.*
(plane); *Zusammenstoss, m.* (auto).
crazy *verrückt.*
cream *Sahne, f., Rahm, m.*
create (to) *schaffen*
creature *Geschöpf, n.; Wesen, n.*
credit *Kredit, m.*
creditor *Gläubiger, m.*
crime *Verbrechen, n.*
crisis *Krise, f.*
crisp *knusperig.*

critic *Kritiker, m.*
critical *kritisch.*
criticize (to) *kritisieren.*
crooked *krumm.*
crop *Ernte, f.*
cross *Kreuz, n.*
crossing *Übergang, m.*
crossroad *Strassenkreuzung, f., Kreuzweg, m.*
crouch (to) *hocken.*
crow *Krähe, f.*
crowd *Menge, f.; Gedränge, n.*
crowd (to) *überfüllen, zusammendrängen.*
crowded *überfüllt, wimmelnd.*
crown *Krone, f.*
crown (to) *krönen.*
cruel *grausam, unmenschlich.*
cruelty *Grausamkeit, f.*
crumb *Krume, f., Krumchen, m. Krumel, m.*
crumble (to) *zerbröckeln.*
crust *Kruste, f.*
crutch *Krücke, f.*
cry *Ruf, m.; Geschrei, n.*
cry (to) *weinen* (weep); *schreien* (shout).
cuff *Manschette, f.*
cunning *listig, verschmitzt, verschlagen.*
cup *Tasse, f.*
cure *Heilung, f.*
curiosity *Neugier, f.*
curious *neugierig.*
curl *Locke, f.*
current *Strom* (noun) *m.; laufend* (adj.),
jetzig (adj.), *gegenwärtig.*
curtain *Vorhang, m., Gardine, f.*
curve *Kurve, f.*
cushion *Kissen, n.*
custom *Sitte, f.*
customary *gebräuchlich.*
customer *Kunde, m.* (-in), *f.*
customshouse *Zollamt, n.*
customs official *Zollbeamte, m.*
cut *Schnitt, m.*
cut (to) *schneiden.*

D

dagger *Dolch, m.*
daily *täglich.*
dainty *zierlich.*
dairy *Milchgeschäft, n.*
dam *Damm, m., Deich, m.*
damage *Schaden, m.*
damage (to) *beschädigen.*
damp *feucht.*
dance *Tanz, m.*
dance (to) *tanzen.*
danger *Gefahr, f.*
dangerous *gefährlich.*
dark *dunkel.*

darkness *Dunkelheit, f.*
dash (to) *sich beeilen, bespritzen* (water), *losstürzen* (auf).
data processing *Datenverarbeitung f.*
date *Datum, n.; Verabredung, f.* (meeting).
daughter *Tochter, f.*
dawn *Morgendämmerung, f.*
day *Tag, m.*
  day after tomorrow *übermorgen.*
  day before yesterday *vorgestern.*
  yesterday *gestern.*
dazzle (to) *blenden, verblüffen.*
dead *tot.*
deaf *taub.*
deal *Teil, m.; Geschäft, n.* (business).
  a great deal of *sehr viel*
  to strike up a deal with
    someone *jemandem ein Geschäft*
    machen
  it's a deal (coll.) *abgemacht!*
  big deal! *gross Wichtigkeit!* (coll.)
deal (to) *ausgeben* (cards), *verteilen, zuteilen, handeln* (mit).
dealer *Händler, m.; Geber, m.* (cards).
dear *lieb; teuer* (also expensive).
death *Tod, m.*
debate *Debatte, f., Verhandlung, f.*
debt *Schuld, f.*
debtor *Schuldner, m.*
decanter *Karaffe, f.*
decay *Verfall, m.* (ruin); *Fäulnis, f.* (rot).
decay (to) *verfallen, verfaulen.*
deceased *verstorben.*
deceit *Falschheit, f.*
deceive (to) *betrügen.*
December *Dezember, m.*
decent *anständig.*
decide (to) *entscheiden.*
decided *entschieden.*
decision *Entscheidung, f.; Entschluss, m.*
decisive *entscheidend.*
deck *Deck, n.*
declare (to) *erklären.*
decline *Untergang, m. Fall, m.*
decline (to) *verfallen, abweisen; deklinieren* (grammar); *untergehen.*
decrease *Abnahme, f.; Verminderung, f.*
decrease (to) *abnehmen, vermindern.*
decree *Verordnung, f.*
dedicate (to) *widmen.*
deed *Tat, f.*
deep *tief.*
deer *Hirsch, m.*
defeat *Niederlage, f.*
defeat (to) *besiegen.*
defect *Fehler, m.*
defend (to) *verteidigen.*
defense *Verteidigung, f.*
defiance *Trotz, m.*

define (to) *definieren.*
definite *bestimmt.*
defy (to) *trotzen.*
degree *Grad, m.*
delay *Verzögerung, f.*
delay (to) *aufhalten.*
delegate *Delegierte(r), m., Bevollmächtigte(r), m.*
delegate (to) *delegieren.*
deliberate (to) *erwägen.*
deliberately *absichtlich.*
delicacy *Delikatesse, f.; Leckerbissen, m.*
delicate *zart.*
delicious *köstlich.*
delight *Freude, f.; Vergnügen, n.*
delighted *erfreut.*
deliver (to) *liefern.*
deliverance *Befreiung, f.*
delivery *Ablieferung, f.; Abgabe, f.*
demand *Forderung, f.; Nachfrage, f.* (business); *Verlangen, n.*
demand (to) *fordern.*
democracy *Demokratie, f.*
demonstrate (to) *demonstrieren.*
demonstration *Darlegung, f.; Demonstration, f.* (political).
denial *Verleugnung, f.*
denounce (to) *denunzieren, offentlich anklagen.*
dense *dicht.*
density *Dichte, f.*
dentist *Zahnarzt, m.*
deny (to) *ableugnen, verleugnen.*
departure *Abreise, f.*
department *Abteilung, f.*
depend (to) *abhängen.*
dependent *abhängig.*
deplore (to) *bedauern, beweinen.*
deposit *Anzahlung, f.*
depreciation *Wertminderung, f.*
depress (to) *niederdrücken.*
depression *Depression, f.*
deprive (to) *berauben, entziehen.*
depth *Tiefe, f.*
deride (to) *verlachen, verhöhnen.*
derive (to) *ableiten.*
descend (to) *abstammen.*
descendant *Nachkomme, m; Abkömmling, m.*
descent *Abstieg, m.; Abstammung, f.* (family).
describe (to) *beschreiben.*
description *Beschreibung, f.*
desert *Wüste, f.*
desert (to) *verlassen.*
deserve (to) *verdienen.*
design *Zeichnung, f.* (drawing); *Absicht, f.* (intention).
designer *Zeichner, m.*
desirable *wünschenswert.*
desire (to) *wünschen.*

desire *Wunsch, m.*
desirous *begierig.*
desk *Pult, n.*
desolate *trostlos.*
despair *Verzweiflung, f.*
despair (to) *verzweifeln.*
desperate *verzweifelt.*
despise (to) *verachten.*
despite *trotz* (gen.).
dessert *Nachtisch, m.*
destiny *Schicksal, n.*
destroy (to) *zerstören.*
destruction *Zerstörung, f.*
detach (to) *ablösen, freimachen*
detail *Einzelheit, f.*
detain (to) *aufhalten.*
detect (to) *entdecken, aufdecken* (crime).
detective *Detektiv, m.*
detective story *Kriminalgeschichte, f.;*
    Detektivroman, m.
determination *Entschlossenheit, f.*
determine (to) *bestimmen.*
detest (to) *verabscheuen.*
detour *Umweg, m.*
detract (to) *abziehen, entziehen, vermindern.*
detrimental *schädlich.*
develop (to) *entwickeln.*
development *Entwicklung, f.*
device *Kunstgriff, m; Gerät, n.*
devil *Teufel, m.*
devise (to) *ersinnen, ausdenken.*
devoid *ohne* (acc.), *bar* (gen.).
devote (to) *widmen*
devour (to) *verschlingen, verzehren.*
dew *Tau, m.*
dial *Zifferblatt, n.* (clock); *Wähler, m.*
    (phone).
dial (to) *wählen.*
dialect *Dialekt, m.*
dialogue *Dialog, m.*
diameter *Durchmesser, m.*
diamond *Diamant, m.*
diary *Tagebuch, n.*
dictate (to) *diktieren.*
dictation *Diktat, n.*
dictionary *Wörterbuch, n.; Lexikon, n.*
die (to) *sterben.*
diet *Diät, f.*
differ (to) *sich unterscheiden.*
difference *Unterschied, m.*
different *verschieden.*
difficult *schwierig.*
difficulty *Schwierigkeit, f.*
dig (to) *graben.*
digest (to) *verdauen.*
dignity *Würde, f.*
dim *trübe.*
dimension *Dimension, f.; Mass, n.;*
    Ausmass, n.

diminish (to) *vermindern.*
dining room *Speisesaal, m.*
dinner *Abendessen, n.*
dine (to) *essen, speisen.*
dip (to) *senken, (ein)tauchen.*
diplomacy *Diplomatie, f.*
diplomat *Diplomat, m.*
direct *direkt.*
direct (to) *den Weg zeigen* (show the way).
direction *Richtung, f.*
director *Direktor, m.*
directory *Adressbuch, n.; Telefonbuch*
    (phone), *n.*
dirt *Schmutz, m.*
dirty *schmutzig.*
disability *Unfähigkeit, f.;*
    Körperbehinderung, f.
disabled *unfähig, behindert.*
disadvantage *Nachteil, m.*
disagree (to) *uneinig sein, nicht zustimmen.*
disagreeable *unangenehm.*
disagreement *Meinungsverschiedenheit, f.*
disappear (to) *verschwinden.*
disappearance *Verschwinden, n.*
disappoint (to) *enttäuschen.*
disapprove (to) *missbilligen, ablehnen.*
disaster *Unglück, n.; Katastrophe, f.*
disastrous *unheilvoll, schrecklich.*
discharge *Entlassung, f.* (dismissal);
    Abfeuern, n. (gun).
discharge (to) *entlassen* (person); *abfeuern*
    (firearm), *abschiessen* (firearm).
discipline *Zucht, f., Disziptin, f.*
disclaim (to) *bestreiten.*
disclose (to) *enthüllen, offenbaren.*
disclosure *Enthüllung, f. Mitteilung f.,*
    Offenbarung, f.
discomfort *Unbehaglichkeit, f.*
disconnect (to) *trennen, abschalten.*
discontent *unzufrieden.*
discontinue (to) *aufhören.*
discord *Zwietracht, f.*
discount *Diskonto, m.* (financial); *Rabatt, m.*
discourage (to) *entmutigen.*
discouragement *Entmutigung, f.*
discover (to) *entdecken.*
discovery *Entdeckung, f.*
discreet *diskret, vorsichtig.*
discretion *Besonnenheit, f.; Urteil, n.*
discuss (to) *besprechen, sich unterhalten*
    (*über*)
discussion *Besprechung, f.; Diskussion, f.*
disdain *Verachtung, f.*
disdain (to) *verschmähen, verachten.*
disease *Krankheit, f.*
disgrace *Schande, f.* (shame); *Ungnade, f.*
disguise *Verkleidung, f.*
disguise (to) *verkleiden.*
disgust *Ekel, m., Abscheu, m.*

disgust (to) *(an)ekeln.*
disgusted *ekelhaft, angeekelt.*
dish *Speise, f.* (food); *Teller, m.* (plate).
dishonest *unehrlich.*
disk *Scheibe, f.*
diskette *Diskette, f.*
dislike *Widerwille, m., Abneigung, f., der Widerwille, m.*
dislike (to) *nicht mögen, nicht lieben.*
dismiss (to) *entlassen.*
     dismissal *Entlassung, f.*
disobey (to) *nicht gehorchen.*
disorder *Unordnung, f.*
dispense (to) *verteilen.*
displace *verschieben, verrücken, verdrängen.*
display *Entfaltung f.* (unfold); *Schau, f.* (exposition).
displease (to) *missfallen, missachten.*
displeasure *Missfallen, n.*
disposal *Verfügung, f.*
dispose (to) *anordnen, verfügen.*
dispute *Streit, m.*
dispute (to) *streiten.*
dissolve (to) *auflösen.*
distance *Entfernung, f.*
distant *entfernt.*
distinct *deutlich.*
distinction *Auszeichnung, f.; Unterschied, m.* (difference).
distinguish (to) *unterscheiden.*
distort (to) *verdrehen.*
distract (to) *verwirren, ablenken.*
distress *Not, f.*
distress (to) *betrüben, beunruhigen.*
distribute (to) *verteilen.*
district *Distrikt, m.*
distrust *Misstrauen, n.*
distrust (to) *misstrauen.*
disturb (to) *stören.*
disturbance *Störung, f.*
ditch *Graben, m.*
dive (to) *tauchen.*
divide (to) *verteilen.*
divine *göttlich.*
division *Teilung, f.; Trennung, f.*
divorce (to) *scheiden.*
divorced *geschieden.*
dizziness *Schwindel, m.*
dizzy *schwindlig.*
do (to) *tun, machen.*
dock *Dock, n.; Anlegeplatz, m.*
doctor *Arzt, m.*
doctrine *Lehre, f.*
document *Urkunde, f. Dokument, n.*
dog *Hund, m.*
doll *Puppe, f.*
dome *Kuppel, f.*
domestic *häuslich; einheimisch* (native).
domestic animal *Haustier, n.*

dominate (to) *beherrschen.*
door *Tür, f.*
dose *Dosis, f.*
dot *Punkt, m.*
double *doppelt.*
doubt *Zweifel, m.*
doubt (to) *zweifeln.*
doubtful *zweifelhaft.*
doubtless *ohne Zweifel.*
dough *Teig, m.*
down *unter* (dat. or acc.); *hinunter, herunter.*
dozen *Dutzend, n.*
draft *Weichsel, m.* (money); *Zeichnung, f.* (drawing); *draft Zug, m.* (air); *ziehen, n.* (milit.); *Bier vom Fass* (beer), *n.*
drag (to) *schleppen.*
drain (to) *entwässern abfliessen lassen.*
drama *Drama, n.*
draw (to) *zeichen.*
draw back (to) *schleppen.*
drawer *Schublade, f.*
drawing-room *Gesellschaftszimmer, n.; Salon, m.; Wohnzimmer, n.*
dread *Furcht, f.*
dread (to) *fürchten.*
dreadful *furchtbar, schrecklich.*
dream *Traum, m.*
dream (to) *träumen.*
dreamer *Träumer, m.*
dress *Kleid, n.*
dress (to) *sich anziehen.*
dressmaker *Schneiderin, f.*
drink *Getränk, n.*
drink (to) *trinken.*
drip (to) *tropfen, tröpfeln.*
drive (to) *fahren.*
drive (computer) *Laufwerk, n.*
driver *Chauffeur, m.*
drop *Fall, m.; Tropfen, m.* (liquid).
drown (to) *ertrinken.*
drug *Droge, f.*
drug addiction *Rauschgiftsucht, f.*
drug dealer *Drogenhändler, m.; Pusher, m.* (coll.).
drugstore *Apotheke, f.; Drogerie, f.*
drum *Trommel, f.*
drunk *betrunken.*
dry *trocken.*
dry (to) *trocknen.*
dryness *Trockenheit, f.*
duchess *Herzogin, f.*
duck *Ente, f.*
due *Verfallszeit, f.; Fälligkeitstermin, m.* (due date), *fällig sein* (to be due).
duke *Herzog, m.*
dull *trübe* (weather); *matt* (color); *dumpf* (sound), *fad(e)* (book).
dumb *stumm; dumm* (stupid).

deaf and dumb *taubstumm.*
during *während* (gen.).
dust *Staub, m.*
dust (to) *abstauben; ausbürsten* (clothes).
dusty *staubig.*
Dutch *holländisch.*
duty *Pflicht, f.; Dienst, m.* (service); *Zoll, m.*
　　(customs).
dwarf *Zwerg, m.*
dwell (to) *wohnen.*
dye *Farbe, f.*
dye (to) *färben.*

E

each *jeder.*
　each other　*einander.*
　each time　*jedesmal.*
eager *eifrig.*
eagle *Adler, m.*
ear *Ohr, n.*
early *früh.*
earn (to) *verdienen.*
earnest *ernst.*
earth *Erde, f.*
ease *Bequemlichkeit, f.* (comfort); *Ruhe, f.*
　　(calm); *Linderung, f.* (relief);
　　Leichtigkeit, f. (facility).
ease (to) *lindern, erleichtern.*
easily *leicht.*
east *Osten, m.*
Easter *Ostern, pl.*
eastern *östlich.*
easy *leicht.*
eat (to) *essen.*
echo *Echo, n.; Widerhall, m.*
echo (to) *widerhallen.*
economical *wirtschaftlich; sparsam.*
economize (to) *sparen.*
economy *Sparsamkeit, f.; Wirtschaft, f.* (of a
　　country).
economy class *Touristenklasse, f.*
edge *Schneide, f.* (blade); *Rand, m.* (rim);
　　Kante, f.; Vorteil (advantage), *f.*
edition *Ausgabe, f.; Auflage, f.*
editor *Redakteur, m.*
editorial *Leitartikel* (noun) *m.; redaktionell*
　　(adj.).
education *Bildung, f.; Erziehung, f.*
effect *Wirkung, f.*
effective *wirkungsvoll.*
efficiency *Leistungsfähigkeit, f.*
effort *Anstrengung, f.; Bestreben, n.*
　　(endeavor).
egg *Ei, n.* (*Eier,* pl.).
egoism *Egoismus, m.; Selbstsucht, f.*
eight *acht.*
eighteen *achtzehn.*

eighteenth *achtzehnt.*
eighth *achte, m. f.*
eightieth *achtzigste, m.f.*
eighty *achtzig.*
either *oder.*
　either . . . or　*entweder . . . oder.*
elastic *elastisch.*
elbow *Ellbogen, m.*
elder *älter.*
elderly *älterer, ältlich.*
eldest *Älteste, m. & f.*
elect (to) *erwählen.*
election *Wahl, f.*
elector *Wähler, m.*
electrical *elektrisch.*
electricity *Elektrizität, f.*
elegant *elegant.*
element *Element, n.*
elementary *elementar.*
elephant *Elefant, m.*
elevator *Aufzug, m.; Fahrstuhl, m.*
eleven *elf.*
eleventh *elfte.*
eliminate (to) *ausscheiden, beseitigen.*
eloquence *Beredsamkeit, f.; Redegabe, f.*
eloquent *beredt, redegewandt.*
else *ander, anders; sonst* (otherwise).
　anyone else　*irgend ein anderer.*
　elsewhere　*anderswo.*
　everybody else　*jeder andere.*
　nobody else　*sonst niemand.*
　someone else　*ein anderer.*
elude (to) *ausweichen, entgehen.*
embark (to) *(sich) einschiffen.*
embarrass (to) *in Verlegenheit bringen.*
embarrassing *unangenehm, beschämend.*
embarrassment *Verlegenheit, f.*
embassy *Botschaft, f.*
embody *verkörpern.*
embrace (to) *umarmen.*
embroidery *Stickerei, f.*
emerge (to) *herauskommen,*
　　hervortreten.
emergency *Notfall, m.*
eminent *hervorragend.*
emotion *Erregung, f.; Rührung, f.*
emperor *Kaiser, m.*
emphasis *Betonung, f.*
emphasize (to) *betonen.*
emphatic *nachdrücklich.*
empire *Reich, n.*
employee *Angestellte, m. or f.*
employer *Arbeitgeber, m.*
employment *Arbeit, f.; Beschäftigung, f.;*
　　Tätigkeit, f.
empty *leer.*
enable (to) *befähigen.*
enamel *Email, n.; Emaille, f.*
enclose (to) *einschliessen.*

enclosure *Anlage, f.* (letter); *Einzäunung, f.* (fence).
encourage (to) *ermutigen.*
encouragement *Ermutigung, f.*
end *Ende, n.*
end (to) *enden, aufhören.*
endeavor *Bestreben, n.; Bemühung, f.*
endeavor (to) *such bemühen.*
endorse (to) *unterzeichnen* (a check), *gutheissen.*
endure (to) *ertragen, aushalten.*
enemy *Feind, m.*
energy *Energie, f.*
energy crisis *Energiekrise, f.*
enforce (to) *durchsetzen.*
engage (to) *anstellen.*
engaged *beschäftigt* (busy); *verlobt.*
engagement *Verpflichtung, f.* (appointment); *Beschäftigung, f.* (business); *Verlobung, f.* (marriage).
engine *Maschine, f.; Lokomotive, f.* (train).
engineer *Ingenieur, m.*
English *englisch.*
engrave (to) *eingravieren.*
enjoy (to) *geniessen, amüsieren.*
  enjoy oneself   *sich amüsieren.*
enjoyment *Vergnügen, n.*
enlarge (to) *vergrössern.*
enlist (to) *sich freiwillig melden* (military); *anwerben* (soldiers); *Dienste in Anspruch nehmen* (one's services).
enormous *ungeheuer.*
enough *genug.*
enter (to) *hineingehen.*
  Enter! *Herein!*
entertain (to) *unterhalten.*
entertainment *Unterhaltung, f., Schau, f.* (show).
enthusiasm *Begeisterung, f.*
enthusiastic *begeistert.*
entire *ganz.*
entitle (to) *berechtigen.*
entrance *Eingang, m.*
entrust (to) *anvertrauen.*
enumerate (to) *aufzählen.*
envelope *Umschlag, m.; Kuvert, n.*
envious *neidisch.*
envy *Neid, m.*
envy (to) *beneiden.*
episode *Episode, f.; Nebenhandlung, f.*
equal *gleich.*
equal (to) *gleichen.*
equality *Gleichheit, f.; Gleichberechtigung, f.* (pol.).
equator *Äquator, m.*
equilibrium *Gleichgewicht, n.*
equip (to) *ausrüsten.*
equipment *Ausrüstung, f.*
era *Zeitalter, n.*

erase (to) *ausstreichen, ausradieren.*
eraser *Gummi, m.*
erect (to) *errichten.*
err (to) *sich irren.*
errand *Auftrag, m.*
error *Irrtum, m.*
escalator *Rolltreppe, f.*
escape *Flucht, f.*
escape (to) *entlaufen.*
escort (to) *begleiten, eskortieren.*
especially *besonders.*
essay *Aufsatz, m.*
essence *Essenz, f.* (extract); *Wesen, n.*
essential *wesentlich.*
establish (to) *errichten, gründen.*
establishment *Gründung, f.*
estate *Vermögen, n.* (wealth); *Gut, n.* (land).
esteem *Achtung, f.*
esteem (to) *(hoch) schätzen, (hoch) achten.*
estimate *Kostenanschlag, m.* (cost); *Schätzung, f.* (appraisal); *Meinung* (opinion).
estimate (to) *veranschlagen, schätzen.*
eternal *ewig.*
eternity *Ewigkeit, f.*
European *Europäer* (noun) *m.; europäisch.* (adj.)
evade (to) *entfliehen.*
evasion *Ausflucht, f.*
eve *Vorabend, m.*
even *eben* (adj.); *sogar* (adv.).
evening *Abend, m.*
  Good evening! *Guten Abend!*
evening clothes *Gesellschaftsanzug, m.*
evening dress *Abendkleid, n.* (woman's).
event *Ereignis, n.*
ever *je, jemals.*
every *jeder*
  everybody   *jedermann.*
  everything   *alles.*
  everywhere   *überall.*
evidence *Beweis, m.; Zeugnis, n.*
evident *offenbar, klar.*
evil *Übel* (noun) *n.; schlecht* (adj.).
evoke (to) *hervorrufen.*
evolve (to) *herausarbeiten, sich entwickeln.*
exact *genau.*
exaggerate (to) *übertreiben.*
exaggeration *Übertreibung, f.*
exalt (to) *erheben, veredeln.*
exaltation *Erhebung, f.*
examination *Prüfung, f.*
examine (to) *prüfen.*
example *Beispiel, n.*
exceed (to) *überschreiten.*
excel (to) *übertreffen.*
excellence *Vortrefflichkeit, f.*
excellent *vortrefflich, ausgezeichnet.*
except *ausgenommen; ausser* (dat.).

except (to) *ausnehmen, ausschliessen.*
exception *Ausnahme, f.*
exceptional *aussergewöhnlich.*
exceptionally *ausnahmsweise.*
excess *Übermass, n.*
excessive *übermässig.*
exchange *Tausch, m.*
exchange (to) *wechseln.*
excite (to) *aufregen.*
excitement *Aufregung, f.*
exclaim (to) *ausrufen.*
exclamation *Ausruf, m.*
exclude (to) *ausschliessen.*
exclusive *auschliesslich.*
excursion *Ausflug, m.*
excuse *Verzeihung, f.; Entschuldigung, f.*
excuse (to) *verzeihen, entschuldigen.*
    Excuse me *Verzeihung!*
      (*Entschuldigung!*)
execute (to) *ausführen* (carry out);
    hinrichten (put to death).
execution *Ausführung, f.* (of plan or idea);
    Hinrichtung, f. (of person).
exempt (to) *befreien.*
exercise *Übung, f.*
exercise (to) *üben.*
exert (to) *sich anstrengen.*
exertion *Anstrengung, f.*
exhaust (to) *erschöpfen.*
exhaustion *Erschöpfung, f.*
exhibit (to) *ausstellen.*
exhibition *Ausstellung, f.*
exile *Verbannung, f.*
exile (to) *verbannen.*
exist (to) *existieren.*
existence *Existenz, f.*
exit *Ausgang, m.*
expand (to) (*sich*) *ausdehnen.*
expansion *Ausdehnung, f.*
expensive *teuer.*
experience *Erfahrung, f.*
experience (to) *erfahren.*
experiment (to) *experimentieren.*
expert *Fachmann, m.*
expire (to) *verscheiden, ablaufen.*
explain (to) *erklären.*
explanation *Erklärung, f.*
explanatory *erklärend.*
explode (to) *explodieren.*
exploit *Heldentat, f.*
exploit (to) *ausnützen.*
explore (to) *erforschen.*
explosion *Explosion, f.*
export (to) *ausführen, exportieren.*
export *Ausfuhr, f.; Export, m.*
expose (to) *aussetzen.*
express *Schnellzug, m.*
express (to) *ausdrücken.*
expression *Ausdruck, m.*

expressive *ausdrucksvoll.*
expulsion *Ausstossung, f.; Vertreibung, f.*
exquisite *vorzüglich, köstlich.*
extend (to) *verlängern, ausdehnen.*
extensive *ausgedehnt.*
extent *Weite, f.* (distance); *Umfang, m.;*
    Verlängerung, f. (time).
exterior *Äussere* (noun) *n.; äusserlich* (adj.).
exterminate (to) *ausrotten.*
external *äusserlich, auswärtig.*
extinction *Erlöschen, n.*
extinguish (to) *erlöschen.*
extra *extra.*
extraordinary *aussergewöhnlich.*
extravagant *verschwenderisch, überspannt.*
extreme *äusserst.*
eye *Auge, n.*
eyebrow *Augenbraue, f.*
eyeglasses *Brille, f.*
eyelash *Wimper, f.*
eyelid *Augenlid, n.*
eyesight *Sehkraft, f.*

F

fable *Fabel, f.*
face *Gesicht, n.*
face (to) *unter die Augen treten,*
    gegenüberstehen.
facilitate (to) *erleichtern.*
facility *Leichtigkeit, f.; Erleichterungen, f.*
facsimile *Telefax, n; Telebrief, m.; Fax, n.*
fact *Tatsache, f.*
    in fact *in der Tat.*
    as a matter of fact *im übrigen.*
factory *Fabrik, f.*
factual *tatsächlich.*
faculty *Fähigkeit, f.* (ability); *Fakultät, f.*
    (school).
fade (to) *welken.*
faded *verschossen, verblichen* (color).
fail (to) *fehlen; unterlassen* (neglect);
    durchfallen (exam).
    without fail *ganz gewiss, unfehlbar.*
failure *Misserfolg, m.*
faint (to) *ohnmächtig werden.*
fainting spell *Ohnmacht, f.*
fair *schön* (weather); *hell* (complexion);
    ehrlich (just), *gerecht, fair.*
    fair play *ehrliches Spiel.*
faith *Glaube, m.* (religion); *Treue, f.*
faithful *treu.*
fall *Fall, m.; Sturz, m.; Herbst, m.* (autumn).
fall (to) *fallen, stürzen.*
false *falsch.*
fame *Ruhm, m.*
familiar *vertraut, bekannt.*
family *Familie, f.*

famine *Hungersnot, f.*
famous *berühmt.*
fan *Ventilator, m.* (ventilator); *Windfahre, f.*
    (of a windmill); *Lüfter, m.* (electric).
fancy *Neigung* (noun) *f.; bunt* (adj.).
fantastic *fantastisch.*
far *weit, fern.*
farce *Posse, f.*
fare *Fahrpreis, m.*
farewell *Abschied, m.*
    Farewell! *Lebe wohl!*
farm *Bauernhof, m.*
farmer *Landwirt, m.*
farming *Landwirtschaft, f.*
farther *weiter, ferner.*
fashion *Mode, f.*
fashionable *elegant, modisch, modern.*
fast *schnell.*
fasten (to) *befestigen.*
fat *Fett* (noun) *n.; fett, dick* (adj.).
fatal *tödlich, fatal.*
fate *Schicksal, n.*
father *Vater, m.*
father-in-law *Schwiegervater, m.*
faucet *Wasserhahn, m.*
fault *Fehler, m.*
favor *Gunst, f.*
    Do me a favor. *Tun Sie mir einen*
    Gefallen!
favor (to) *vorziehen, bevorzugen,*
    begünstigen.
favorable *günstig, vorteilhaft.*
favorite *Günstling, m.; Liebling, m.;*
    Lieblings-, (adj.)
fax *Telefax, m; fax, m.*
fear *Furcht, f.*
fear (to) *fürchten.*
fearless *furchtlos.*
feather *Feder, f.*
feature (*Gesichts)zug, m.;* (facial) *Merkmal,*
    n.; Film, m. (movie).
February *Februar, m.*
federal *Bundes-, föderativ* (adj.).
federation *Staatenbund, -e, m.; Bundesstaat,*
    -en, m.
fee *Gebühr, f.*
feeble *schwach.*
feed (to) *füttern.*
feel (to) *fühlen.*
feeling *Gefühl, n.*
fellow *Kamerad, m.*
fellowship *Kameradschaft, f.;*
    Gemeinschaft, f.
female *weiblich.*
feminine *fraulich.*
fence *Zaun, m.*
fencing *Fechten, n.*
fender *Kotflügel, m.*
ferocious *wild.*

ferry *Fähre, f.*
fertile *fruchtbar.*
fertilize (to) *befruchten.*
fertilizer *Düngemittel, n.; Dünger, m.*
fervent *inbrünstig, feurig.*
fervor *Inbrunst, f.*
festival *Fest, n.*
fetch (to) *holen.*
fever *Fieber, n.*
few *wenige.*
    a few *ein paar.*
fiction *Dichtung, f.*
field *Acker, m.; Feld, n.*
fierce *wild.*
fiery *feurig*
fifteen *fünfzehn.*
fifteenth *fünfzehnte.*
fifth *fünfte.*
fiftieth *fünfzigste.*
fifty *fünfzig.*
fig *Feige, f.*
fight *Kampf, m.*
fight (to) *kämpfen.*
figure *Figur, f.; Ziffer* (number).
file *Feile, f.* (tool); *Registratur, f.;*
    Briefordner, m.
fill (to) *füllen.*
filling (tooth) *Füllung, f.*
film *Film, m.*
filthy *schmutzig.*
final *endgültig.*
finance *Finanz, f.*
finance (to) *finanzieren.*
financial *finanziell.*
find (to) *finden.*
fine *Geldstrafe* (noun) *f.; fein* (adj.) (opp. of
    coarse); *schön* (adj.) (elegant).
finger *Finger, m.*
finish (to) *beenden.*
fire *Feuer, n.*
fireman *Feuerwehrmann, m.*
fireplace *Kamin, m.*
firm *Firma,* (noun) *f.; fest, stark* (adj.).
first *erster.*
    at first *zuerst.*
fish *Fisch, m.*
fish (to) *fischen.*
fisherman *Fischer, m.*
fishing *Fischen, n.; Angeln, n.*
fist *Faust, f.*
fit *Anfall,* (noun) *m.; passend* (adj.)
    (becoming); *tauglich* (adj.) (capable).
fitness *Angemessenheit, f.; Eignung, f.*
five *fünf.*
fix (to) *reparieren.*
flag *Fahne, f.*
flame *Flamme, f.*
flank *Seite, f.*
flash *Blitz, m.* (lightning); *Aufflammen, n.*

flashlight *Taschenlampe, f.; Blitzlicht, n.,*
   (camera flash).
flat *flach.*
flatter (to) *schmeicheln.*
flatterer *Schmeichler, m.*
flattery *Schmeichelei, f.*
flavor *Aroma, n.; Geschmack, m.*
fleet *Flotte, f.*
flesh *Fleisch, n.*
flexibility *Biegsamkeit, f.*
flexible *biegsam.*
flight *Flug, m.*
fling (to) *werfen, Schleudern.*
flint *Kieselstein, m.; Feuerstein, n.*
float (to) *treiben.*
flood *Überschwemmung, f.; Flut, f.*
flood (to) *überschwemmen.*
floor *Boden, m.; Stock, m.* (story).
floppy disc *Floppy-disk, f.; Diskette, f.*
flourish (to) *blühen.*
flourishing *blühend.*
flow (to) *fliessen, strömen.*
flower *Blume, f.*
fluid *flüssig.*
fly *Fliege, f.*
fly (to) *fliegen.*
foam *Schaum, m.*
fog *Nebel, m.*
fold *Falte, f.*
fold (to) *falten.*
foliage *Laubwerk, n.*
follow (to) *folgen.*
following *folgend.*
fond *zärtlich, liebevoll.*
fondness *Zärtlichkeit, f.*
food *Essen, n.*
fool *Narr, m.*
foolish *töricht, lächerlich.*
foot *Fuss, m.*
football *Fussball, m.; Fussballspiel, m.*
footstep *Schritt, m.*
for *für* (acc.); *zu* (dat.); *wegen* (gen.) (on
   account of); *denn* (because).
   as for me   *was mich betrifft.*
   for a year   *während eines Jahres.*
   for example   *zum Beispiel.*
   word for word   *Wort für Wort.*
forbid (to) *verbieten.*
force *Kraft, f; Gewalt, f.*
force (to) *zwingen.*
foreground *Vordergrund, m.*
forehead *Stirn, f.*
foreign *fremd, ausländisch.*
foreigner *Fremder, m.; Ausländer, m.*
forest *Wald, m.*
forget (to) *vergessen.*
forgetfulness *Vergesslichkeit, f.*
forget-me-not *Vergissmeinnicht, n.*
forgive (to) *vergeben, verzeihen.*

forgiveness *Vergebung, f.*
fork *Gabel, f.*
form *Form, f.*
formal *offiziell, formell.*
formation *Bildung, f.*
former *fruher; erster* (as opposed to latter),
   vorherig, ehemalig.
formerly *vormals.*
formula *Formel, f.*
forsake (to) *verlassen.*
fort *Festung, f.*
fortieth *vierzigste.*
fortunate *glücklich.*
fortunately *glücklicherweise.*
fortune *Vermögen, n.; Glück, n.* (luck).
forty *vierzig.*
forward *vorwärts.*
forward (to) *absenden, nachscheicken.*
foster (to) *pflegen.*
foul *faul.*
found (to) *gründen.*
foundation *Gründung, f.; Grundlage, f.*
founder *Gründer, m.*
fountain *Brunnen, m.*
fountain pen *Füllfeder, f.*
four *vier.*
fourteen *vierzehn.*
fourteenth *vierzehnte.*
fourth *vierte.*
fowl *Geflügel, n.*
fox *Fuchs, m.*
fragile *zerbrechlich.*
fragment *Bruchstück, n.*
fragrance *Duft, m.*
fragrant *duftig.*
frail *zart, gebrechlich.*
frame *Rahmen, m.*
frame (to) *rahmen.*
frank *aufrichtig, freimütig.*
frankness *Offenheit, f.*
free *frei.*
freedom *Freiheit, f.*
freeze (to) *frieren.*
freight *Fracht, f.*
French *französisch.*
frequent *häufig.*
frequently *oft, öfters*
fresh *frisch.*
friction *Reibung, f.; Friktion, f.*
Friday *Freitag, m.*
fried *gebraten.*
friend *Freund, m.*
friendly *freundlich.*
friendship *Freundschaft, f.*
frighten (to) *erschrecken.*
frightening *schrecklich, erschreckend.*
fringe *Rand, m.*
frivolity *Leichtsinn, f.*
frog *Frosch, m.*

from *von, aus* (dat.)*; nach* (dat.) (according to).
  from morning till night *von früh bis spät.*
  from time to time *von Zeit zu Zeit.*
  from top to bottom *von oben bis unten.*
front *Vorderseite, f.; Front, f.* (military).
frozen *gefroren.*
fruit *Frucht, sing. f.; Obst, coll., n.*
fry (to) *braten*
  fried eggs *Spiegeleier, pl.*
  fried potatoes *Bratkartoffeln, pl.*
frying pan *Bratpfanne, f.*
fuel *Brennstoff, m.; Treibstoff, m.*
fulfill (to) *erfüllen.*
full *voll.*
fully *voll.*
fun *Scherz, m.; Spass, m.*
  to have fun *sich amüsieren.*
  to make fun *sich lustig machen.*
function *Funktion,* (math) *f.; Tätigkeit, f.; amtliche Pflicht, f.*
function (to) *funktionieren.*
fund *Fonds, m.; Kapital, m.*
fundamental *grundlegend; wesentlich.*
funeral *Begräbnis, n.*
funny *komisch.*
fur *Pelz, m.*
furious *wütend, rasend.*
furnace *Ofen, m.*
furnish (to) *möblieren.*
furniture *Möbel, f.*
furrow *Furche,* (agric.) *f.; Runzel* (on skin)*, f.*
further *weiter.*
fury *Wut, f.*
future *Zukunft* (noun) *f.; zukünftig* (adj.).

G

gaiety *Fröhlichkeit, f.; Heiterkeit, f.*
gain *Gewinn, m.*
gain (to) *gewinnen; zunehmen* (weight).
gallant *tapfer, ritterlich.*
gallery *Galerie, f.*
gallop *Galopp, m.*
gamble (to) *spielen.*
game *Spiel, n.*
garage *Garage, f.*
garbage *Abfall, m.; Müll, m.*
garden *Garten, m.*
gardener *Gärtner, m.*
garlic *Knoblauch, n.*
gas *Gas, n.*
gasoline *Benzin, n.*
gate *Tor, n.; Sperre, f.* (railroad).
gather (to) *sammeln, sich versammeln*
gay *lustig.*
gear *Getriebe, n.; Gang, m.* (motor).

gem *Edelstein, m.*
general *General, m.* (military); *allgemein* (adj.).
generality *Allgemeinheit, f.*
generalize (to) *verallgemeinern.*
generation *Generation, f.*
generosity *Freigebigkeit, f.; Grossmut, f.* (magnanimity).
generous *grosszügig.*
genius *Genie, n.*
genteel *fein, vornehm.*
gentleman *Herr, m.*
gentleness *Sanftheit, f.*
genuine *echt.*
geographical *geographisch.*
geography *Geographie, f.*
germ *Keim, m.; Bakterien* (us. pl.); *Bazillus, m.*
German *Deutsche*(r) (noun) *m.; deutsch* (adj.).
gesture *Gebärde, f.*
get (to) *bekommen, erwerben, holen* (fetch); *werden* (become).
  get down *hinunterkommen.*
  get off *absteigen.*
  get up *aufstehen.*
ghastly *grässlich.*
ghost *geist, m.*
giant *Riese, m.*
gift *Geschenk, n.*
gifted *begabt.*
girl *Mädchen, n.*
give (to) *geben.*
  to give back *zurückgeben*
glad *froh.*
gladly *gern.*
glance *Blick, m.*
glass *Glas, n.*
glasses *Brille, f.*
gleam *Schein, m.; Schimmer, m.*
gleam (to) *scheinen, glänzen*
glitter *Glanz, m.; Glitzen, n.*
globe *Kugel, f.; Globus, m.*
gloomy *düster.*
glorious *glorreich.*
glory *Ruhm, m.*
glove *Handschuh, m.*
glow *Glut, f.; Glühen, n.*
glue *Leim, m.*
go (to) *gehen.*
  to go away *weggehen, fortgehen.*
  to go back *zurückgehen.*
  to go in *hineingehen.*
  to go out *herausgehen, ausgehen.*
  to go to bed *zu Bett gehen.*
God *Gott, m.*
godchild *Patenkind, n.*
godfather *Pate, m.*

godmother *Patin, f.*
gold *Gold, n.*
golden *golden.*
golf *Golf* (*spiel*), *n.*
good *gut.*
  Good afternoon! *Guten Tag!*
  Good evening! *Guten Abend!*
  Good morning! *Guten Morgen!*
  Good night! *Gute Nacht!*
good-bye *Auf Wiedersehen!*
good-looking *gut aussehend.*
goodness *Güte, f.*
goods *Waren, pl.*
goodwill *guter Wille, m.*
goose *Gans, f.*
gossip *Klatsch, m.; Geschwätz, n.*
gossip (to) *klatschen.*
govern (to) *regieren.*
grace *Gnade, f.; Anmut, f.* (charm).
graceful *anmutig, hold, graziös.*
grade *Grad, m.*
grain *Korn, n, Getreide, n.; Körnchen, n.* (sand).
grammar *Grammatik, f.*
grand *grossartig.*
grandchild *Enkelkind, n.*
granddaughter *Enkelin, f.*
grandfather *Grossvater, m.*
grandmother *Grossmutter, f.*
grandson *Enkel, m.*
grant *Bewilligung, f.; Schenkung, f.*
grant (to) *bewilligen, gestatten.*
grape *Weintraube, f.*
grapefruit *Pompelmuse, f.*
grasp *Griff, m.*
grasp (to) *greifen, fassen.*
grass *Gras, n.*
grateful *dankbar.*
gratitude *Dankbarkeit, f.*
grave *Grab,* (noun) *n.; ernst* (adj.).
gravy *Sauce, f.; (Braten) sosse, f.*
gray *grau.*
grease *Fett, n.*
great *gross, herrlich* (coll.); *wunderbar* (coll.).
greatness *Grösse, f.*
greedy *gierig, gefrässig.*
green *grün.*
greet (to) *grüssen.*
greeting *Gruss, m.*
grief *Kummer, m.*
grieve (to) *sich grämen.*
grin (to) *grinsen.*
grind (to) *mahlen.*
groan *Stöhnen, n.*
groan (to) *stöhnen.*
grocer *Kolonialwarenhändler, m.*
grocery store *Kolonialwarenladen, m.*
gross *grob.*

ground *Boden, m.*
group *Gruppe, f.*
group (to) *gruppieren.*
grow (to) *wachsen; an* (*bauen*) (crops); *züchten* (animals).
growth *Gewächs, n.*
grudge *Groll, m.*
guaranteed *garantiert.*
guess *Vermutung, f.*
guess (to) *raten.*
guide *Führer, m.*
gum *Zahnfleisch, n.* (teeth).
  chewing gum *Kaugummi, n.*
gun *Gewehr, n.*
gush *Guss, m.*
gush (to) *hervorströmen.*

H

habit *Gewohnheit, f.*
habitual *gewöhnlich.*
hail *Hagel, m.*
hair *Haar, n.*
hairdo *Frisur, f.*
hairdresser *Frisör, m.; Friseuse, f.*
hairpin *Haarnadel, f.*
half *halb.*
hall *Halle, f.; Saal, m., Diele, f.*
ham *Schinken, m.*
hammer *Hammer, m.*
hand *Hand, f.*
hand (to) (*über*) *reichen.*
handbag *Handtasche, f.*
handful *Handvoll, f.*
handkerchief *Taschentuch, n.*
handle *Griff, m.*
handle (to) *anfassen, behandeln*
handsome *stattlich, hübsch, schön.*
handy *handlich.*
hang (to) *hängen.*
happen (to) *geschehen.*
happiness *Glück, n.*
happy *glücklich.*
harbor *Hafen, m.*
hard *hart.*
hard disk *Hartplatte, f.; Magnetplatte, f.*
harden (to) *härten.*
hardly *kaum.*
hardness *Härte, f.*
hardware *Eisenwaren, pl.*
hardware store *Eisenwarengeschäft, n.*
hardy *abgehärtet, robust, kräftig.*
hare *Hase, f.*
harm *Schaden, m.*
harm (to) *schädigen.*
harmful *schädlich*
harmless *harmlos.*
harmonious *harmonisch.*

harmony *Harmonie, f.*
harsh *rauh, hart* (touch)*; sauer* (taste)*; grell* (sound/color)*; schroff.*
harvest *Ernte, f.*
haste *Eile, f.*
hasten (to) *eilen.*
hat *Hut, m.*
hate *Hass, m.*
hate (to) *hassen.*
hateful *gehässig.*
hatred *Hass, m.*
haughty *hochmutig, arrogant.*
have (to) *haben.*
haven *Hafen, m.; Zufluchtsort, m.; Asyl, n.*
hay *Heu, n.*
he *er.*
head *Kopf, m.* (of a person)*; Chef, m.* (of a firm)*; Haupt, n.* (of a government).
headache *Kopfschmerzen, pl.*
headphones *Kopfhörer* (pl.).
heal (to) *heilen.*
health *Gesundheit, f.*
healthy *gesund.*
heap *Haufen, m.*
heap (to) *(auf)häufen.*
hear (to) *hören.*
hearing *Gehör, n.*
heart *Herz, n.*
heaven *Himmel, m.*
heavy *schwer.*
hedge *Hecke, f.*
heel *Ferse, f.* (of the foot)*; Absatz, m.* (of a shoe).
height *Höhe, f.*
heir *Erbe, m.*
hell *Hölle, f.*
helm *Ruder, n.*
help *Hilfe, f.*
help (to) *helfen.*
helpful *behilflich.*
hem *Saum, m.*
hen *Huhn, n.; Henne, f.*
her *ihr* (pers. pr., dat.)*; poss. adj.)*; sie* (pers. pr., acc.).
herb *Kraut, n.; Gewürzkraut, n.* (culinary).
herd *Herde, f.*
here *hier.*
herewith *hiermit.*
hero *Held, m.*
heroic *heldenhaft, heroisch.*
heroine *Heldin, f.*
herring *Hering, m.*
hers *ihr(er, -e, -es).*
herself *sie (ihr) selbst; sich.*
hesitate (to) *zögern.*
hide (to) *verstecken.*
hideous *scheusslich.*
high *hoch.*
higher *höher.*

hill *Hügel, m.*
him *ihn* (acc.)*; ihm* (dat.).
himself *er (ihm, ihn) selbst; sich.*
hinder (to) *hindern.*
hint *Wink, m.*
hint (to) *andeuten.*
hip *Hüfte, f.*
hire (to) *mieten.*
his *sein* (poss. adj.)*; sein(er, -e, -es)* (pron.).
hiss (to) *zischen.*
historian *Geschichtsschreiber, m.*
historical *historisch.*
history *Geschichte, f.*
hoarse *heiser.*
hoe *Hacke, f.*
hold *Halt, m.*
hold (to) *halten.*
hole *Loch, n.*
holiday *Feiertag, m.*
holidays *Ferien, pl.* (vacation).
holy *heilig.*
homage *Huldigung, f.*
home *Heim, n.*
homosexual *homosexuell* (adj.), *Homosexuelle(r), m./f.*
honest *ehrlich.*
honesty *Ehrlichkeit, f.*
honey *Honig, m.*
honeymoon *Flitterwochen, pl.; Hochzeitsreise, f.* (honeymoon trip)
honor *Ehre, f.*
honor (to) *ehren.*
honorable *ehrenvoll.*
hood *Kapuze, f.; Haube n.* (car), *Verdeck, n.*
hoof *Huf, m.*
hook *Haken, m.*
hope *Hoffnung, f.*
hope (to) *hoffen.*
hopeful *hoffnungsvoll.*
hopeless *hoffnungslos.*
horizon *Horizont, m.*
horizontal *horizontal.*
horn (auto) *Hupe, f.*
horrible *schrecklich.*
horse *Pferd, n.*
horseback (on) *zu Pferde.*
hosiery *Strümpfe, f.; Strumpfwaren, pl.*
hospitable *gastfreundlich.*
hospital *Krankenhaus, n.; Hospital, n.*
host *Gastgeber, m.; Wirt, m.*
hostess *Gastgeberin, f.; Wirtin, f.*
hostile *feindlich.*
hot *heiss.*
hotel *Hotel, n.; Gasthof, m.*
hour *Stunde, f.*
house *Haus, n.*
household *Haushalt, m.*
housekeeper *Haushälterin, f.*
housemaid *Hausmädchen, n.*

how *wie*
> How are you? *Wie geht's?*

however *dennoch, wie . . . auch immer.*

howl *Heulen, n.*

howl (to) *heulen.*

human *menschlich.*

humane *human.*

humanity *Menschlichkeit, f.*

humble *demütig.*

humid *feucht.*

humiliate *erniedrigen, demütigen.*

humility *Demut, f.*

humor *Humor, m.*

hundred *hundert.*

hundredth *hundertste.*

hunger *Hunger, m.*

hungry *hungrig.*

hunt *Jagd, f.*

hunter *Jäger, m.*

hurricane *Orkan, m.*

hurry *Eile, f.*
> Hurry up! *Beeilen Sie sich!*

hurt (to) *verwunden; verletzen.*

husband *Mann, m.; Gatte, m.*

hush (to) *schweigen.*

hyphen *Bindestrich, m.*

hypocrite *Heuchler, m.*

I

I *ich.*

ice *Eis, n.*

ice cream *Eis, n.; Speiseeis, n.*

icy *eisig.*

idea *Idee, f.; Einfall, m.*

ideal *Ideal,* (noun) *n.; ideal* (adj.).

idealism *Idealismus, m.*

idealist *Idealist, m.*

identical *identisch.*

identity *Identität, f.*

idiot *Idiot, m.*

idle *müssig, träge, unbeschäftigt.*

idleness *Müssigkeit, f.; Faulheit, f.; Trägheit, f.*

if *wenn, ob.*

ignoble *unedel.*

ignorance *Unwissenheit, f.*

ignorant *unwissend.*

ignore (to) *ignorieren, nich beachten.*

ill *krank.*

illegal *gesetzwidrig, ungesetzlich, illegal.*

illness *Krankheit, f.*

illusion *Täuschung, f.*

illustrate (to) *illustrieren.*

illustration *Abbildung, f.*

image *Einbildungskraft, f.; Ebenbild, n.; Bild, n.*

imagination *Fantasie, f.*

imagine (to) *sich einbilden.*

imitate (to) *nachahmen.*

imitation *Nachahmung, f.*

immediate *unmittelbar.*

immediately *sogleich, sofort.*

immigrant *Immigrant, m.*

imminent *bevorstehend, unmittelbar.*

immobility *Unbeweglichkeit, f.*

immoral *unmoralisch.*

immorality *Unsittlichkeit, f.*

immortal *unsterblich.*

immortality *Unsterblichkeit, f.*

impartial *unparteiisch.*

impassible *gefühllos.*

impatience *Ungeduld, f.*

imperfect *Vergangenheit* (noun) *f.* (in grammar); *unvollkommen* (adj.).

impertinence *Unverschämtheit, f.*

impetuosity *Ungestüm, n.*

import *Einfuhr, f.; Import, m.*

import (to) *einführen, importieren.*

important *wichtig.*

imported *importiert.*

importer *Importeur, m.*

impossible *unmöglich.*

impress (to) *Eindruck machen, beeindrucken.*

impression *Eindruck, m.*

imprison (to) *einsperren.*

improve (to) *verbessern.*

improvement *Verbesserung, f.*

improvise (to) *improvisieren.*

imprudence *Unvorsichtigkeit, f.; Unklugheit, f.*

imprudent *unklug.*

impulse *Antrieb, m. Anregung, f.*

impure *unrein.*

in *in* (dat.).

inadequate *unzulänglich, ungenügend.*

inaugurate (to) *eröffnen.*

incapable *unfähig.*

incapacity *Unfähigkeit, f.*

inch *Zoll, m.*

incident *Vorfall, m.*

include (to) *einschliessen.*

included *eingeschlossen.*

income *Einkommen, n.*

income tax *Einkommensteuer, f.*

incomparable *unvergleichlich, nicht vergleichbar.*

incompatible *unvereinbar.*

incompetent *unfähig, unzulänglich.*

incomplete *unvollständig.*

inconvenient *lästig, unbequem, beschwerlich.*

incorrect *unrichtig.*

increase *Erhöhung, f.*

increase (to) *sich vermehren, erhöhen.*

incredible *unglaublich.*

indebted *verschuldet; verpflichtet.*

indecision *Unentschlossenheit, f.*

indeed *tatsächlich.*
independence *Unabhängigkeit, f.*
independent *unabhängig.*
index *Inhaltsverzeichnis, n.*
index *Register* (in a book).
index card *Karteikarte, f.*
index finger *Zeigefinger, m.*
indicate (to) *hinweisen, andeuten, bezeichnen.*
indicative *Indikativ* (noun) *m.* (in grammar); *anzeigend* (adj.); *hinweisend* (adj.).
indifference *Gleichgültigkeit, f.*
indifferent *gleichgültig.*
indigestion *Verdauungsstörung, f.*
indignant *empört.*
indignation *Entrüstung, f; Empörung, f.*
indirect *indirekt.*
indiscreet *indiskret.*
indiscretion *Unbedachtsamkeit, f.; Indiskretion, f.* (polit.).
indispensable *unentbehrlich.*
individual *einzeln, persönlich.*
indolent *träge.*
indoors *im Hause, zu Hause.*
induce (to) *veranlassen, verursachen.*
indulge (to) *sich hingeben.*
indulgence *Verwöhnung, f.*
indulgent *nachsichtig.*
industrial *industriell.*
industrious *fleissig.*
industry *Industrie, f.*
inefficient *unfähig.*
infancy *Kindheit, f.*
infant *kleines Kind, n.; Baby, n.; Säugling, m.*
infantry *Infanterie, f.*
infection *Infektion, f.*
inferior *minderwertig.*
infernal *höllisch.*
infinite *unendlich.*
infinity *Unendlichkeit, f.*
influence *Einfluss, m.*
influence (to) *beeinflussen.*
inform (to) *benachrichtigen.*
information *Auskunft, f.; Nachricht, f.* (news).
ingenious *geistig.*
ingenuity *Scharfsinn, m.*
inhabit (to) *bewohnen.*
inhabitant *Einwohner, m.*
inherit (to) *erben.*
inheritance *Erbgut, n.*
inhuman *unmenschlich.*
initial *Anfangsbuchstabe, m.*
initial (adj.) *anfänglich, ursprünglich*
initiate (to) *anfangen, einleiten, einführen.*
initiative *Initiative, f.*
injection *Einspritzung, f.; Spritze, f.*
injury *Verletzung, f.*

injustice *Ungerechtigkeit, f.*
ink *Tinte, f.*
inkwell *Tintenfass, n.*
inland *Binnenland, n.; innenländisch,* (adj.).
inn *Gasthof, m.; Gasthaus, n.*
innkeeper *Gastwirt, m.*
innocent *unschuldig.*
innocence *Unschuld, f.*
inquire (to) *sich erkundigen, nachfragen.*
inquiry *Erkundigung, f.; Anfrage, f.; Nachfrage, f.*
insane *geisteskrank.*
inscription *Inschrift, f.*
insect *Insekt, n.*
insensible *unempfindlich.*
inseparable *unzertrennlich.*
inside *drinnen.*
insight *Einsicht, f.*
insignificant *unbedeutend.*
insincere *unaufrichtig, heuchlerisch.*
insinuate (to) *andeuten.*
insist (to) *bestehen auf.*
insistence *Beharren, n.; Bestehen, n.*
inspect (to) *besichtigen, untersuchen.*
inspection *Besichtigung, f.; Untersuchung, f.*
inspiration *Inspiration, f., Begeisterung, f.*
inspire *begeistern, erwecken.*
install (to) *einstellen, installieren.*
installment *Rate, f.; Teilzahlung, f.*
instance *Beispiel, n.; Fall, m.*
instant *Augenblick, m.*
instantly *sofort.*
instead of *anstatt* (gen.).
institute (to) *einführen, gründen.*
institution *Anstalt, f.*
instruct (to) *unterrichten.*
instructor *Lehrer, m.; Erzieher, n.*
instruction *Anweisung, f.; Unterricht, m.* (teaching).
instrument *Instrument, n.*
insufficient *ungenügend.*
insult *Beleidigung, f.*
insult (to) *beleidigen.*
insurance *Versicherung, f.*
insure (to) *versichern.*
intact *unversehrt, unberührt.*
intellectual *intellektuell.*
intelligence *Intelligenz, f.*
intelligent *intelligent.*
intend (to) *beabsichtigen.*
intense *intensiv.*
intensity *Heftigkeit, f.*
intent *Absicht, m.; Plan, m.*
intent (adj.) *eifrig, beschäftigt* (mit), *gerichtet, gespannt.*
intention *Absicht, f.*
interest *Interesse, n.*
interesting *interessant.*

interfere (to) *sich einmischen, dazwischentreten.*
interior *Innere, n.*
intermediate *mittel.*
intermission *Pause, f.*
international *international.*
interpret (to) *interpretieren, übersetzen; deuten* (emotion), *dolmetschen.*
interpreter *Dolmetscher, m.*
interrupt (to) *unterbrechen.*
interval *Pause, f.; Zwischenzeit, f.*
interview *Interview, n.; Besprechung, f.*
intimacy *Vertrautheit, f.*
intimate *vertraut, zu verstehen geben.*
into *in* (dat. or acc.).
intolerant *unduldsam, intolerant.*
intonation *Tonfall, m.* (phonetics).
introduce (to) *vorstellen.*
introduction *Vorstellung, f.*
intuition *unmittelbare Erkenntnis, f.; Anschauungsvermögen, n.* (intuitive faculty).
invade (to) *einfallen, eindringen* (*in*), *angreifen.*
invent (to) *erfinden.*
invention *Erfindung, f.*
inventor *Erfinder, m.*
invert (to) *umkehren, umdrehen.*
invest (to) *investieren; anlegen* (money).
investment *Kapitalanlage, f.*
invisible *unsichtbar.*
invitation *Einladung, f.*
invite (to) *einladen.*
invoice *Faktura, f.; Warenrechnung, f.*
invoke (to) *anflehen, beschwören.*
involve (to) *verwickeln.*
iodine *Jod, n.*
Irish *irländisch.*
iron *Eisen, n.* (metal); *Bügeleisen, n.* (for ironing).
iron (to) *bügeln, plätten.*
irony *Ironie, f.*
irrefutable *unwiderlegbar.*
irregular *unregelmässig.*
irresistible *unwiderstehlich.*
irritate (to) *reizen, ärgern.*
island *Insel, f.*
isolate (to) *absondern, isolieren.*
Israel *Israel, n.*
Israeli *israeli* (adj.), *Israeli, m./f., Israelit(in), m./f.*
issue *Ausgabe, f.*
it *es.*
Italian *Italiener* (noun) *m.; italienisch* (adj.).
itch (to) *jucken.*
its *sein* (poss. adj.); *sein(er, -e, -es)*, (poss. pron.), *ihr, dessen, deren.*
itself *selbst*, (emphatic), *sich* (refl.), *für sich* (by itself), *an sich* (in itself).

ivory *Elfenbein, n.*
ivy *Efeu, n.*

J

jacket *Jacke, f., Jackett, m.*
jail *Gefängnis, n.*
jam *Marmelade, f.*
January *Januar, m.*
Japanese *Japaner* (noun) *m.; japanisch* (adj.).
jar *Krug, m.*
jaw *Kiefer, m.*
jealous *eifersüchtig.*
jealousy *Eifersucht, f.*
jelly *Gelee, n.*
jewel *Juwel, m.*
jeweler *Juwelier, m.*
Jewish *jüdisch.*
job *Arbeit, f., Stellung, f. Posten, m., Job, m.*
join (to) *sich ausschliessen an, verbinden, zusammenfügen* (mit).
joint *Gelenk, n.*
joke *Witz, m.; Scherz, m.; Spass, m.*
joke (to) *scherzen.*
jolly *lustig.*
journalist *Journalist, m.*
journey *Reise, f.*
joy *Freude, f.*
joyous *freudig.*
judge *Richter, m, Schiedsrichter, m.* (sports).
judge (to) *urteilen.*
judgment *Urteil, n.; gerichtliche Entscheidung, f.*
judicial *gerichtlich.*
juice *Saft, m.*
July *Juli, m.*
jump *Sprung, m.; Satz, m.*
jump (to) *springen.*
June *Juni, m.*
junior *jünger.*
jungle *Dschungel, m.*
just *recht* (fair); *gerecht* (justice); *gerade* (recent).
justice *Gerechtigkeit, f.*
justify (to) *rechtfertigen.*

K

keen *scharf.*
keep (to) *behalten* (retain); *hindern;* (hinder), *aufbewahren.*
keep off   *abhalten.*
keep on   *fortfahren.*
keep up   *aufrechterhalten.*
kernel *Kern, m.*

kettle *Kessel, m.*
key *Schlüssel, m.*
keyboard (computer) *Tastatur, f.*
kick *Fusstritt, m.*
kick (to) *ausschlagen, treten, einen Fusstritt geben.*
kidneys *Nieren, pl.*
kill (to) *töten.*
kin *Blutsverwandtschaft, f.*
kind *Art* (noun) *f.; gütig* (adj.).
kindly *freundlich.*
kindness *Güte, f.; Freundlichkeit, f.*
king *König, m.*
kingdom *Königreich, n.*
kiosk *kiosk, m.; Verkaufsstand, m.*
kiss *Kuss, m.*
kiss (to) *küssen.*
kitchen *Küche, f.*
kit *Werkzeugtasche, f.*
kite *Drache, m.*
knee *Knie, n.*
kneel (to) *knieen.*
knife *Messer, n.*
knight *Ritter, m.*
knit (to) *stricken.*
knock *Schlag, m.; Hieb, m.* (beating); *Klopf, m.; Griff, m.* (door).
knock (to) *klopfen, schlagen, hauen, stossen; anklopfen* (door).
knot *Knoten, m.*
know (to) *wissen* (have knowledge of); *kennen* (be acquainted with).
knowledge *Kenntnis, f.*

L

label *Etikett, n.; Marke* (brand), *f.*
labor *Arbeit, f.*
laboratory *Laboratorium, n.*
laborer *Arbeiter, m.*
lace *Spitze, f.* (ornamental); *Senkel, m.* (of a shoe).
lack *Mangel, m.*
lack (to) *mangeln.*
lady *Dame, f.*
lake *See, m.*
lamb *Lamm, n.*
lame *lahm.*
lamp *Lampe, f.*
land *Land, n.*
land (to) *landen.*
landscape *Landschaft, f.*
language *Sprache, f.*
languish (to) *schmachten.*
languor *Schlaffheit, f.*
lantern *Laterne, f.*
large *gross.*
laser *Laser, m.*

laser beam *Laserstrahl, m.*
laser printer *Laserdrucker, m.*
last *letzt.*
   last year   *voriges Jahr.*
last (to) *dauern.*
lasting *dauernd.*
latch *Klinke, f.* (knob); *Drücker.*
late *spät.*
lately *kürzlich.*
latter *letzter.*
laugh (to) *lachen.*
laughter *Gelächter, n.*
lavish *freigebig.*
lavish (to) *überhäufen.*
law *Gesetz, n.; Recht, n.* (code).
lawful *rechtmässig.*
lawn *Rasen, m.*
lawyer *Rechtsanwalt, m.*
lay (to) *legen.*
layer *Schicht, f.*
lazy *faul.*
lead *Blei, n.*
lead (to) *führen.*
leader *Führer, m.*
leadership *Führung, f.*
leaf *Blatt, n.*
leak *Leck, n.*
leak (to) *durchsickern.*
lean (adj.) *mager.*
lean (to) *lehnen.*
leap (to) *springen, hupfen.*
leap *Sprung, m.*
learn (to) *lernen.*
learned *gelehrt.*
learning *Gelehrsamkeit, f.*
least *wenigste.*
   at least   *mindestens, wenigstens.*
leather *Leder, n.*
leave (to) *verlassen* (abandon); *weggehen* (on foot); *wegfahren* (by vehicle).
lecture *Vortrag, m.*
left *link, links.*
   to the left   *links.*
leg *Bein, n.*
   leg of lamb   *Hammelkeule, f.*
legal *gesetzmässig, gesetzlich.*
legend *Sage, f.*
legislation *Gesetzgebung, f.*
legislator *Gesetzgeber, m.*
legitimate *legitim.*
leisure *Freizeit, f.*
lemon *Zitrone, f.*
lemonade *Limonade, f.*
lend (to) *(aus) leihen, verleihen.*
length *Länge, f.*
lengthen (to) *verlängern.*
lesbian *lesbich* (adj.), *Lesbierin, f.*
less *weniger.*
lesson *Stunde, f.; Lektion, f.* (in book).

let (to) *lassen; gestatten* (allow); *vermieten* (rent).
letter *Buchstabe, m.* (alphabet); *Brief, m.* (correspondence).
level *Niveau, n.*
liable *haftbar.*
liar *Lügner, m.; Lügnerin, f.*
liberal *liberal.*
liberty *Freiheit, f.*
library *Bibliothek, f.*
license *Erlaubnis, f.; Führerschein, m.* (driver's license).
lick (to) *lecken.*
lie *Lüge, f.*
lie (to) *lügen* (falsify); *liegen* (rest).
lieutenant *Leutnant, m.*
life *Leben, n.*
lift (to) *heben, hochheben, aufheben.*
light *Licht* (noun) *n.; leicht* (adj.).
light (to) *anzünden* (match, fire).
   to light up   *erleuchten.*
lighten (to) *erhellen* (brightness); *erleichtern* (weight).
lighter *Feuerzeug, n.*
lighthouse *Leuchtturm, m.*
lighting *Beleuchtung, f.*
lightning *Blitz, m.*
like *wie* (as); *ähnlich* (similar).
like (to) *gern haben, mögen, gefallen.*
   I'd like to   *ich möchte.*
likely *wahrscheinlich.*
likeness *Ähnlichkeit, f.*
likewise *gleichfalls.*
liking *Vorliebe, f.*
limb *Glied, n.*
limit *Grenze, f.; Beschränkung, f.* (limitation).
limit (to) *begrenzen, beschränken.*
limp (to) *hinken, humpeln.*
line *Linie, f.*
line up (to) *sich anstellen.*
linen *Wäsche, f.* (household); *Leinwand, f.* (fabric).
linger (to) (*ver) weilen, sich lange aufhalten.*
lingerie *Damenwäsche, f.*
lining *Futter, n.*
link *Glied, n.*
link (to) *verbinden, verknüpfen.*
lion *Löwe, m.*
lip *Lippe, f.*
lipstick *Lippenstift, m.*
liquid *Flüssigkeit* (noun) *f.; flüssig* (adj.).
liquor *Alkohol, m.; Likör, m.* (liqueur).
list *Liste, f.*
literary *literarisch.*
literature *Literatur, f.*
little *klein.*
   a little   *ein wenig.*
live *lebend.*

live (to) *leben.*
lively *lebhaft, lebendig, munter.*
liver *Leber, f.*
load *Last, f.* (burden); *Ladung, f.* (cargo).
load (to) *laden.*
loan (*ver)leihen.*
lobby *Vorhalle, f., Foyer, n.*
local *lokal, örtlich.*
locate (to) *orientieren, finden, festlegen.*
location *Platz, m.; Lage, f.*
lock *Schloss, n.*
lock (to) *zuschliessen, verschliessen, abschliessen.*
locomotive *Lokomotive, f.*
log (*Holz) Klotz, m.*
logic *Logik, f.*
logical *logisch.*
loneliness *Einsamkeit, f.*
lonely *einsam.*
long *lang.*
   long ago   *vor langer Zeit; längst.*
   for a long time   *seit langer Zeit; seit langem.*
long (to) *sehnen.*
   long for   (to) (*sich) sehen (nach)*
longer *länger.*
longing *Sehnsucht, f.*
look *Blick, m.*
look (to) *schauen; aussehen* (appear).
   Look!   *Sehen Sie her!*
   Look out!   *Passen Sie auf!*
   to look forward   *sich freuen auf* (rejoice); *entgegensehen.*
loose *lose.*
loosen (to) *losmachen, loslassen.*
lose (to) *verlieren.*
loss *Verlust, m.; Schaden, m.*
lost *verloren, verschwunden.*
lot (a) *viel* (much).
   a lot of   *eine Menge.*
loud *laut.*
love *Liebe, f.*
love (to) *lieben.*
lovely *schön, reizend.*
low *niedrig.*
lower (to) *niederlassen, herunterlassen, vermindern* (decrease).
loyal *treu.*
loyalty *Treue, f.*
luck *Glück, n.*
lucky *glücklich.*
luggage *Gepäck, n.*
luminous *leuchtend.*
lump *Klumpen, m.*
lunacy *Wahnsinn, m.*
lunch *Mittagessen, n.*
lung *Lunge, f.*
luxurious *prächtig, luxuriös.*
luxury *Luxus, m.; Aufwand, m.*

M

machine *Maschine, f.*
mad *verrückt.*
madam *gnädige Frau.*
made *gemacht.*
madness *Wahnsinn, m.*
magazine *Zeitschrift, f.*
magistrate *Magistrat, m.*
magnificent *prachtvoll, glänzend, herrlich.*
maid *Dienstmädchen, n.* (servant).
mail *Post, f.*
main *haupt*
   the main thing   *die Hauptsache.*
mainly *hauptsächlich.*
maintain (to) *erhalten; unterhalten*
   (support).
maintenance *Unterhalt, m.*
majesty *Majestät, f.*
major *Major, m.*
majority *Mehrheit, f.*
make (to) *machen.*
man *Mann, m.; Mensch, m.* (human being).
manage (to) *führen, verwalten, wissen*
   umzugehen mit (coll.).
management *Leitung, f.*
manager *Leiter, m.; Regisseur, m.* (theater);
   Manager, m.
manicure *Maniküre, f.*
mankind *Menschheit, f.*
manner *Art, f.; Weise, f.*
manners *Benehmen, n.*
manufacture *Fabrikation, f.; Herstellung, f.*
manufactured *hergestellt.*
many *viele.*
map *Landkarte, f.*
marble *Marmor, m.*
March *März, m.*
march *Marsch, m.*
march (to) *marschieren.*
margin *Rand, m.*
marine *Marine, f.*
mark *Kennzeichen, n.*
mark (to) *markieren* (score); *notieren,*
   aufschreiben.
market *Markt, m.*
marketplace *Marktplatz, m.*
marriage *Heirat, f.*
married *verheiratet.*
marry (to) *heiraten, sich verheiraten; trauen*
   (perform the ceremony).
   to marry off   *verheiraten.*
marvel *Wunder, n.*
marvel (to) *sich wundern.*
marvelous *wunderbar.*
masculine *männlich.*
mask *Maske, f.*
mask (to) *maskieren.*

mason *Maurer, m.*
mass *Masse, f.; Messe, f.* (church).
massage *Massage, f.*
master *Meister, m.*
master (to) *meistern.*
masterpiece *Meisterwerk, n.; Meisterstück, n.*
match *Streichholz, n.* (incendiary); *Gleiche,*
   n. (comparative).
match (to) *zusammenpassen; gewachsen sein*
   (to be a match for).
material *Material, n.*
maternal *mütterlich.*
mathematics *Mathematik, f.*
matter *Angelegenheit, f.* (affair); *Stoff, m.*
   (substance).
   What's the matter?   *Was ist los?*
mattress *Matratze, f.*
mature *erwachsen, reif.*
May *Mai, m.*
may *dürfen* (to be allowed); *mögen* (to be
   likely).
mayor *Bürgermeister, m.*
me *mich* (acc.); *mir* (dat.).
meadow *Wiese, f.*
meal *Mahl, n.*
mean *übel* (unkind), *Mittel* (Math).
mean (to) *meinen* (to be of the opinion);
   bedeuten (to signify).
   What does it mean?   *Was bedeutet das?*
meaning *Bedeutung, f.* (significance).
means *Mittel, n.*
meanwhile *inzwischen.*
measure *Mass, n.*
measure (to) *messen.*
meat *Fleisch, n.*
mechanic *Mechaniker, m.*
mechanical *mechanisch.*
medal *Medaille, f.* (jewel).
medical *ärztlich.*
medicine *Medizin, f.* (science); *Arznei, f.*
   (medication).
mediocre *mittelmässig.*
mediocrity *Mittelmässigkeit, f.*
meditate (to) *grübeln, sinnen, nachdenken.*
meditation *Nachdenken, n.*
medium *mittel.*
meet (to) *treffen.*
   Pleased to meet you.   *Sehr erfreut, Sie*
   kennenzulernen.
meeting *Versammlung, f.*
melon *Melone, f.*
melt (to) *schmelzen.*
member *Mitglied, n.*
memorize (to) *auswendig lernen.*
memory *Gedächtnis, n.*
mend (to) *reparieren.*
mental *geistig.*
mention (to) *erwähnen.*
menu *Speisekarte, f.*

merchandise *Ware, f.*
merchant *Kaufmann, m.*
merciful *barmherzig, mitleidvoll.*
merciless *unbarmherzig.*
mercury *Quecksilber, n.*
mercy *Barmherzigkeit, f., Gnade, f.*
merit *Verdienst, n.*
merit (to) *verdienen.*
merry *fröhlich, heiter, lustig.*
message *Nachricht, f.*
messenger *Bote, m.*
metal *Metall, n.*
metallic *metallisch.*
method *Methode, f.*
Mexican *Mexikaner* (noun) *m.; mexikanisch* (adj.)
microphone *Mikrofon, n.*
microwave oven *Mikrowellengerät, n., Mikrowellenherd, m.*
middle *Mitte, f.*
middle aged *von mittlerem Alter*
Middle Ages *Mittelalter, n.*
midnight *Mitternacht, f.*
midway *halbwegs.*
might *Macht, f.*
mighty *mächtig.*
mild *leicht, mild, sanft.*
mildness *Milde, f.*
mile *Meile, f.*
military *militärisch.*
milk *Milch, f.*
milkman *Milchhändler, m., Milchmann, m.*
milky way *Milchstrasse, f.*
mill *Mühle, f.*
miller *Müller, m.; Müllerin, f.*
milliner *Modistin, f.*
million *Million, f.*
millionaire *Millionär, m.*
mind *Verstand, m.; Sinn, m.*
mind (to) *beachten* (to pay heed)*; aufpassen* (also to watch over).
mine *Grube, f.* (coal).
mine (poss. pr.) *mein* (*er, -e, -es*).
miner *Bergmann, m.*
mineral *mineralisch.*
mineral *Mineral, n.*
minister *Minister* (state), *m.; Geistliche, m.* (church).
ministry *Ministerium n.* (state); *Amt, n.* (church).
mink *Nerz, m.*
minor *Minderjährige(r), m.*
minority *Minderheit, f.*
minute *Minute, f.*
    Just a minute! *Einen Augenblick!*
    Wait a minute! *Warten Sie einen Augenblick!*
    Any minute now! *Jeden Augenblick!*
miracle *Wunder, n.*

mirror *Spiegel, m.*
miscellaneous *gemischt, verschieden.*
mischief *Unfug, m.*
mischievous *boshaft.*
miser *Geizhals, m.*
miserly *geizig.*
misfortune *Unglück, n.*
Miss *Fräulein, n.*
miss (to) *versäumen, fehlen.*
mission *Mission, f., Aufgabe, f.* (someone).
mist *Nebel, m.*
mistake *Fehler, m.*
mistaken *irrtümlich.*
    You are mistaken. *Sie sind im Irrtum.*
Mister *Herr.*
mistrust (to) *misstrauen.*
misunderstand (to) *missverstehen.*
misunderstanding *Missverständnis, n.*
misuse (to) *missbrauchen.*
mix (to) *mischen.*
mixture *Mischung, f.*
mob *Pöbel, m.*
mobile *beweglich.*
mobilization *Mobilmachung, f.* (mil.), *Mobilisierung, f.*
mobilize (to) *mobilisieren.*
mock (to) *verspotten.*
mockery *Spott, m.; Spotterei, f.*
mode *Mode, f.*
model *Modell, n.*
moderate *mässigen.*
moderation *Mässigkeit, f.*
modern *modern.*
modest *bescheiden.*
modesty *Bescheidenheit, f.*
modification *Veränderung, f.*
modify (to) *verändern.*
moist *feucht.*
moisten *anfeuchten.*
moment *Augenblick, m.; Moment, m.*
    Just a moment. *Einen Augenblick.*
monarchy *Monarchie, f.*
monastery *Kloster, n.*
Monday *Montag, m.*
money *Geld, n.*
monitor *Bildschirm, m.; Monitor, m.; Fenster, m.*
monk *Mönch, m.*
monkey *Affe, m.*
monologue *Monolog, m.*
monorail *Einschienbahn, f.*
monotonous *eintönig.*
monotony *Eintönigkeit, f.*
monster *Ungeheuer, n.*
monstrous *ungeheuer.*
month *Monat, m.*
monthly *monatlich.*
monument *Denkmal, n.*
monumental *monumental, kolossal.*

mood *Stimmung, f.; Laune, f.* (temper).
moody *launisch.*
moon *Mond, m.*
moonlight *Mondschein, m.*
mop *Mop, m.*
moral *Moral, f.*
morality *Sittlichkeit, f.*
more *mehr.*
moreover *darüber hinaus.*
morning *Morgen, m.*
morsel *Bissen, m.; Brocken, m.*
mortal *sterblich.*
morality *Sterblichkeit, f.*
mortgage *Hypothek, f.*
mortgage (to) *verpfänden.*
mosquito *Mücke, f.*
most *am meisten.*
    most of   *die meisten.*
mostly *meistens.*
moth *Motte, f.*
mother *Mutter, f.*
mother-in-law *Schwiegermutter, f.*
motion *Bewegung, f.*
motionless *bewegungslos.*
motivate (to) *anregen, begründen, motivieren.*
motor *Motor, m.*
mount (to) *montieren; aufkleben* (paste); *besteigen* (horse).
mountain *Berg, m.*
mountainous *bergig.*
mourn (to) *trauern.*
mournful *traurig.*
mourning *Trauer, f.*
mouse *Maus, f.*
mouth *Mund, m.*
move (to) *bewegen.*
movement *Bewegung, f.*
movies *Kino, n.*
moving *rührend.*
much *viel*
    How much?   *Wieviel?*
mud *Schlamm, m.*
muddy *schlammig.*
mule *Maultier, n.; Maulesel, m.*
multiply (to) *multiplizieren.*
multitude *Menge, f.*
mumble (to) *murmeln.*
municipal *städtisch.*
munition *Munition, f.*
murder *Mord, m.*
murder (to) *ermorden.*
murderer *Mörder, m.*
murmur (to) *murmeln, rauschen.*
muscle *Muskel, m.*
museum *Museum, n.*
mushroom *Pilz, m.*
music *Musik, f.*
musical *musikalisch.*

musician *Musiker, m.*
must *müssen.*
mustache *Schnurrbart, m.*
mustard *Senf, m.; Mostrich, m.*
mute *stumm.*
mutton *Hammelfleisch, n.*
my *mein.*
myself *ich (mich, mir) selbst.*
mysterious *geheimnisvoll.*
mystery *Geheimnis, n.*

N

nail *Nagel, m.*
nail (to) *nageln.*
naive *harmlos, naïv.*
naked *nackt.*
name *Name, m.*
    first name   *Vorname, m.*
    last name   *Zuname, m.; Familienname* (family name).
    What is your name?   *Wie heissen Sie?*
namely *nähmlich.*
nap *Schläfchen, n.*
napkin *Serviette, f.*
narrow *eng.*
nasty *garstig, ekelhaft.*
nation *Nation, f.*
national *national.*
nationality *Nationalität, f.*
native *Eingeborene, m., f., n.*
    native country   *Heimat, f.*
natural *natürlich.*
naturally *natürlich.*
nature *Natur, f.*
naughty *unartig.*
naval *See-.*
navy *Flotte, f.; Kriegsmarine, f.*
near *nah.*
nearly *beinahe.*
neat *nett, ordentlich.*
neatness *Niedlichkeit, f.; Sauberkeit, f.*
necessary *notwendig.*
necessity *Notwendigkeit, f.*
neck *Hals, m.*
necklace *Halsband, n.*
necktie *Krawatte, f.; Schlips, m.* (colloquial).
need *Not, f.; Bedürfnis, f.*
need (to) *brauchen.*
needle *Nadel, f.*
needless *unnötig.*
needy *dürftig, bedürftig.*
negative *Negative, m.*
neglect *Vernachlässigung, f.*
neglect (to) *vernachlässigen.*
negotiate (to) *verhandeln, abschliessen* (treaty); *nehmen* (a curve in road).

negotiation *Unterhandlung, f.;*
  Verhandlung, f.
neighbor *Nachbar, m.*
neighborhood *Nachbarschaft, f.*
neither *kein(er, -e, -es).*
  neither . . . nor *weder . . . noch.*
nephew *Neffe, m.*
nerve *Nerv, m.*
  What a nerve! *So eine Frechheit!*
nervous *nervös.*
nest *Nest, n.*
net *Netz, n.*
neuter *Neutrum, n.*
neutral *neutral.*
never *niemals, nie*
  Never mind! *Das macht nichts!*
nevertheless *trotzdem; auf alle Fälle.*
new *neu.*
news *Nachrichten, pl.*
newspaper *Zeitung, f.*
next *nächst.*
nice *nett.*
nickname *Spritzname, m.*
niece *Nichte, f.*
night *Nacht, f.*
nightgown *Nachthemd, n.*
nightmare *Alpdrücken, n.; Alptraum, m.*
nine *neun.*
nineteen *neunzehn.*
ninety *neunzig.*
ninth *neunte.*
no *nein; kein* (adj.).
  no longer *nicht mehr.*
  no matter *ungeachtet* (gen.)
nobility *Adel, m.*
noble *adlig, eder* (fig).
nobody *niemand.*
noise *Geräusch, n.*
noisy *geräuschvoll.*
nominate (to) *ernennen.*
nomination *Ernennung, f.*
none *kein(e, -er, -es).*
nonsense *Unsinn, m .*
noon *Mittag, m.*
nor *noch, auch nicht* (nor I).
normal *normal.*
north *Norden, m.*
northern *nordisch, nördlich.*
northeast *Nordosten, m.*
northwest *Nordwesten, m.*
nose *Nase, f.*
nostril *Nasenloch, n.*
not *nicht.*
note *Note, f.*
note (to) *notieren.*
notebook *Notizbuch, n.*
nothing *nichts.*
notice (to) *bemerken.*
notification *Benachrichtung, f.*

notify (to) *benachrichtigen.*
notion *Idee, f.; Begriff, m.*
noun *Name, m.*
nourish (to) *nähren.*
nourishment *Nahrung, f.*
novel *Roman, m.*
novelty *Neuheit, f.*
November *November, m.*
now *jetzt*
  now and then. *dann und wann;*
      manchmal.
nowadays *heutzutage.*
nowhere *nirgendwo.*
nuclear *Kern-, Atom-,*
  weapon *Kernwaffe, f.; Atomwaffe, f.*
  fission *Kernspaltung, f.*
  physics *Kernphysik, f.*
nude *nackt, bloss.*
nuisance *Unfug, m.*
null *null*
  null and void *null und nichtig.*
numb *gefühllos.*
number *Nummer, f.*
numerous *zahlreich.*
nun *Nonne, f.*
nurse *Krankenschwester, f.* (for the sick);
    Kindermädchen (for children).
nursery *Kinderstube, f.* (children); *Gärtnerei,*
    f. (trees).
nursery rhyme *Kinderlied, n.*
nut *Nuss, f.*
nutcracker *Nussknacker, m.*

O

oak *Eiche, f.*
oar *Ruder, n.*
oat *Hafer, m.*
oath *Eid, m.*
obedience *Gehorsam, m.*
obedient *gehorsam.*
obey (to) *gehorchen.*
object (to) *einwenden, dagegen sein.*
objection *Einwand, m.*
objective *objektiv.*
objectively *sachlich.*
obligation *Verpflichtung, f.*
oblige (to) *verpflichten.*
obliging *gefällig.*
obscure *unklar, verborgen, unbekannt.*
obscurity *Dunkelheit, f.*
observation *Beobachtung, f.*
observatory *Sternwarte, f.*
observe (to) *beobachten.*
obstacle *Hindernis, no.*
obstinacy *Eigensinn, m.*
obstinate *eigensinnig.*
obvious *klar.*

obviously *offenbar, deutlich.*
occasion *Gelegenheit, f.*
occasional *gelegentlich.*
occasionally *zuweilen, dann und wann.*
occupation *Beschäftigung, f.*
occupy (to) *besitzen; besetzen* (military);
    bewohnen (house).
occur (to) *vorkommen* (an event); *einfallen*
    (a thought), *vorfallen.*
occurrence *Vorfall, m.*
ocean *Ozean, m.*
October *Oktober, m.*
odd *ungerade* (uneven); *sonderbar*
    (unusual); *seltsam.*
odor *Geruch, m.*
of *von* (dat.); *aus* (dat.) (made of).
    of course   *natürlich.*
off *fort, weg.*
    off and on   *ab und zu.*
offend (to) *beleidigen.*
offense *Beleidigung, f.*
offensive *beleidigend.*
offer (to) *anbieten,* (*dar*) *bieten.*
offering *Angebot, n.*
office *Büro, n.*
official *offiziell.*
often *oft, oftmals, öfters, häufig.*
oil *Öl, n.*
old *alt.*
olive *Olive, f.*
olive oil *Olivenöl, n.*
on *auf* (dat. or acc.); *an* (dat. or acc.) (date).
once *einmal; vormals, einst* (formerly).
    at once   *sofort.*
    once and for all   *ein für allemal.*
    once in a while   *manchmal.*
    once more   *noch einmal.*
one *eins* (number), *ein(er, -e).*
one (pr.) *man.*
oneself *sich, sich selbst.*
onion *Zwiebel, f.*
only *nur.*
open *offen.*
open (to) *öffnen.*
opener *Öffner, m.*
opening *Öffnung, f.*
opera *Oper, f.*
operate (to) *operieren* (med.); *betätigen;*
    funktionieren, wirken.
operation *Operation, f.*
opinion *Meinung, f.*
opponent *Gegner, m.*
opportune *gelegen, günstig.*
opportunity *Gelegenheit, f.*
oppose (to) *sich widersetzen gegen,*
    gegenüberstehen.
opposite *gegenüber.*
opposition *Widerstand, m.*
oppress (to) *unterdrücken.*

oppression *Unterdrückung, f.*
optician *Optiker, m.*
optimism *Optimismus, m.*
optimistic *optimistisch.*
or *oder.*
orange *Apfelsine, f. Orange, f.*
orange juice *Apfelsinensaft, m.*
orator *Redner, m.*
orchard *Obstgarten, m.*
orchestra *Orchester, n.*
ordeal *Prüfung, f.; Qual, f.* (fig.).
order *Ordnung, f.* (neatness); *Bestellung, f.*
    (commercial); *Befehl, m.* (command);
    Orden, m. (decoration).
    out of order   *kaputt.*
    to put in order   *in Ordnung bringen.*
order (to) *ordnen* (regulate); *bestellen*
    (commercial); *befehlen* (command).
ordinary *gewöhnlich.*
organ *Orgel, f.* (music); *Organ, n.*
    (anatomy).
organization *Organisation, f.*
organize (to) *organisieren.*
Orient *Orient, m.*
oriental *orientalisch.*
origin *Ursprung, m.* (source); *Herkunft, f.*
    (descent).
original *original, ursprünglich.*
originality *Originalität, f.*
ornament *Ornament, n.*
orphan *Waisenkind, n.*
orthodox *orthodox.*
other *ander.*
other than *anders als, verschieden* (*von*).
ought (to) *sollen.*
ounce *Unze, f.*
our *unser.*
ours *unser(er, -e, -es).*
out *aus* (dat.); *hinaus, heraus.*
    out of   *ausser* (dat.)
outcome *Folge, f.; Ergebnis, n.*
outdo (to) *übertreffen.*
outdoors *im Freien.*
outer *äusser.*
outlast *überdauern.*
outlaw *Geächtete(r), m.*
outlaw (to) *achten, verbieten.*
outlay *Auslage, f., Ausgabe, f.*
outlet *Auslass, m.; Absatz, m.* (market).
outline *Umriss, m.*
outlook *Aussicht, f.*
output *Produktion, f.; Leistung, f.* (machine).
outrage *Unverschämtheit, f.; Schandtat, f.;*
    Frevel, m .
outrageous *frevelhaft, empörend, schändlich.*
outside *Aussenseite* (noun) *f.; draussen*
    (outdoors); *ausserhalb* (besides).
oval *oval.*
oven *Ofen, m.*

over *über* (acc.); *vorbei* (finished).
over and over *wieder und wieder.*
overboard *über Bord.*
overcoat *Mantel, m.*
overcome (to) *überwinden.*
overflow (to) *überfliessen.*
overlook (to) *übersehen.*
overrun *überrennen, überlaufen.*
overseas *nach Übersee.*
overthrow *umstürzen, stürzen* (govt.).
overwhelm (to) *überwältigen.*
owe (to) *schulden.*
owl *Eule, f.*
own *eigen.*
own (to) *besitzen* (possess); *bekennen
zugeben* (admit).
owner *Besitzer, m.*
ox *Ochse, m.*
oxygen *Sauerstoff, m.*
oyster *Auster, f.*
ozone *ozon, n.*

P

pace *Schritt, m; Tempo, n.*
pace (to) *schreiten.*
pacific *friedlich.*
pack *Kartenspiel, n.* (cards).
pack (to) *(ein)packen, verpacken, Packung,
f.* (cigarettes); *Rucksack, m.;
Tornister, m.*
package *Paket, n.*
page *Seite, f.*
pager *Pager, m.; Beeper, m.*
pain *Schmerz, m.*
pain (to) *schmerzen.*
painful *schmerzhaft.*
painless *schmerzlos.*
paint *Farbe, f.*
paint (to) *malen* (art); *(an)streichen* (a
wall), *spritzen lassen* (car).
painter *Maler, m.*
painting *Gemälde, n.*
pair *Paar, n.*
pajamas *Pyjama, m.*
palace *Palast, m.*
pale *blass.*
palm *Palme, f.*
pamphlet *Broschüre, f.*
pan *Pfanne, f.*
pancake *Pfannkuchen, m.*
pane *Scheibe, f.*
panic *Panik, f.*
panorama *Panorama, n.*
panties *Schlüpfer, m.*
pants *Hose, f.*
paper *Papier, n.*
parachute *Fallschirm, m.*

parade *Parade, f.*
paragraph *Paragraph, m; Absatz, m.*
parallel *parallel.*
paralysis *Lähmung, f.*
paralyzed *gelähmt.*
parcel *Paket, n., Päckchen, n.*
pardon *Verzeihung, f; Entschuldigung, f.*
pardon (to) *vergeben, entschuldigen.*
parenthesis *Klammern, f.*
parents *Eltern, pl.*
Parisian *Pariser, m.*
park *Park, m.*
park (to) *parken.*
parliament *Parlament, n.*
parrot *Papagei, m.*
parsley *Petersilie, f.*
part *Teil, n.* (share); *Ersatzteil*
(replacement).
part (to) *teilen, sich trennen* (separate);
auseinander gehen.
partial *teilweise.*
partiality *Vorliebe, f.*
particular *besonder(er, -e, -es).*
particularly *besonders.*
partner *Partner, m.; Sozius, m.*
party (political) *Partei, f.; Gesellschaft, f.*
(society); *Party; f.* (social).
pass *Ausweis, m.*
pass (to) *durchgehen, vorbeigehen; bestehen*
(exam); *überholen* (overtake a car).
passage *Durchgang, m.; Überfahrt, f.*
(travel).
passenger *Passagier, m.*
passion *Leidenschaft, f.*
passionately *leidenschaftlich.*
passive *Passiv, n.*
passport *Pass, m.*
past *Vergangenheit* (noun) *f.; vorbei, vorig*
(time); *nach* (on the clock).
ten past six   *zehn nach sechs.*
last month   *vorigen Monat*
last week   *vorige Woche*
last year   *voriges Jahr*
paste *Kleister, m. Teig* (cul.).
paste (to) *kleistern, kleben.*
pastry *Gebäck, n.*
pastry shop *Konditorei, f.*
patch *Flicken, m.*
patch (to) *flicken.*
patent *Patent, n.*
paternal *väterlich.*
path *Weg, m; pfad, m.; Bahn, f.* (elec.).
pathetic *pathetisch.*
patience *Geduld, f.*
patient *Patient* (noun) *m.; geduldig* (adj.).
patriot *Patriot, m.*
patriotic *patriotisch.*
patron *Gönner, m.; Patron, m.; Förd-
erer, m.*

patronage *Begünstigung, f.; Schutz, m.*
patronize (to) *unterstützen.*
pattern *Muster, n.*
pause *Pause, f.*
pave (to) *pflastern.*
pavement *Pflaster, n.*
paw *Pfote, f.*
pay *Lohn, m.; Bezahlung, f., Gehalt, n.*
pay (to) *zahlen, bezahlen.*
payment *Bezahlung, f.*
pea *Erbse, f.*
peace *Frieden, m.*
peaceful *friedlich.*
peach *Pfirsich, m.*
peak *Gipfel, n.*
peanut *Erdnuss, f.*
pear *Birne, f.*
pearl *Perle, f.*
peasant *Bauer, m.*
pebble *Kiesel(stein), m.*
peculiar *sonderbar.*
pedal *Pedal, n.*
pedantic *pedantisch.*
pedestrian *Fussgänger, m.*
peel *Rinde, f.; Schale, f.*
peel (to) *schälen.*
pen *Feder, f.*
    fountain pen *Füllfeder, f.*
penalty *Strafe, f., Todesstrafe* (death).
pencil *Bleistift, m.*
penetrate (to) *durchdringen.*
peninsula *Halbinsel, f.*
penitence *Reue, f.*
pension *Pension, f.*
people *Leute, pl.*
pepper *Pfeffer, m.*
peppermint *Pfefferminz, m.*
per *pro.*
perceive (to) *wahnehmen.*
percentage *Prozentsatz, m.*
perfect *vollkommen.*
perfection *Vollkommenheit, f.*
perfectly *gänzlich; völlig.*
perform (to) *verrichten; aufführen;*
    vortragen (theater); *durchführen.*
performance *Vorstellung, f.; Aufführung, f.*
perfume *Parfüm, n.*
perfume (to) *parfümieren.*
perhaps *vielleicht.*
period *Periode, f.; Punkt, m.* (typ.).
periodical *periodisch; Zeitschrift, f.*
permanent *ständig.*
permission *Erlaubnis, f.*
permit *Erlaubnisschein, m.*
permit (to) *erlauben.*
peroxide *Hyperoxyd, n., Superoxyd, n.*
perpetual *immerwährend, andauernd,*
    fortwährend.
perplex *verwirren.*

persecute (to) *verfolgen.*
persecution *Verfolgung, f.*
perseverance *Ausdauer, f.*
persist (to) *beharren.*
person *Person, f.*
personal *persönlich.*
personality *Persönlichkeit, f.*
perspective *Perspektive, f.*
perspiration *Schweiss, m.*
persuade (to) *überzeugen, überreden.*
pertaining *betreffend.*
petrol *Benzin, n.*
petticoat *Unterrock, m.*
petty *kleinlich.*
pharmacist *Apotheker, m.*
pharmacy *Apotheke, f.*
phenomenon *Phänomen, n.*
philosopher *Philosoph, m.*
philosophical *philosophisch.*
philosophy *Philosophie, f.*
phonograph *Plattenspieler, m.*
photograph *Fotografie, f., Aufnahme, f.*
photograph (to) *aufnehmen.*
photographer *Fotograf, m.*
photostat *Photokopie, f.; Fotokopie.*
phrase *Frase, f.*
physical *körperlich.*
physician *Arzt, m; Doktor, m.*
piano *Klavier, n.*
pick (to) *pflücken.*
pick up (to) *aufheben, abholen.*
picnic *Picknick, n.*
picture *Bild, n.*
picturesque *malerisch.*
pie *Torte, f.*
piece *Stück, n.*
pier *kai, m.; Landungssteg, m.*
pig *Schwein, n.*
pigeon *Taube, f.*
pile *Haufen, m., Stapel, m.*
pile (to) *aufhäufen, (auf) stapeln.*
pilgrim *Pilger, m.*
pill *Pille, f.*
pillar *Säule, f.*
pillow *Kissen, n.*
pilot *Pilot, m.*
    automatic pilot *Steuergerät, n.*
pin *Stechnadel, f.*
pinch (to) *kneifen.*
pink *rosa.*
pious *fromm.*
pipe *Pfeife, f.* (tobacco); *Rohr, n.*
    (plumbing).
pirate *Seeräuber, m.; Pirat, m.*
pistol *Pistole, f.*
pitiful *mitleidig.*
pity *Mitleid, n.*
place *Platz, m.; Stelle, f.* (spot, situation);
    Ort, m. (locality).

take place *stattfinden.*
place (to) *stellen, legen, setzen.*
plain *Ebene* (noun) *f.; einfach* (adj.).
plan *Plan, m.* (project); *Entwurf, m.*
plan (to) *ausdenken.*
plane *Flugzeug, n.*
planet *Planet, m.*
plant *Pflanze, f.*
plant (to) *pflanzen.*
plaster *Verputz, m.; Pflaster, n.* (med.).
plastic *Kunststoff* (noun) *m.; plastisch* (adj.).
plate *Teller, m.*
platform *Bahnsteig, m.* (station).
platter *Platte, f.*
play *Spiel, n.; Stück, n.* (theater).
play (to) *spielen.*
plea *Gesuch, n.; Einrede, f.*
plead (to) *plädieren* (law); *inständig bitten; anflehen.*
pleasant *angenehm.*
please *bitte.*
please (to) *gefallen.*
pleasure *Vergnügen, n.*
pledge *Pfand, n. Verspechen, n.*
plenty *genug* (enough); *reichlich* (abundance).
plot *Verschwörung, f.* (conspiracy); *Handlung, f.* (of a story).
plot (to) *anstiften, heimlich planen.*
plow *Pflug, m.*
plow (to) *pflügen.*
plum *Pflaume, f.*
plumber *Klempner, m.*
pneumonia *Lungenentzündung, f.*
pocket *Tasche, f.*
poem *Gedicht, n.*
poet *Poet, m.; Dichter, m.*
poetic *poetisch.*
poetry *Dichtung, f.*
point *Punkt, m.; Spitze, f.*
point (to) *spitzen, hinweisen, richten auf.*
pointed *spitz(ig).*
poise *Gleichgewicht, n. (Körper) haltung, f.*
poison *Gift, n.*
poison (to) *vergiften.*
poisonous *giftig.*
polar *polar.*
pole *Pol, m.*
police *Polizei, f.*
policeman *Schutzmann, m.; Polizist, m.*
policy *Politik, f.; Police, f.* (insurance).
Polish *polnisch.*
polish *Glanz, m., Politur, f.*
polish (to) *glänzend machen, polieren.*
polite *höflich.*
politeness *Höflichkeit, f.*
political *politisch.*
pollution *Verschmutzung, f.*
pond *Teich, m.*

pool *Schwimmbad, n.*
poor *arm.*
Pope *Papst, m.*
popular *volkstümlich; beliebt* (liked).
population *Bevölkerung, f.*
pork *Schweinefleisch, n.*
port *Hafen, m.*
porter *Träger, m.*
portrait *Bild, n.; Porträt, n.*
Portuguese *Portugiese* (noun) *m.; portugiesisch* (adj.).
position *Stellung, f.* (job), *Lage, f.* (site).
positive *bestimmt, positiv.*
possibility *Möglichkeit, f.*
possible *möglich.*
post *Post, f.; Stelle, f.* (job).
postage *Porto, n.*
postcard *Postkarte, f.*
poster *Plakat, n.*
posterity *Nachkommenschaft, f.*
post office *Postamt, n.*
pot *Topf, m.*
potato *Kartoffel, f.*
pound *Pfund, n.*
pour (to) *giessen.*
poverty *Armut, f.*
powder *Pulver, n.* (gun); *Puder, m.* (cosmetic).
powder (to) *pudern.*
power *Macht, f., Gewalt, f.*
powerful *mächtig.*
practical *praktisch.*
practice (to) *üben.*
praise *Lob, n.*
praise (to) *loben, rühmen.*
prank *Streich, m.*
pray (to) *beten.*
prayer *Gebet, n.*
preach (to) *predigen.*
preacher *Prediger, m.*
precaution *Vorsicht, f.*
precede (to) *vorangehen.*
preceding *vorangehend.*
precept *Vorschrift, f.; Beispiel, n.* (example).
precious *kostbar, unschätzbar.*
precise *genau; steif* (formal).
precision *Genauigkeit, f.*
predecessor *Vorgänger, m.*
predict *voraussagen, vorhersagen.*
preface *Vorwort, n.*
prefer (to) *vorziehen.*
preference *Vorzug, m.*
pregnant *schwanger.*
prejudice *Vorurteil, n.*
preliminary *einleitend, vorbereitend.*
preparation *Vorbereitung, f.*
prepare (to) *vorbereiten, zubereiten.*
prepay (to) *vorauszahlen.*
prescribe (to) *verschreiben.*

prescription *Rezept, n.*
presence *Gegenwart, f.; Anwesenheit, f.*
present *Gegenwart, f.* (grammar), *Geschenk, n.* (gift), *anwesend* (adj.).
preserve (to) *erhalten; konservieren* (food); *bewahren.*
preserves *Konserven, f.; Eingemachte, n.; Konfitüren, f.* (jellies, jams).
preside (to) *präsidieren.*
president *Präsident, m.*
press *Presse, f.*
press (to) *drücken; bügeln* (clothes).
pressing *dringend.*
pressure *Druck, m.; Blutdruck* (blood-); *Drücken, n.*
prestige *Prestige, n.; Ansehen, n.*
presume (to) *vermuten.*
pretend (to) *vorgeben, vortäuschen.*
pretext *Vorwand, m.*
pretty *hübsch, nett.*
prevail (to) *vorherrschen, siegen.*
prevent (to) *verhindern.*
prevention *Verhinderung, f.*
previous *frühere.*
prey *Raub, m.*
price *Preis, m.*
price-cutting *Preissenkung, f.*
price tag *Preisschild, n.*
price war *Preiskrieg, m.*
pride *Stolz, m.*
priest *Priester, m.*
prince *Prinz, m.*
principal *haupt-* (adj.); *Haupt-, n.*
principle *Grundsatz, m.; Prinzip, n.*
print (to) *drucken.*
printer *Drucker, m.*
prison *Gefängnis, n.*
prisoner *Gefangene, m.*
private *privat.*
privilege *Vorrecht, n.*
prize *Preis, m.*
prize (to) *schätzen.*
probable *wahrscheinlich.*
problem *Problem, n.* (math); *Schwierigkeit, f.*
procedure *Verfahren, n.*
proceed (to) *fortschreiten.*
process *Verfahren, n.; Prozess, m.; Verlauf, m.*
procession *Prozession, f.*
proclaim (to) *bekanntmachen.*
produce (to) *erzeugen, hervorbringen, herstellen.*
production *Erzeugung, f.; Produktion, f.; Herstellung, f.; Fabrikation, f.*
productive *fruchtbar, schöpferisch, erzeugend.*
profession *Beruf, m.*
professional *beruflich, berufsmässig.*

professor *Professor, m. Lehrer, m.* (school).
profile *Profil, n.*
profit *Gewinn, m; Profit, m.*
profit (to) *gewinnen, profitieren.*
program *Programm, n.*
progress *Fortschritt, m.*
progress (to) *vorwärtskommen, weiterkommen.*
progressive *fortschrittlich.*
prohibit (to) *verbieten.*
prohibition *Verbot, n. Untersagung, f.*
project *Projekt, n.; Unternehmen, n.*
project (to) *hervorstehen, entwerfen.*
promise (to) *versprechen.*
prompt *schnell, sofortig.*
pronoun *Fürwort, n.*
pronounce (to) *aussprechen.*
pronunciation *Aussprache, f.*
proof *Beweis, m.*
propaganda *Propaganda, f.*
proper *passend, anständig* (decent).
property *Eigentum, n.*
proportion *Verhältnis, n.; Mass, n.*
proposal *Vorschlag, m.*
propose (to) *vorschlagen.*
prose *Prosa, f.*
prospect (to) *Aussicht, f.*
prosper (to) *gedeihen.*
prosperity *Wohlstand, m.*
prosperous *gedeihlich, blühend.*
protect (to) *schützen.*
protection *Schutz, m.*
protector *Beschützer, m.*
protest *Einspruch, m.; protest, m.*
protest (to) *protestieren, sich auflehnen* (gegen).
Protestant *Protestant, m.*
proud *stolz.*
prove (to) *beweisen, bestätigen.*
proverb *Sprichwort, n.*
provide (to) *versorgen.*
provided that *vorausgesetzt dass.*
province *Provinz, f.*
provincial *provinziell.*
provision *Lebensmittelvorrat, m.; Beschaffung, f., Besorgung, f.*
provoke (to) *herausfordern, reizen.*
prowl *herumschleichen, herumstreichen.*
proximity *Nähe, f.*
prudence *Vorsicht, f.*
prudent *klug, vorsichtig, umsichtig.*
prune *Backpflaume, f.*
psychological *psychologisch.*
psychology *Psychologie, f.*
public *Publikum* (noun) *n.; öffentlich* (adj.).
publication *Herausgabe, f.* (literary); *Veröffentlichung, f.* (notification).
publish (to) *herausgeben* (book); *veröffentlichen* (announcement).

publishing house *Verlag, m.*
publisher *Verleger, m.*
pull (to) *ziehen.*
pump *Pumpe, f.*
punish (to) *bestrafen.*
punishment *Strafe, f.*
pupil *Schüler, m; Schülerin, f.*
purchase (to) *kaufen.*
purchase *Einkauf, m.*
pure *rein.*
purity *Reinheit, f.*
purple *Purpur, m.*
purpose *Absicht, f., Zweck, m.*
purse *Geldtasche, f., Portemonnaie, n.; Handtasche, f.*
pursue (to) *verfolgen, nachgehen.*
push (to) *stossen.*
put (to) *legen* (lay)*; setzen,* (set)*; stellen* (place).
  put down *aufschreiben.*
  put off *aufschieben.*
  put on *anziehen.*
  put up *aufstellen.*
  put into practice *einsetzen.*
  put a question to someone *eine Frage richten an.*
puzzle *Rätsel, n.*
puzzle (to) *verwirren.*

quaint *seltsam.*
qualify *befähigen, qualifizieren.*
quality *Qualität, f.*
quantity *Quantität, f.*
quarrel *Streit, m.*
quarter *Viertel, n.*
queen *Königin, f.*
queer *seltsam, eigenartig.*
quench (to) *löschen* (thirst)*; auslöschen* (fire).
question *Frage, f.*
question (to) *fragen.*
quick *schnell, geschwind, rasch.*
quiet *ruhig.*
quit (to) *verlassen, aufgeben.*
quite *ganz.*
quote (to) *anführen* (a fact)*; zitieren* (a passage).

R

rabbi *Rabbiner, m.*
rabbit *Kaninchen, n.; Hase, m.* (hare).
race *Rennen, n.* (contest)*; Rasse, f.* (species).
radiate (to) *strahlen.*

radiator *Heizkörper, m.; Kühler* (motor).
radio *Radio, n; Rundfunk, m.*
rag *Lappen, m.*
rage *Wut, f.*
ragged *zerlumpt, zerfetzt.*
rail *Schiene, f.*
railroad *Eisenbahn, f.*
railroad car *Eisenbahnwagen, m.*
rain *Regen, m.*
rain (to) *regnen.*
rainbow *Regenbogen, m.*
raincoat *Regenmantel, m.*
rainy *regnerisch.*
raise (to) *erhöhen.*
raisin *Rosine, f.*
rake *Rechen, m.; Harke, f.*
rank *Rang, m.; Glied, n.* (mil.).
rapid *schnell.*
rapidly *schnell, geschwind, rasch.*
rapture *Entzücken, n.*
rash *Hautausschlag* (noun) *m.* (skin)*; hastig* (adj.).
rat *Ratte, f.*
rate *Kurs, m.* (exchange)*; Preis, m.*
rate (to) *(ab)schätzen.*
rather *ziemlich, lieber, eher.*
ration *Ration, f.*
rational *vernünftig.*
rave (to) *schwärmen.*
raw *roh.*
ray *Strahl, m.*
razor *Rasiermesser, n.*
razor blade *Rasierklinge, f.*
reach (to) *erreichen, greifen* (nach).
reach *Reichweite, f.*
react (to) *reagieren, entgegenwirken.*
read (to) *lesen.*
reading *Lesen, n.; Lektüre, f.*
ready *fertig.*
real *wirklich.*
realization *Verwirklichung, f.*
realize (to) *verwirklichen.*
really *wirklich.*
rear *Hintergrund* (noun) *m.; hinter* (adj.).
rear (to) *grossziehen, aufziehen* (children)*, züchten* (animals).
reason *Grund, m.* (cause)*; Vernunft, f.* (intelligence).
  it stands to reason *es versteht sich.*
reason (to) *logisch denken, vernüftig urteilen.*
reasonable *vernünftig.*
reasoning *Schlussfolgerung, f.; Urteilen, n.*
reassure (to) *beruhigen.*
rebel *Rebell, m.*
rebel (to) *sich auflehnen, rebellieren.*
rebellion *Empörung, f.; Aufstand, m.*
recall (to) *sich erinnern* (memory)*; zurückrufen* (to summon back).

receipt *Quittung, f.*
receive (to) *empfangen, erhalten, bekommen.*
receiver *Empfäger, m.*
recent *neu.*
recently *neulich.*
reception *Empfang, m.*
recess *Ferien f.* (school); *Pause, f.*
reciprocal *gegenseitig.*
recite (to) *aufsagen; rezitieren* (drama).
recognize (to) *erkennen.*
recollect (to) *sich erinnern an.*
recollection *Erinnerung, f.*
recommend (to) *empfehlen.*
recommendation *Empfehlung, f.*
reconcile (to) *versöhnen.*
record *Rekord, m.* (sports).
    phonograph record *(Schall)platte, f.*
recover (to) *sich erholen* (illness),
    zürückerhalten (to get back); *neu*
    uberziehen (quilt, sofa).
recruit *Rekrut, m.* (mil.).
recruit (to) *rekrutieren, (an)werben.*
red *rot.*
Red Cross *Das Rote Kreuz, n.*
redeem (to) *erlösen.*
reduce (to) *herabsetzen; abnehmen* (weight).
reduction *Nachlass, m.; Verminderung, f.*
reed *Schilf, n.*
reef *Riff, n.*
refer (to) *sich beziehen.*
reference *Bezugnahme, f.*
referring (to) *mit Bezugnahme auf.*
    in reference to (corresp.) *Betreff/Betrifft.*
refine (to) *verfeinern.*
refinement *Verfeinerung, f.*
reflect (to) *zurüchstrahlen; widerspiegeln.*
reflection *Widerschein, m.* (image);
    Überlegung, f. (thoughts).
reform *Besserung, f.*
reform (to) *sich bessern, reformieren.*
refrain (to) *sich enthalten.*
refresh (to) *erfrischen.*
refreshment *Erfrischung, f.*
refrigerator *Kühlschrank, m.*
refuge *Zufluchtsort, m.*
    take refuge *flüchten.*
refugee *Flüchtling, m.*
refund *Rückzahlung, f.*
refund (to) *zurückzahlen.*
refusal *Verweigerung, f., Ablehnung, f.*
refuse (to) *ablehnen, verweigern.*
refute (to) *widerlegen.*
regard *Ansehen, n.*
regardless *ungeachtet, ohne Rücksicht auf.*
regime *Regime, n.*
regiment *Regiment, n.*
register (to) *eintragen* (membership);
    einschreiben (letter); *sich*
    immatrikulieren (university).

regret *Bedauern, n., Reue, f.*
regret (to) *bedauern.*
regular *regelmässig.*
regulate *regulieren.*
regulation *Vorschrift, f.*
rehearsal *Probe, f.*
rehearse (to) *Probe halten.*
reign *Herrschaft, f.*
reign (to) *herrschen.*
reinforce (to) *verstärken.*
reject (to) *ablehnen.*
rejoice (to) *sich freuen.*
relapse *Rückfall, m.*
relate (to) *erzählen.*
relation *Verwandtschaft, f.*
relationship *verwandtschaftliche Beziehung,*
    f.; Verhältnis, n.
relative *Verwandte, m./f.*
relax (to) *entspannen.*
relaxation *Entspannung, f.*
release *Befreiung, f.*
release (to) *freilassen.*
reliable *zuverlässig.*
relic *Überbleibsel, n.; Relique, f.;* (religious).
relief *Erleichterung, f.; Linderung, f.* (of
    pain).
relieve (to) *erleichtern, lindern.*
religion *Religion, f.*
religious *religiös.*
relinquish (to) *aufgeben.*
relish (to) *mit Appetit geniessen.*
relish *Geschmack, m.; Genuss (an), m.*
reluctance *Widerwille, n.*
reluctant *widerwillig.*
rely (to) *sich verlassen (auf).*
remain (to) *bleiben.*
remainder *Rest, m.*
remark *Bemerkung, f.*
remark (to) *bemerken.*
remarkable *bemerkenswert.*
remedy *Arznei, f.* (medicine); *Hilfsmittel, n.*
    (cure).
remember (to) *sich erinnern (an).*
remembrance *Erinnerung, f.*
remind (about) (to) *mahnen.*
remorse *Reue, f.*
remote *entfernt* (distance); *rückständig;*
    abgelegen (distance).
removal *Beseitigung, f.*
remove (to) *entfernen.*
renew (to) *erneuern.*
renewal *Erneuerung, f.*
rent *Miete, f.*
rent (to) *mieten.*
repair *Reparatur, f.*
repay (to) *zurückzahlen.*
repeat (to) *wiederholen.*
repent (to) *bereuen.*
repetition *Wiederholung, f.*

replace *zurückerstatten* (things taken);
    ersetzen.
reply *Antwort, f.*
reply (to) *antworten.*
report *Bericht, m.; Zeugnis, n.* (report card).
report (to) *berichten.*
reporter *Reporter, m.*
represent (to) *vertreten.*
representation *Vertretung, f.*
representative *Vertreter, m.*
repress (to) *unterdrücken.*
represson *Unterdrückung, f..*
reprimand *Verweis, m; Tadel, m.*
reprimand (to) *tadeln.*
reprisal *Vergeltungsmassnahme, f.*
reproach *Vorwurf, m.*
reproach (to) *vorwerfen.*
reproduce (to) *reproduzieren.*
reproduction *Reproduktion, f.;*
    Vervielfältigung, f.
republic *Republik, f.*
repulse *zurücktreiben, zurückschlagen.*
reputation *Ruf, m.; Ansehen, n.*
request *Bitte, f.; Ersuchen, n.*
request (to) *bitten.*
require (to) *benötigen.*
requirement *Bedarf, m.*
rescue (to) *retten.*
research *Forschung, f.*
resent (to) *verübeln.*
resentful *aufgebracht, ärgerlich.*
resentment *Verdruss, m.*
reservation *Reservation, f.*
reserve (to) *reservieren.*
reservoir *Behälter, m.*
residence *Wohnstätte, f.*
resident *Bowohner, m.*
resign (to) *aufgeben, austreten* (Aus.).
resignation *Rücktritt, m.*
resist (to) *widerstehen.*
resistance *Widerstand, m.*
resolute *entschlossen.*
resolution *Beschluss, m.*
resolve (to) *sich entschliessen* (decide);
    lösen; aufklären (problem).
resort *Kurort, m.* (health); *Luftkurort, m.;*
    Erholungsort, m.; Zuflucht, f.
    (recourse); *als letzter Ausweg* (as a
    last resort).
resource *Hilfsmittel, n.*
respect *Achtung, f.*
respectful *ehrfürchtig, achtungsvoll.*
responsibility *Verantwortlichkeit, f.*
responsible *verantwortlich.*
rest *Ruhe, f.*
rest (to) *ruhen; sich ausruhen.*
restaurant *Restaurant, n.*
restless *unruhig.*
restoration *Wiederherstellung, f.*

restore (to) *wiederherstellen,*
    restaurieren.
restrain (to) *zurückhalten.*
restraint *Zurückhaltung, f.*
restrict (to) *beschränken.*
restriction *Einschränkung, f.;*
    Beschränkung, f.
result *Resultat, n.; Ergebnis, n.; Folge, f.*
result (to) *folgen; sich ergeben.*
resume (to) *wiederaufnehmen, wieder*
    anfangen.
retail *Einzelverkauf, m.; Kleinhandel, m.*
retail (to) *im Kleinhandel verkaufen.*
retain (to) *behalten.*
retaliate (to) *vergelten.*
retaliation *Vergeltung, f.*
retire (to) *sich zurückziehen, in den*
    Ruhestand treten.
retirement *Zurückgezogenheit, f.;*
    Pensionierung, f.
retract *widerrufen; zurückziehen.*
retreat *Rückzug, m.*
retreat (to) *sich zurückziehen.*
return *Ruckkehr, f.*
return (to) *zurückkehren.*
reveal (to) *offenbaren, enthüllen.*
revelation *Offenbarung, f.*
revenge *Rache, f.*
revenge (to) *rächen.*
revenue *Einkommen, n.*
reverence *Ehrerbietung, f.*
reverend *ehrwürdig.*
reverse *Rückseite, f.; Kehrseite* (side of a
    coin).
reverse (to) *umkehren.*
review (to) *überprüfen; rezensieren* (critical);
    wiederholen.
review *Überblick, m. Parade, f.* (army);
    Revue, f. (theater), *Rezension, f.*
    (book).
revise (to) *revidieren* (critique);
    überarbeiten.
revive *auffrischen, wieder zu Bewusstsein*
    bringen.
revival *Wiederbelebung, f.*
revoke (to) *widerrufen.*
revolt *Aufstand, m.*
revolt (to) *sich empören.*
revolution *Revolution, f.*
revolve (to) *sich drehen.*
reward *Belohnung, f.*
reward (to) *belohnen.*
rhyme *Reim, m.*
rhyme (to) *reimen.*
rib *Rippe, f.*
ribbon *Band, n.*
rice *Reis, m.*
rich *reich.*
richness *Reichtum, m.*

rid (to get) *loswerden.*
riddle *Rätsel, n.,*
ride *Fahrt, f.*
ridiculous *lächerlich.*
rifle *Gewehr, n.*
right (noun) *Recht, n.*
right *richtig* (correct); *rechts* (position).
    all right   *ganz gut.*
righteous *gerecht.*
rigid *steif, fest, starr.*
rigor *Strenge, f.*
rigorous *streng, scharf, hart.*
ring *Ring, m.*
    wedding ring   *Trauring, m.*
ring (to) *ringen, läuten; schellen* (bell).
rinse (to) *spülen, ausspülen.*
riot (to) *Aufruhr, f.*
ripe *reif.*
ripen (to) *reifen.*
rise *Steigung, f.*
rise (to) *aufstehen* (get up); *steigen*
    (increase, mount), *aufgehen* (sun).
risk *Gefahr, f.*
risk (to) *riskieren, wagen.*
rite *Ritus, m.*
ritual *rituell.*
rival *Rivale, m.; Konkurrent, m.*
rivalry *Mitbewerbung, f., Konkurrenz, f.*
river *Fluss, m.*
roach *Schabe, f.; Schwabe, f.*
road *Weg, m.*
roar (to) *brüllen.*
roast *Braten, m.*
roast (to) *braten.*
rob (to) *rauben.*
robber *Räuber, m.*
robbery *Diebstahl, m.*
robe *Morgenrock, m.*
robot *Roboter, n.*
robust *stark, kräftig.*
rock *Felsen, m.*
rock (to) *wiegen, schaukeln.*
rocky *felsig.*
rocket *Rakete, f.*
rod *Rute, f.; Stab, m.*
roll *Rolle, f.* (cylinder); *Brötchen, n.* (bread);
    Semmel, f. (Aust.).
roll (to) *rollen.*
Roman *Römer* (noun) *m.; römisch* (adj).
romantic *romantisch.*
roof *Dach, n.*
room *Zimmer, n.* (of a house); *Weltraum, m.*
    (space).
    There is no room.   *Da ist kein Platz.*
roomy *geräumig.*
root *Wurzel, f.*
rope *Seil, n.; Strick, m.*
rose *Rose, f.*
rot (to) *faulen; vermodern.*

rough *rauh* (coarse); *roh* (crude); *stürmisch*
    (stormy).
round *Runde* (noun) *f.; rund* (adj.).
round *um* (acc.); *herum.*
round-trip *Rundreise, f.*
rouse (to) *aufwecken; erregun* (to stir up).
routine *Routine, f.*
row *Reihe, f.*
row (to) *rudern.*
royal *königlich.*
rub (to) *reiben.*
rubber *Gummi, m.*
ruby *Rubin, m.*
rude *grob, unhöflich.*
ruffle (to) *ausser Fassung bringen* (to
    upset); *kräuseln.*
ruin *Ruine, f.*
ruin (to) *ruinieren.*
rule *Regel, f.*
rule (to) *regieren, herrschen.*
ruler *Lineal, n.*
rum *Rum, m.*
rumor *Gerücht, n.*
run (to) *rennen, laufen.*
    run away   *weglaufen.*
rural *ländlich.*
rush (to) *Sturz, m.; Andrang, m.* (crowd).
Russian *Russe* (noun) *m.; russisch* (adj.).
rust (to) *rosten.*
rusty *rostig.*
rye *Roggen, m.*

S

sacred *heilig.*
sacrifice *Opfer, n.*
sacrifice (to) *opfern.*
sacrilege *Entweihung, f.*
sad *traurig.*
sadden (to) *betrüben.*
saddle *Sattel, m.*
sadness *Traurigkeit, f.*
safe *Schliessfach* (noun) *m.* (of a bank);
    wohlbehalten (adj.) (in safekeeping);
    sicher (adj.) (secure).
safety *Sicherheit, f.*
sail (to) *segeln.*
sail *Segel, n.*
sailor *Matrose, m.*
saint *Heilige, m. & f.*
    patron saint   *Schutzheilige, m. & f.*
sake (for the ... of) *um ... willen.*
salad *Salat, m.*
salami *Salami, f.*
salary *Gehalt, n.*
sale *Verkauf, m.; Ausverkauf, m.* (bargain).
saleslady *Verkäuferin,f.*
salesman *Verkäufer, m.*

salmon *Lachs, m.*
salt *Salz, n.*
salute *Gruss, m.*
salute (to) *grüssen.*
salvation *Rettung, f.*
Salvation Army *Heilsarmee, f.*
same *der- (die-, das-) selbe*
  the same as   *der-, die-, dasselbe wie.*
  all the same   *es spielt keine Rolle.*
sample *Muster,n.*
sanctuary *Zufluchtsort, m.*
sand *Sand, m.*
sandal *Sandale, f.*
sandwich *belegtes Butterbrot, n.*
sandy *sandig.*
sanitary *hygienisch.*
sap *Saft, m.*
sapphire *Saphir, m.*
sarcasm *Sarkasmus, m.*
sarcastic *sarkastisch.*
sardine *Sardine, f.*
satiate (to) *sättigen.*
satin *Seiden, m.*
satisfaction *Befriedigung, f.*
satisfactory *zufriedenstellend.*
satisfy (to) *befriedigen.*
saturate (to) *durchtränken, imprägnieren,*
  (chem.).
Saturday *Samstag, m.; Sonnabend, m.*
sauce *Sauce, f.; Sosse, f.*
saucer *Untertasse, f.*
sausage *Wurst, f.*
savage (adj.) *wild, ungezähmt.*
save (to) *sparen* (hoard), *retten* (rescue).
saving *Ersparnis, f.*
savior *Erretter, m.*
say (to) *sagen.*
scale *Schuppe, f.; Tonleiter, f.* (music).
scales *Waage, f.*
scalp *Skalp, m.; Kopfhaut, f.*
scan (to) *flüchtig überblicken.*
scandal *Skandal, m.*
scanty *knapp, dürftig.*
scar *Narbe, f.*
scarce *knapp.*
scarcely *kaum.*
scare (to) *erschrecken.*
scarf *Schal, m.*
scarlet *scharlachrot.*
scattered *verstreut.*
schedule *Stundenplan, m.* (time)*; Fahrplan*
  (train, bus).
scheme *Schema, n.; Entwurf, m.*
scholar *Gelehrte, m. & f.*
school *Schule, f.*
schoolteacher *Lehrer, m.; Lehrerin, f.*
science *Wissenschaft, f.*
scientific *wissenschaftlich.*
scientist *Wissenschafter, m.*

scissors *Schere, f.*
scold (to) *schelten.*
scorn *Verachtung, f.*
scorn (to) *verachten.*
scornful *verächtlich, höhnisch.*
Scottish *schottisch.*
scrape (to) *kratzen; schaben* (vegetables).
scraper *Schaber, m.*
scratch *Schramme, f.; Kratzwunde,f.*
scratch (to) *kratzen.*
scream *Schrei, m.*
scream (to) *schreien.*
screen *Schirm, m.*
  movie screen   *Leinwand, f.*
screw *Schraube, f.*
scribble (to) *kritzeln.*
scruple *Skrupel, m.*
scrupulous *gewissenhaft.*
scrutinize (to) *genau prüfen.*
scuba diving *(Sport)tauchen, n.*
sculptor *Bildhauer, m.*
sculpture *Bildhauerei, f.*
sea *Meer, n.*
seal *Siegel, n.; Seehund, m.* (animal).
seal (to) *siegeln.*
seam *Naht, f.*
search *Suche, f.; Untersuchung, f.* (customs).
search (to) *suchen, untersuchen.*
seashore *Seeküste, f.*
seasickness *Seekrankheit, f.*
season *Jahreszeit, f.; Saison, f.* (events).
seat *Sitz, m.*
seat (to) *setzen; Platz verschaffen.*
seat belt *Sicherheitsgurt, m.*
second *zweit(er, -e, -es).*
secret *Geheimnis* (noun) *n.; geheim,* (adj.).
secretary *Sekretär, m.; Sekretärin, f.*
sect *Sekte, f.*
section *Teil, m.*
secure *sicher.*
secure (to) *sichern.*
security *Sicherheit, f.*
see (to) *sehen.*
seed *Samen, m.*
seek (to) *suchen.*
seem (to) *scheinen.*
seize (to) *ergreifen, fassen.*
seldom *selten, rar.*
select (to) *(aus)wählen.*
selection *Auswahl, f.*
selfish *selbstsüchtig; egoistisch.*
selfishness *Selbstsucht, f.*
self-service *Selbstbedienung.*
sell (to) *verkaufen.*
semicolon *Semikolon, n.*
senate *Senat, m.*
senator *Senator, m.*
send (to) *senden.*
senior *Ältere(r).*

sensation *Gefühl, n.* (feeling); *Sensation, f.* (excitement); *Sinnesempfindung, f.*
sense *Sinn, m.*
senseless *sinnlos.*
sensibility *Vernünftigkeit, f.*
sensible *vernünftig.*
sensitive *empfindlich.*
sensitivity *Empfindlichkeit, f.*
sensual *sinnlich.*
sensuality *Wollust, f., Sinnlichkeit, f.*
sentence *Urteil, n.* (legal); *Satz, m.* (grammar).
sentiment *Gefühl, n.*
sentimental *sentimental.*
sentimality *Sentimentalität, f.*
separate *einzeln, getrennt.*
separate (to) *trennen.*
separately *besonders, getrennt.*
separation *Trennung, f.*
September *September, m.*
serene *heiter, friedlich.*
sergeant *Sergeant, m.; Unteroffizier, m.*
series *Serie, f.*
serious *ernst.*
seriousness *Ernsthaftigkeit, f.*
servant *Diener, m.*
serve (to) *dienen.*
service *Dienst, m.; Gottesdienst, m.* (church service).
session *Sitzung, f.*
set (adj.) *festgelegt.*
set *Sammlung, f.* (collection); *Untergang, m.;* (sun); *Satz, m.* (series); *Service, n.* (dishes).
set (to) *setzen; stellen* (clock).
  to set the table *decken.*
settle (to) *abrechnen* (accounts); *erledigen* (conclude); *festsetzen.*
  . . . in a territory *sich niederlassen.*
  . . . in a place *ansässig werden.*
settlement *Begleichung, f.; Erledigung, f.; Siedlung, f.* (houses).
seven *sieben.*
seventeen *siebzehn.*
seventeenth *siebzehnte.*
seventh *siebte.*
seventieth *siebzigste.*
seventy *siebzig.*
several *mehrere.*
  several times *mehrmals.*
severe *streng* (stern, rigorous); *heftig* (pain).
severity *Strenge, f.*
sew (to) *nähen.*
sewage *Kloakenwasser, n.*
sewer *Abwasserkanal, m.*
sex *Geschlecht, n.*
shabby *schäbig.*
shade *Schatten, m.*
shadow *Schatten, m.*

shady *schattig.*
shake (to) *schütteln; zittern* (tremble).
  handshake *Händedruck, m.*
shallow *seicht, oberflächlich* (fig.).
shame *Schande, f.* (disgrace); *Scham, f.* (modesty).
shameful *schändlich.*
shameless *schamlos.*
shampoo *Shampoo, n.; Haarwaschmittel, m.*
shape *Form, f.*
share *Teil, m.; Anteil, m. Aktie, f.* (stock).
share (to) *teilen, (sich) beteiligen.*
shareholder *Aktionär, m.*
sharp *scharf.*
sharpen *schärfen.*
shave (to) *sich rasieren.*
she *sie.*
shed *Hütte, f.*
shed (to) *vergiessen* (spill); *abwerfen* (discard).
sheep *Schaf, n.*
sheer *rein, lauter.*
sheet *(Bett)laken, n.; Blatt, n.* (paper).
shelf *Brett, n.*
shell *Muschel, f.; Geschoss, n.* (artillery).
shelter *Unterkunft, f.; Luftschutzraum, m.* (air raids).
shelter *unterstellen* (from exposure); *schützen* (from danger); *beherbergen.*
shepherd *Schäfer, m.*
shield *Schild, n.*
shield (to) *schützen.*
shift *Schicht, f.* (workers).
shift (to) *schieben, versetzen, umstellen.*
shine (to) *scheinen; putzen* (shoes).
ship *Schiff, n.*
ship (to) *senden, verschiffen, verfrachten.*
shipment *Verladung, f.; Verschiffung, f.; Beförderung, f.* (conveyance of goods).
shirt *Hemd, n.*
shiver *Schauer, m., Zittern, n.*
shiver (to) *(er)schauern.*
shock *Schlag, m.* (blow); *Stoss, m.*
shock (to) *anstossen* (scandalize); *erschüttern, schockieren.*
shoe *Schuh, m.*
shoemaker *Schuhmacher, m.*
shoot (to) *schiessen.*
shop *Laden, m.; Geschäft, n.*
shopping center *Einkaufszentrum, n.*
short *kurz.*
shorten (to) *kürzen.*
shorthand *Kurzschrift, f.; Stenographie, f.*
shorts *Unterhosen, pl.* (men's underwear); *kurze Hosen* (short pants).
shot *Schuss, m.*
shoulder *Schulter, f.*
shout *Schrei, m.*

shout (to) *schreien.*
shovel *Schaufel, f.*
show *Vorstellung, f.* (play); *Ausstellung, f.* (exhibition).
show (to) *zeigen, aufführen, ausstellen.*
showcase *Vitrine, f.; Schaukasten, m.*
shower *Schauer, m.* (rain); *Dusche, f.* (shower-bath).
shrill *schrill, gellend.*
shrimp *Garnele, f.*
shrink (to) *einlaufen.*
shrub *Strauch, m.; Busch, m.*
shrubbery *Gebüsch, n.*
shun (to) *meiden, sich fern halten (von).*
shut *geschlossen.*
shut (to) *schliessen.*
shy *schüchtern.*
sick *krank.*
sickness *Krankheit, f.*
side *Seite, f.*
sidewalk *Bürgersteig, m.*
siege *Belagerung, f.*
sigh *Seufzer, m.*
sight *Aussicht, f.; Anblick, m.*
sign (to) *seufzen, unterschreiben, unterzeichnen.*
sign *Zeichen, n.*
signal *Signal, n.*
signal (to) *signalisieren.*
signature *Unterschrift, f.*
significance *Bedeutung, f.*
significant *bezeichnend.*
signify (to) *bezeichnen* (indicate); *bedeuten* (mean).
silence *Schweigen, n.*
silent *still, schweigend, schweigsam.*
silk *Seide, f.*
silken *seiden.*
silly *dumm, albern, lächerlich.*
silver *Silber, n.*
silvery *silbern.*
similar *ähnlich.*
similarity *Ähnlichkeit, f.*
simple *einfach.*
simplicity *Einfachheit, f.*
simply *einfach, nur* (only).
simulate (to) *simulieren, vortäuschen.*
simultaneous *gleichzeitig.*
sin *Sünde, f.*
sin (to) *sündigen.*
since *seit* (dat.); *da, weil* (because).
sincere *aufrichtig, im Ernst.*
sincerity *Aufrichtigkeit, f.*
sing (to) *singen.*
singer *Sänger, m.; Sängerin, f.*
single *einzeln; ledig* (unmarried).
singular *einzigartig; seltsam* (strange).
sinister *unheilvoll, böse.*
sink *Gussstein, m.; Ausguss, m.*

sink (to) *sinken.*
sinner *Sünder, m.; Sünderin, f.*
sip (to) *nippen.*
sip *Schluck, m.; Schlückchen, n.*
sir *Herr, m.*
sister *Schwester, f.*
sister-in-law *Schwägerin, f.*
sit (to) *sitzen* (be seated); *sich setzen* (sit down).
   to sit for an exam   *sich einer Prüfung unterziehen.*
   to sit for a portrait   *sich malen lassen.*
site *Lage, f.; Bauplatz, m.* (of a building); *Stelle, f.*
situation *Lage, f.; Umstände, pl.*
six *sechs.*
sixteen *sechzehne.*
sixteenth *sechzehnte.*
sixth *sechste.*
sixtieth *sechzigste.*
sixty *sechzig.*
size *Grösse, f.*
skate *Schlittschuh, m.*
skate (to) *Schlittschuh laufen.*
skeleton *Gerippe, n.; Skelett, n.*
sketch *Skizze, f.*
sketch (to) *skizzieren.*
skill *Geschicklichkeit, f.*
skillful *geschickt, kundig.*
skin *Haut, f.*
skirt *Rock, m.*
skull *Schädel, m.*
sky *Himmel, m.*
skyscraper *Wolkenkratzer, m.*
slam (to) *zuschlagen.*
slander (to) *verleumden.*
slap *Klaps, m.; Ohrfeige, f.* (in the face).
slate *Schiefer, m.; Dachschiefer.*
slaughter (to) *schlachten.*
slave *Sklave, m.; Sklavin, f.*
slavery *Sklaverei, f.*
sleep *Schlaf, m.*
sleep (to) *schlafen.*
sleeve *Ärmel, m.*
sleigh *Schlitten, m.*
slender *schlank.*
slice *Schnitte, f.; Scheibe* (bread).
slice (to) *in Scheiben schneiden.*
slide (to) *gleiten, rutschen.*
slight *gering, leichte Erkältung.*
slip (to) *(aus)rutschen, gleiten.*
   to slip on   *anziehen* (clothes).
   to slip away   *entschlüpfen.*
   to slip in   *hineinschieben in.*
   to slip up   *sich irren, im Irrtum sein.*
slip *Fehler, m.* (mistake); *Unterrock, m.* (lingerie).
slope *Abhang, m.*
slot *Einwurf, m. Schlitz, m.* (mail).

slow *langsam.*
slumber *Schlummer, m.*
slumber (to) *schlummern.*
sly *schlau.*
small *klein.*
smart *elegant* (clothes); *gescheit* (clever).
smash (to) *zerschmettern.*
smear (to) *beschmieren, einreiben.*
smell *Geruch, m.*
smell (to) *riechen.*
smile *Lächeln, n.*
smile (to) *lächeln.*
smoke *Rauch, m.*
smoke (to) *rauchen.*
smooth *glatt.*
smother (to) *ersticken.*
smuggle (to) *schmuggeln.*
snail *Schnecke, f.*
snake *Schlange, f.*
snapshot *Aufnahme, f.*
snatch (to) *ergreifen.*
sneer (to) *verhöhnen.*
sneeze (to) *niessen.*
snore (to) *schnarchen.*
snow *Schnee, m.*
snowstorm *Schneesturm, m.*
so *so.*
   and so on   *und so weiter.*
soak (to) *einweichen, durchnässen* (drench).
soap *Seife, f.*
sob *Schluchzen, n.*
sob (to) *schluchzen.*
sober *nüchtern.*
social *gesellschaftlich.*
society *Gesellschaft, f.*
sock *Sock, f.; kurzer Strumpf, m.*
soda *Sodawasser, n.; Sprudel, n.*
soft *weich.*
soften (to) *erweichen, aufweichen.*
software *Software f.*
soil (to) *beschmutzen.*
soil *Erde, f.; Boden, m.*
soiled *schmutzig, beschmutzt.*
solar energy *Sonnenenergie, f., Solarenergie, f.*
soldier *Soldat, m.*
sole *Sohle, f.*
solemn *feierlich.*
solemnity *Feierlichkeit, f.*
solicit (to) *bitten, ersuchen.*
solid *fest, solide.*
solitary *einsam* (lonely); *einzeln* (one).
solitude *Einsamkeit, f.*
solution *Lösung, f.*
solve *lösen.*
some *einige* (a few); *etwas* (partial).
somebody *jemand.*
somehow *irgendwie.*
something *etwas.*

sometimes *zuweilen, manchmal.*
somewhat *etwas, einigermassen.*
somewhere *irgendwo.*
son *Sohn, m.*
song *Lied, n.*
son-in-law *Schwiegersohn, m.*
soon *bald.*
soot *Russ, m.*
soothe (to) *besänftigen; lindern* (pain).
sore *Geschwür* (noun) *n.; wund, schmerzhaft* (adj.); *empfindlich, verärgert* (annoyed).
   sore throat   *Halsschmerzen, pl.*
sorrow *Kummer, m.*
sorry *bekümmert.*
   I am sorry.   *Es tut mir leid.*
sort *Sorte, f.; Art, f.*
sort (to) *sortieren, einordnen.*
sound *Laut, m.; Geräusch, n.*
sound (to) *lauten, läuten* (telephone).
soup *Suppe, f.*
sour *sauer.*
source *Quelle, f.* (spring); *Ursprung, m.* (origin).
south *Süden, m.*
southeast *südöstlich* (adj.); *Südosten, m.*
southern *Süd-; südlich.*
southwest *südwestlich; Südwesten, m.*
sovereign *Herrscher, m.; Herrscherin, f.; Soverän, m.*
sow (to) *säen.*
space *Raum, m.; Zwischenraum, m.* (space between).
spacious *(ge)räumig.*
spade *Spaten, m.; Pik, n.* (cards).
Spanish *spanisch.*
spare *spärlich.*
spare (to) *entbehren, schonen.*
spark *Funke, m.*
sparkle (to) *funkeln, glänzen.*
sparrow *Sperling, Spatz, m.*
speak (to) *sprechen.*
special *besonders, extra.*
specialty *Spezialität, f.*
specific *eigen, spezifisch, genau.*
specify (to) *spezifizieren, anführen.*
spectacle *Schauspiel, n.; Schaustück, n.*
spectator *Zuschauer, m.*
speculate (to) *spekulieren.*
speech *Sprache, f.; Rede, f.*
speed *Geschwindigkeit, f.*
speedy *schnell, geschwind.*
spell *Zauber, m.* (charm).
spell (to) *buchstabieren, schreiben.*
spelling *Buchstabieren, n.*
spend (to) *ausgeben.*
sphere *Sphäre, f.*
spice *Gewürz, n.*
spice (to) *würzen.*

spicy *würzig.*
spider *Spinne, f.*
spill (to) *verschütten, vergiessen.*
spin (to) *spinnen.*
spine *Rückgrat, n.; Wirbelsäude, f.*
spirit *Geist, m.*
spiritual *geistig.*
spit (to) *spucken.*
spite *Bösartigkeit, f.*
 in spite of *trotz* (gen.), *trotzdem* (gen. or
  dat.).
splash (to) *(be)spritzen.*
splendid *prachtvoll.*
 Splendid! *Wunderbar!*
splendor *Pracht, f.; Glanz, m.*
split *Spalt, m.; Trennung, f.; Spaltung, f.*
split (to) *spalten.*
spoil (to) *verderben; verwöhnen* (child).
sponge *Schwamm, m.*
spontaneous *spontan.*
spoon *Löffel, m.*
spoonful *Löffelvoll, m.*
sport *Sport, m.*
spot *Fleck, m.* (stain); *Stelle, f.* (place).
spread (to) *verbreiten; bestreichen* (on
 bread).
spring *Frühling, m.* (season); *Sprung, m.*
 (jump); *Quelle, f.* (source).
spring (to) *springen.*
sprinkle *sprenkeln, bestreuen, sprengen.*
sprout *Sprössling, m.; Spross, m.*
spur *Sporn, m.*
spur (to) *anspornen.*
 on the spur of the moment *spontan.*
spurn (to) *verschmähen* (an offer);
 zurückstossen (a person).
spy *Spion, m.*
spy (to) *spionieren.*
squadron *Schwadron, f.; Eskadron, f.* (mil.);
 Batallion (tanks).
square *Quadrat, n.*
squeeze (to) *(aus)drücken.*
squirrel *Eichhörnchen, n.*
stabilize (to) *stabilisieren.*
stable *fest* (adj.); *stabil.*
stack *Stoss, m.* (wood).
stack (to) *aufstapeln, aufhäufen.*
stadium *Stadion, n.*
staff *Stab* (military), *m.; Personal, n.*
 (business).
stage *Bühne, f.* (theater); *Stadium, n.*
stain *Fleck, m.; Färbemittel* (dye), *n.*
stain (to) *(be)flecken, färben.*
stairs *Treppe, f.*
stammer (to) *stottern.*
stamp *Briefmarke, f.* (postage); *Stempel, m.*
stance *Haltung, f.; Stellung, f.*
stand *Stand, m.*
 Stand still *Stillstehen.*

 to stand pain *den Schmerz aushalten.*
 to stand on ceremony *Umstände machen.*
 to stand back *zurücktreten.*
star *Stern, m.*
starch *Stärke, f.*
stare (to) *(an)starren.*
start *Anfang, m.*
start (to) *beginnen, anfangen.*
starve (to) *(ver)hungern.*
state *Staat, m.* (country); *Zustand, m.*
 (condition).
state (to) *angeben, vorbringen, erklären.*
stately *stattlich.*
statement *Erklärung, f.; Aufstellung, f.*
 (account).
stateroom *Kabine, f.; Prunksaal, m.*
station *Bahnhof, m.* (railroad); *Stellung, f.*
 (position).
statistics *Statistik, f.*
statue *Statue, f.*
stay *Aufenthalt, m.*
stay (to) *bleiben.*
steady *fest.*
steak *Beefsteak, n.*
steal (to) *stehlen.*
steam *Dampf, m.*
steamer *Dampfer, m.*
steel *Stahl, m.*
steep *steil.*
steer (to) *steuern.*
stem *Stengel, m.* (plant).
stenographer *Stenotypistin, f.*
stenography *Kurzschrift, f.;*
 Stenographie, f.
step *Schritt, m.; Stufe, f.* (stairs).
step (to) *schreiten.*
sterilized *sterilisiert.*
stern *ernst.*
stew *Ragout, n.; Eintopfgericht, n.*
stew (to) *schmoren, dünsten.*
steward *Steward, m.*
stick *Stock, m.*
stick (to) *stecken; ankleben* (paste).
stiff *steif.*
stiffen (to) *(ver)steifen; verstärken.*
stiffness *Steifheit, f.*
still *still, ruhig* (adj.); *jedoch, noch* (adv.).
still (to) *stillen, beruhigen.*
stimulant *Anregungsmittel, n.*
stimulate (to) *anregen.*
sting *Stich, m.*
sting (to) *stechen.*
stinginess *Geiz, m.*
stingy *geizig.*
stir (to) *rühren, bewegen.*
stirrup *Steigbügel, m.*
stitch *Stich, m.* (surgery); *Masche, f.* (sew).
stitch (to) *heften; nähen,* (sew).
stock *Warenbestand, m.; Vorrat, m.*

stocks and shares *Aktien und Wertpapiere (pl.).*
stock exchange *Borse, f.*
stocking *Strumpf, m.*
stomach *Magen, m.*
stone *Stein, m.*
stool *Schemel, m.*
stop *Haltestelle, f.*
stop (to) *halten, aufhören, haltmachen.*
 Stop! *Halt!*
store *Laden, m.; Warenhaus, n.; Geschäft, n.*
store (to) *lagern, aufbewahren; speichern (on computer disk).*
stork *Storch, m.*
storm *Sturm, m.*
story *Geschichte, f.; Erzählung, f.; Stockwerk, n.*
stove *Ofen, m.*
straight *gerade.*
 straight on *geradeaus.*
straighten *gerade machen, aufrichten.*
strain *Anstrengung, f.*
strange *seltsam, sonderbar.*
stranger *Ausländer, m.; Fremde, m.*
strap *Riemen, m.*
straw *Stroh, n.; Strohhalm, m.* (for drinking).
strawberry *Erdbeere, f.*
stream *Strom, m.*
street *Strasse, f.*
streetcar *Strassenbahn, f.*
strength *Kraft, f.*
strengthen *verstärken; kräftigen.*
strenuous *angestrengt.*
stress *Druck, m.; Betonung, f.* (accentuation).
stretch *Strecke, f.*
stretch (to) *strecken.*
strict *streng.*
stride *Schritt, m.*
string *Bindfaden, m.; Schnur* (cord)*, f.*
 no strings attached *ohne Bedingungen.*
strip (to) *abstreifen, abziehen; entkleiden (of clothes).*
stripe *Streifen, m.*
strive (to) *streben.*
stroke *Strich, m.* (of a brush, pen)*; Schlaganfall, m.* (med.).
stroll *Spaziergang, m.*
stroll (to) *spazierengehen.*
strong *stark.*
structure *Bau, m.*
struggle *Kampf, m.*
struggle (to) *kämpfen.*
stubborn *hartnäckig.*
student *Schüler, m.; Schülerin, f.; Student, m.; Studentin, f.* (college, univ.).
studio *Studio, n. Atelier, n.* (artist).
studious *lernbegierig, fleissig, arbeitsam.*
study *Studium, n.*
study (to) *studieren.*

stuff *Stoff, m.; Material, n.*
stuff (to) *stopfen, verstopfen.*
stumble (to) *stolpern.*
stump *Stumpf, m.*
stun (to) *betäuben.*
stunt *Sensation, f.; Kunststück, n.*
stupendous *fantastisch.*
stupid *dumm.*
stupidity *Dummheit, f.*
stupor *Betäubung, f.*
sturdy *kräftig.*
stutter (to) *stottern.*
style *Stil, m.*
subdue (to) *unterwerfen.*
subject *Angelegenheit, f.;* (matter)*; Fach, n.* (school); *Fachgebiet, n.*
subjugate (to) *unterwerfen.*
subjunctive *Konjunktiv, m.*
sublime *erhaben.*
submission *Unterwerfung, f.*
submissive *unterwürfig.*
submit (to) *unterwerfen.*
subordinate *untergeordnet.*
subordination *Unterordnung, f.*
subscribe (to) *abonnieren.*
subscription *Abonnement, n.*
subsist (to) *bestehen, sich ernähren von, weiterbestehen.*
substance *Substanz, f.*
substantial *beträchtlich, wesentlich.*
substitute (to) *ersetzen.*
substitution *Ersatz, m.*
subtle *fein, raffiniert.*
subtract *abziehen.*
subtraction *Substraktion, f.*
suburb *Vorstadt, f.*
subway *Untergrundbahn, f.*
succeed (to) *gelingen* (achieve).
success *Erfolg, m.*
successful *erfolgreich.*
succession *Nachfolge, f.*
successor *Nachfolger, m.*
such *Solch-.*
 Such a scandal! *Solch ein Skandal!*
sudden *plötzlich.*
sue (to) *verklagen.*
suffer (to) *leiden.*
suffering *Leiden, n.*
sufficient *genügend.*
sugar *Zucker, m.*
suggest (to) *andeuten, vorschlagen.*
suggestion *Vorschlag, m.*
suicide *Selbstmord, m.*
suit *Anzug, m.; Kostüm, n.* (lady's).
suitable *passend.*
sulk (to) *schmollen, trotzen.*
sullen *mürrisch, düster.*
sum *Summe, f.*
summary *Zusammenfassung, f.*

summer *Sommer, m.*
summit *Gipfel, m.*
summon (to) *vorladen, einberufen.*
sumptuous *prächtig, kostbar.*
sum up *zusammenfassen.*
sun *Sonne, f.*
sunbeam *Sonnenstrahl, m.*
Sunday *Sonntag, m.*
sunny *sonnig.*
sunrise *Sonnenaufgang, m.*
sunset *Sonnenuntergang, m.*
sunshine *Sonnenschein, m.*
superb *herrlich, vorzüglich.*
superficial *oberflächlich.*
superfluous *überflüssig.*
superintendent *Inspektor, m.; Direktor, m.;*
  Verwalter, m.
superior *Vorgesetzte, m. & f.*
superiority *Überlegenheit, f.*
superstition *Aberglaube, m.*
supervise (to) *beaufsichtigen.*
supper *Abendessen, n.*
supplement *Nachtrag, m.; Anhang, m.;*
  Beilage, f. (of a newspaper).
supplementary *ergänzend.*
supply (to) *versorgen, beschaffen.*
support *Stütze, f.; Unterstützung, f.*
support (to) *(unter)stützen.*
suppose (to) *vermuten, annehmen.*
suppress (to) *unterdrücken.*
supreme *höchst, oberst.*
sure *gewiss, sicher.*
surety *Sicherheit, f.*
surface *Oberfläche, f.*
surgeon *Chirurg, m.*
surgery *Chirurgie, f.*
surname *Zuname, m.; Nachname, m.*
surpass *übertreffen.*
surprise *Überraschung, f.*
surprise (to) *überraschen.*
surrender *Übergabe, f.; Kapitulation, f.*
surrender (to) *aufgeben, übergeben.*
surroundings *Umgebung, f.*
survey *Übersicht, f.; Vermessung, f.*
survey (to) *besichtigen, vermessen.*
survive (to) *überleben.*
susceptibility *Empfänglichkeit, f.*
susceptible *empfänglich, empfindlich.*
suspect (to) *verdächtigen.*
suspense *Ungewissheit, f.; Spannung, f.*
suspicion *Verdacht, m.*
suspicious *verdächtig.*
sustain (to) *ernähren.*
swallow *Schluck, m.* (gulp); *Schwalbe, f.*
  (bird).
swallow (to) *verschlucken.*
swamp *Sumpf, m.*
swan *Schwan, m.*
swear (to) *schwören.*

sweat *Schweiss, m.*
sweat (to) *schwitzen.*
sweep (to) *kehren; fegen.*
sweet *süss.*
sweetness *Süsse, f.*
swell (to) *(an)schwellen.*
swift *schnell, rasch.*
swim (to) *schwimmen.*
swindle (to) *schwindeln.*
swindler *Schwindler, m.*
swing (to) *schwingen, schaukeln.*
Swiss *Schweizer* (noun) *m.; schweizerisch*
  (adj.).
switch *Schalter, m.*
sword *Schwert, n.*
syllable *Silbe, f.*
symbol *Symbol, n.*
symbolic *symbolisch.*
symbolize *symbolisieren.*
symmetrical *symmetrisch.*
sympathetic *mitfühlend.*
sympathize (to) *mitfühlen.*
sympathy *Sympathie, f.; Verständnis, n.*
symptom *Symptom, n.*
syrup *Sirup, m.*
system *System, n.*
systematic *systematisch, methodisch,*
  planmässig.

T

table *Tisch, m.*
tablecloth *Tischtuch, n.*
tacit *stillschweigend.*
taciturn *schweigsam.*
tact *Takt, m.*
tactful *taktvoll.*
tactless *taktlos.*
tail *Schwanz, m.*
tailor *Schneider, m.*
take (to) *nehmen.*
  to take an exam   *eine Prüfung ablegen.*
  to take heart   *Mut fassen.*
  to take a vacation   *Ferien machen; Urlaub*
    nehmen.
  to take time   *dauern.*
  to take an oath   *einen Eid ablegen.*
  to take part   *teilnehmen (an).*
  to take place   *stattfinden.*
  to take pleasure in   *Vergnügen finden an.*
  to take one's temperature   *Fieber messen.*
  to take a walk   *einen Spaziergang*
    machen.
  to take over   *übernehmen.*
tale *Erzählung, f.*
talent *Talent, n.; Begabung, f.*
talk *Rede, f.; Vortrag, m.*
talk (to) *reden, plaudern, sprechen.*

talkative *gesprächig.*
tall *hoch; gross* (people).
tame *zahm.*
tame (to) *zähmen.*
tangle (to) *verwickeln.*
tank *Tank, m.*
tapestry *Wandteppich, m.*
tar *Teer, m.*
tardy *spät.*
target *(Ziel)scheibe, f.*
tarnish (to) *trüben, anlaufen* (metal).
task *Aufgabe, f.*
taste *Geschmack, m.*
taste (to) *schmecken.*
tax *Steuer, f.*
taxi *Taxi, n.*
tea *Tee, m.*
teach (to) *unterrichten.*
teacher *Lehrer, m.; Lehrerin, f.*
team *Gruppe, f.; Mannschaft, f.* (sports).
tear *Träne, f.* (teardrop); *Riss, m.* (rip).
tear (to) *(zer)reissen.*
tease (to) *necken, ärgern.*
teaspoon *Teelöffel, m.*
technical *technisch.*
technique *Technik, f.*
technology *Technik, f.*
tedious *langweilig, ermüdend.*
telecommunications *Fernmeldewesen, n.*
telefax *Telefax, n.*
telegram *Telegramm, n.*
telegraph (to) *telegrafieren.*
telephone *Telefon, n.*
    telephone operator   *Telefonistin, f.*
telephone (to) *telefonieren, anrufen.*
tell (to) *sagen, erzählen.*
temper *Laune, f.*
temperate *gemässig, mässig.*
temperature *Temperatur, f.*
tempest *Sturm, m.; Gewitter, n.*
temple *Tempel, m.; Schläfe, f.* (head).
temporary *vorübergehend, vorläufig.*
tempt (to) *versuchen, verlocken.*
temptation *Versuchung, f.*
ten *zehn.*
tenacious *zäh, hartnäckig.*
tenacity *Zähigkeit, f.; Hartnäckigkeit, f.*
tenant *Mieter, m.*
tend (to) *sich neigen zu.*
tendency *Neigung, f.*
tender *zart, empfindlich.*
tennis *Tennis, n.*
tense *gespannt.*
tense *Zeitform, f.* (grammar).
tension *Spannung, f.*
tent *Zelt, n.*
tenth *Zehntel* (noun) *n.* (fraction); *zehnt-*
    (adj.).
tepid *lauwarm.*

term *Ausdruck* (expression), *m.; First*
    (time), *f.*
  to be on good terms   *auf gutem Fusse*
    stehen.
  not to be on speaking terms   *nicht*
    miteinander sprechen.
terrace *Terrasse, f.*
terrible *schrecklich.*
terrify (to) *(er)schrecken.*
territory *Gebiet, n.*
terror *Schrecken, m.*
test *Prüfung, f.*
test (to) *prüfen.*
testify (to) *bezeugen.*
testimony *Zeugnis, n.*
text *Text, m.*
textbook *Lehrbuch, n.*
than *als.*
thank (to) *danken.*
    Thank you! *Danke schön!*
thankful *dankbar.*
that *das* (demonstrative)*; der, die, das, welch*
    (*er, -e, -es*) (relative)*; dass, damit*
    (conjunction).
thaw *Tauwetter, n.*
thaw (to) *tauen.*
the *der, die, das.* (nom.).
theater *Theater, n.*
their *ihr.*
theirs *ihr(er, -e, -es).*
them *sie* (acc.)*; ihnen* (dat.).
theme *Thema, n.*
themselves *sie (ihnen) selbst, sich.*
then *dann, damals.*
theory *Theorie, f.*
there *dort, da.*
    there is, there are   *es gibt.*
thereafter *danach.*
thereby *dadurch.*
therefore *deshalb, daher.*
thereupon *darauf.*
thermometer *Thermometer, n.*
these *diese.*
thesis *These, f., Doktorarbeit* (university).
they *sie.*
thick *dick.*
thief *Dieb, m.*
thigh *Schenkel, m.*
thimble *Fingerhut, m.*
thin *dünn.*
thing *Sache, f.; Ding, n.*
think (to) *denken.*
third *dritte.*
Third World *Dritte-Welt, f.*
thirst *Durst, m.*
thirteen *dreizehn.*
thirteenth *dreizehnte.*
thirtieth *dreissigste.*
thirty *dreissig.*

this *dieser (-e, -es)*.

thorn *Dorn, m.*

thorough *gründlich*.

though *zwar, obwohl, obgleich*.

thought *Gedanke, m.*

thoughtful *nachdenklich*.

thoughtless *rücksichtslos*.

thousand *tausend*.

thrash (to) *dreschen*.

thread *Faden, m.*

threat *Drohung, f.*

threaten (to) *drohen*.

three *drei*.

threshold *Schwelle, f.*

thrift *Sparsamkeit, f.*

thrifty *sparsam*.

thrill *spannendes Erregnis, m.*

thrill (to) *begeistern, packen*.

thrilling *ergreifend, begeisternd*.

thrive (to) *gedeihen*.

thriving *gedeihend, blühend*.

throat *Kehle, f.; Hals, m.*

throb (to) *klopfen*.

throne *Tron, m.*

throng *Menge, f.*

through *durch* (acc.); *hindurch*.

throughout *durchaus*.

throw (to) *werfen*.

thumb *Daumen, m.*

thunder *Donner, m.*

thunder (to) *donnern*.

Thursday *Donnerstag, m.*

thus *so, auf diese Weise*.

thwart (to) *vereiteln*.

ticket *Karte, f.; Fahrkarte, f.* (train).

ticket window *Schalter, m.*

tickle (to) *kitzeln*.

ticklish *kitzlig*.

tide *Flut, f.* (high); *Ebbe, f.* (low).

tidiness *Ordentlichkeit, f.*

tidy *ordentlich*.

tie *Band, n.* (bond); *Krawatte, f.* (necktie).

tie (to) *binden*.

tiger *Tiger, m.*

tight *eng*.

tile *Ziegel, m.* (roof); *Kachel, f.* (wall); *Fliese, f.* (kitchen).

till *bis*.

till now   *bisher, bis jetzt*.

tilt (to) *kippen*.

timber *Bauholz, n.*

time *Zeit, f.*

in the nick of time   *zur rechten Zeit*.

time of arrival   *Ankunftszeit, f.*

time of departure   *Abfahrtszeit, f.*

at the present time   *gegenwärtig*.

time is up   *Die Zeit ist abgelaufen*.

Once upon a time . . .   *Einmal; Vor Zeiten . . .*

to waste time   (*die*) *Zeit verschwenden* (*vertreiben*).

for the last time   *zum letzten Mal*.

behind the times   *rückständig*.

from time to time   *von Zeit zu Zeit*.

on time   *pünktlich*.

to have a good time   *sich vergnügen, sich amüsieren*.

what time is it?   *Wie spät ist es?*

timid *furchtsam, ängstlich*.

timidity *Furchtsamkeit, f.*

tin *Zinn, n.*

tiny *winzig*.

tip *Spitze, f.* (end); *Trinkgeld, n.* (money).

tip (to) *Trinkgeld geben*.

tire *Reifen, m.*

tire (to) *ermüden*.

tired *müde*.

tireless *unermüdlich*.

tiresome *langweilig, ermüdend*.

title *Titel, m.*

to *zu* (with infinitive); *nach, zu* (dat.); *an* (dat. or acc.).

toad *Kröte, f.*

toast *Toast, m.*

tobacco *Tabak, m.*

today *heute*.

toe *Zehe, f.*

together *zusammen*.

toil (to) *schwer arbeiten*.

toilet *Toilette, f.*

token *Andenken, n.; Münze, f.* (coin).

tolerable *erträglich*.

tolerance *Toleranz, f.; Duldung, f.*

tolerant *duldsam, tolerant, geduldig* (patient).

tolerate (to) *dulden*.

toll (to) *läuten, schlagen* (hours).

tomato *Tomate, f.*

tomb *Grab, n.*

tomorrow *morgen*.

ton *Tonne, f.*

tone *Ton, m.*

tongs *Zange, f.*

tongue *Zunge, f.*

tonight *heute abend*.

too *auch* (also); *zu* (excessive).

tool *Werkzeug, n.*

tooth *Zahn, m.*

toothbrush *Zahnbürste, f.*

toothpaste *Zahnpasta, f.*

toothpick *Zahnstocher, m.*

toothpowder *Zahnpulver, n.*

top *Gipfel, m.; Oberst, n.; Spitze, f.*

topic *Gesprächsstoff, m.; Thema, n.*

torch *Fackel, f.*

torment *Qual, f.*

torment (to) *quälen*.

torture *Folter, f.*

torture (to) *foltern*
toss (to) *werfen.*
toss *Wurf, m.*
total *Gesamtsumme, f.; gesarnt* (adj.)*; völlig* (adj.).
totally *gänzlich.*
touch (to) *berühren.*
touching *rührend.*
touchy *überempfindlich.*
tough *hart, zäh.*
tour *Rise, f.; Rundreise, f., Tour, f.*
tour (to) *herumreisen, durchreisen.*
tourist *Tourist, m.*
tournament *Turnier, n.*
toward *zu, nach* (dat.)*; gegen* (acc.).
towel *Handtuch, n.*
tower *Turm, m.*
town *Stadt, f.*
toy *Spielzeug, n.*
trace *Spur, f.*
trace (to) *durchzeichnen* (drawing), (*nach*) *zeichnen.*
track *Spur, f.*
trade *Handel, m.*
tradition *Tradition, f.; alter Brauch, m.*
traditional *traditionell, üblich.*
traffic *Verkehr, m.*
tragedy *Tragödie, f.*
tragic *tragisch.*
trail *Pfad, m.; Weg, m.; Fährte, f.* (hunting).
train *Zug, m.*
train (to) *erziehen, schulen* (children)*; trainieren* (athletes).
training *Erziehung, f.*
traitor *Verräter, m.*
trample (to) *niedertreten.*
tranquil *ruhig.*
tranquility *Ruhe, f.*
transaction *Verhandlung, f.; Transaktion, f.*
transfer (to) *übertragen*
transit *Durchgang, m.*
transition *Übergang, m.*
transitory *vergänglich.*
translate (to) *übersetzun, f.*
translation *Übersetzung, f.*
translator *Übersetzer, m.*
transmission *Übersendung, f.*
transmit (to) *übersenden, übertragen.*
transparent *durchsichtig.*
transport *Transport, m.*
transport (to) *transportieren.*
transportation *Beförderung, f.; Überführung, f.; Transport, m.*
trap *Falle, f.*
trap (to) *fangen, ertappen.*
trash *Abfall, m.; Auswurf, m.*
travel *Reisen, n.*
travel (to) *reisen.*
traveler *Reisende, m. & f.*

tray *Tablett, n.*
treacherous *treulos, verräterisch.*
treachery *Treulosigkeit, f.*
treason *Verrat, m.*
treasure *Schatz, m.*
treasurer *Schatzmeister, m.*
treasury *Schatzamt, n.*
treat *Hochgenuss, m.*
treat (to) *behandeln, bearbeiten, spendieren.*
treatment *Behandlung, f.*
treaty *Vertrag, m.*
tree *Baum, m.*
tremble (to) *zittern.*
trembling *Zittern, n.*
tremendous *ungeheuer.*
trench *Graben, m.; Schützengraben, m.* (military).
trend *Neigung, f.*
trial *Probe, f.; Prozess, m.* (law).
triangle *Dreieck, n.*
tribe *Stamm, m.*
tribunal *Tribunal, n.*
tribune *Tribüne, f.*
tribute *Ehrung, f.; Hochachtung, f.*
trick *Kniff, m.; Trick, m.*
trifle *Kleinigkeit, f.*
trifling *kleinlich* (petty)*; gering* (minor).
trim (to) *stutzen* (hedges)*; kürzen* (hair).
trimming *Verzierung, f.; Garnierung, f.*
trip *Fahrt, f.*
trip (to) *stolpern.*
triple *dreifach.*
triumph *Triumph, m.; Sieg, m.*
triumph (to) *siegen.*
trivial *geringfügig.*
trolley car *Strassenbahnwagen, m.*
troop *Truppe, f.*
trot *Trab, m.*
trot (to) *traben.*
trouble *Unannehmlichkeit, f.; Schwierigkeit, f.*
  to go to the trouble *sich Umstände machen.*
  to save oneself the trouble *sich die Mühe ersparen.*
trousers *Hose, f.*
truck *Lastwagen, m.*
true *wahr.*
truly *wahrhaftig; aufrichtig.*
  yours truly *hochachtungsvoll.*
trump *Trumpf, m.*
trump (to) *trumpfen.*
trumpet *Trompete, f.*
trunk *Koffer, m.*
trust *Vertrauen, n.*
trust (to) *trauen.*
trustworthy *zuverlässig.*
truth *Wahrheit, f.*
truthful *wahrhaft, genau.*

truthfully *aufrichtig, ehrlich gesagt, wahrhaftig.*
truthfulness *Ehrlichkeit, f., Wahrheit, f.*
try (to) *versuchen, probieren.*
tube *Rohr, n.*
tumble (to) *stürzen, stolpern.*
tumult *Getümmel, n.*
tune *Melodie, f.*
tune (to) *stimmen.*
tunnel *Tunnel, m.*
turf *Rasen, m.*
turkey *Truthahn, m.*
turmoil *Aufruhr, f.; Unruhe, f.*
turn (to) *drehen.*
   turn back   *zurückkehren.*
   Turn left   *Biegen Sie links ein!*
   to turn around   *sich undrehen.*
   to turn pages   *umblättern.*
   to turn upside down   *auf den Kopf stellen.*
   It's your turn   *Sie sind dran.*
   to turn against   *sich wenden gegen.*
turnip *weisse Rübe, f.*
twelfth *zwölfte.*
twelve *zwölf.*
twentieth *zwanzigste.*
twenty *zwanzig.*
twice *zweimal.*
twilight *Zwielicht, n.*
twin *Zwilling* (noun) *m.; doppelt* (adj.).
twist (to) *drehen, wickeln.*
two *zwei.*
type *Modell, n.; Typ, m.*
type (to) *mit der Schreibmaschine schreiben.*
typewriter *Schreibmaschine, f.*
tyranny *Tyrannei, f.*
tyrant *Tyrann, m.*

U

ugliness *Hässlichkeit, f.*
ugly *hässlich.*
ultimate *(aller) letzt.*
umbrella *(Regen)schirm, m.*
umpire *Schiedsrichter, m.*
unable to *unfähig.*
unanimity *Einmütigkeit, f.; Einstimmigkeit, f.*
unanimous *einstimmig.*
unawares *unversehens.*
unbearable *unerträglich.*
unbelievable *unglaublich.*
unbutton (to) *aufknöpfen.*
uncertain *unsicher.*
uncertainty *Unsicherheit, f.*
unchangeable *unveränderlich.*
uncle *Onkel, m.*
uncomfortable *unbequem.*
uncommon *ungewöhnlich.*
unconscious *bewusstlos.*

unconsciousness *Ohnmacht, f.*
uncouth *ungebildet.*
uncover (to) *aufdecken; offenbaren* (feelings).
undecided *unentschieden.*
undefinable *unerklärbar, unerklärlich.*
undeniable *unleugbar, unbestreitbar.*
under *unter* (dat. or acc.).
undergo (to) *durchmachen, erleiden* (suffer).
underground *Untergrund* (noun) *n.; unterirdisch* (adj.)*.; Untergrundbahn, f.* (subway).
underline (to) *unterstreichen.*
underneath *unten, unterhalb.*
understand (to) *verstehen.*
understanding *Verständnis, n.*
undertake (to) *unternehmen.*
undertaker *Leichenbestatter, m.*
undertaking *Unternehmen, n.*
underwear *Unterwäsche, f.*
undesirable *unerwünscht.*
undignified *würdelos.*
undo (to) *aufmachen; auflösen* (untie).
undress (to) *sich ausziehen.*
uneasy *beunruhigt.*
uneasiness *Beunruhigung, f.*
unemployed *arbeitslos.*
unequal *ungleich.*
unequaled *unvergleichlich.*
uneven *uneben.*
uneventful *ereignislos.*
unexpected *unerwartet.*
unfair *ungerecht.*
unfaithful *untreu.*
unfavorable *ungünstig.*
unforgettable *unvergesslich.*
unfortunate *unglücklich.*
unfortunately *unglücklicherweise, leider.*
ungrateful *undankbar.*
unhappily *leider.*
unhappy *unglücklich.*
unharmed *unverletzt.*
unhealthy *ungesund.*
unheard (of) *unerhört.*
uniform *Uniform* (noun) *f.; gleichförmig* (adj.).
uniformity *Gleichförmigkeit, f.*
uniformly *gleichförmig.*
unify (to) *vereinigen.*
unimportant *unwichtig.*
unintentional *unabsichtlich.*
union *Vereinigung, f.; Verband, m.; Gewerkschaft, f.* (trade union).
unit cost *Stückkosten* (pl.).
universal *universal.*
universe *Weltall, n.*
university *Universität, f.*
unjust *ungerecht.*
unkind *unfreundlich.*

unknown *unbekannt.*
unlawful *ungesetzlich.*
unless *es sei denn dass; ausgenommen wenn.*
unlike *unähnlich, anders als.*
unlikely *unwahrscheinlich.*
unlimited *unbeschränkt.*
unload (to) *abladen, ausladen.*
unluckily *unglücklicherweise.*
unnecessary *unnötig.*
unoccupied *unbesetzt; unbeschäftigt.*
unpack (to) *auspacken.*
unpleasant *unangehehm.*
unpublished *unveröffentlicht.*
unquestionably *fraglos.*
unravel (to) *enträtseln, auflösen.*
unreal *unwirklich.*
unreasonable *unvemünftig.*
unreliable *unzuverlässig.*
unrestrained *ungezwungen.*
unroll (to) *abwickeln, entrollen.*
unsafe *unsicher.*
unsatisfactory *unbefriedigend.*
unsatisfied *unbefriedigt.*
unscrupulous *bedenkenlos, skrupellos.*
unselfish *selbstlos.*
unsteady *unsicher, wackelig.*
unsuccessful *erfolglos.*
unsuitable *unpassend.*
untidy *unordentlich.*
untie (to) *aufbinden, losbinden.*
until *bis, an, zu* (dat.).
    until now   *bisher.*
untrue *unwahr; untreu* (faithless).
unusual *ungewöhnlich.*
unwell *unwohl.*
unwholesome *ungesund.*
unwilling *widerwillig, unwillig.*
unwise *unklug.*
unworthy *unwürdig.*
up *auf* (dat. or acc.); *aufwärts; oben.*
uphold (to) *stützen, aufrechterhalten* (fig.).
upkeep *Instandhaltung, f.*
upon *auf, über* (dat. or acc.).
upper *ober.*
upright *aufrecht.*
uprising *Aufstand, m.*
upset *beunruhigt, aufgeregt.*
upset (to) *umkehren; aufregen* (distress).
upside down *drunter and drüber.*
upstairs *oben.*
upward *steigend, aufwärts.*
urge (to) *dringen, drängen, auffördern.*
urgent *dringend.*
us *uns.*
use *Gebrauch, m.; Verwendung, f.* (utility).
use (to) *gebrauchen; verwenden.*
used to (to be) *gewöhnt sein.*
useful *nützlich.*
useless *nutzlos.*

usual *gewöhnlich.*
utensil *Werkzeug, n.; Gerät, n.*
utility *Nützlichkeit, f.*
utilize (to) *nutzbar machen.*
utmost *äussert.*
    to the utmost   *aufs Äusserste.*
utter (to) *äussern, aussprechen.*
utterly *durchaus.*

V

vacant *frei, leer, unbesetzt.*
vacation *Ferien, pl.; Urlaub* (from job).
vaccination *Impfung, f.*
vaccination certificate *Impfschein, m.*
vacuum (all purpose) *Allzwecksauger, m.,
    Staubsauger* (vacuum cleaner), *m.*
vaguely *unbestimmt.*
vain *eitel.*
    in vain   *vergebens, umsonst.*
valiant *tapfer.*
valid *gültig.*
validity *Gültigkeit, f.*
valley *Tal, n.*
valuable *wertvoll.*
value *Wert, m.*
value (to) *schätzen.*
valued *geschätzt.*
valve *Ventil, n.*
vanilla *Vanille, f.*
vanish (to) *verschwinden.*
vanity *Eitelkeit, f.*
vanquish (to) *besiegen.*
vapor *Dampf, m.*
variable *veränderlich, wechselnd.*
variation *Abweichung, f.* (deviation),
    Variation, f.
varied *verschieden.*
variety *Abwechslung, f.; Mannigfaltigkeit, f.*
various *verschieden(e), mehrere.*
varnish (to) *lackieren.*
vary (to) *verschieden.*
vase *Vase, f.*
vast *ungeheuer* (gross); *weit.*
vault *Gewölbe, n.; Schatzkammer* (bank), *f.*
veal *Kalbfleisch, n.*
vegetable *Gemüse, n.*
vehicle *Fahrzeug, n.*
veil *Schleier, m.*
veil (to) *verschleiern.*
vein *Ader, f.* (body and mineral); *vene, f.*
velvet *Samt, m.*
venerable *ehrwürdig.*
venerate (to) *verehren.*
veneration *Verehrung, f.*
vengeance *Rache, f.*
ventilation *Lüftung, f.*
ventilator *Ventilator, m.; Lüftungsanlage, f.*

venture (to) *versuchen.*
verb *Zeitwort, n.*
verdict *Urteil, n.*
verge *Rand, m.*
  on the verge of   *am Rand* (gen).
verification *Bestätigung, f.*
verify (to) *bestätigen.*
verse *Vers, m.; Dichtung, f.* (poetry).
version *Version, f.;* (translation);
              Darstellung, f. (account).
very *sehr.*
vest *Weste, f.*
veterinarian *Tierarzt, m.*
VHS recorder *VHS Recorder, m.*
vice *Untugend, f.*
vice-president *Vizepräsident, m.*
vice versa *umgekehrt.*
vicinity *Nähe, f.; Nachbarschaft, f.*
victim *Opfer, n.*
victor *Sieger, m.*
victorious *siegreich.*
victory *Sieg, m.*
view *Aussicht, f.; Ansicht, f.* (opinion).
vigorous *kräftig.*
vile *abscheulich.*
village *Dorf, n.*
vine *Weinstock, m.; Rebe, f.*
vinegar *Essig, m.*
vineyard *Weingarten, m.*
violence *Gewalttätigkeit, f.; Heftigkeit, f.*
violent *gewaltig, heftig.*
violet *Veilchen, n.*
violet *violett.*
violin *Geige, f.*
violinist *Geiger, m.*
virtue *Tugend, f.*
virtuous *tugendhaft.*
visible *sichtbar.*
vision *Sehen, n.; Erscheinung, f.* (ghost).
visit *Besuch, m.*
visit (to) *besuchen.*
visitor *Besucher, m.*
visualize (to) *sich vorstellen.*
vital *lebens-; vital.*
vitality *Lebenskraft, f.*
vivacious *lebhaft.*
vivacity *Lebhaftigkeit, f.*
vivid *lebendig; leuchtend* (color).
vocabulary *Wortschatz, m.*
vocal *stimmlich.*
vocation *Beruf, m.*
vogue *Mode, f.*
voice *Stimme, f.*
void *Leere* (noun) *f.; leer* (empty); *ungültig*
    (invalid).
volcano *Vulkan, m.*
volume *Umfang, m.*
voluntary *freiwillig.*
vote (to) *wählen.*

vote *Stimme f.*
vow *Gelübde, n.*
vow (to) *geloben.*
vowel *Vokal, m.*
vulgar *gemein, niedrig.*
vulnerable *verwundbar, verletzbar.*

W

wager *Wette, f.*
wager (to) *wetten.*
wages *Gehalt, n.*
waist *Taille, f.*
wait (to) *warten.*
  waiting room *Wartezimmer, n.*
waiter *Kellner, m.; Kellnerin, f.*
wake (to) *aufwecken.*
wake up (to) *aufwachen.*
walk *Spaziergang, m.*
walk (to) *gehen.*
  take a walk   *spazierengehen, einen*
         Spaziergang machen.
wall *Wand, f.*
wallet *Brieftasche, f.*
walnut *Walnuss, f.*
wander (to) *wandern.*
wanderer *Wanderer, m.*
want *Mangel, m.; Not, f.* (poverty).
want (to) *wollen.*
war *Krieg, m.*
ward *Station, f.* (hospital); *Mündel (m./f.)*
    (law).
ward off (to) *abwehren.*
wardrobe *Kleiderschrank, m.; Garderobe, f.*
ware *Ware, f.*
warehouse *Warenhaus, n.*
warm *warm.*
warm (to) *wärmen.*
warmth *Wärme, f.*
warn (to) *warnen.*
warning *Warnung, f.*
warrior *Krieger, m.*
wash (to) *waschen.*
washroom *Waschraum, m.*
waste *Verschwendung, f.*
waste (to) *verschwenden.*
watch *Uhr, f.*
watch (to) *wachen, achtgeben, aufpassen;*
    zusehen (to watch someone do work).
watchful *wachsam.*
water *Wasser, n.*
waterfall *Wasserfall, m.*
waterproof *wasserdicht.*
wave *Welle, f.*
wave (to) *schwenken; winken, wellen* (hair).
wax *Wachs, n.*
way *Weg, m.* (road); *Weise, f.* (manner).
we *wir.*

weak *schwach.*
weaken (to) *schwächen.*
weakness *Schwachheit, f.; Schwäche, f.*
wealth *Reichtum, m.*
wealthy *reich.*
weapon *Waffe, f.*
wear (to) *tragen, anhaben.*
weariness *Müdigkeit, f.; Langweile, f.*
weary *müde.*
weather *Wetter, n.*
weave (to) *weben.*
wedding *Hochzeit, f.*
Wednesday *Mittwoch, m.*
weed *Unkraut, n.*
week *Woche, f.*
weekend *Wochenende, n.*
weekly *wöchentlich.*
weep (to) *weinen.*
weigh (to) *wiegen.*
weight *Gewicht, n.*
welcome *Empfang, m.* (reception);
    freundliche Aufnahme, f.
welfare *Wohlfahrt, f.*
well *gut, wohl.*
well *Brunnen, m.*
   oil well *Ölquelle, f.*
west *west, Westen, m.*
westwards *westwärts.*
wet *nass, feucht.*
whale *Walfisch, m.*
what *was; welch(er, -e, -es)* (which)
   what kind of *was für ein.*
whatever *was auch.*
wheat *Weizen, m.*
wheel *Rad, n.*
when *wenn, als; wann* (interrogative).
whenever *so oft wie.*
where *wo; wohin* (whereto).
whereas *da, nun.*
wherever *überall wo.*
whether *ob.*
which *der (die, das); welch(-er, -e, -es).*
   which one *welch(-er, -e, -es).*
while (noun) *f.; indern, während*
   (conj.).
whim *Laune, f.; Einfall, m.*
whip *Peitsche, f.*
whisper (to) *flüstern.*
whistle *Pfeife, f.*
whistle *pfeifen.*
white *weiss.*
who *der (die, das), welch(er, -e, -es)*
   (pron.); *wer* (inter. pron.).
whoever *wer auch immer.*
whole *Ganze* (noun) *n.; ganz* (adj.).
wholesale *Grosshandel, m.*
wholesome *heilsam, gesund; Engrosgeschäft*
   (wholesale business), *n.*
whose *dessen (deren); wessen* (inter.)

why *warum.*
wicked *böse.*
wide *breit.*
widen (to) *breiten, erweitern.*
widow *Witwe, f.*
widower *Witwer, m.*
width *Weite, f. Breite, f.*
wife *Frau, f.*
wig *Perücke, f.*
wild *wild.*
wilderness *Wildnis, f.*
will *Wille, m.; Testament, n.* (legal).
will (to) *wollen.*
willing *gewillt.*
willingly *gern; mit Vergnügen.*
win (to) *gewinnen.*
wind *Wind, m.*
wind (to) *winden, aufwickeln.*
windbreaker *Anorak, m.*
window *Fenster, n.*
windy *windig.*
wine *Wein, m.*
wing *Flügel, m.*
wink *Blinzeln, n.; Augenzwinkern, n.*
wink (to) *blinzeln, zwinkern.*
winner *Sieger, m.*
winter *Winter, m.*
wipe (to) *wischen; ausrotten* (wipe out).
wire *Draht, m.*
wire (to) *kabeln, telegraphieren.*
wisdom *Weisheit, f.*
wise *weise.*
wish *Wunsch, m.*
wish (to) *wünschen.*
wit *Witz, m.; Geist, m.*
witch *Hexe, f.*
with *mit* (dat.)
withdraw (to) *zurückziehen; zurücknehmen*
   (statement); *abheben* (money).
wither (to) *verwelken.*
within *drinnen.*
without *ohne* (acc.).
witness *Zeuge, m.*
witness (to) *bezeugen.*
witticism *witzige Bemerkung, f.*
witty *witzig, geistreich.*
woe *Weh, n.*
wolf *Wolf, m.*
woman *Frau, f.*
wonder *Wunder, n.*
wonder (to) *sich wundern, sich fragen.*
wonderful *wunderbar, herrlich.*
wood *Holz, n.*
woods *Wald, m.*
woodwork *Holzwerk, n.*
wool *Wolle, f.*
word *Wort, n.*
   word by word *Wort für Wort.*
word processor *Textverarbeiter, m.*

work *Arbeit, f.*
  work of art *Kunstgegenstand, m.*
work (to) *arbeiten; sich beschäftigen.*
worker *Arbeiter, m.*
workshop *Werkstatt, f.*
world *Welt, f.*
worldly *weltlich.*
worried *besorgt.*
worry *Sorge, f.; Plage, f.*
worry (to) *besorgen; plagen.*
  Don't worry *Sorgen Sie sich nicht!*
    (*Machen Sie sich keine Sorgen!*)
worse *schlechter.*
worship *Gottesdienst, m.*
worship (to) *anbeten, verehren.*
worst *schlechtest.*
worth *Wert, m.*
worthless *wertlos.*
worthy *würdig.*
wound *Wunde, f.*
wound (to) *verwunden.*
wounded *verwundet.*
wrap (to) *einpacken,* (*ein*)*wickeln.*
wrath *Zorn, m.*
wreath *Kranz, m.*
wreck *Wrack, n. Schiffbruch, m.*
wreck (to) *zertrümmern, scheitern.*
wrestle (to) *wringen; sich quälen* (with a
  problem).
wrestler *Ringkämpfer, m.*
wrestling *Ringkampf, m.*
wretched *elend, unglückselig.*
wring (to) *ringen.*
wrist *Handgelenk, n.*
write (to) *schreiben.*
writer *Schreiber, m.; Schriftsteller, m.*
writing *Schreiben, n.; Schrift, f.* (work).
  in writing *schriftlich.*
wrong *unrecht, falsch.*
  You are wrong. *Sie haben Unrecht.*

X

X-ray *Röntgenstrahlen* (pl.).

Y

yacht *Yacht, f.*
yard *Hof, m.* (courtyard).
yarn *Garn, n.*
yawn *Gähnen, n.*
yawn (to) *gähnen.*
year *Jahr, n.;*
yearly *jährlich.*
yearn (to) *sich sehnen.*
yearning *Sehnen, n.; Sehnsucht, f.*

yeast *Hefe, f.*
yell (to) *schreien.*
yellow *gelb.*
yes *ja, doch.*
yesterday *gestern.*
yet *noch* (also besides); *doch, dennoch*
  (however).
yield (to) *aufgeben* (give up); *erzeugen*
  (produce).
yoke *Joch, n.*
yolk (*Ei*) *Dotter, n.* (of an egg); *Eigelb, n.*
you *Sie, du* (familiar sing.); *ihr* (familiar
  pl.); *Sie, dich, euch* (acc.); *ihnen, dir,*
  euch (dat.).
young *jung.*
  young lady *junge Dame, f.; Fräulein, n.*
your *ihr, dein, ihr.*
yours *ihr* (*-er, -e, -es*); *dein*(*-er, -e, -es*).
yourself *Sie* (*ihnen*) *selbst; du* (*dich, dir*)
  selbst; ihr (*euch*).
youth *Jungend, f.*
yuletide *Weihnachtzeit, f.; Weihnachten, n.*

Z

zeal *Eifer, m.*
zealous *eifrig.*
zebra *Zebra, n.*
zero *Null, f.*
zipper *Reissverschluss, m.*
zone *Zone, f.*
zoo *Tierpark, m.; Zoo, m.*
Zoology *Zoologie, f.*

GLOSSARY OF PROPER NAMES

Albert *Albrecht.*
Alfred *Alfred.*
Andrew *Andreas.*
Ann *Anna.*
Anthony *Anton.*
August *August.*
Barbara *Barbara.*
Bernard *Bernhard.*
Bertha *Bertha.*
Charles *Karl.*
Charlotte *Lotte.*
Edward *Eduard.*
Elisabeth *Elisabeth, Else.*
Elsie *Ilse.*
Emily *Emilie.*
Eric *Erich.*
Ernest *Ernst.*
Eugene *Eugen.*
Frances *Franziska.*

179